# Be The Instrument

## Doug Giesler

Giesler Systems, LLC

# Praise for

# 'Be The Instrument'

"*Doug Giesler's Be the Instrument stands on its own as a book designed to help the reader "convert fear to faith". It's a journey written about by countless authors, in a myriad of ways. This book manages to help the reader travel side by side with Doug, intimately connected with him as he insightfully explores the mental processes awakened in a reader dedicated to self exploration and growth. The format is powerful. One can have a conversation with him by reading simply a paragraph, a page, or a chapter. On these merits, I would highly recommend this book!*"

Patricia G. Simmons, M.D.
Board Certified in Psychiatry & Neurology

"*A thought provoking and motivational work. 'Be The Instrument' breaks down in easily digestible steps how to get you out of your own way and achieve the goals you set for yourself. The everyday practical knowledge and real life stories of the author helps shift the mindset towards action right now! It's an exceptional motivational work!*"

Jaie Hart
Author: *Changing Perspectives, So It's Over, Now What?, Understanding Forgiveness,* and *Expanding Horizons.*

*"I've just finished my first reading of 'Be the Instrument' by Doug Giesler, and let me tell you, it's been a wild ride of self-discovery! I've been an avid nerd/geek/zealot for Personal Development, Self Help, Enhanced Human Potential, and Spiritual Growth content for the last 42 years and this was refreshing. This book isn't your typical self-help fluff—it's a heartfelt journey that'll make you laugh, cry, and probably do a happy dance or two.*

*Doug's writing style? It's like having a chat with your wisest friend over a cup of coffee. He's got this knack for breaking down complex ideas into bite-sized nuggets of wisdom that'll stick with you long after you've turned the last page.*

*What I absolutely adore about this book is how Doug weaves together practical tips with soulful insights and personal stories. It's not about becoming a productivity machine—it's about finding that sweet spot where your ambitions dance in harmony with your inner peace. Trust me, it's magical!*

*I found myself nodding along, scribbling notes, and even getting teary eyed in a few spots (don't tell anyone!) as I worked through the exercises. Doug's approach is like a gentle nudge that helps you uncover layers of yourself you didn't even know existed.*

*If you're feeling stuck, overwhelmed, or just in need of a perspective shift, 'Be the Instrument' is your new best friend. It's not about following a rigid set of rules—it's about tuning into your own unique melody and letting it guide you towards a life that feels authentically YOU.*

*So, grab a copy, find a cozy spot, and prepare to uncover new possibilities that'll leave you feeling inspired, empowered, and ready to rock your world. Doug Giesler, you've created something truly special here. Thank you for this gift!"*

Garry Johnson
Infinite Mastery Consultant, Retired Master Hypnotherapist

*"Be The Instrument is masterfully written to challenge your inner genius. Doug delightfully guides you on an educational tour of your hidden beliefs. He then expertly leads you on a journey of personal empowerment that will touch every area of your life. If you are seeking a more fulfilling life this book is a must read. I would pick up 10 copies to share with your friends and family. They will thank you for it!"*

Jim Britt
15X international best-selling author and world's top 20 Success coach and top 50 most influential speaker.
www.JimBritt.com

# Contents

# INTRODUCTION

T HE PURPOSE OF THIS book is to show you the mechanics, step by step, thought by thought, and challenge by challenge how to convert fear to faith. How to get in the ZONE! That is, after all, what the great teachers try to teach, right? The problem is that they lack **DETAILS** and / or are somewhat cryptic! Attitude, while important, just isn't enough if there is underlying negativity and/or false beliefs that are acting as anchors and running contrary to your best intentions! Dragging that weight around as you take each step is not only counterproductive, but probably wearing you down! It's not necessary, I'll show you why!

This book is about cracking the code, uncovering these secret saboteurs, neutralizing them with the light of awareness, and leveling the playing field in the mind! You can't be who you were and who you intend to be at the same time. Take that next step, take back your POWER, I'll show you how!

At their core, the great spiritual philosophies seem to have the same basic underlying themes. Fascinating, I agree, yet again, that doesn't solve the "How to" question! These themes are great to point us in the right direction, and give us a positive attitude, however, specific detailed instruction / understanding is truly the next step. By dissecting this and really drilling down on details, I'll show you the "mind hacks" I used to take that next step and make it meaningful from an operative standpoint. This book shows you real world techniques on implementation, TODAY, NOW...in your life! How do you turn the light of awareness "ON"? Where are you amplifying your power and where are you literally giving it away? Your success and / or failure depends on it and living from this new perspective will help!

What these philosophies attempt to show us is not flawed, but vague and vague just doesn't get it done! YES, absolutely, "narrow is the gate"! It is razor thin FOR SURE, 100%...but where is it?! Jesus spoke of this in parables, that I didn't understand, and until I understood... I struggled. While I don't like to admit it, I was blind and dumb, just as He described! (Shaking my head in disbelief!) NO MORE... the blinders are off! What was revealed to me was instrumental...in fact, a major discovery that really helped me turn the corner and see from a whole new light. I don't want you to struggle like I did. I'll show you this discovery. You too can read between the lines and understand the secret of all secrets, the way to the TRUTH, in layman's terms, with real world examples! Believe me when I tell you that it will make all the difference... **IT WILL MAKE ALL THE DIFFERENCE!**

# 1

# SETTING THE STAGE / PRELIMINARY THOUGHTS

THE UNAWARE MIND CAN be tricked into believing ANYTHING! In fact, it is completely untrustworthy much of the time unless you make a REAL effort to ascertain what IT really intends to do moment by moment by moment. In other words, in fractions of a second, on cutting edge of the "NOW" moment... You MUST be hyper focused, highly alert, energized, aware, and PRESENT, else the mind will deceive you!

Pay attention, and focus... What EXACTLY is the mind focused on...NOW, and NOW and NOW? Not like in a general sense...like theme, or tone... I mean by the microsecond...with vigilance and a stupendous amount of focused awareness. Did you even notice? Seriously, it's kind of funny actually, one minute it tells you to do something, and the very next moment it literally takes the opposite vantage point. Quite possibly it may even criticize the "You" that made the decision a moment ago... Did you ever notice this happening? What I intend to show you is that with enough **ENERGY**, and **AWARENESS**, **FOCUS** and **GUIDANCE**... The mind can be used to create amazing things!

Equally important is the opposite side of the coin, though. Understanding is power, and given the "wrong" circumstances, or the wrong focus and / or a lack of attention, well then... "BAD" things can happen! I will explain good and bad later. First though, I will show you how to tell where your power is or isn't for that matter... if you are giving it away, to whom, when, how, as well as how to reclaim it, and take it back!

Let's start by understanding that we all have different backgrounds, upbringings, environments, desires, wants, "needs", etc. We are all affected differently by early and ongoing influencers, influences, coaching, training, parental, sibling, relatives, teachers, Doctors and / or other caregivers' ineptitudes! (NOT making excuses here, so please hear me out!). In essence, we are who we are because of our previous decisions and current values/beliefs. These folks, as well as our environment have had at least something to do with shaping our current beliefs and **beliefs MATTER**!!!! They shape everything we think, and what we think colors our world. We all see the world with different eyes, and what our eyes are seeing is somewhat "tainted" by our beliefs about it. If you take 10 people into a room, an event happens, and then each has to tell you exactly what happened, you will get ten different stories about what just happened!

If you are not paying attention to what's going through your mind presently, well then, the mind and its decisions will revert to your core beliefs and whether you make one or not, a decision is being made. That decision will be made by a "You". YES...but which one? I know I know; you might say well the only one that's here... No, that's not what I mean. I mean, literally, what version of you? Some examples might be that I am trying to be a good father, or mother, or employee, etc. So, a decision was made, was it made by a "you" acting as any of these type people below, or acting as an "**Archetype**"[1] of a particular type of person? In other words, what was your mindset, and who was driving that mindset within you as you made the decision?

1. The Father, Mother, Grandmother, Grandfather, Cousin, Sister, Brother, Son, Daughter

2. Employee, Boss, Loyal Countryman, Teammate, Coach, Teacher, Sports fan

3. Soldier, Warrior, President, CEO, COO, CFO, Manager

4. HERO, Friend, Lover, Spouse, Caregiver, provider

These are just a few examples of "WHO" you could be "acting as" or from, as the "driver" or thinker in that situation, at that time, and where your current mind is. In other words, your vantage point at the moment the decision is made. If we are taking on that perspective, which we are...then that perspective is "tainted" and "biased" with eyes that see the world differently than if I had chosen to look at the world through the eyes of a different "version of self". What I am hoping to show you is that when you wake up to see these different versions of "self" taking over the mind and making decisions FOR you, AS you, it really matters!

You'll ultimately see that depending on the situation, who is there, what is happening, and a million different possible influences, any number of these "selves" could be jockeying for position in the mind to take over the virtual steering wheel (YOU) at any given moment. You must be aware enough to see it happening though. So, your job throughout the day is to wake up and see these various "selves" and who won this time (in the mind). Who was it that actually made the decision? We know that a decision was made, whether it was a good decision or a bad one, not as important at this juncture. Pay attention to what "Me" made the decision, where your focus and attention was...and if the "I" that was acting as me was actually PRESENT, AWAKE and AWARE enough to make it. A decision is being made every moment of every day...what I want to know is WHO MADE IT? Was I truly PRESENT... and if not, why not?! Laziness, from a mind perspective, is NOT an option if you want to see where your power is. That is why I say that it requires a stupendous amount of awareness, and FOCUS, by the microsecond!

If you can muster the energy, and truly concentrate on being present to the mind and WITHIN vs having a focus that is primarily "out there", this vantage point will show you where your power is! More specifically to WHOM is in control of the mind, (what version of "self") and what their priorities might have been that influenced that decision. Our focus and attention are driving our results every moment of every day...and we actually do have the ability to change our focus. First we MUST be aware! This alone will highlight for us what our deep core values are. Our values, or what is important to us, affects everything!

What is important to us, in other words, who we are in every moment, and from what paradigm we are reacting from, colors what we see...like it or not! Said differently, what we see in this world is biased, based on core beliefs. (programming) In essence, our beliefs shape our reality, and that reality drives our desires and fears! Our desires and / or fears carry weight in the mind, based on our priorities and beliefs situationally. If the mind had a scale that weighed desire vs fear, that would be a really good gauge to pay attention to! That scale would help us to determine what has the power, desire or fear, or something else. What tells us the answer? EMOTION! Our emotions are literal gauges that HIGHLIGHT for us every moment of every day where we are focused and what we are focused on. What we are focused on totally drives our results.

## "Where attention goes energy flows"[2]

This is HUGE! Pay attention to your emotions/feelings, and where you are focusing your energy. This is the easiest way to understand where your power is or if you are giving it away. This is a true KEY element to how the "I" or "YOU" arrives presently (or not) in the moment to play this game of life!

#1 are you present? #2 Are you focused on what you **WANT** or what you don't want? The positive or negative? Desire or fear? Peaceful or worried? Relaxed or "stressed"? These are really IMPORTANT clues as to where your focus is... PAY ATTENTION!

If there is a general lack of energy and / or awareness, an inability to SEE or HEAR properly (without distraction)...if you are rooted or focused on something other than what you want, or even just completely unaware of your own CORE beliefs. Well, that is of MAJOR significance because if you are unaware of these core beliefs, you have no power to override them and many an effort will essentially be squashed before it even has a chance of developing into something "Good"! Why? Because being unconscious, or unaware is a big part of the problem...the biggest, IMHO. In fact, results are often somewhat random, based on the abilities I mentioned, or to the extent that you master these abilities, these new skills! So, let's progressively develop these skills with some strategies that are geared towards identifying opportunities we may be missing.

Let's start by understanding that much of what we believe was likely generated in our childhood, and again, not implying "blame" on anyone, that is a whole separate conversation. I am NOT going to give you excuses which would prolong your learning curve. What you need to see, with awareness, is how to assess what those beliefs are, where they came from, and whether or not they are truly important to you NOW. I think, if you had a choice, which you do, you would likely agree that it is important to understand this right?! In fact, in order to progress you'll need to own up to your beliefs, can you do that? BE HONEST!

With understanding, you will be able to make choices that coincide with what is important to you, at this time, in this place, in this situation, NOW. It seems that a lot of times we make decisions that are not aligned with what we actually want today, it's like we forgot to update the software in our own head! Why? Well, that is why I am writing this to you. The essence of that is primarily because of the way the mind operates. Our CORE beliefs, positionalities and programs are running behind the scenes to the unaware mind. Because of this, we miss opportunities that can make a big difference in our lives, and it's mainly because we were never told how to see them, where to look! We start with a somewhat dated machine with old, outdated software, then on top of that, we also have to consider the way the EGO interjects itself in between the "YOU" or "I" (me) and the "NOW". I will explain how it does this...and understanding this is very powerful!

In the meantime, you may be asking, who am I to tell you how to "think" and why bother trying to think differently anyway? What is this ability I am talking about? It is a SKILL, and a way of looking at things! It is very likely that it is from a different vantage point than what you are traditionally trained and currently able to do consistently. It takes effort, and focus, and a tremendous amount of energy if this is not something you have been accustomed to doing. I sure wasn't and it took years to even start seeing this way. In fact, it is so powerful and so effective, that if done properly and with enough energy, it can generate results very quickly once you really GET IT!

So, to answer the question, why am I sharing this? From a very general perspective, I just like to help people and without this information, life can be tough! With this information it can give you the power to SEE and HEAR from a whole new level and this will empower you to make life changing decisions that can have a HUGE impact on your results, happiness, and satisfaction... basically your ability to enjoy being here.

## A LITTLE ABOUT DOUG

I can't stand to see people in pain... crying people tear me up! Rather, I truly LOVE to see people succeed, for lots of reasons! Seeing their enthusiasm, the contagious smiles, the positivity, sharing, and caring attitudes it can generate, the true vibrance and GLOW that energy brings out in people. I really value a positive attitude, and let's face it, smiling and LOVING people like this are a lot more fun to be around. I do my best to help people smile, in whatever ways I can. I gain tremendous satisfaction in seeing people overcome a personal barrier and achieve something truly special as that seems to amplify and bring out even more of the "good"! Maybe it was that formerly they did not think they could do something, but with a little guidance and a small push, in the right direction, and the right focus, it was just the stepping stone they needed to launch an amazing success story...because after I showed them that one thing, the stepping stones just laid out in front of them and they just went right through every other obstacle that seemed to arrive in front of them! It could be a small victory, or a MAJOR milestone, major victory, major accomplishment. You see, that was me. I was the student, now I want to be the teacher or coach...for YOU!

Thankfully, I have had a lot of victories. Appreciation goes out to a LOT of people! I have had a lot of help. Yes, I had to work very hard at it, and I am very competitive. I am also very appreciative, and I paid very close attention to what worked and what didn't work...IN DETAIL, which is really important!

Bottom line, I never liked to lose, I don't give up easily and I listen to coaching, advice, etc. The problem for me, years ago, was that if I lost it would damage my fragile ego. I can handle losing a lot more graciously now, however, I still don't like to lose. LOL. Having said that, I owe a lot of gratitude to a lot of people. I have either read their courses, been on their websites, or taken their online courses, read their books, listened to their audio, or whatever other varieties of learning exist! Thanks in a MAJOR part to my parents, who have been behind me and with me throughout my journey! I am SO very appreciative for who they are, that I was blessed enough to have such AMAZING parents, and the fact that they have ALWAYS been there for me through thick and thin! They literally pushed me and prodded me, and questioned me, and set me up for success over and over again. Quite honestly, one of the bigger pushes that set the stage for a lot of victories for me was their insistence that I play sports as a kid. I would have never played sports, but they made me, and I LOVED IT!!!! I was fortunate to have some great coaches in sports as well, so thanks to them, winning was always a big motivator for me, and again, a lot of the teams I was on won a lot. I liked to think that I had a lot to do with that, ha-ha!

Anyway, I was as shy as a kid could be. Embarrassingly shy! You would never believe that...I know. It's true. To this day, I do not have much desire to talk or even be amongst people in general. I totally prefer to be alone. I have always been kind of afraid of people. I would tolerate it, but only after a massive amount of effort and focus, and if I was in a large group, it would take me some time to recover... still does!! There is just way too much energy there for me to process. I am an empath, I feel everything! In large groups there is a ton of energy swirling around, too much to make sense of, it is overwhelming. As a kid, I did not know how to deal with that, it was just plain nervous energy, I did not know where it came from NOR how to process it... quite honestly it is still a bit of a challenge for me. In fact, I would be perfectly content not saying anything at all and being alone! I was always afraid...of authority, of getting in trouble, of doing the wrong thing, of not succeeding, anything really. I guess you could say I was just generally afraid.

Now, let me pause to say that there was no real reason for this. Like as in, I was not abused, or treated badly... I was loved, grew up in a favorable environment, with phenomenal parents that love me a TON, and a sister that I get along famously with. She is as AWESOME as awesome gets! I love my whole family to the end of the earth, my amazing wife, Joelle, and her family included! Never would I have an inkling of a complaint about any of them! Why then was I so afraid? I did not know, and while it did not stop me from doing things, it did make it less fun, and sometimes quite uncomfortable. Again, no real reason, per se, I just knew that I was afraid, tense, stressed...all the time! It was obvious to me, trust me I felt it, but I was embarrassed, and I certainly didn't want to admit my "flaw"...not to anyone out there for sure, no less to myself! So, what is a man to do? I ran straight into the wind... buried it and plowed onwards...until I just couldn't do it anymore! That ultimately is what I will explain and what made all the difference...UNDERSTANDING. Sheer force just isn't enough at some point against a strong headwind. The underlying mechanism eventually wins if you give it enough power! That is EXACTLY what I was doing, giving it power. So "IT" did win, and so I lost...temporarily! The good thing is that although it was painful, and it took many years for me to recover, I did recover, and I did find out what made me fail. ME!!!!

The essence of it was that I was unconscious, unaware, and just barreling through life by sheer determination and a bullheadedness that was unparalleled, with virtual blinders on and ear plugs in as well. I knew what I wanted and that is all that was in front of me. Tunnel vision! Since I did not understand the feelings, or what they were there for, I did my best to shut them off...to the extent that I could. I had lots of methodologies too. Bury them, ignore them, resist them...medicate them, you name it...thankfully not with drugs! I filled my mind with better thoughts, affirmations, and tried to reprogram my mind thinking that would eliminate these useless feelings eventually. I read books like **Napoleon Hill "The LAW of success"**[3], **"Think and Grow RICH"**[4], and **"The magic of believing" by Claude M Bristol**[5]! I read a ton of books searching for answers. I was very motivated, and yes, I guess you might call me a dreamer. I truly thought that if I made enough money, there would be nothing more that could scare me, there would be no reason to be afraid. So, in the name of security, and comfort... I plowed on and I plowed through stuff. With enough money, I could "buy my freedom" so to speak! From a mental standpoint, that was essentially my attitude. I will say that I was always very respectful throughout my driven ness. I did not go through people; I was always courteous and mindful of others. At least I had that going for me!

Ultimately, it worked for a long time. As I buried the fears and emotions, I went around the problems, and I did pretty OK... for a long while! It took roughly 34 years to catch up with me. Then I literally hit the wall, I couldn't take it anymore, I was working way too much and way over stressed, had a phone on both ears at the same time and working for two companies that were merging, 18-hour days. Uh Oh... oh no, I am doing that again. LOL! I am doing it much differently though now. (BY CHOICE...not need, big difference!) You will see... back then I was a different person, and I was quite literally at the end of my rope! I was stretched super thin, and my foundation was weak! Talk about a house of cards... Yep, that was me! So, I crumbled, and fell on my face...and it hurt...so I laid low for quite a while trying to figure myself out. I guess you could say soul searching, which is just what I needed.

Thankfully, I had made a bunch of money, and banked it, so it wasn't a huge crisis. It bought me some time! Having been fired for the first time in my life, my ego was bruised, and I was "spent". I was tired, burnt out! I needed to step back and assess, and assess I did...I assessed the situation, and more importantly the ME that was in it!

That was from the psychological side of things. From a professional side of things, I decided not to go back to work right away, and with a decent bank account, I dove into the stock market! I freakin LOVED the stock market...and I had made a bunch of money "trading" too so I studied everything I could get my hands on to get even better at it. This was a major passion for me. I read many books, bought courses, went into online trading forums, etc. While I saw huge potential with stocks, I was being told that with all the manipulation in stocks, it's easier and more profitable to trade commodities. So, that's what I wanted to do... forget stocks, ha-ha...let's trade commodities! I studied everything! I spent thousands of dollars on courses, and materials, computers, software, data...and watched the charts endlessly! Massive amounts of screen time, tick by tick. Days on end would disappear...I freakin LOVED the charts (still do!). I have always loved puzzles and trying to figure stuff out, and this was a huge challenge for me.

I hadn't failed at too many things in life, so far, and while this seemed like it would be easy, it has been one of the most difficult things to truly understand. I was determined though, and when I wasn't studying the charts, or watching the market, I was studying mental / psychological books and programs or trying to gain some other kind of spiritual help. Why? Because the underlying problem (My emotions) was still there. At my core, I had not changed. I was still carrying around a lot of emotional "baggage" so I was analyzing and trying to figure that out as well!! I was learning a TON and I was super excited about this newfound "career"! TRADING!!!! YEAHHHHH, I was ridiculously excited about trading... Why? 2 main reasons. First, I could make a ton of $$$, AND Second I did NOT have to deal with anyone other than myself! This was a total WIN-WIN for me, I mean seriously!

So, I traded everything, gold, silver, the British Pound, US dollar, corn, soybeans, wheat, cotton, coffee, cocoa, bonds...just to name a few, I could go on and on. S&P, Nasdaq futures...I wasn't very good at it, but I wasn't terrible either... I made money here and there and lost some too. Essentially, I knew enough to keep myself out of trouble, but I wasn't making enough to live on...so I kept studying, and even taught myself how to program in this new language called **"Easy language"**[6]. I think that I may have spent a few years learning to code my own stuff and that really helped me to understand the markets a lot better. **Tradestation** is an amazing platform. Not only could I use this to try stuff, but it was the ultimate bull**** detector. There were, and still are, a lot of self-proclaimed ALL STAR professional traders out there...and believe me I bought a lot of their courses! It seemed to me though that they were selling only pieces of their programs, not enough to really use, and / or they were not successful at it to begin with. The other possibility is that they were not very good teachers, or I wasn't a very good student. HAHA!!! There are a lot of gray areas in trading, and this is where their intimate knowledge of their own system was probably one of the keys to make or break things that was virtually unexplainable. I was learning though, getting better and this was the early stages of the internet, so things were changing rapidly!

I kept buying stuff and programming my own indicators and strategies by combining the old with the new knowledge repeatedly! Finally, I came to understand the markets really well, particularly the financials. Also, there are some legit teachers out there, and quite honestly, each system I bought had a tidbit of functionality, I learned something useful that I added to the databank! I learned a TON about the markets, and trading! I was seriously on to something, for sure, but I wasn't quite there yet. The systems were cool, my programming was developing, but I was personally, from a developmental stage, and emotional stage, still BROKEN!

The long and the short of it was that unfortunately, now that I understood what to do...I was incapable of doing it because I had my back to the wall financially and you just can't trade successfully from that mental vantage point! Ask any successful trader. In fact, the basis for the understanding of this mental dynamic in the mind is that you can't focus on what you don't want (fear) and get what you want (desire)! It just doesn't work. Trading is what showed me this phenomenon, and it is very powerful. My focus was "out there", and I was watching the charts in front of me tick by tick, on faster and faster timeframes. Gradually, in addition to that, I started to look "in here", as in watching the mind as it was processing the information in front of me, at lightning-fast speeds! While I was watching the charts, I was also paying attention to myself and studying myself, tick by tick...on faster and faster timeframes! That started to show me something different, but my education was just in the early stages of development.

All that STUDY, all that programming, all that knowledge was GREAT... I mean SUPER GREAT, but holy moley...12 years had passed, and I still wasn't making enough trading to sustain us! I didn't understand completely yet, but I was starting to turn the corner on this new insight. You can't really get a positive result when you are focused on what you "don't want"...You can't trade the markets with money you can't afford to lose. FEAR will win! You will lose your money!

Fortunately, I wasn't actually losing money, but I wasn't making any either, not enough anyway...so I had to call a spade a spade. While I hadn't given up, because I was truly getting dialed into the markets, I had to go make some money elsewhere, build up my capital on two fronts:

1. Emotionally

2. Dollars or risk capital to trade with!

12 years had passed, just living off my previous earnings and profits, and my accounts were drawn down to the point where we were a little stressed. I even drew down My 401k and sold what would be MAJOR winners in the stock market. One of the stocks I sold went from $2 to $300 recently, and I had 1000 shares that I bought at 2 and 7/8. Dang, there were others too... that would have meant hundreds of thousands of dollars today. Hindsight is 20/20, RGEN was one of them. Anyway, we still had some funds, and a bunch of equity in the house, but I had to get a job, and we were looking to relocate. The combination would free up the equity in the house and give us a fresh start somewhere. That somewhere ended up being Lake Murray, in South Carolina! We spent 3 years searching the Southeast for the best lake, and Lake Murray is it, by FAR!!!! Amazing Lake, and area! It took us 3 years to sell the "farm", due to the market timing and the Lehman collapse. We then bought a house for cash in SC, and both found jobs. A year later, I got into real estate and the rest is history, I guess...what a ride! Trading and real estate are amazing, they give you a lot of opportunities to watch the mind. It has been an amazing education!

To back track a bit, I had learned a TON of spiritual and psychological "angles" to help me on the emotional side of things, yet I was still somewhat fragile. When we arrived in SC, it was a fresh start, and I was a man on a mission. I had a great NEW theoretical mindset now, and I had to prove to myself that all these new mental angles actually worked. I was pretty much down and out emotionally, and financially, but what I did have was a huge amount of book knowledge and a little bit of courage. My intention was to prove that this stuff worked in the real world. The mental "STUFF" I had learned. You see, I had spent a good portion of the 12 years studying not only the charts, and the spiritual stuff, but I was also studying MYSELF in relation to that stuff! I was looking at ME, just like the charts, TICK BY TICK! I literally learned what made me "tick", like as in, at MY CORE and what the mind was doing as a result. YES, I was still driven, and I was much more aware of myself too, as a result of this new vantage point. In addition, and because I wanted to amplify that ability, I had bought a lifetime subscription to **"HOLOSYNC"**[7] and I was using it regularly! This a product by **Centerpointe Research**, which is designed to increase awareness even more! IT WORKS, Thank You **Bill Harris**, rest in peace, your product is phenomenal, and I still use it every day!

Somewhere along the line, I believe several years before I turned the corner emotionally, and financially for that matter, I got some good advice. My Dad told me that I should not be moving to get away from something, but towards something. I don't think that I really understood the actual power in that statement and advice, but it did resonate with me. It totally made sense, I agreed, and it aligned with all that MIND STUFF that I had read. I forget the actual sentence he said. The essence of it was don't run AWAY from something but DO run towards something! That's some amazing advice! We will talk more about that extensively, but when I was younger, I did not understand the wisdom in that statement. Now I do...it has to do with FEAR vs DESIRE, and FOCUS... where your attention is and what's driving you. To what are you giving your power? More on that later, but it really does make all the difference! Thanks Dad :)

While this is somewhat embarrassing for me, I don't tell you this for no reason! It is to show what I went through. It was a lot of years in trials and mental challenges, difficult mind stuff to deal with. I was trying to figure out a puzzle, the mind, mine! I wanted full control of my mind because I could see that I was missing opportunities. That meant being committed to it, and I mean REALLY COMMITTED! I have had to give up a lot of stuff along the way because once I committed, I was ALL IN! Early on that meant quitting the use of Copenhagen. That was a huge step for me because I loved that stuff...and it was one of the first things I did so that the chemical and habit was not controlling me and affecting this super important tool I was working on, MY MIND! That was most definitely one of the more difficult early challenges, I felt like I had lost my best friend! I also had the emotional baggage of being fired from a job...that had never happened to me. So, I was rebuilding the foundation from the ground up. That is the reason for the explanation, not because I am proud of the fragility of my ego back then, or that I had literally failed MYSELF!

So, having drained my accounts over 12 years just living and having some fun...
I had rebuilt my "self" and was out to light up the world. I was full of vigor,
rested up emotionally, and with a full tank of gas and a whole new set of beliefs,
my little "self" that was merging into my bigger "SELF" was ON FIRE burning
on all cylinders. Well, Ok I was ramping up, and I had a great attitude! While it
wasn't perfect, I was saying bring it on world, here I come.  I was starting over
though, well not over...over, I had a couple bucks rolling around in the bank. We
had freed up the equity from the house sale and "downsized" to give us a fresh
start. So, me and this new "SELF" set out a new, with BETTER BELIEFS, a ton
of affirmations, visualizations, and good intentions! So, let's talk about beliefs!

# 2

# BELIEFS

D O YOU KNOW WHAT your beliefs are? I am not talking about surface level, like as in stated beliefs, like the standards by which you try to hold yourself to, or general philosophies that maybe you have just adopted along the way in one way or another. I am talking about DEEP CORE beliefs, like as in; is the world a good place, a friendly one, or something to be afraid of? What are your beliefs, where are they? When do they show up? When do they matter? Are you able to SEE THEM, respond to them, and use them, or does your mind even have the ability to see them TO honor them? Have you ever specifically looked for them, or tested them? Have you watched your mind try to violate them and paid attention to when? What situation, who was there? What caused the attempted violation, what emotion was present, what was your mind "thinking about"? If you were blindsided by yourself, what took you OUT of the moment long enough to temporarily BLIND you? This is a serious question, and I am challenging you to find out for yourself. When you say you believe in something, is your mind able to stand its ground, dig its heels in and honor that belief?

My guess is that sometimes YES, and sometimes NO. Have you ever analyzed when you can and when you can't? Situationally, with what people, with what environment, stressors, state of health, awareness, energy, focus? Were you HUNGRY? Or should I say hangry... Ha-ha! Bottom line, WHEN are you aware enough moment to moment to moment to moment to honor your beliefs? I do not need an answer to this question, please don't call me and explain yourself. This is a question for YOU! You are the only one that can answer it... and you literally need to call yourself out on it! Why is it important? BECAUSE this knowledge, this level of awareness and focus allows you to see your BLIND

SPOTS... **<u>BEFORE they blind you</u>**! These are the situations, things, events, people, and whatever else that TRIGGER YOU. One way or another, even with your best intentions, these are the moments where you need to increase your focus and awareness and pay attention, with hyper vigilance and MASSIVE amounts of energy, to the point where time actually slows down! THAT IS FOCUS. You are THAT dialed in and PRESENT... It's actually called being "IN THE ZONE", and I will explain how to get there!

**<u>LESSON KEY:</u> Listen and pay attention to the various vantage points, and paradigms you are subscribed to during your day. Pay attention to your thoughts.**

If something is bothering you and you just can't seem to shake it, stop for a moment, and really sit with it so that you can understand it a little more deeply! You don't need to do anything about it just yet. Just try to be aware at this point. Also, for fun and to use as a reminder, maybe for the next week, try listening to the song **"Stand My Ground"**[8] by **Within Temptation**. Are there things that are haunting your mind, as described in the song? If so, why? What are the emotions and / or paradigms that are driving this "attachment"? Use this song as a reminder to explore these feelings a little bit. Stand your ground and don't walk away from them, just listen and watch. YOU CAN DO IT! Take the step you know you must!

# 3

# AWARENESS

I T's ONE THING TO know these things, but without awareness, none of it can be used. You MUST become AWARE of what the mind is doing **IN THE MOMENT**...**NOW**. If you are not present to the moment in the moment, then it is impossible to see the various beliefs as they surface and operate. You are gaining a SKILL, and you must exercise this skill, as often as possible to amplify your ability to use it! In the last chapter, the lesson key was to pay attention to thoughts and feelings in general and stop periodically to think about them. Now, we need to take that to the next level, and be watchful with a heightened level of awareness AS THEY COME UP!

Bottom line, this is a real simple chapter. If you are not aware of a core belief, then you have ZERO ability to even make a choice about whether or not you honor it. IT (the Mind / Ego) will decide for you without the present "YOU"...being in the moment to change your mind. Change only happens in the moment of NOW. If you are aware enough to SEE, and HEAR as the mind processes, PRESENTLY... THEN and ONLY THEN do you have an actual choice!

The other alternative, of course, is that the choices are made on autopilot, based on core beliefs and this is basically driven by previous versions of self, archetypes, or programming. That is our comfort zone, and we go on and on...human nature resists change and so we allow our "selves" to run the show between our ears until we make a crucial decision. We decide, once and for all, to commit to showing up in life to take over the reins for our "SELF", with AWARENESS!!! This is why I refer to and try to highlight the different vantage point from the higher "SELF" vs lower "selves"! AWARENESS is the key, and energy is required to maintain that presence. The higher "SELF" vantage point, its presence and AWARENESS is required to affect our ability to make effective decisions moment by moment by moment. NOW! And NOW...and NOW! This is where we can SEE these beliefs, and patterns and how they affect us, as well as our results!

The difference now is that we are going to see it sooner, not in retrospect, but with awareness, sooner, as in NOW!!

**Lesson KEY: Awareness is a SKILL, work on the skill! Be ALERT, FOCUS, and pay very close attention to WHERE your attention is, WITHIN that awareness, moment by moment.**

Try to stay present in the "NOW". Your attention and awareness are required here, that's a part of the skill. Now, observe that they are two SEPARATE internals that make up that one thing. Try to break it down, and watch! This is an important distinction because what I want you to notice is when the attention part of that dynamic is being drawn to the past, when it is being drawn to the future, and when it is just distracted. In addition, what type things are doing this to you? What are the drivers of this? How long does it last? Try to distinguish the difference between being present in the moment, and the times when you are taken out of the moment and only see it in retrospect, after the fact. As often as possible, come back and do your best to maintain presence, NOW. This is going to be difficult at first and require a lot of energy so you may be extra tired at the end of the day as you adjust to this perspective. It will be more difficult as the day progresses and/or when you have less energy too. You are working on a new skill, and this is NOT easy, so be patient, and just keep at it, keep trying.

This is also a multi-step progressive assignment:

1. First you MUST be PRESENT, work on that, and continue to work on that!

2. Second you MUST be AWARE of that presence and where your attention is within it AS you are being present.

In trying to accomplish this as a 1,2 punch try to distinguish the difference between being hyper focused and really drilled down on the task, like IN THE TASK, as in within an orientation that is IN the task vs. watching the attention and focus, with awareness OF the doing of the task. The difference is the perspective, orientation, or vantage point. The way that I see this is as an IN vs ABOVE perspective. Try to see this. It is with where your awareness is, <u>WITHIN the vantage point</u> from where you are present to yourself! By all means, FOCUS on the task at hand, that is as important as ever! It will keep you safe and hopefully out of harm's way. What I want you to try to do is BOTH! While not sacrificing the detail and skill with which you are accomplishing the task, maintain an overarching awareness of this dynamic happening WITHIN...watch the DOER, as it is DOING, watch the thinker as it is thinking! That's the awareness factor and represents this higher "SELF" vantage point I will continually reference.

This vantage point, and skill, as you develop it, is a TOOL. You are now sharpening that tool to be able to SEE thoughts and actions from a perspective that allows you to use the tool to dissect them. Within this dichotomy is a microscopic view of your beliefs and patterns of beliefs. Pay attention to these as they surface within this awareness for you, this will provide you BIG gains and a very powerful ad "vantage" point!

This is going to require some effort, and a lot of energy. So, let's talk about ENERGY!!

# 4

# ENERGY

A GAIN, IT'S ONE THING to know these things, but without energy, it is an uphill battle. We really just need something to be excited about to keep that energy alive and well...but not TOO excited. LOL. Blind belief, overzealous, cocky, etc. can also make us miss important details. A great book series about energy flow is **"The Celestine Prophecy"**[9], by **James Redfield**...what an amazing series! It's fun to read and provides a lot of insights into energy dynamics between people. I really enjoyed that a lot and it really helped me to understand the energy perspectives.

When my wife, Joelle and I were right out of college, we would lay on the floor and dream about what we wanted in life and visualize it together. We took a course, and another one, and I'd say that over the years I have spent a lot of money on books courses and if you add that all up in time, dollars, and cents, and all...as well as profits and losses, investments, machines, programming, mental and computer...We are talking hundreds of thousands of dollars! Thousands of hours of study, hyper focused INTENSE laser sharp highly caffeinated and adrenalized study... not only of what was in front of me, but what was going on in my mind as the things crossed my screen. Not my computer screen, but the MIND screen. There is a BIG difference! That required a lot of energy, consistently.

Bottom line, you need massive amounts of ENERGY and FOCUS, with AWARENESS to see from this perspective! You must find the energy and know where to look!

The first step in this process, from the previous chapters, is to WATCH YOUR THOUGHTS! In his course and book. Ken Roberts said it this way:

## "1000 times a day, come back to NOW"[10]

Great advice. For sure! Watching your thoughts, as a task, doesn't seem like it should be hard. I mean, at first glance, this should not be difficult right? In the beginning though, when really attempting to do it, I thought that this was the most difficult thing in the world. I was amazed at how hard it was, and how much energy it took to do it. Please do this consistently, find the energy! Try with all your energy and all your focus to stay present, in the NOW moment. Pay attention to everything that's going on "out there", with a focus and attention to what's going on "in here" as well...as in, within THE MIND!!! It isn't easy to maintain that perspective, so cut yourself a little slack here and there, and take a breath! It really isn't as easy as it sounds. The next step after learning to watch your thoughts in this manner, with awareness, is to pay attention to the who, what, where, and when, people, situations, and things, take us OUT OF the moment. Next is the observation of the energy being exchanged, to whom, by what, and of course how and when! Holey Moley, that's a lot to take in. Yep, I get it. Just start slowly, and make the effort, it will be worth it! This is also described very nicely in the celestine prophecy books I mentioned.

The energy dynamic between people involved situationally, as well as internally, is really important to pay attention to. You need to understand and SEE what version of self is arriving in your mind to each of these "moments" and situations, when certain people are there! The perspective will help you to understand what "IT" (the mind) wants out of the moment FROM these people or the situation, or both. That is where you can gain the insights that help you take that next step, because that insight / understanding just revealed something to your "SELF" about your "self"! What you actually WANT is going to reveal to the higher "SELF" the mind gears that kick in and just got activated as a result of that wanting! If that didn't register, please read it again, because it is really important! You are watching the mind gears "in here" as everything is going on "out there"! Pay close attention to the GEARS of the mind that get activated, or "triggered" and how IT re-acts in and to these various situations. Observation skill and your ability to process all of this is going to be affected by your overall state, energy level, the people involved, and the situation as well. Everything affects everything. Be conscious of this, particularly the energy dynamic as things develop, while they are happening, and after the fact!

**LESSON KEY: BEWARE!!!!! Or should I say, BE AWARE!? Heightened awareness is able to take in and observe significantly more available in-formation than attention can, you must use this! As you are using this,**

**pay attention to it as it relates to energy and flow of energy. You must do both, be aware, yes...AND pay attention! It is a broad-based field awareness without sacrificing the acute focus and attention to detail. This requires more energy, so we must find ways to maximize it, and use it more efficiently.**

Attention is of course needed, and ULTRA important for task completion; however, it tends to block information out because it is too dialed in to the task! Obviously, you need both, and will use both. Awareness is more all-encompassing / over-arching / ALL SEEING! To use both takes ENERGY! So, who is there with you? What do you want / NEED... from them, or the situation? This is driving the "you" that arrives to the moment. Now, watch your thoughts and actions, YES...and with this added skillset, let's notch it up to the next level again: Pay attention now to WHO is there, WHERE you are physically and mentally, what the situation is, what you want from it, what they want from you, and the **ENERGY DYNAMIC** that develops in the moment as all of that is happening! As you are aware and paying attention "out there" LOOK WITHIN as well...be watchful and AWARE "in here", not only of the thoughts and beliefs it triggers, but of your ENERGY, and re-actions to it, ALL OF IT! What I want for you to be able to pinpoint is WHEN, at what precise moment your mind gets taken out of the moment!?! Were you present? If not, when did the switch flip off? In addition, was there tension, stress, nerves, anxiety...or was there a sense of excitement, anticipation? What was the energy? Were you really high energy wise, really low, or somewhere in the middle? When did that change, if it changed? Why? DIG!

Observe what was activated within you, and WHEN it was activated! I want you to SEE and understand how you FEEL, before, during, and after events and situations occur, ALL KINDS! Make note, in particular how you feel after an experience. Some people, and some situations energize you, others drain you. Pay attention, there is a reason for this, so revisit and play it back. Where did it go? Only you can answer this, and why! At first it will be seen, after the fact, in most cases. From this point forward, I want you to see it sooner! You are developing a mindful surveillance skill to see this faster and faster... AS it is happening, WHILE it is happening! Energy is being exchanged constantly. Take this next step of discovery, work on this monitoring capability to advance the skill. Watch your thoughts, as you have been, with an added focus on energy IN THE MOMENT, as it is happening! It has to do with where your attention is and being attentive to the evolution of the moment with awareness! What I want you to be able to do is MAXIMIZE the controlled usage of energy IN THE MOMENT! Emotion creates energy, YOU must manage and direct that energy to amplify your SKILL!

Remember please that replaying scenarios is NOT to put you in the past for more than the time required to assess what happened and dissect the evolution of the moment. What I want you to see is the actual unfolding of it, moment by moment, frame by frame, in order to understand exactly what the mind was doing as it unfolded, NOT to be critical of it. This is an extremely important distinction! BLAME is NOT the goal here; in fact, we will talk about that shortly! The goal here is to SEE something, WHERE and WHEN and WHY, and HOW, and WITH WHOM, in WHAT situation, at what TIME, under what circumstances, in what frame of mind, and now at what energy level am I taken out of the moment? What was the energy, how was it affected, where did it go? When? Why? Did I have enough, did I use it effectively? Where & when could I have used the energy more efficiently, preserved it, gained some, and / or managed it better, maybe even channeled it?

This is a TON of information to process, and this is why we need to develop this skill, sharpen it, and ensure that it has enough ENERGY to work properly! PRACTICE, and observe... WATCH! This is an education, and it is FREE, just don't miss class, because you are teaching it to your "SELF"! Higher "SELF" that is! The education is being provided by these lower "selves"; they just don't know it yet! (ha-ha). We need to see where they are using energy effectively, or wasting it, depleting it, being used by it...so that we can preserve it, manage it, and energize the systems. We want and need to maximize its usage efficiently moment by moment! This means being conscious, aware, and observant from many angles all at the same time! Kind of a catch 22 if you really think hard about this. We need energy to maximize the usage of energy. It's like we are finding ways to recapture it and manage it better as situations evolve, but we need energy to do so!

# 5

# THE LAW OF ATTRACTION

T HIS HAS TO DO with our CORE, the underlying THEME within! Or
should I say themes? There are beliefs inside of us! We have programs running on the surface, as well as behind the scenes. In many ways, at multiple levels,
we have a "way" about us, a certain configuration or composition. Call it karma,
the Law of Attraction, magnetism, subconscious mind "stuff" or whatever else.
All of that adds up and a metamorphosis of sorts happens within us as it all
intermixes and blends together. This mass of "stuff" inside us, at our core, has a
way of magnetizing or polarizing us as a collective! In doing so, these underlying
themes create repeating patterns in our lives, have you been noticing this? As
we proceed through our lives, we magnetize some things, and we repel others!
For some things we see them abundantly. They seem to be drawn towards us
consistently, and yet others are scarce if we see them at all! It's like we hold them
off, drive them off, or even chase them away in some cases yet we feel as if nothing
even happened to warrant such a propensity! Something is internally driving this,
and it is different moment to moment...pay close attention. This is driven by the
law of attraction, and we need to see it in operation as it is operating!

The sum total of our stuff, once it all permeates through us, has a way of produc-
ing a generalized "tone" within us and this affects our lives positively or negatively.
It truly transforms and reconstructs us moment by moment, hour by hour, and
day by day. Dynamic and "electric" patterns within us can emerge in an instant,
and be gone in a flash, or they can be prolonged and extend out for many years in
some cases, if we allow them to. This disposition can be powerfully compelling,
seemingly irresistible on some days, and on a different day, at a different time
these tendencies are somewhat muted or seem to have little effect on anything!

This can change in theme, as well as specifics, and we can see it in others as well! When we do drill down on specifics, it can be seen that it truly affects everything. It goes from a general gravitational pull all the way down to the knitty gritty. Lots of inner interdependencies, gears within gears. When it's all said and done, you might call this our overall consciousness engineering. This inner construction & gearing determines the overarching influence we have relative to our "universe". This ranges from BIG THEMES, to minute little patterns and simple occurrences. This, as a whole, represents our inner constitution. In fact, you may as well call it a bill of rights, because it essentially determines what is "allowed" into our lives, our "Governor" as it relates to the Law of attraction.

The net of it all is that by adding up all our good stuff and bad stuff, everything we know, and are, there is a certain "me" or "self" with which we arrive to our life to represent! Everything sort of weighs in on this intricate scale that kind of "measures" us, and configures us. The net of this "stuff" is counterbalanced out in fractions of a second readying us for life as we enter the day, the moment! We either hop out of bed on the "right" side or the alternative and either way, once our feet hit the darn thing, that scale weighs us and our stuff! From the second our feet hit the floor; it seems that often times that initial tone carries us right through the day! The result is a certain stigma or "energy" with which "I" arrive to that day. Each day, in fact, each MOMENT is different because we arrive differently. As a result of how we arrive, in aggregate, we have a certain "draw"! We arrive at the moment with a state of allowing towards some things, and towards others it can be quite contradictory. Internal conflict? No, that never happens. Ha-ha. (sarcasm). The point is, we arrive on some days with somewhat of an attitude because of our inner constitution (good or bad), and this most definitely affects our results. It could mean that proverbial black cloud actually follows us around on any given day, right? It can also mean we arrive to the day with a sense of irresistibility, no clouds at all, and blue bird skies! Just got crazy good night's sleep and we are off to the races. We are larger than life, we cannot be denied, everything seems to go our way!

Let's face it, some people just give off really good vibes, right? We can feel it in other folks as well as within ourselves, the vibe! The alternative, of course, is that maybe the vibe we are giving off is not positive at all. We have all been around a "downer" personality type, we may even be that type at times. People can tend to avoid us on any given day as a result of this! Basically, we give off a vibration and / or operate on a certain frequency, which changes all the time as our internals adapt to what we are experiencing "out there". Our wavelength either aligns with stuff, and people, or it doesn't. This means, we can be on, or off...we can be in tune with our "selves" and others, or we can feel somewhat disconnected. It is quite spectacular, once seen! Pay attention, it matters.

Once again, this truly affects everything, from the way that we carry ourselves, and the way that we appear to others, to how we feel internally, and that inner gearing holds sway over what we are attracting into our lives! We may be walking tall in the AM one day with a commanding presence, and then at the end of that very long day, feel beaten down and tired...so our slouched demeanor reflects a different tone all together. It all matters, smile / frown, all manner of facial expressions, the eyes, the way we stand, sit, walk, talk, eat, drink, etc. They say body language speaks volumes. It really does. It is a reflection of our internals, people see it, and feel it, and we literally resonate a vibration...like we are playing a tune! The tune and tone changes as we meet life moment by moment and the external world affects us. It is heard, it is seen, and it is felt! The question, more importantly, is are you seeing it within?

There is a constant exchange and stabilization going on as we enter each moment. This is important because obviously it can have a significant impact on what is going on internally, WITHIN, moment to moment! Not only do other people see it and feel it, but the universe, our universe responds to it! What we are putting out as we adjust determines what we are resonating, at our core, which reflects right back to us in what is delivered! It's like this constant state of reverberation as we proceed through life. It is so ridiculously consistent that it is almost dependable if we can truly drill down on the mechanics of it. It's almost like an echo, we scream, and then only moments later...we hear a slightly toned-down version of that scream come right back to us. The interesting thing is that it comes back to us multiple times! That's how the law of attraction works, so we need to monitor this attractor factor. The problem, and the reason it isn't 100%, is that there are just too many cross currents. We live in a complex world, with a lot of other magnets. Hundreds of millions of them, and they are poles apart! In the end, that does come into play, so we do need to be cognizant of it, as an overall factor.

Never-the-less, as a result of this magnetic chemistry, similar types of things, people and "results" seem to come into our life, over and over again, right? Our stuff seems to align with their stuff or that stuff! Have you noticed that this is amplified when you are in certain moods? This applies to situations as well, or when we show up to life with a certain "energy", whether that be charismatic, or maybe some alternative to that! This can obviously be good or bad, just notice the difference. We are prone to _____. We have a propensity towards _____. Fill in the blanks! It's an invitation game. We are sending out thousands of invitations each day, yet the universe, OUR UNIVERSE, only hears a select few of them. Our internal magnet is predominantly facing a definite direction and it is magnetizing something, what is it? If we look around, we'll see. Funny thing though, this isn't interchangeable amongst other folks, certainly we see an array of people with an infinite amount of "stuff", and they are all attracting different things, it seems. Some have a ton of it, others, not so much. In fact, our ability to get a response from the universe isn't even the same within us on any given day, is it? It's like some messages are received and others are totally NOT. Some days we seem to get all we could ever want, and others, we feel as if we should have stayed in bed. I must have left my magnet in the dam drawer, or it fell out of my pajamas, and it is still in the bed. Ha-ha! Truth be told, our attractor factor can make a U-Turn in a fraction of a second, with the right stimulus and / or trigger! The fact is our internal chemistry can change really FAST! It's almost imperceptible, at times. Consequently, we are unendingly schooled on this attraction phenomenon. We can miss important details as to why things went a certain way because it happens so fast. So, these things, and these ways find a way to come back to visit us, AGAIN! We got what we got, and we'll get it again, assuming we use the same methodology. Our internals have a lot to do with that, if not everything to do with it. That is why we need to be watchful.

## The LAW is written within...we need to learn our own language!

Bottom line, we need more chalk talk! That's our internal chalkboard, some good ole positive, encouraging, SELF talk. Teaching our "selves" with some internal sticky notes and reminders! We need more awareness, to be quite frank about it. So, in order to get the education that we have been missing, we need to realize and SEE these similar situations and things as they present themselves repeatedly! We need to wake up to it, be on the lookout. First, we need to see it happen as it arrives...and then understand WHY! Sometimes these things and situations will show up more frequently than others. These are opportunities to have a breakthrough so don't ignore them! We are continuously attracting our life, in other words, our life is the result of what we are "attracting" into it at all times! In all things, at our core, we are responsible for what is showing up, at some level. Every bit of it. Now is the time to understand WHY it is showing up as it does, in all the various ways! We want to know and understand when the law of attraction is working for us and pay particular attention to when it's seemingly NOT working! Actually, we need to wake up to the fact that it is actually working all the time, every moment of every day. It's just that sometimes it is working for us, and sometimes against! So, we need to observe when. Sometimes we are an attracting machine, and other times we are literally pushing things away, the people, things, and situations... particularly the ones that we want. This can happen by accident or unconsciously if we are not paying attention, and unaware of our core magnetism momentarily. This can recur over long stretches of time too, if we continue to ignore the signs that we are headed in the wrong direction! We can certainly get and feel stuck, and this is why! Bottom line, we can just as easily magnetize what we don't want and bring MORE of it into our life vs attracting what we want and this can happen by habit, patterns within us...or unconsciousness. We are simply not seeing them.

We need to wake up and see the law of attraction working, and how it is working! It is quite revealing, when, how, how much, and even why is typically discoverable with investigation and a bit of awareness! Something to see, for sure. The stream and the internals that drive it, the major influencing factors, as well as the CORE overall TONE are changeable! We can become aware of what we are attracting. All we need to do, in reality, is look around and then back up for a quick hot second! More specifically though, and early on in this process of discovery, we need to go back into it a little bit mentally. Like hitting the rewind button. This probably means we need to see things arrive in retrospect. It kind of puts the pieces back together for us. We end up with a somewhat surprised acknowledgement. Like "*ohhhhh, now I see why that happened, why I got what I got, when I got it*"! I pretty well asked the universe for it, without speaking the actual words. It is the proverbial wake-up call! Eyes wide open NOW! That typically has to happen before we can see it sooner in the progression though, and sort of affect the process before it affects us adversely, or otherwise! With awareness, we can see it sooner and sooner, faster, and faster!

### The law of attraction is ALWAYS working!
### The question is:
### What are you attracting?

Pay attention to EVERYTHING, as silly as it might seem, stupid stuff even, like whenever you are in a rush, every light is RED!!!!! Whenever you NEED to send a text...the lights are all green! Ha-ha. I love this stuff. It's hilarious really. Wait a minute, NO TEXTING and driving! Seriously, your attention can be very easily diverted, what I am trying to show you is when, how, where, with whom, under what situations, at what times of day, after what type of food you have eaten, caffeinated, decaffeinated, etc. certain stuff, people, and situations show up in your life. It is not a coincidence!

Once seen, THEN, and only then can you see that in that situation, at that time, under these circumstances, we were RIPE for a lesson! We, in fact, brought it on ourselves! It is THEN, that the "you" gets taken over by a "false self" in the mind, and that "you" does something that the real "YOU" didn't intend. In other words, the "you" in your mind at that exact moment reacted in a way that was less than stellar...and so was the result, just SEE IT! Our ability to attract to ourselves the lessons we need is something to behold, undoubtedly. It is extremely impressive! EYE OPENING!

What you will see if you watch, is that there are repeating THEMES, and they repeat in very specific areas of your life. We all have different "stuff", trust me, we are NOT the same. Not by any stretch, we are driven by different things, like different things, and different things motivate us, which also means that different things REPEL us as well. Sometimes those things can generate fear, and fear is a BIG motivator. We tend to flip flop between FEAR and DESIRE, what we want vs what we don't want. At least that is a common pattern I have seen as prevalent within myself. If I am generally attracted to something, like having money for instance...I kind of like having some, so I tend to want more of it. What I have noticed, in a pronounced way is that in years gone past, I was FEARFUL of its opposite...as in NOT HAVING MONEY, or having it taken away, giving it up! It's a dynamic in the mind, like a toggle. We all have stuff we don't want to give up...and it matters! In situations where money was involved years ago, I would get nervous because I didn't want to lose it. That affected my decisions, and those decisions affected my life. Bottom line, if a thought pattern is negatively affecting you the only way to "fix" it is to know that it's there to begin with! The only way to know that it's there is to BE PRESENT with enough energy and awareness, and a highly focused attention NOW to SEE IT!!!!! Remember that **"Where attention goes energy flows"**[11], thanks **James Redfield**! That means being present to oneself and paying attention as to whether this thing is driving us from the positive side or the negative side. Attraction or aversion. Am I attracting something and magnetizing it towards me or am I doing the opposite? If I am doing the opposite, then I am quite literally PUSHING IT AWAY! I may be acting as either one or neither! I could be an attractor in this moment, and a detractor in the next, depending on what the moment presents and who I AM in it. In fact, I may be neutral, but the see saw will typically be weighted more heavily to one side than the other. The point is to see this as it is happening, because it can change in an instant!

The Law of attraction comes into play with everything! We are attracting or averting, constantly. We need to be diligent, in that surveillance mode, observing consciously what we are attracting or averting moment by moment as well as tone wise, situationally. This has to do with fear vs desire, what we want vs what we don't want, and the overall internal chemical energy that is involved as a result. This affects our magnetism, which is our CORE! That CORE is a MAGNET, it can be a tiny little magnet, or HUGE. It can work for you, or completely against you... lightly, or HEAVILY! What we need to see, by paying attention, is what our magnet is magnetizing?! Is it magnetizing anything? Is it even working? How much, how strong is it? Is it working against me, or FOR ME? The sum total of our beliefs is generating an attractor factor, that's our magnet. We need to become conscious of what our magnet is doing. That is the law of attraction! Some days it's watered down. Some days it is so strong you can almost smell it. It's vibrant and alluring.

We will be seeing the law of attraction come up throughout this book and in operation all through our lives. This chapter is merely an introduction to the idea. This is something we will want to be paying attention to, consciously, studiously, at all times! Very, very important!

**LESSON KEY: Watch for the underlying themes! These themes are a result of a magnet, that magnet is YOU! What are you magnetizing? How is that showing up in your life? Your core magnet is your attractor factor! Pay attention to how the law of attraction is affecting your life!**

In the previous chapters we have been very focused on and really drilling down on thought, watching thought, and situational observation of me...looking WITH-IN! NOW, take a few steps back and assess. The question to ask yourself at this point is: Am I seeing recurring patterns, consistent themes, or similar type people over and over again? What, specifically, am I "attracting" into my life? Am I moving TOWARDS or AWAY from anything in particular, people, situations, things, events? AM I attracted to, or repelled from them? As with previous keys, continue to be watchful of thoughts. Now add this new vantage point, that is more all-seeing. Pay attention to the underlying themes and your re-ACTIONS to them as they show up in your life. NOW! Then, if you missed it, look at it after the fact. Am I seeing similar reactions within my "selves" as these situations present themselves in my life? What are the patterns? What are the thoughts? What are the themes? What are my reactions? This is a process of self-discovery, and you are learning more and more about these "selves" that are driving your thoughts and behaviors.

Your REACTIONS are the KEY to SEE! The skill you are developing is to be able to see them faster and faster. The patterns of thought are patterns because of the beliefs and paradigms that you live by each day. With this amplified and expanded awareness, NOW this higher version of YOU will see them, faster, and sometimes IN THE MOMENT as they drive your decisions and actions! <u>You are attracting and repelling constantly, see it happen!</u> What are the fears and /or desires that are driving this? Now combining all of these new skills, and pumping them up with energy, you are able to get to the moment just a little bit faster. It is as if you can almost see the reaction within yourself BEFORE it happens. See if you can see this!

For a fun song to listen to regarding underlying themes, and how we need to put them in this spotlight so to speak, check out the **RUSH** song, **"Limelight"**[12]. I think that this offers a wonderful perspective. Starting with a genuine curiosity watching thoughts and themes will be very helpful, if not fascinating, as portrayed in the song. The intent here is to reveal something to ourselves. It is highlighting for us what the driving forces are, and how the law of attraction is operating in our lives, and that begins with thoughts, and themes of thoughts! They generally hang out together, in other words, thoughts of a similar type! Pay attention to them as they show up, when they show up, and the re-actions within the mind as they do! You are basically shining a light on them... bringing them to the surface, for observation, with awareness and focus!

# 6

# MONEY

M ONEY CAN BE A big positive as well as a big negative. It can be a trigger for people as well, in both ways, and a very influential one! For that reason, let's revisit this concept of FEAR vs DESIRE as it relates to money. I want to explain this very thoroughly from two different times in my life as an example. In one period, I was driven primarily by DESIRE, and in another FEAR. The results I was getting were very much correlated to which one had the power! I want you to see the details as to why though, because it's an important mind element! This should also help you to understand why this is its own chapter. It's a BIG one for a lot of people, and this relationship is a key driver.

Please understand that this is NOT about me, per se, it is being used to explain a mind dynamic so that you can understand the toggles and gearing within the mind, as it relates to money, and the influence it can have! Important to note that how this relates to me may be the same, or somewhat different than how it relates to you. You may want to question whether it is relevant to you first, and then if so, how much? Then take it to the next level and evaluate it a little deeper, like how it may relate to other potential toggles (within you) that are either interdependent or affect you in similar ways! Keep this in mind from that perspective as money can often be a significant contributor to a particular challenge / lesson. Sometimes, what we see at the surface is truly just the tip of the iceberg. So as always, dig deeper! Looking at this superficially is probably not going to get you down to the elemental factors that are pushing and pulling the gears within. So, having said that, don't focus on the "Doug" aspect of this! On the contrary, DO try to understand the mindset or paradigm that I was operating

FROM, as it relates to money, and how that may relate to how you look at things! This will be more beneficial to you from that perspective.

When I was first developing my strategies to trade stocks, I was making a whole bunch of money... In my psychology, way back then, I was not really attached to the outcome. I wanted them to do well, but quite honestly, I was so busy and focused on my career that I wasn't able to pay as much attention. Secondly, I believed the book that I had read and did what it said to do, so I just expected it to work. In the grand scheme, psychologically speaking, it really did not matter whether the stocks went up or the book I read was "right"...there was no stress around money at that time in my life. All my stocks went up!!!! All of them, I mean, I bought a stock at 2 dollars, it went to 100, I bought another at 52 cents, it went to like 23 dollars +. My account went from a few thousand to a few hundred thousand. I really wasn't even paying attention! Yes, I was excited, but I was busy at my "day job"!

Flip the coin: several years go by, the stock market tanks...I cashed out a bunch of stocks, but the Lion's share of them "lost" a lot of paper money. Easy come easy go, right? I just thought everything went up forever, I didn't have an exit plan! LOL. Anyway, that created a bit of a pain point for me, kind of irked me! Well, it's easy to see that as a future trigger, right?! Make a note of that. It did not register at that time, quite honestly, because I was not stressed relative to money. However, if / when you have a fragile ego, being "right" or "wrong" can be associated with winning or losing. When identified with it in that fashion, it can be particularly painful, or the opposite. What I want to emphasize here is that we can identify with it relative to our self-worth, as we win or lose, or as our account values go up or down! In a stock or money account, "worthiness" can be reflected in the dollar values of wins or losses, account balances, or the result of the last trade we took. That is particularly true if we don't have a good relationship with money! When I say good, I really mean "BALANCED"! Money, in my opinion, is not good or bad, it is simply a means of exchange. Just keep that in mind.

A few more years go by, I was still making a lot of money but then I lost my job. Uh Ohhhh...income stream gone; confidence shaken... I had never been fired from anything. I was more than a bit shaken; I was embarrassed. How could this happen? Well, get up dust yourself off and go at it again... Well, I could not do it. I was burnt out, tired, and somewhat broken! So, I took a step back, took some time off and literally studied everything I could get my hands on...for 12 YEARS!!!!! Ok, maybe it had a little bit bigger impact on me than I thought! That's a pretty long time.

During that timeframe, I banged my head against the wall quite a bit, not literally, but it was a trying period for me. I had pretty much figured out the markets and was trading them in a simulated environment, but for whatever reason, I couldn't really put the final pieces together. I could see the patterns, and really understood them. What I learned though was that in that situation, with my back to the wall financially (no income) and having a more limited amount of money to trade with, I could not trade successfully. The FEAR was winning every time. Why? Because I NEEDED the money. You can't trade that way, it's not balanced. The weight is too heavily on the side of fear, and that drives the decisions. In trader land, the fear will win until you either overcome the fear or have a little more insulation from losses...or both! I determined that I would change course, make some money elsewhere, then return to the markets later. You see, quite easily from this perspective, that I did not have a balanced relationship with money and, of course, it was affecting my results!

The reason I am telling you this is because it is a perfect example of how fear operates in the mind. Something had obviously changed within me, and I saw this happen right in front of my own eyes, as I was trading, REAL TIME! I knew exactly what to do, but due to the "trigger", and my situation, the mind would step in and get in my way! That "self" was fearful of LOSING, and that version of self, "I" NEEDED to WIN...or at a minimum, NOT LOSE! My trading system would say, take the trade here, my mind would stutter, delay, or not even take the trade...it was amazing to me to watch it. That "self" was stepping in and BLINDING me because it was operating from a mindset of pain avoidance! The good news is that this new higher version of me, the new "I" was starting to gain this new perspective and the lower version of "self" was starting to be seen. I was waking up and now conscious of it, seeing it happen! Unfortunately, I missed a lot of good trades that way. I watched as it was happening in my own mind, right in front of me...IN THE MOMENT, with full on awareness. I saw it happen repeatedly, as the moment would slip away! I was so close, yet it would slip right through my fingers, so to speak. This opened my eyes to a whole new world. So that is where, when, and how my TRUE education began as I applied it to every aspect of life as I knew it! Seeing that  this mind gearing truly affects everything was a major and very impactful epiphany for me!

As a result, I was able to create some psychological "hacks" and just kept working at it, HARD...and when I say HARD, I mean, like 18 hours a day hard, massive amounts of screen time. A LOT of frustration! Part of me was trying to work around the problem, ME, by using more strategies and indicators, and then refining them with programming. The other part of me was working my way through it... with education, OF ME, and refining ME, with more programming!

This meant massive amounts of watchful study, programming, research, tuning, fine tuning, and then more programming, endlessly, virtually 24 hours a day, to the extent that I could keep my focus, and my eyes open. As soon as I woke up, I'd be right back at it again. I had an inner resolve to master this, and it was a red hot burning desire! I probably reprogrammed about everything in Tradestation, exaggeration...but I have spent a ton of time making my own indicators and strategies. Over time, and thousands of hours of screen time, I had created a way to look at the markets that was ridiculously accurate...and I was also "in the zone" a lot of the time! I was getting a little bit better at this thing called me as well! I saw the markets, on lightning-fast timeframes, and had literally slowed time to the point where I was picking the EXACT low tick on the E Mini S&P or Soybean futures markets. I had it all fine-tuned, figured out...and then I ran desperately short on funds. Many years had passed, and I hadn't made any real money! I was still learning to control this aspect of myself, so I was trading in a simulated environment. Ultimately, while this new illuminated perspective was enthralling, due to this money thing, I had to go back to work! The cool thing was that I had figured this stuff out, this MIND STUFF, trading was just the tool I needed to see it, real time. What a blessing...to see such a thing, powerful!

I was NOW set out to light it up, set the world on fire, and show everyone that this MIND STUFF actually works. I was excited about it. First, I had to prove it to myself though. It was a redirection of sorts, for sure, however, I was working on the same mind concepts. On top of that, I was reassessing everything, and really working super hard on my awareness. I was creating a virtual mind blueprint for myself that detailed the evolution of the moment in extremely minute detail. I broke it down, over and over again in my mind. Seeing the "slow motion" trades where time had truly slowed down right in front of me...and learning how to focus the mind that hard really opened my eyes to how "IT" (the mind) really works. The important thing that I kept coming back to was that sometimes it can actually get us in our own way, mentally. Actually, A LOT!!!! This was a major key. So, during that timeframe, I was really digging in and paying attention to when my mind would get in my own way, when I made poor decisions, and when I made good ones. What was I focused on in that moment? I would dissect it. This was instrumental in learning and moving forward! It really played a huge role in my own development! That's why I explain it in such detail, everything is interrelated. It's really important to pay attention to the things that drive you, and then pay attention to how the mind and body react as a result of that "attachment"! This is very beneficial, if not pivotal!

So back to money, it was obviously a big motivator for me. I wanted a lot of stuff, for all the wrong reasons. As I "grew up", I thought that I was getting wiser...and the need for money did change a bit, from wanting stuff to wanting security. I think I was more motivated by the fear of NOT having money, especially in that timeframe, than motivated by the stuff that money can buy. Yes, I do like my toys...they just make me smile. I do like comfortable things, and seriously why not have them? I was never a showboat, mainly just like what I like, and I like to be comfortable. To an extent you do need a few dollars rolling around to take care of yourself and others. So back to the point:

## Pay attention to what is driving you!

Are you motivated by fear or desire? Is that always, or just towards certain things, situationally? Where is that coming from? How does it make you feel? It's not wrong, and I am not judging, the question is for YOU...so that you can understand the inner workings of your own mind. Dig deeper.

Remember what my dad asked, which is a GREAT QUESTION:

## "Are you running towards something, or away from something?"[13]

What do you want? What motivates you? What is the antithesis to that? Which one is carrying the weight? Health vs sickness or dis-ease is a popular one for a lot of people too...as an example. Some folks are truly fearful of getting sick, so they constantly think about ailments, looking them up online, analyzing symptoms, naming them, and identifying more. YIKES! If the information is generating more fear, vs "answers", or solutions, please stop. Fear is FEAR, I don't care what it is aimed at, it isn't helping! As a start, find just 1 thing to feel good about. Focus on health, even if you have to imagine it initially! If you need help, go to the Doctor, get help! Maybe that is required to point you in the right direction, mentally and / or physically. We get what we focus on, and it expands! Sometimes a little mental steering is all that is required, other times, maybe we need a little professional help. Just saying, pay attention to which side of the coin is driving you, whether you go to the Doctor, or not. Heck, if you go to the Dr. and wonder, "What if the medicine doesn't work"? Well, that's probably not the best use of your mind! Is that thought doing you any good? Where does it lead the mind? YOU? Is this question leading you towards the positive side, or the negative? My suggestion is to ask a better question! Funny actually, and maybe worth mentioning. Do you happen to realize how often placebo's work? I am not a doctor, and I make no claims here, nor am I making any recommendations relative to using them, but the stats are actually quite impressive! If placebo's work, then the mind must be pretty powerful if used properly! Imagine if you had a powerful placebo effect, and some medicine! How cool would that be. I am obviously playing, but think about it, real medicine, and MIND medicine! I tend to be a believer though, so I guess I have to ask. Are you a half full type, or half empty? Is this relative to everything, or just some things? The negative side, focusing on what you don't want is not helping!

**LESSON KEY:** **Watch your thoughts and behaviors surrounding MONEY, and if that's not important to you, determine what is! Specifically! Health? Beauty? Security? Safety? Relationships? Food? Challenges? Puzzles? Achievement? Power? Love? Truth? Knowledge? What ranks for you? These are just a few examples...now pay attention to the opposite of that, and how you relate to it. Are you more motivated to move towards what you want, or away from what you don't want? This is a huge clue that will help you determine how you are weighing these different things, as well as which is tipping the scale to lean one way or the other! That's your focus, your rudder, and it determines which way your magnet is facing!**

Assess this, continuously, in the moment! As in, what is the driver? Once you see what is driving you to do the things you do, then you can make more educated decisions about whether to keep doing them or not. Kind of simple, really, but as you start to dissect your thoughts and pay attention moment by moment by moment, you may be surprised by what is driving the "you" and your thoughts and actions. It is super ridiculously important to understand the mechanisms driving you to do what you do...in ALL THINGS! Pay attention though... particularly around MONEY, or the key drivers in your life! Work on your awareness and maintaining a balanced perspective! As often as possible, come back to being awake and aware, with presence...NOW! How are you feeling, what are you thinking, where are your hands, feet, legs, arms, eyebrows, teeth...are they tapping, clinched, relaxed, stressed, tight, loose? Why? What EXACT thought, or train of thought, is causing this feeling, reaction, status within you? Is it steering you one way or another? What are your present motivators, are you anxious, excited, optimistic, pessimistic...does money have anything to do with it? if not, what does? What are the influencing factors? Are you expecting a good result, bad result, don't know? More money, less money? Just pay attention to your thoughts around money and how they make you feel, this will be an education in itself! It may take some time, so please give yourself some additional patience vitamins!

There are obviously a lot of other things that motivate people, certainly not just money. I chose to drill down on money because it is easy for me to explain, and there are not a lot of grey areas! Money does affect a lot of other things too, so it tends to be a core issue, or be involved in others, one way or another. Other examples might be achievement, relationships, security, adrenaline, power, control, pride, risk, peace, love, intimacy, health, food, physical appearance, and there are many more. Understand that in all things there will be a MIND tendency to PUSH towards or PULL away from them. This is the mind RE-action relative to having it or NOT having it. A desire for it, or a FEAR of not having. An attraction to or an avoidance of. A wanting of or NOT wanting the alternative. Having a focus geared towards abundance or lack. Belief / faith in and trust or Non-belief! Half full, half empty. Attracted to or repelled from. The key is to SEE which side of this mental equation you are operating from, REAL TIME, NOW! Seeing this in the moment is showing you what has the power within! Are you trying to move towards something, or away from the opposite of it? In the actual moment of the decision, what is the deciding factor? Pleasure seeking, pain avoidance, or maybe towards some things it might be more neutral, balanced, and unbiased? Notice the differences as the moment is unfolding. Answer the question with your awareness of this dynamic as it is happening in your mind! Try as much as possible to really drill down on the moment, with your awareness of the "within" aspect as life is unfolding, particularly as meaningful decisions are being made. Having particular "NEEDS" or must have things and situations is going to change this dynamic within. Seeing this is key, it will open your eyes. The drivers of these decisions are going to come much more into focus as you pay attention to the way that life is unfolding, and where the mind is placing "importance", which will heighten SELF understanding, and this will, in turn, create opportunities for growth.

Awareness & presence dialed up and tuned in shows us aspects of our "selves" we would not ordinarily see. Pay attention! Whether we show up to a moment with an attitude that is smiling and optimistic is a huge contrast to one of dread and an expectation of an undesirable result. The body can give us important clues as to which way we are leaning! It does it in many ways too. In some folks, it may show up as sweaty hands, or arm pits. In others, it might be an uneasy stomach, indigestion, diarrhea in anticipation of something or later. The entire "body language" of the self that arrives to the moment is often very insightful, assuming we are paying attention! POOR thoughts and patterns of thoughts are very telling! We see it in others, by the way that they carry themselves, speak, their demeanor, enthusiasm, facial expressions, mannerisms, etc. but do we see it in our "selves"? Are we paying attention to the thoughts that are generating the responses within? Which way are the sides of your mouth facing? Are your eyebrows furrowed? Pay attention to this, and other important clues.

The physical attributes reflect where the mind is focused, possibly on the negative as an example, which would show up in the body in an undesirable way.

We may be resisting something, and / or even just resisting the actual reaction in the body! Nervousness, anxiety, unnecessary sweat, stress, tension. These all affect EVERYTHING that the body does, from the way it holds itself to the way it processes food and supports itself. Everything matters and it begins with thought. Ever get a tension headache? This didn't just happen, it is the result of a progression, thoughts upon thoughts, and patterns of thought. So, what is the thought that you are thinking that is driving this "lack of health", lack of ease, or frown WITHIN? Be watchful! Maybe, you could change your focus to an abundance of health, a big smile, or better thoughts that are geared towards it! Think of it this way, is my mind presently in a state of "EASE" or uneasiness? Also called disease or DIS-ease! Coincidence? I think not. Where, when, with whom, and possibly situationally, how much am I seeing this DIS-ease? To what extent? Here lies a story, and weight, possibly a NEED! Uncover it, dig a little, SEE IT! Then change your mind.

Funny thing is, once seen with presence, the thoughts that drive these things can be changed. Once this is done the physical association is GONE, and so the body is "healed", sometimes instantly! I am not promising some miracle, but I will say that a healing could range from a "no sweat" attitude, to no more allergies, to seeing more serious ailments go away as well. Again, I AM NOT A Doctor, nor do I encourage you to go it alone should you need medical attention, this is just something that I have experienced myself, so I know it to be true! I was told I would never throw again due to a shoulder injury, yet I healed, and in fact, I learned to throw with both hands! I proceeded to play quarterback for the football team a year later as well. I was told I needed nasal surgery, NOT, I somehow "gave up" allergies after 30 years of nose sprays within a fairly short period! I have "healed" from many physical ailments, and I promise you that the mind has a lot to do with it! I had one situation years ago that debilitating back pain vanished overnight from nothing more than a mental insight! It was from reading a really good book, nothing more, no drugs, no operation, nothing! BIG thanks to **Dr. John E. Sarno**, and his book **"Healing back pain"**! This really helped me understand more deeply how the mental affects the physical! He has another book, **"The Mindbody Prescription"**[14] that is geared to more than just back pain! Brilliant books. I know firsthand that this stuff works! My wife can attest to it. Amazing perspectives and powerful mind angles dealing with and processing emotions! Awareness can erase years of mental negativity in an instant, once seen, and understood! Mental health and its physical corollary can benefit quite quickly! We will get more into the emotions, and emotional intelligence in chapter 8. First, let's talk about resistance!

# 7

# RESISTANCE

R ESISTANCE COMES FROM NON-BELIEF in what you want, or if you want to put it in different perspective, it is FAITH in the OPPOSITE of what you want! It is having a focus on, and belief in what you don't want, whether conscious or unconscious. It is a program (core belief) that believes in the OPPOSITE and so it is focused there. It is an underlying theme that is often below the surface of your conscious mind that is acting as a MAGNET to what you don't want! The UNAWARE mind not knowing that it believes something that goes AGAINST what it "WANTS" is a secret saboteur of your best laid plans to "get what you want". This can be related to our health, wealth, and pretty much everything else! Really, take that in for a moment, everything is affected, ALL, the whole kit and caboodle...our "universe"!

So, having said that, wouldn't it be wise to know what these underlying themes are? Would it make sense to uncover these "CORE" beliefs with awareness in the moment so that you can remove the magnetism to the opposing force? Often that means to that which is FEARED. If you find yourself "worrying" a lot... for instance, that is a clue that you are focused, in one way or another on the OPPOSITE of what you want. Worry is essentially a negative visualization...and YOU ARE CHOOSING to focus on FEAR, or the negative! STOP! When fear is the focus, you get what is feared. Remember that slogan, **"where attention goes energy flows"**[15]! When you worry or when you focus on FEAR... that is, you, ALLOWING the law of attraction to work against you! Wouldn't you like for the Law of attraction to work in your favor vs attracting what you don't want? What you need to see is that depending on which "magnet" has more power, you will either attract what you want or REPEL IT. Paying attention to what you are focused on, the emotions being generated, and the attitudes that prevail in your mind on a moment-to-moment basis will show you in REAL TIME, what you are focused on...and then of course you see the result! Pay attention to that dynamic.

That dynamic will be determined by a lot of things, some of which you don't have control. What you do have control of is your mind, and what you are focused on. (Your thinking) With awareness, you can gain a tremendous amount of power. Power is generated two ways: First, by cancelling the magnets that are working against you. Second, by amplifying the magnets that are working for you!

How? WITH AWARENESS! By understanding that you can only shift what you are focused on when you are aware enough to see it. If you can't see it, you can't change it. That means that you are unaware, or it is in your subconscious. Resistance that is unconscious, is a program running behind the scenes that does NOT have your best interests in mind. Think DIS-ease vs EASE! Where is the mind? DIS-ease or negative emotion = resistance! It will magnetize that which you don't want until or unless you become aware enough as that decision is made <u>CONSCIOUSLY</u> to SEE IT! You MUST become vigilant about paying attention as your life happens, as in hyper aware, NOW! Did you ever notice that in certain situations, at certain times, you get what you want...and in others you get what you resist, or you are afraid of, or what you don't want? This an underlying theme, which needs to NOT be an underlying theme. As you gain awareness, your underlying themes can go away by using your new SKILLS, and you eliminate the opposing magnets. Cancel your subscription to the magnets that are not serving you by uncovering them, exposing them, seeing, and understanding them!

**<u>LESSON KEY:</u> Where is my focus? I NEED TO KNOW where the Law of attraction is working for me or against me and understand how this shows up within me!**

From this elevated vantage point, with awareness, all your energy and all this skill you have been developing... watch your thoughts and determine one more thing. **<u>Am I focused on what I WANT, or what I Don't want?</u>** This is really important, not only to see situationally but to know how it shows itself within. This is going to highlight for you a KEY MIND ELEMENT which is determining your MAGNETISM! Your magnetism is given its power to be magnetic by whichever you are focused on and how much emphasis you are giving it. To that degree, whichever you are focused on is where your energy is being directed. Directed = direction, like as in, which way is it pointed? Where your energy goes is where your FAITH is being pointed! To which are you giving your faith? PAY ATTENTION! Am I driven by and having faith in what I am attracted to, or what I am repelled from, and to what degree? Like how strong is this DRIVE to run towards something or away from something? Am I afraid of, worried about, and focused on avoiding the bad result or optimistic, expecting and visualizing a good result? Your focus is being driven by these underlying beliefs, and the patterns of thought you are bringing into the moment! Optimism, pessimism, your paradigm, your expectation for example in that situation, relative to that thing...is DRIVING the RE-action (in the mind), watch this! Are the pictures / scenes that are being generated in the mind what you would consider to be "good" or "bad", what you want and are aiming for or what you don't want? The images / thoughts are generating the re-action / re-sponse! The "RE" part of that RE=action or RE-sponse is determining the RESULT, until YOU arrive to the moment to make a NEW CHOICE! A NEW CHOICE is a NEW ACTION, vs a RE-action which is NOT, and that is why I highlight that difference repeatedly! If you are not in the moment, if this "RE" part of the chain re-action in that fraction of a second is allowed to RE-spond then it is an <u>automatic reaction, and NO NEW CHOICE is made here</u>!

SEE THIS, when you are asleep at the wheel, unaware, unconscious! Are you focused and aware enough to see this? WAKE UP! NOW! See if this was a RE-action or a NEW ACTION?! If you are not awake, aware, and PRESENT, then you are giving your power away to these former and / or future hypothetical "selves" who will gladly step into the moment and decide (RE-act) for you, AS YOU, because they want to be you and stay you! It happens FAST, lightning fast! The problem is that the response is generated from an imagined "self", one that is focused on the past or future and not this NEW YOU that is PRESENT NOW!! In any given moment these "selves" could be focused on what you don't want, out of habit, a strong belief, or un "conscious" ness! Pay attention and SEE this. What are you are inviting into your life, moment by moment? You must TAKE YOUR POWER BACK if you are not focused! With MASSIVE awareness, determine where your focus is PRESENTLY, on what you want, or what you don't want! That is the power of intention, you are intentionally and now CONSCIOUSLY directing your FAITH, PRESENTLY, NOW and NOW...and NOW! In doing so, **YOU are <u>consciously CHOOSING</u> what you want to invite into your life!**

## EMOTION, highlights resistance!

So, let's talk about emotion!

# 8

# EMOTION

Y ES, WE HAVE THEM. Yes, sometimes they suck, and YES, sometimes they
are GREAT!!! Did you ever think about how awesome, awesome feels
though...and that awesome would not feel so awesome if there was no comparison? In other words, awesome feels awesome because it compares to sucks! It
is in relation to, and the opposite of SUCKS! You can't have one without the
other. While I was growing up, I just wanted awesome, and I was always afraid
of SUCKS!!!! Everything seems to happen in waves though...up waves don't last
forever and just the same, down waves don't last forever either...it is important to
understand this! We get less caught up in the extremes this way, and we are less
prone to being swept away by the emotions of life. Bottom line, when we are not
afraid of "SUCKS", when we don't RESIST the bad stuff...awesome happens a
lot more of the time...and that's AWESOME!!!!

Here's the deal though. To see emotion, it requires a little bit of a different vantage
point, or lens so to speak. Emotions tend to sweep us up and carry us away very
quickly, so what we have done is generated our own "learned responses" to them,
so we don't have to "think" or even "feel" them at all in some cases. The emotions
kind of just happen in the background, and we ignore them, right? NO...NO!
NOT ANYMORE! Now, we are having an intervention! LOL. Seriously though,
I want you to see this as it is happening. What we tend to do is try to avoid
or ignore the painful emotions and just have the good ones! Some emotions
we acknowledge, and others we really don't. In order to gain "understanding"
though, we need a different methodology because ignorance and avoidance gain
us NOTHING! There is quite an array of emotions, and they are all telling us
different things. These are valuable moments of insight, and they are slipping

right through our fingertips a lot of the time when we fall asleep at the wheel! We have trained our "selves" to just dismiss them and move on, or whatever else! Your new lens will see this maneuvering, and instead this new higher "YOU" will get the needed information in the moment! Emotions are there for a reason, they highlight and alert us that something important is happening, a LESSON...so WAKE UP!! A STORYLINE is being revealed to you, you must SEE IT!

Pay very close attention to your "triggers"! These are instances where emotions tend to get dialed up really quick. You will see some common themes here, and you will see them faster and sooner than you did before! GOOD WORK! When they come up, do your best to try to slow down and breathe. I know life happens fast, just do your best. Try to NOT get caught up inside the actual emotion itself. YOU NEED TO WATCH IT, not ignore it. Watch it as if it were not yours though! You can't watch emotion if you are all caught up IN IT! You must maintain a detached vantage point from it and just watch with this new lens. The key here is to watch the mind as these emotions come up because there is a storyline BEHIND the emotion...try to SEE IT! Watch what the mind is doing / thinking / feeling in all of these different "states of mind" as these emotions come up. I realize this is a tall task, as there are an infinite number of situational things that can bring up an infinite amount of "stuff". For me it helped to use a product called **"HOLOSYNC"**[16]. It took an intense amount of effort and focus to drill down on and expand my awareness. Over time, this has helped me to uncover a lot of these "Me's", the little "selves" I refer to as they generate emotions. Awareness is the key to see the programming behind them and learn what that programming is attached to. That "attachment" is ultimately what generated the emotion, but we don't take the time, nor do we focus hard enough with awareness to see behind it. In this way, we can see how important it is. Emotion is telling us and highlighting it for us as a feeling when to be most alert so that WE CAN SEE these various "selves" and their storylines as they develop!

As a result of the emotional clue to pay attention, and NOW your amplified awareness, you will discover what these selves are concerned with and attached to! Ask yourself...what's driving this emotion / feeling, what is pushing, and pulling them? Their priorities, the EGO mechanisms that drive these "selves" all have attachments. These attachments carry weight, that weight is determined by what "I" personally call GOOD vs what I call BAD and how much of a priority it is to want to move towards or away from it! That boils down to what I WANT vs what I don't want, right? We need to know which version of "Me" is driving the "Me" bus (in the mind) and know what that version of me WANTS or is attached to. What is driving its decisions, determines how successfully YOU can accomplish the task at hand. It will determine what other emotions come up, which is driven by the various EGO attachments! By knowing all of that and being present to the moment, YOU can't be blindsided, and YOU CAN decide for yourself. It all starts with a twinge, the twinge is the clue...as that twinge of emotion begins to arise, you activate the window, this new lens, and watch! With awareness, YOU have choice. Say it, with awareness "I" have choice!

With CHOICE, YOU can choose a NEW thought and make a NEW decision, take a NEW ACTION in the moment! This is the skill you must consistently work on, otherwise, human nature is to stay the same...whether that is good or bad. We just don't like change! This always reminds me of a song called **"Vital signs"**[17], by the band **RUSH**. RUSH, the way that I hear their songs, have endless vantage points about the mind, EGO, alter egos, spirituality, etc., and this song is one of the best songs that I have heard that seems to explain this phenomenon! This song, in my opinion, describes the mind gears in a very cool manner! It also explains what I was doing when I was "trading"...yes, I was trading, but I was also watching the mind as it processed the information and I "acted" or "RE-acted"...like as in "Pusha de button" to take the trade! That's my dad's funny way of saying push the button. It makes me laugh, literally just by saying it! This was my methodology to discover the actual timing of decisions, and whether or not I was able to be present to make it. If I did push the button, or I didn't, and if it was early or late, I made every effort to be PRESENT and SEE IT, see the decision being made, NOW.

The reason I bring up emotion and dwell on it so much is to make undoubtedly clear that emotion is THAT THING that highlights the triggers. Once triggered, the emotion sweeps in and right then alongside the whooooosh of emotion, right behind it, who steps in while we are sidetracked? The false self, one of the lower "selves"! Emotion tends to step in and assist the little "selves" and their programming **IN BLINDING US!** Be on the lookout! The way it happens, in a very simplified manner, is that we enter a situation, we get attached to a certain outcome, the "fear" (stress and anxiety) about NOT having the thing that we want kicks up an emotion, and that emotion sweeps us up and GRABS US (the mind). As it does this, in a fraction of a second it OUTWEIGHS the positive "desire" for the "good" result. The one we want! As the FEAR enters the mind, the EMOTION of it literally tips the scale towards focusing on what we don't want, and in an instant, the MIND is incapable of deciding otherwise because it takes us out of the moment...and fear wins. How does fear win? Fear won because in essence, the emotion of it SHUT DOWN the processor, and you no longer had access to the "ability" to decide. A RE-action was generated, and the RE-action was from the "self" that RE-acted, WITHIN! YOU failed to man your post, with your new skill, and were not in the moment to REPRESENT! Man your post!

This is military jargon for be on your guard, watching. In essence that means that you were unaware and not present from an operative standpoint, so WAKE UP! You have to see this happen. The decision, in that moment, was made for you, but it wasn't the real higher YOU that made it... YOU MUST be on the cutting edge of the moment of NOW to see this as it happens! Keep working on this SKILL!

Another discovery that helped me was that I spent some time researching the lizard brain and understanding how the mind literally changes where it processes from and that actually does matter. Trading drove me to that too. Emotion is the trigger that flips the switch, and by flipping the switch / hitting your "TRIGGER"...the mind goes from processing in the front which I think that is the prefrontal cortex if I remember correctly...to the BACK, the amygdala! It essentially removes the "YOU" from the decision-making process and without getting too spiritual on you...**THAT IS THE GATE**! When they say that narrow is the gate, the gate is the razors edge between yesterday and tomorrow...a moment ago and the moment to come. Narrow is the gate. YES, that's pretty darn narrow!

**LESSON KEY: Watch early for emotions/feelings as they arise and when your mind gets triggered or disconnects as a result!** This is a methodology to truly expand and empower your emotional intelligence!

Whenever the mind is triggered, it tends to disconnect in one way or another and / or it goes into fight or flight mode! Watch this. The decisions that are made in these moments are "RE-actions" not NEW actions! Watch your "self" get taken out of the moment. SEE these RE-actions as they happen! In order to do that you will need to wake up, pay attention, and energize the higher "SELF" to be alert, awake, aware and PRESENT, NOW! These situations are often preceded by an emotion, watch for this CLUE to pay attention, and heighten your awareness. Without presence, your life goes on the way it was...with presence YOU have choice to move in a different direction, if you choose to! INTEND to BE PRE-SENT to CHOOSE, and then CHOOSE WISELY with awareness and focus, NOW!

# 9

# GOOD & BAD, BLACK & WHITE, PREFERENCES!

O NCE YOU REALLY DIGEST and understand this stuff, the good news is that you will ultimately GET and ENJOY a lot more of what you PREFER! GOOD, in your eyes, will happen a lot more than bad! The cool thing is that you can go on preferring all you want, while not being afraid of the opposing dynamic!

Chapter 9 / 10 is about putting it all together. I want this higher "YOU" getting in THE ZONE with even MORE CONSISTENCY! Keep the progress going. I want to get a little more analytical to really dissect the thinking aspects of this understanding. For me it really helped me to kind of see it in charts and what not to assess things situationally! This is where the rubber meets the road. Tying it all up, putting all the pieces together. Each insight is a level gained in understanding which amplifies your power to access THE ZONE and shows you how to get there in a more RELIABLE and CONSISTENT manner!

This is a progression, so stay with it! It will include some amazing music and quotes to explore from some talented and insightful people! The lessons are not always blatantly obvious, and they will hit you from different angles too, so take some time to explore in order to assess what each of these may mean to you vs. accepting what it means to me as I explain or mention them! I will introduce songs and artists, and music, and of course I'll tell you what they are saying to me, which may also be in line with what you see or hear. It may not, you may hear something different, which is fine! Take the time to look up the lyrics and listen to the music though to be sure you get the most out of it! These are very powerful examples in my opinion, and because of the way these artists deliver them, in tone, speed, various voices, etc. they will help with "processing" this information! Hearing these ideas & themes from different vantage points helps. These insights will challenge the way you think in a fairly dramatic way if you really hear, see, and ponder them. Carefully examining and understanding these inclusions at more than just a surface level will make it more impactful for you and more fun too! Just thinking about thinking and watching thought can be a little labor some, I get it! It's nice to hear the same lessons from other sources and angles, and people that also appear to be challenging "thought"!

So, I am going to mix it up a little bit for you with links to videos, quotes from some notable authors, and some musical examples that will break things up a little bit and really make you think! Dig deep and analyze the way these examples may phrase things just a little bit differently, yet they are saying the same or similar things. I can't emphasize enough that what I explain that I hear may be different than what you hear, which may be different than what the band intended...so please assess, so that you may gain from the assessing! Pay attention as always to what it brings up within you. What I think is cool is that using different words, and emphasis, and angles, a lot of people are coming to the same conclusions and providing similar "instructions" in various ways...It's REALLY refreshing! That's also NOT a coincidence... so, let's go ahead and GET IN THE ZONE!

# 10

# GETTING IN THE ZONE

T HE DIAGRAM BELOW WAS in a write-up by **Bill Harris** who was the owner of **Centerpointe research**. (Rest in peace Bill, Thank you!) He developed a product called **"HOLOSYNC"**[18], which is designed to help you increase your awareness using brain entrainment/meditation. He also wrote some really good stuff in his blog, and book: **"Thresholds of the mind"**[19]. Seeing this diagram below made me think about sports, and life of course, and then I sent these ideas to my sister for her and her sons, in an effort to explain how top athletes access the "ZONE". They were going into little league at the time, and I guess I thought that I wish I knew then, at their age, what I know now...and I don't have kids, so I wanted to pass this knowledge along! In any case, it is equally powerful in other applications, at any age, for anyone, and honestly...every moment where performance may or may not measure up, hope it is helpful, and by all means let me know how it helps you! This is edited more for a general audience...rather than being directed towards Donna, Troy & Tyler.

This is **about motivations, accessing the moment, achievement IN the MO-MENT**, the understanding of **"FLOW states"**[20] and getting in **THE ZONE**! Take everything that you have learned so far, dissect it even further, and move forward with me progressively! The result is a super amplified and focused perception. Build this SKILL, your ability to access the zone with presence!

**DIAGRAM BELOW:** The "ZONE" is top right. Situations can, and do begin anywhere on the chart, depending on a variety of factors as well as who is involved and their relationship to you, among other things. For ease, let's begin at the bottom left, as you would normally, and proceed to the right, as if you are reading. If you ascend 45 degrees up and to the right...like a good stock chart, you are growing! If you proceed directly north, up the left side, you may be a "worry wart", or caught up in a cycle of fear one way or another, bumping your head against some resistance, or whatever else which may be keeping you from the things you want (FEAR). If you proceed to the right along the bottom, you might be breezing through life, with very little challenging you, or not challenging yourself at all? Possibly the other end of the spectrum in that "Ignorance is bliss" so to speak or you have attained SELF mastery, and everything is EASY because you are in the ZONE!!

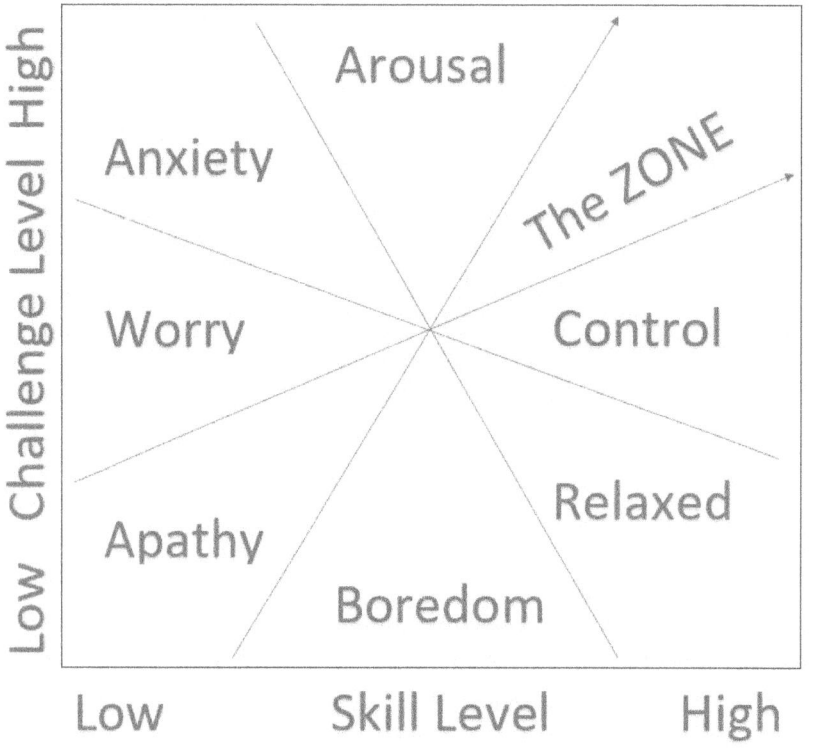

Keep in mind that it is NEVER that simple! We all start from different places, different levels of awareness, and different upbringings. That being said, every moment, every situation is different and everyone in it has a differing "LENS" with which they look at it and ARRIVE FROM! The people involved may not be the same as the last moment we were in, the situational components are always different, and the "attachments" that weigh on you and them, can be different as well. So, lets approach this knowing that in every situation, we could be starting from a different point on this chart! Again, to assess, let's start bottom left. Starting with disinterest, or apathy towards the content of the moment (situationally) and expanding towards stuff that you actually DO care about!

This is a schematic of what the mind does, as a processor in various situations, as it enters them. This is what that looks like from an analytical brain perspective...what I want to do is back off and analyze it. I have been working for the better part of my life to amplify my abilities, not only physically, but more importantly, mentally. The mental side of the equation is super ridiculously powerful, not necessarily from a "thinking" mind only, but more importantly from an awareness perspective.

What I have come to realize is that with practice, it does become easier to access the zone, and that for some situations, it is most definitely easier than others. In addition, that is going to differ for everyone, based on conditions, attachments, awareness, and talent, both physically and mentally. On top of that, the level of awareness / consciousness matters. The attachments and conditioning will be driven by EGO mind, and awareness, or lack of it, and that (skill level) will determine the individual's ability to cycle through the various quadrants in the diagram to end up in "FLOW", or to get into the zone. (Or NOT).

There are many other variables that also affect the ability to access the ZONE, including physical conditioning, or stamina, mental ability, or the ability to handle various stressors, and whether you are full of energy or tired, hungry, or affected in some other way for instance. And then after all of that come the mental blocks that you need to work through, or EGO "blind spots"...and that is where your awareness is just not there, you get taken out of the moment, mainly because you can't see it, the EGO gets in the way, and you are seeing an illusion instead of reality!

So, with all that being said, this section is diving more into THE DETAILS! With hard work, you are discovering them, right? The truth, in some situations, as we see it...is clear as day! In other situations, other environments, or with certain people, under certain circumstances, the truth is right in front of us, yet we can't see or hear it! Why? The short answer is because the mind has blocked us out of the moment (TIME)! We are literally blind and deaf to it because we are not even in the moment...so how do we take the blinders off!?! GET IN THE ZONE! That's how. NOW!

I spend a lot more time in the ZONE than I used to, and that's why I wanted to explain this perspective to my family! It is really powerful place to live from! I took you through the progression for me because you were obviously not familiar with my story and I wanted you to see that it wasn't something that was just gifted to me, I had to work really hard at it! In addition, drilling down on this in detail should give you key angles and ideas to use yourself as you process this information.

So, as another example from my life, in my senior year at Rutgers, I was the field goal kicker and my % successful was 93%. Again, that's not to brag, it's really not, it's to point out the fact that I had a very high degree of focus, even at times when 100,000 fans were screaming at the top of their lungs. That was also when I was much younger, dumb, untrained, and unaware from a logistical mental processing perspective. From this chart, I was probably in the top right quadrant, but in all honesty, I didn't know how I got there. I was very competitive and had a lot of practice at that particular challenge though. Notable, is that I did not know a fraction of what I know now, and what I am sharing with you! Although my physical ability to kick a football is not with me anymore, my mental abilities are 1000 times what they were back then!

Bottom line, I have been in the zone, plenty of times, yes, and I can explain now what it takes to get there! I have also NOT been in the zone, and made a lot of mistakes! Maybe my physical attainments were not demonstrated the dramatic fashion of a Michael Jordan, but I did kick a game winning field goal here and there! I was also the quarterback, in days gone by, and could throw an incredibly accurate dart (football) to a moving target going down the field with plenty of distractions...consistently! I was also the pitcher for the baseball team, and in one 7 inning game I threw 14 strike outs! I have made some incredible golf shots, won tournaments, hit home runs, delivered In many situations personally and professionally, many venues, and in many ways...not all that would be notable in a newspaper, but certainly relevant to the lives of the people I have helped. I most definitely understand it...and use it, all the time, and it is more than just situational awareness and focus! I don't say it to brag. I say it and share this because it seems to me that this MIND "stuff", getting in the zone, used outside of sports and in "life" in the right ways, makes the world a better place to live and breathe! Please remember that this ability is just as relevant in high achievers, not necessarily in just athletes, but also in your personal and business life as well. It is something you will use your entire life, so check this out.

From a super simplified perspective: Where you start on this chart from a mental standpoint is going to be determined by:

1. YOU

2. The situation

3. What you want out of the situation, or from the person / people involved IN the situation

4. Your level of attachment to that outcome and your relationship to THOSE people in THAT situation

5. Your level of awareness to 1 through 4

6. Challenge level of the situation

7. Your Skill level relative to that specific challenge, as well as that situation, with whomever else is involved and THEIR SKILL level

The RESULT will be based on your ability to BE PRESENT and use that awareness in the moment to make a new decision! (Use your skills) That is the essence of getting in the zone, or flow states, as Bill called them...super ridiculous LASER focus and awareness, in the moment. 100% PRESENCE!

Your progression in this diagram, in differing situations, is going to look slightly or maybe even A LOT different! The above is just an example, and I encourage you to analyze it. Keep in mind that the brain doesn't go in a straight line from bottom left to top right, it flip-flops, like a wavelength up and down along that path...so from apathy, as an example, we go to worry, worry to boredom, boredom to anxiety. As we grow, and become aware, anxiety to relaxation. As we challenge the status quo, we move through arousal and control to the flow state. That's in a super simplified world, but our world is far from simple, isn't it? So, let's look harder at it...understanding that as the mind changes, perspective changes, relationships to the situation change, and your point on this chart can change as a result, INSTANTLY! I drew a hypothetical example of what that might look like above...but let's dissect it further...

As your "Challenge level" goes up (left side), unless your skill level (bottom) also goes up you will fail in certain situations. That's life, so here is how growth occurs. You increase your ability to handle the "stress" associated with your current scenarios, mentally, physically, emotionally, etc. That ability or lack of ability produces feelings / emotions associated with that particular "Challenge". (If negative emotion, you are going up the left side). We are constantly brought to challenges to go through them, not around them! So, we really need to understand this dynamic, and the fact that we must learn to:

## BE COMFORTABLE BEING UNCOMFORTABLE

...it is the only place where growth can occur (detachment / nonattachment / and being in the moment with awareness help). Keep in mind that positive emotion can just as easily steal the moment from you as negative emotion! (**"irrational exuberance"**[21], as an example: **Alan Greenspan**).

Some of life's best moments are when we have just overcome a personal challenge, where we met the moment and conquered it, vs. it conquering us (you)! In life, you must raise your SKILLS! These are the skills we have been talking about, and progressively working on. (Bottom of this chart) This is a requirement for you to be able to handle the constant flow of challenges in your life (left side of chart) Why? Because they never stop...in fact, your life **"STREAM"**[22] is going to continue to flow faster and faster. YOU must grow to that speed and skill level. Life as we know it is moving faster by the minute, right? For fun, Listen to the song **"Faster"**[23] by **Within Temptation**! Incredible band. It's amazing and really speaks to this in my opinion. This, the way I see and hear it, is a great reminder to increase your skills to access the moment, faster! That's where growth occurs. You must grow your ability to handle life's moments and you do that with AWARENESS / PRESENCE!

As we grow, we enter periods of anxiety and from a wavelength perspective, we go from top left to bottom right, as we master things, get relaxed, catch our breath, and then go after it hard again it puts us in the top left again. As we grow, the wavelength narrows and we glide towards the top right, but only with the proper mindset/ SKILL. With awareness, we go from flip flopping between anxiety and relaxation, to flip flopping between arousal and control...but ONLY as our skill level increases. As our skill level increases, the anxiety level decreases, and naturally faith and trust increase as a result. Note that anxiety has a negative expectation, whereas arousal implies a state of positive expectancy. There is a big difference, because where your focus is matters! Positive expectation without demanding control of situations is the ultimate place to be. Bottom line, you must get to the moment, faster and faster...that's where change happens! Thanks again to Within Temptation, the band, for amplifying that point to me again most recently in their song! Listening to their music has really helped me because there are a lot of lessons in the lyrics, in my opinion! The band is amazing :)

With awareness and practice, your skill level increases relative to THAT specific challenge, you move upwards and outwards towards the top right, or as **Bill Harris**[24] called it a **"FLOW"** state. This is what elite athletes may refer to as the "ZONE" and so I labeled it The Zone in the diagram! Babe Ruth as Bill described could see the laces rotating on the ball as it approached home plate. I have heard athletes describe the end of games where the game was on the line, pressure was on, and super ridiculous focus was needed to make something happen to win the game. This was a place where time was moving extremely slowly, almost standing still. That is the top right part of the chart, THE ZONE! You cannot just show up and get in the zone, it takes practice, effort, personal expansion and challenging yourself as well as a huge amount of awareness. With the combination of laser focused practice, and the ENERGY of the moment, (arousal in the chart) that combination of forces pushes us into the ZONE where adrenaline, awareness and focus literally bring on that FLOW state in us. We become the best version of ourselves in that moment. There are no anxious thoughts about what if I fail, no regret or animosity if the ball bounces the wrong way, there are no distractions, NOTHING in our mind is preventing that perfect execution in that moment and we ultimately rise above the moment as the "winner".

Understand though that this is not a requirement in the moment, to win. It really doesn't matter win or lose in the game; it is a win vs. other forces within us that may have prevented us from even being there in some cases! It is a win to be a better version of our "SELF" than we were just a moment ago, a day ago, a year ago. There are no regrets in this version of self. You really need to see that we must show up in life, and if we are going to show up, we may as well bring the best version of ourselves. With constant practice and putting ourselves endlessly in growth mode (the moment) and experiencing new and expansive ways of "living", our ability to handle life's challenges is always getting better / bigger, in all situations. The level of "stress" required to push us into that top left corner is more and more and more...meaning as we grow our SKILLS, we experience less and less and less levels of stress UNLESS we are pushing the envelope so to speak! (Pushing yourself past a former version of yourself, OUT OF YOUR COMFORT ZONE) Whether you are showing up for an exam, a practice, the first game of the season, or the national championship... you are driven to challenge yourself to move towards that upper right area of this chart. It is a state of MASTERY, and the best athletes, CEO's and successful people in the world have figured out a way to master themselves and their game. It is also why we admire people like that, we see something in them that is in us, and we long to see that version of ourselves (me/you!)!

We want to see that "ME"! The mind projects us there, and then because the next instant, only fractions of a second later we realize we are not there yet, it brings a tear to our eye! So, if it brings a tear to your eye to see that something, or someone, or something coming out in life for someone else...it means that you have yet to master that part of YOU, so get to it! My guess is that most of them probably don't even understand this chart, they **"JUST DO IT"**[25]... but you can't just do it until you get off your ass and challenge yourself. TAKE THAT STEP! As your challenge level and skill level increase, you are gifted the opportunity to get in that "ZONE" or **"flow state"**[26]. That is such an amazing place, it can be accessed easier over time, and it is one of almost a "witness perspective". If you ask these elite athletes to describe the moment, it was probably effortless, and often they might describe it as TIMELESS as well... they just knew, without thinking...it just happened, they just did it! Amazing, imagine living your life from that perspective! I challenge you to approach life from this vantage point, you'll be glad you did. But how...?

Take a moment to notice something pretty cool. This diagram shows us that we can feel good about the result no matter what happens. Not blatantly obvious within the diagram so why do I say that? Understanding this chart shows us that we are constantly and forever going to meet moments that are bigger than us...so it is with life. That means that we are not going to win every time, however, from a different perspective, as long as we are pushing ourselves to bigger and bigger moments, we are ultimately ALWAYS a winner... even as we lose from time to time. Wait...what? As we consistently meet more and more moments, and WIN...and WIN, and WIN...we grow into bigger moments, and better versions of our "SELF". As we consciously direct our energies with ultra-focused awareness, arousal and control in BIG moments push us into flow states where we can achieve things we had not even dreamed of. This requires failing sometimes, and not just sometimes, a LOT!!!! It's part of the learning curve...isn't that exciting? It puts a different spin on failure and allows you to actually appreciate it!

Sometimes we just need something to be excited about, right?

The president and CEO of my company **Glenn Phillips**[27] just posted this on Facebook, do you think he knows a secret?

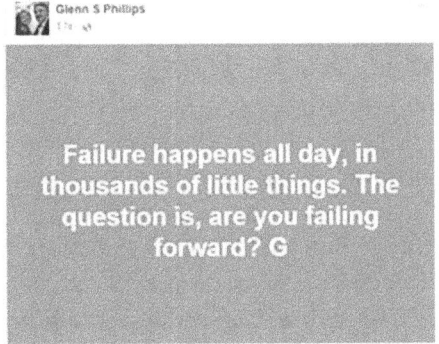

The beauty in this statement is that with understanding, the regret, the disappointment, and the negative states associated with the "LET DOWN", or one of the supposed "losses" go away almost instantly, if they ever show up at all...WHY? Because we can stand tall and know that I am challenging myself, and that's a good thing, not a bad thing. (appreciation). If I were in that bottom left corner, in apathy, worry or boredom...surely, I would not be in situations where I even have a chance to succeed, AT ANYTHING! Put yourself in situations where you can stand tall and succeed... sure, you'll get knocked down a bit, you will fail, and fail you must.

I remember **Michael Jordan**[28] talking about failure, pretty powerful angle too, check this clip out:

https://youtu.be/GuXZFQKKF7A

So, fail forward fast...Just get up, dust yourself off and try again...all the better for the lesson... and NO REGRET! PAY ATTENTION, be awake and aware, do not retreat into regret and disappointment as that only delays your ultimate victory. Shift deliberately to appreciation instead.

In a previous post my amazing CEO posted this:

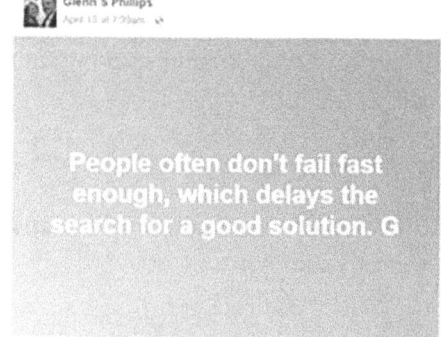

By shifting to appreciation, instead of the alternatives, it allows you to move FORWARD much more quickly in a positive frame of mind. The mind doesn't get bogged down in the negative states. If you want the victory, understand that it is an INTERNAL game. It is a victory over yourself, and your "self" and your "self" onwards and upwards, you are always GROWING into a better version of yourself. ALWAYS. Each version of YOU is met with new challenges because you have grown. If you are not growing, you are very likely seeing the same or similar things and staying in the bottom and left quadrants, and who the hell wants to be there over and over again?

Is boredom fun? Is worry FUN? Is fear, fun? Wouldn't you like to move through that stuff? I mean like really know how to, specifically, with guidance and confidence?

Worry is just a nice way to say I am scared to death to do something! Fear can be crippling, until you walk right through it. Fear is an illusion generated by a past/future projection (THE LIES, from the song FASTER, IMHO). The NEW YOU, with presence is bigger...faster...stronger! With awareness, focus and skill...fear vanishes the instant you <u>decide to NOT listen to it</u>. You can do this with massive CONFIDENCE! It's a LIE, this type of fear is an illusion, and it only exists in the past or future, never in the moment. The moment is where you meet the new YOU and GROW into the version of yourself that you "INTEND" to be and to that version of "YOU" fear is understood! Important distinction, the fear that gets you out of the way of a fast-moving train is there for a reason, illusory fear of the "self" created kind is NOT!

Worry, boredom, apathy, anxiety, ignorance, avoidance, and resistance produce the same things over and over again in your life, it cycles but never changes. You must move, YOU must act, you must challenge yourself to get better, not necessarily only at what you are doing...but how you think while you are doing it. That difference is a difference maker. It takes the energy away from the negative spin and "ALLOWS" a version of you that is unattached to the result to DO IT, and therefore that "YOU" is capable in that moment to ACT without distraction, without negative associations, without FEAR! Anxiety converts to AWARE-NESS with AROUSAL and FOCUS combining to give it an additional push. Then with that wind at your back, in the moment of the contest or challenge, YOU show up and that version of you is always a winner! Why, because you are not worried about losing, you are a new version of YOU that is consistently better than the previous version too, growing. Positive expectancy, without fear of its alternative is the place where you can live life to the fullest and it truly is a happy place. Quite honestly, when acting from this perspective, winning happens a lot more! So, to me that sounds like MASTERY...let's take a look what the internet says! Thanks **GOOGLE**[29] These are some of the words I see in general search land:

Proficiency, genius, ability, capability, knowledge, understanding, comprehension, familiarity, command, grasp, grip, skill, expertise, expertism, dexterity, finesse, prowess, know-how, control, superiority, supremacy, the upper hand, rule, power, authority, dominion, sovereignty.

**Miriam-Webster** puts it this way, more specifically:

> **"a: the authority of a <u>master</u> : DOMINION**
> **b: the upper hand in a contest or competition : SUPERIORITY,**
> **ASCENDANCY**
> **2a: possession or display of great skill or technique**
> **b: skill or knowledge that makes one master of a subject: COM-**
> **MAND"[30]**

(Thank you, **Miriam-Webster** & **Google**, for these words and definitions!)

Notice the same and similar words come up, and synonyms like ability, skill, proficiency, COMMAND, DOMINION, understanding. Please don't read this to assume or THINK you can control every situation, you cannot and will not, although at times it may feel like you do, because things do tend to go your way when you gain this "ability", but to control everything is impossible, there are just too many variables. Remember, other people have differing agendas which makes it even more complicated! "GET A GRIP" does not mean of the situation, it means of the YOU that's in it!!!! Of what's going on in your mind! Understand that what you can control is YOUR REACTION TO and IN each moment. The "I" or you and YOUR thinking is what you need to master. Situations, events, and things are constantly changing, evolving, growing. YOUR MASTERY, your ZONE is between your ears, GET A GRIP ON THAT!

There is actually an easy way to tell if you are in the bottom left, or the left side of the chart in general... So how do you know? Well, if you don't ***HAVE A GRIP*** then it is very likely you are not smiling. That is, at a minimum, a HUGE CLUE, a wakeup call, a HELL NO I am not going to stay here in this foul attitude where nothing positive can happen. **STAND YOUR GROUND**[31]! Examples are regret, sour faces, bad attitudes, being angry at oneself for losing, or anything / any attitude that puts you in the PAST or FUTURE w/ a negative attitude towards it. You will not allow those kinds of demons to take over your mind, because with awareness, you can **CHOOSE a better thought**, a more productive one, and SMILE in the face of adversity! With a smile, you are better than the version of you that would previously get caught up in all that negativity! See through the lies!

The "attitude" is that I am driven to a level of command of my "SELF" that only I can control. No one else can remove this smile from my face... NO one, NO thing, NO situation! It is immovable. Similar to the words of the **"Cowardly Lion"**[32] from the **Wizard of Oz**, if you were KING of your MIND, and in command of your THINKING, then not NOBODY not NO HOW could that smile be removed from your face. That's the way I look at it anyway. You don't need a WIZARD to fix you, all you need is the awareness of what is preventing you from mastering you. What is it? Understanding. There is a thought that you are thinking that is the cause, however, that thought is generated from a previous version of you and responding to something that was yesterday or tomorrow, a moment ago or anticipating a moment to come. Whatever it is, understand that it is NOT YOU, it is an IMPOSTER, acting and thinking AS you because you have authorized it to think FOR YOU as you in this moment! Take that in for a moment. The conquest is of you...not what's OUT THERE, it is of what's inside you. A CHOICE! YOU DECIDE what you think, until you are not aware enough to make the decision to think what you think, and in THOSE MOMENTS, you are blinded by "STUFF" that seems to just happen. Why? It is because you, the REAL YOU was not present in this moment to ACT for yourself, to CHOOSE! What actually happened was that a former version of you showed up and acted AS you FOR you...The NEW you that you intended to be didn't or couldn't show up! THAT is the times where you seem to lose, or get poor results, over and over again for the same exact reason, you were not PRESENT in that moment to get the lesson. Why? I hate to say it but let's be blunt...you got in your own way!

Here's a fun clip to the King of the Forest, **The cowardly Lion, Wizard of OZ**[33]:

https://youtu.be/gOCNY9pJ850

Notice how the KING of the forest commands respect and is treated as such. Consider yourself the KING of your forest: **THE MIND**, in COMMAND of EVERY THOUGHT. There are big thoughts that carry with them lots of weight and others that you have already mastered, have command over. If you didn't already make the correlation, the way I am seeing this is that the thoughts are the little creatures in the forest, like the cowardly lion describes. As an analogy, some creatures (thoughts) are bigger than others, right? Courage is not the absence of FEAR, it is the understanding that growth requires I walk right through it. It is an understanding that I cannot proceed through this moment as who I WAS, I must BECOME NEW in this moment, new means UNATTACHED to a previous version of me and what that me did or was. It means completely present and aware. It means UNATTACHED TO EXPECTATION and RE-SULTS. Although we may desire a certain outcome, I am going to smile no matter what happens, so I will just allow the moment to unfold naturally. Will I try to steer it, of course...but with a detached focus, that WITNESS perspective. This ultra-focused ZONE, or FLOW state simply ALLOWs the best outcome, and that's usually what happens. You see by being unattached to the outcome, the FEAR that would be associated with what we perceive as a negative outcome VANISHES. What replaces the fear is AWARENESS / PRESENCE...and in that moment, I can be the new ME! Why? Because with presence, I NOW have a choice! Previously I was not present to make the choice at all! Former, attached, and / or scared me showed up! With awareness and my new lenses, I HAVE CHOICE!

**LESSON KEY: LOOK WITHIN. Continue to LOOK WITHIN with more and more AWARENESS! Try to ascertain when you are able to be "in the zone" and when you bring anything less than this higher version of SELF to the moment!**

That is where answers will present themselves. YOU MUST be present to hear and see them! Keep working on this SKILL, analyze it when you miss the moment, and try to understand why. EXACTLY, what happened? Break it down! Do not be critical of yourself, this is not to beat yourself up, or blame anyone, it is ONLY to understand what happened, what <u>exactly</u> took you out of the moment, how, and when? Very important, worth repeating and highlighting: THIS IS <u>NOT</u> TO BLAME! It is to understand, so that the next time, you are more skillful and maybe just ever so slightly faster at arriving to the moment! Remember please you are working on a SKILL, this has everything to do with amplifying that skill, and NOTHING to do with anyone else. See the next section, the blame game!

# My Gift To You!

## Stop Living on Autopilot

*Discover How to Tune Into*

*Your Authentic Self in Just 3 Steps!*

*Are you feeling out of sync with your life's purpose? Do you find yourself going through the motions, knowing deep down that you're capable of so much more?*

*You're not alone. I've been there too.*

*I'm Doug Giesler, and I want to share a story with you. Not long ago, I was living a life that looked successful on the outside, but inside, I felt empty and disconnected. I was out of tune with my true self, my mission, and my vision.*

*But then, everything changed.*

## Discover The 3
## Simple Practices

*That Transformed My Life*
*(And Can Transform Yours Too)*

## Get Your Copy

## BeTheInstrument.com

# The Journey To Your Best Self Begins With A Single Step. Will You Take It?

*Don't let another day pass feeling out of tune with your life's purpose. The world needs your unique gifts and talents. It's time to step into your power and become the instrument of positive change you were meant to be.*

*Visit the website to get instant access to the Attuned Living Starter Kit. Your transformation begins now.*

## Get Your Copy
## BeTheInstrument.com

*Remember, the life you've always dreamed of is within reach. But you must take action. The choice is yours.*

**Stop Settling for Less! Learn How to**

**Achieve Extraordinary Peace of Mind and Success!**

*Still on the fence? Consider this: A year from now, you'll wish you had started today. Don't let fear or doubt hold you back any longer.*

**Claim your free Attuned Living Starter Kit now and take the first step towards the life you deserve.**

## Get Your Copy
## BeTheInstrument.com

# THE BLAME GAME

## GETTING IN THE ZONE I

To BLAME IS TO avoid or miss the lesson, regardless of whether you blame your "self", someone else, the situation, the past, or whatever else you can come up with. We already know that resistance and avoidance are not going to help us. Blaming anything is a waste of precious energy, and you miss the lesson, double trouble! Don't engage in the blame game. Preserve your energy and use that energy to further assess and amplify your skills!

Let's dive deeper into how to accomplish this and why it is so important. First of all, we should recognize this tendency to place blame as a very prominent lesson that can come up quite a bit for us, and yet often times we don't even see the lesson amongst the myriad of other things that are blazing through our mind cylinders. Error is at the core of the issue to begin with, right? Had there not been an error, or a bad situation, then blame would not even be presenting itself as an option! The lesson in this "error" situation was to observe and SEE what mind element <u>within</u> our "selves" brought this to us in one way or another. If it was an actual error, on our part, then what was it that grabbed our attention long enough to distract us and take us out of the moment? While we were distracted, something went awry! The lesson was to discover what it was that took us out of the moment, so that the next time it doesn't do that! Once we see the lesson, everything changes, we have choice. So, we need to understand when the lesson is available so that we can keep an eye out for it, heighten our awareness so that we are ready!

BIG CLUE: It's right about the same "time" / mind juncture that we pivot from taking responsibility or shifting to "blame". So, to revisit the lesson from the last chapter, let's use fear as the lesson of choice and see how that might relate to blame and where the opportunity gets missed. What can happen is the lessons can actually piggyback on each other, and so we can often miss one or both because we are looking in the wrong direction!

In this example, fear and blame from a previously missed moment combine to pack a double whammy in this one and then the same, or another error is made. Another bad situation results. Let's project a possible scenario. Fear generated an emotion, fight or flight mode was "triggered", we got distracted, and something bad happened. Immediately, we blamed something or someone from the situation, which is where? IN THE PAST! Where was the fear generated from? Fear is a "self" generated illusion (past or future), and it is generated from that version of "self" which was just triggered. In an instant, that little "self" created an imaginary visualization of that past or a hypothetical projected "bad" future, the one that it was fearful of. The "self", in a flash, projected that illustration onto our current mind screen. So, that's what we were looking at...in a fraction of a second. In this example, the AWARE "I" was essentially asleep at the wheel and not PRESENT because it was taken over by one of the little "selves" and that "self" was essentially "in charge" of the mind as the decision was made. What was seen and responded to? The "self" was watching the projected visualization in a virtual movie theatre of the mind vs REALITY! That's what it responded to! What's the lesson? Don't let IT (past/future little self) get YOU (present higher SELF) caught up in fear or sitting in a virtual mind generated movie theatre instead of here and NOW, PRESENT in your life! Not only is it creating an illusion for us to respond to on the mind screen, but it also takes us out of the moment and puts us in that past / future, so we are not responding to reality in the PRESENT MOMENT! In fact, WE, as in the "I", the higher SELF is not responding at all, one of the lower "selves" is, and they are responding to an ILLUSION! Do you see this?

To break it down, the higher "SELF" was not present in the moment, that moment just passed. In that moment, we were separated by more than just time. The situation wasn't even the same situation. Please see this! Since it was a self-created visualization that was created by the self in a fraction of a second, that illusion is what generated the RE-action...the RE-action could be to something that was slightly different than reality! Depending on the weight of the emotion, the imaginary projection may be VERY different than REALITY! The images the mind can project are quite dramatic sometimes, particularly when prompted by FEAR! Don't live in the past, or future, GET PRESENT! A BIG LESSON was missed here. The imagery and scenery the mind can put on our mind screen can be very "moving" sometimes, pay attention, but don't get stuck in this virtual theatre longer than it takes to get the lesson it brought you there for!

OK, so moving on, in this example, we miss the first lesson, and then we compound the "succumbing to fear" (resistance) error by immediately shifting to blame and blame puts us where? The past, yep...right back in the past and so again, we are not present. (avoidance) DANGIT! The lesson was first resisted and then avoided, AGAIN! WHO DUNNIT!? The "selves" do it while we are not awake and aware, they take us over! They think they are making an educated decision, it's not necessarily malicious. The unfortunate thing is that they are responding to a complete illusion so how accurate can this RE-action really be? Just like the last time, this wham bam happened so fast we missed it and so nothing changed! We missed the lesson again! Like the wounded ship headed for a rocky shoreline and taking on water, we had 2 opportunities to fix the hull, and we missed them both, putting us deeper in the water and more vulnerable to the rocks we are headed towards. Apparently, we haven't had enough pain, change was not required, YET. The "I" either didn't see it at all or didn't see it as a necessary or desirable option. Let's face it, without presence, the "right" CHOICE was not even available to be seen, we were momentarily blinded by the self, not in the moment, and then the pivot towards the lesson vs blame was not taken! Pain ahead... WHY? Unconsciousness! Lack of consciousness, lack of awareness, lack of presence, or the SKILL to get PRESENT was not developed well enough yet! Keep working at it.

So, how can this go differently with more skill, and by getting the lesson? UNDERSTANDING! How can fear be present to begin with if I am going to be happy no matter what? The weight of the moment goes away, doesn't it? Meaning that had I received that lesson previously, I would be less likely to be in this predicament to begin with! Understanding is POWER in the moment, so understanding doesn't create the courage necessary to overcome fear, it completely ERASES the fear to begin with. This is an important discovery. Understand this dynamic, it will help you preserve energy, and that's energy you need to GET TO THE MOMENT! Having received the lesson, fear is less likely to be the distractor factor (resistance) and cause an error to begin with. Since a bad situation did not happen at all, well then, we didn't need to break out our avoidance tool either, BLAME!

As long as there is fear present, then you can be sure that your focus is on some level or in some way distracted. That is affecting your energy and remember that ENERGY is one of your KEYS to heightened awareness. Your PRESENCE is ensuring that the attractor factor WITHIN is not a distractor factor! It's super important, do you see this now? It's all tied together, a chain reaction. It could be associated with a negative outcome, or demanding control of a situation that cannot be controlled...in other words you are attached to a certain outcome.

The point is that if that outcome doesn't happen, then UGLINESS follows. REGRET, sorrow, disappointment, sulking, crying...upset, anger, animosity towards others and then BLAME. It happens FAST! The blame game is the natural tendency to instantly look to where we can offload that responsibility (pain) and blame it on ANYTHING! We do this because pain doesn't feel good, and we do it as fast as possible, preferably on anything other than ME! Typically, the easiest, fastest, and most efficient way to do it is to offload that disappointment on to someone else because the burden is just too much for me (you) to bear. Please, don't. Instead, pause... BEAR the disappointment, not forever, just for a moment, to understand what produced it, and LET IT GO... don't ever offload that onto another human being...EVER. It is YOU; it is YOU who controls that...always YOU! BTW, don't offload it onto your pet either, or your wall, house, car, building, self...anything! The point is to get the lesson, so that you can move forward. Offloading ENSURES that you will get the lesson AGAIN! Just understand the lesson, and then immediately, LET IT GO!

So, disappointment and the pain, stem from not thinking about something from the correct vantage point, right? With this understanding, would you ever stay in these negative states longer than the fraction of a second it takes to understand what produced it, and then grow from that level of self so the next time you can produce a different result? You see now that ultimately there isn't anything to bear, it is an opportunity, a lesson... that's ALL! It only takes a moment to grab that lesson, appreciate it, and move on! Because we are here NOW, with PRESENCE... we get the lesson! WELL DONE!!! If we skip past it, avoid it, suppress it, or remain in the negative state it produces, the next time will be no different, change cannot occur. You cannot drag your old "self" into each new moment and expect a different result! In the same spirit of discovery, you can't offload responsibility with blame and learn anything either. TAKE responsibility to understand and GROW your SKILLS! If you offload pain, it WILL come back and bite you, and this is WHY! If you internalize it, you bite yourself! Either way, we did not receive the lesson that was given, we did not pass the test, and therefore we do not move on to the next grade in the life classroom! We got held back, by our "selves"! Worse yet, we let them do it. Get PRESENT, MAKE THE GRADE, Pass the test! Next...

**Change ONLY occurs in the moment**, not the past and not the future, NOW! Again, Understanding is POWER! Awareness and being present to the moment create the opportunities needed to enter flow states and move forward with our lives. This is THE MOMENT where we access the "ZONE". **GOOD THINGS HAPPEN HERE!** The zone is where we can learn & grow and become better versions of "SELF"! Another beautiful thing is that this **GROWTH PRE-**

**VENTS ERRORS**! If we are trapped in the past, succumbing to worry, or even frozen in fear, it's a comfort zone! Comfort zones are fine, but that eventually will put you back on the bottom of the chart, in boredom. Who wants to stay there? Worry, fear, boredom, what fun is that? Life is meant to be lived, and that is not living. If allowed to exist or even compound, the lessons are not learned, and then as you can see, the result is really not fun. That is retreating into a personal hell that keeps getting smaller and smaller and smaller...a comfort zone that is shrinking, like the comfort walls are getting thicker as well as closer and closer. On top of that, the way out is less visible. Not a pretty picture... this ultimately becomes apathy and death shortly follows. Not to be morbid, but that is NO WAY TO LIVE! Take the opportunity to grow, the walls are a self-created illusion, TEAR THEM DOWN! How? With understanding. When? NOW!

To expand on that concept a little, why can't we do this over and over...it seems so easy! Why? Several reasons really:

1. Because it requires a lot of energy, which we don't have, and

2. It requires that I DIE to myself (these former "selves") over and over again which we don't want to do! (EGO)

We love our "selves"! This is not literally dying physically, but the death of, or the "END" of a former "self" from a growth perspective. It is a former self that I have outgrown, RELEASED, and LET GO of. Again, not physical death. Like a snake shedding its skin, I am new, and new and new each time I release a "self" that no longer serves me. In some cases, letting go of a "me" is easier than others, particularly if we have been living as that "me" for a long time. In this case, we need to move from the melancholy "self" that cherishes who it was and doesn't want to let go, to the more excited "self" that wants to learn and grow. Just realize this is a choice!

As for that old self, certainly that version of me/you is a little attached to itself, to it staying, living...so that is of course a hurdle. Just another part of the under-standing...you need to see that version of self for what it is, a FORMER "self"! After that, I realize that the former more "limited" version of me must go away to allow more space for this more expanded version of me. I must die to that version of "self" to BECOME my newest and BEST version, over and over and over again! Remain in the past, stay comfortable, SULK or whatever it is you do in these situations, or move forward. With understanding comes CHOICE.

Understanding is that older versions of me were only capable of doing what older versions of me were capable of, that's not my current version of Me's fault, so the choice is to learn, and then LET GO!!!!! Now that's something to get excited about(energy)! Imagine releasing that baggage and then oh MY, the possibilities! By NOT BLAMING, and on the contrary, taking responsibility with the insight just gained from the moment to RELEASE THE PAST and the former versions of self that were unable to meet the moment with what was needed IN THAT MOMENT, we GROW, AMPLIFY our SKILL, and take another step forward...with more ENERGY!! Not only am I excited to move forward which energizes me by the nature of it, but I also just lightened the load! My mood is better as a result, INSTANTLY! Completely different attitude...in a flash!

So, what is it then that causes these negative states when we don't meet the moment? ME!!! Yes, it is! It is our little "selves"...the unskilled ones! Looking at it in detail, it is of course, OLD me...BLAMING OLD me for doing something wrong, for not measuring up, for making a "bad" decision. It is for falling short in one way or another, let's call it an unmet desire, a disappointment, a failure! I wanted THIS to happen and then THAT happened instead, I didn't measure up, in one way or another so now the "self" that wanted this vs that, resorts to sulking, or blaming or whatever else, and those re-actions are exactly what keeps the old "self" alive, instead of progressing to a new and better version of ME, as higher "SELF". I am either identified with what I just won or identified with what I just lost...either way, I am identified with a former version of myself. WHAT? YES, read it again, it means that **the "I" that I was, is still me...I have not grown, I did not receive the lesson!**

Lessons are available in winning as well, but harder to see. Why? Because when we lose, the lesson is much more obvious, we feel pain! Emotional pain, regret, animosity, anger, frustration, etc. These are not fun emotions and so we want to part with them as fast as we possibly can and that's why we miss the opportunity. It happens ridiculously FAST. We offload pain, FAST! We need to wake up and see it happen. These emotions are the clues that we need to WAKE UP and SEE that former "I" that was just me a moment ago and get the lesson. This is what is required, so that the next time I am in that situation or one similar, I can increase my awareness, focus, and SHOW UP to the battle to represent as my higher NEW "SELF" (get in the zone). The battle is in the MIND. **FOCUS!!** Once I see it, I am NOT going to let the former little "self" step into the moment and pinch hit anymore! I WANT TO PLAY THIS GAME OF LIFE, as the higher "SELF" not some ill-equipped former little self...you get it?

OK, great...so what's the lesson in winning? The biggie that comes to mind is impermanence. Another might be pride. Another might be gratitude/appreciation/humbleness. Let's look at an example: Yes, we just overcame a high hurdle, major achievement, maybe it was a huge mountain we climbed and maybe we even got an award! The victory was a milestone, and surely it felt really good. So, what does the mind do? It goes BACK to relive it! What's the problem with that? That victory just ended (impermanence) and there is a higher peak just ahead. Oh, and the road isn't always straight to get there, it could TRIP you up by looking backwards again! WAKE UP, pay attention, GET PRESENT. Ever heard of pride before the fall? It's not the pride, per se, that does it, but what does the pride do? It takes you to the past, OUT OF THE MOMENT! While you were in the past admiring your "self" or the amazing result that you created, you tripped over the stone on your path, or ran face first into a boulder! Understand? OK, so let's not go there, let's stay present instead!

There is a difference between a positive and productive attitude that is energized, spirited, alert and ready vs that of arrogance, gloating and cockiness. One has a bullseye on it and a chip on their shoulder that is about to get knocked off!

So NOW I am energized, and with deliberate effort and FOCUS, it's always the absolute BEST version of me showing up, all the time, as long as I am awake aware and PRESENT! I cannot be stuck in the past and I cannot be projecting some future ideal. I know better! In either of those scenarios, I would be represented by some fictional self: the lie, the false self, the little self, the blind, dumb or even prideful self, among other emotional selves. If that happens, then "I" am not present to be in the FLOW, in the ZONE. The only way to be in the zone is to make sure that former me and future me don't get in the way! The only way to do that is with a heightened awareness, to:

## BE in THIS MOMENT, NOW...with PRESENCE!

There is NOTHING preventing you from smiling right now, NOTHING. (Although your mind and the "selves" might argue!) If the thought in your mind is telling you something different, like NOT to smile, then you can be sure it is a former you or future you, stealing your life! Wake up, and ask yourself...what is it doing? Pay attention, it is blaming something, JUSTIFYING IT?! What is it? That's the EGO wanting to stay YOU! Don't let it do that! See the emotion, yes, but then open your eyes, SEE...what's underneath the emotion, why? To UNDERSTAND! It's the situation, the players, the former self, future self, or whatever imagery is being projected onto your mind screen. It's a LIE, and it's just a projection, YOU can turn it off! While that situation may have happened in the past, or it is a projected hypothetical future, either way it is an illusion, imagined or recreated, and it is being projected onto your mind screen. It is selling you a story and trying to keep you in that theatre in the LEADING ROLE! You are a STAR in this role, and it's ALL ABOUT YOU, and you get all caught up in it, don't you? Be honest!

The only thing preventing you from smiling this instant is a thought you thought was yours, but it is simply you NOT being present to yourself to think something different, to choose a different thought, a better one. Snap out of the "role", wake up from the projection...and smile in spite of that thought! SMILE BIG TOO, because that older version of you has just been replaced with a better version of you (appreciation). It is more up to date, more up to speed and more and more capable of getting in the zone the next time! WHY? Because every time we do this, every time we step up to the plate in life in this fashion, we more ready ourselves, we increase our awareness, we are carrying less and less baggage from the past which amplifies our ability to access the moment, and when we access the moment, we are in the zone. THIS IS THE SKILL! When we are not carrying with us all the stupid stuff from yesterday or a moment ago (The past), and we are not attaching huge weight onto a certain result for tomorrow (The future) we are FREE!!!! I am free to be ME, NOW, I am the higher version of ME and not some former limited version of me. As a result, I am free to choose, and choose I do... forever expanding, moment by moment by moment! **"FASTER"**[34]. Thank you again **Within Temptation** for the awesome song :)

**LESSON KEY:** **Take responsibility to understand the reasons for your results. Live on the cutting edge of NOW, get the lessons it provides, and move on...say, THANK YOU, NEXT!**

There is always one key element to every situation that comes along, you are in it! That is why I ask, which version! The mind can be used in many ways; however, blame is not to be used as a tool or a weapon. Used in that manner, it can be hurtful to yourself and often times others too! Regardless of how it is used, and where it is directed, understand that blame is primarily hurting <u>ME</u>! Blame hurts the blamer; it eliminates the ability for the blamer to move forward with their life and prolongs any pain that resulted from the situation that just occurred. Why? Because it prevents that person from getting the lesson that was available and from moving on. That lesson is the one we NEED to amplify our skills and move forward with our life so that the next time this situation presents itself, which it will, we are ready for it. You & I must arrive IN THE MOMENT and GET THE LESSON to take that next step!

There is a very powerful tool that is available every moment that can assist you in moving forward with your life, it is called <u>FORGIVENESS</u>! In other words,

<u>LET IT GO</u>! Forgiveness moves you forwards, blame takes you backwards, it's that simple. Live in the past, or move forward, it's a choice. The choice is available, and you are going to have to be extremely FAST to be able to use it. Work on your speed!

This means not only forgiving your "self", but others, and even the situation as well. Whatever it takes, stop pointing fingers and take responsibility. This is not in the form of blaming, and badgering yourself, or anyone... it is taking responsibility to use the energy created in the moment to amplify your skills, get the lesson, and make a NEW CHOICE! If an error is made, here's how to proceed: First, BE AWARE, notice how quickly the mind moves to and through this process of blame. Second, Recognize and SEE THE CHOICE, the choice is to move towards forgiveness vs blame.

Immediately, do it FAST! Blame is fast, YOU must be FASTER! Once you get the lesson and understand, you forgive the "self" that was just you a moment ago, and / or whatever else must be forgiven, leave that self and situation behind! LET IT GO, and instantly you become the NEW YOU, energized and ready for the next moment, the next lesson! It is easy, fast, less painful and then you don't drag that "self" and/or that ugliness through the next moment, or the rest of your life (baggage)...you let it go in a flash! There's no one to blame, it's just a lesson. YOU got it...and with appreciation for having received the lesson that was just provided, say NEXT!

There is a cool song, also by **Within Temptation** that reinforces this principle of growth and letting go in my opinion. Once again, this is just the way I hear it and see it, and I think it is really cool if you look at the EGO and former "selves" from this perspective: **"Shed My Skin"**[35]. I know snakes are not typically well thought of, but in this case, it's a really good illustration of shedding the "selves" with full understanding of why! The first line is a really powerful start, and the rest of the song is brilliant too. Definitely worth checking out the song and lyrics as this really seems to deliver the lesson key in a song! Worth mentioning, "kill" as depicted in the song, in my opinion, is relative to the former "self" / ego, not literal! Same as dying to our "selves", growing out of the former selves. As they "die" we grow...into the HIGHER SELF! Notice when they use a different voice too... there is probably a reason for that! Maybe It is higher SELF vs lower self, and an UNDERSTANDING! My opinion, as always. Another amazing song! I encourage you to take a listen to see what you hear; it may be something different than what I hear and / or the band intended!

# YIN / YANG AND MAGNETISM

## GETTING IN THE ZONE II

Y IN / YANG...BLACK / White = perception/balance/contrast in whatever you want to put on the left and right side of this symbol! This is a perceptual vantage point. While this could include gender, race, age, etc. that is not the point of this discussion. This is not racial, and my way of looking at it is not associated with the occult. It is simply a way of dissecting and looking at things, again, with a slightly different lens because we are primarily looking WITHIN as we are processing what is "out there" so to speak! How we perceive things varies depending on what we are looking at, and that can change situationally, with different people, locations, circumstances, etc.! This perception can also change based on what we want FROM the situation, or the people in it. What is good, what is bad, what do you like, what do you not like...what causes you distress, and what equals peace for you? WHY? Do you prefer black, or white (two different things)? Choose yellow vs blue, green vs red if you prefer, or any other comparison. Is that in ALL situations or just some? With certain people, in some situations, do you have a little bit of a chip on your shoulder, or are fearful, relaxed, angry, edgy, suspicious, etc.? Is this true relative to a spouse, sibling, relative, authority figure, child, your child, someone else's child, etc. Is that always, or because they didn't give you what you wanted the last time you saw them, or when you were younger? Maybe they did something nice for you, or the opposite? Did that affect your "lenses"? Are they on / not on your "good side" today, always / never? Does this Include a particular group, family, company, state, country, profession, authority, etc. These are just a few examples and there are many, many more! The essence of it though is that the "lens" with which we are looking at things, people, and situations is determining what we see and where these virtual lines are being drawn in the mind. We want to be observant, AWARE, and able to perceive the way that the mind is differentiating!

Let's face it, a lot of things can affect our lenses, sometimes that affects us a little, and sometimes a LOT! The question is, are YOU, with awareness, in this moment, SEEING where these virtual lines are being drawn in the mind and what that does to you? Are they valid lines, and edges? Where do they start, and where to they stop? Are they easy to see? Are they a moving target? When do they change? Under what circumstances, with whom, when, how, where, at what times, how much? Do you make note of it and adjust, or plow onwards? As an example, my blood pressure might kick up a notch when I go to the doctor or dentist office, or in a classroom, or amongst a certain group, or with a certain person. That might affect what I see, hear, and feel. Another example might be that I am very receptive to suggestions and willing to listen to challenges at work, or socially, but not from THAT person, or in that situation, or relative to that subject/thing. It may be a spouse, parent, a particularly attractive person, by whatever definition that means to you, or the opposite of that. The point is that our outward AND inward demeanor changes in certain situations, as well as with certain people, and that also changes situationally, and with location and time amongst an infinite number of other variables. This is not intended to point them all out. This is just a starting point because this is about looking WITHIN, in ALL kinds of environments and with all types of people in all types of situations! I want to emphasize here is that although the symbol is black and white, that represents 2 things, so don't let the colors get in the way of the point. It represents perception, contrast, balance & peace between those 2 things, whatever they might be. What is "out there" in our field of vision and situationally affects what is going on "in here" WITHIN. The question is, what is that doing to ME and how is that affecting the way I feel, what I see and what I hear as well as what I don't see and don't hear in the mind! This is taking two things and comparing: with/without this/that relative to peace/not peace balance/not balance WITHIN and how that affects what I FEEL, SEE and HEAR... and then depending on all of that, am I able to maintain my energy, focus, attention, awareness and ultimately

PRESENCE? Which of these components/variables knocked me off balance, and took my PEACE/BALANCE? That's where this begins...

One of the things that this SKILL teaches us with awareness and ongoing self-observation, is to notice when "I" am at peace, calm, happy, at ease, comfortable, or relaxed and smiling vs when the opposite may be true in varying degrees. The insights available via our ability to use this skill are going to be more difficult to see when there is a virtual hurricane storming through the mind vs when the mind is calm, quiet, and peaceful. As you develop this skill, your mind will be at peace more of the time, which certainly helps, and then the smaller disturbances are much more easily recognized, understood, and "processed". THAT'S GOOD NEWS, it means that your hard work is paying off! Keep at it...this is progressive! In the end, after a lot of processing, it all becomes small stuff!

One way to look at this would be to imagine the mind as the surface of water. When a virtual hurricane is going on, the top of the water is rough, with a lot of waves, and chop, so it would be tough to see when a stone even hits the water! (The stone is a thought in your mind) When the mind is "BALANCED", it is calm, like a pristine lake with no wind. It looks like a mirror...and the smallest disturbance is easily seen. Throw a stone, even a pebble in there... even the smallest ripple is pinned down to exactly where something hit the water, and you see the ripples (the result)! That's YOUR MIND with this highly developed skill. In other words, it is going to be easier for you to recognize when the balance is disturbed, and where the disruption came from (which thought). Because YOU are balanced, it will be easier for you to see, understand and process it. The mind has no trouble accomplishing 1 thing, while focused and energetic, with awareness. Pile on several things, or a multitude of things, the level of focus required is much more demanding, and the energy required is enormous! Try juggling 100 things with 2 eyes. Awareness helps, but let's just say that the success rate is still going to take a hit. When a number of these juggled items (tasks, as an example) fall and hit the water at the same time, they make waves, and then not only do we need to navigate the waves, but these waves hit each other, and it can get somewhat choppy very quickly with waves going in different directions! If the mind gets overwhelmed, which it will, it can easily lose track of what thought caused which wave! Processing in this environment is not easy if it is possible at all. The clarity with which we are able to SEE, and then process affects our BALANCE and PEACE in this moment, and then if we don't process, it will affect the next one! This has a cumulative, and progressively more negative effect over time.

Said differently, if we fail to process, the level of uncertainty increases, while balance and peace decrease. It is possible to have balance and peace so keep watching the mind, particularly when it is out of balance or off kilter. Remember to keep processing! The more you achieve balance, the easier it will be to maintain! Less obvious but worth mentioning is that the ongoing maintenance required is easier, faster, and less painful if you don't let the processing backlog accumulate! If you are keeping up, and maybe even eat into the backlog a bit here and there, the waves become smaller and smaller, and then it seems they don't even come up as much. When they do, they typically just dissipate and fade back into the mirror that they came from without much of a fuss at all! Once this is accomplished, and the skill is unwavering, this makes for a really solid CORE PEACE, and BALANCE. You might even call it happiness!

This symbol is another way to look at this perspective. Using black and white is just a way to keep it simple, nothing more. It is a visual example of this balance / peace perspective. I look at this a little bit differently though, so let me give you some examples so that you can understand the power in it! It's not just a nice symbol to look at, but a really powerful tool, if looked at properly! Yes, this is a nicely balanced symbol, and it is pretty cool with nice lines and clear edges but there is MUCH more to it, so let's take this a little further.

Look at the symbol above from a different perspective. The lines and the dots are very clear, right? Black and white offer very nice contrast. It is easy to see the white dot within the black side, and the black dot within the white side, they are in alignment and perfectly balanced! Now make believe for a second that this is your mind, and move the black dot, or the white dot within their respective side. It is easy to recognize that something has changed, the balance has been disturbed, and it is easily seen where the change occurred. In fact, throw a couple white dots and a few more black dots into the mix as well. Again, more than likely, these dots will be easily seen as the symbol is still fairly pristine. It is not going to be all that disruptive, or that difficult to see, sort, understand, process, and get back to balance in this scenario.

Now, alternatively, let's take a look at another scenario. Imagine moving the white dot to within the white side and the black dot to within the black side. In this scenario we lose the edge where the dot was. We can no longer see it. If this were the mind, this could be an issue because we no longer know how to identify the edge of that dot, so we would be creeping up and moving more slowly, sort of feeling our way towards it so that we don't bump into it, or fall over the edge, so to speak. Can you see how this would or could be bad, maybe "fearful" in the mind? At a minimum, it would disturb the peace. Now, throw a few more black dots into the black side, and a few more white dots into the white side. Uh Oh, we have a whole bunch of edges now inside, and yet we have no clue where they are, there is no contrast! We can't see the edges of the dots at all. In the mind, this is a BIG problem! That is what would correlate to the "unknown". The mind does NOT like the unknown! This is not peace.

As an example. If I were walking or driving down a dark street, with no street-lights, no headlights, no moon, no light at all, and there was a manhole cover missing, would I be able see or know where it was? NO, there's no contrast, I could just fall into the hole or blow out a tire, maybe even take out an axle. I have no clue where these holes are! What if there were random holes and potholes here and there too? With no light on this road, it would be nearly impossible to navigate safely. In the mind, this would be the equivalent of fear. The same would be true if the road was white and the holes were white... If we don't know where the holes are, we can't navigate the road very effectively, or peacefully. "Progress" would most definitely be slow, with a lot of dangerous holes, and potential damage to the vehicle (ME). NOT FUN! Even though there are not a lot of edges, per se, we can't see them, so from a mind perspective, we would be "edgy" if not nervous all the time! We are essentially blind...but we keep driving anyway, what other choice do we have, may as well close our eyes to it and hit the gas...same difference. (sarcasm) If something hits me, well then so be it...it is what it is, we say! Like the proverbial bumper cars, we just keep bumping into the sides, and other cars along the way, and plow forward with a jolt here and there. Some are a little more stirring than others, particularly when they hit us from the back, or side...but every now and then we hit one head on and that is truly a jarring experience. Let's face it, we just didn't see that coming at all, so we never even slowed down! This is the mind when it cannot see where the edges are!

Last scenario, imagine if the whole circle was filled with 1000 dots or more, just randomly scattered throughout. Let's use the road example again. Imagine driving down this road, the dots are now randomly placed black and white cob-blestones and they cover the whole road so there are edges everywhere. There are so many of them that they cover over the center line, and they even used them for the curbs and sidewalks too so we can't really identify where the lanes are anymore. We have to drive down the road to get where we are going, but we can't progress at all without running over the dots, so that's what we have to do. This is a BUMPY road to begin with and now, since the dots cover the whole road, we have lost sight of the middle line, we can no longer see it at all! Now throw in a bunch more dots, nothing changes in terms of what we see, right? It just gets a little bumpier when we run over one of these new cobblestones that got thrown into the road, or one that may have jumped up out of its place, and is sitting on top of the road, even if we do see them and / or the hole it left!? There are just too many dots to note where the edges are and when a new one gets thrown on our path, we can hardly see it either. The road looks the same, no matter where we look, just a sea of black n white. Driving on cobblestone is rough enough, and LOUD too as the tires hit the inconsistencies in the road! In this scenario, it is nearly impossible to discern where the edges are on any of the dots! We have a bumpy, loud road, and we also have risk, oncoming traffic with no lane markers, and nearly invisible curbs! Everything is covered with dots so we can't differentiate one thing from another! God help the people on the sidewalk. LOL.

Navigating this road is dangerous, and loud, but we NEED to go down it to get where we are going, so what do we do? We start slowly, and as we get more impatient, we start driving a little faster even though it's getting louder, and a little riskier, so we turn up the music! Nice, now we can't hear the tires thumping along anymore, and since we bought some new shock absorbers to "insulate" us from the pain of this rough experience we just keep driving, faster and faster. The shocks seem to work better as we gain speed because they are evening out the bumps, so we drive even faster so we can't feel the bumps in the road hardly at all. Aside from the volume increasing, which is annoying, we just ignore it all! In the mind, this is the equivalent to putting blinders on, and using coping mechanisms ("ignore"-ance & avoidance)! In fact, it's so loud in here that we really can't hear anything in this vehicle, the phone rings with an amazing opportunity, and we miss it because we can't even hear it or see the flashing lights! Every now and then we see a really big dot get thrown into the road, which stands out amongst all the smaller ones and all we do is swerve to avoid it, we don't even slow down... just keep driving! (avoidance).

If this is the mind, our state is somewhat numb to the sight of the edges because they are everywhere. While we can see them a little, they are flying by so fast it's all a blur! We can't hear the noise of the tires anymore because we turned up the music, and the suspension of this new car is wonderful, so we can no longer feel anything either! (Turned off our feelings). Since we are driving really fast now, we hit some big dam cobblestones here and there, the car jumps a bit, and we swerve a little, but because we are so numb to the pain of this experience, we just keep driving. Even hitting these really big cobblestones it's like we hear and feel a big badunk...but just keep right on going because we want this craziness to end (resistance). We MUST "get there"! Regardless of the fact that the car we are driving doesn't feel so hot anymore, it is sputtering, making funny noises, grunting, groaning, and complaining, onwards we go, dents, chips, damaged rims, dings and even cracks and mud on the windshield. Every now and then, with impaired vision we come to a dot that is so big we are forced to slam on the breaks, and while it shakes us up a little, somehow, we manage to avoid the danger. In the mind this means, RESIST, and proceed with caution, sometimes trembling! (Resistance/ Fear). Because of this, after a while, we just have to stop and rest for a minute, it's just too much, we need to take a breather, so we pull off to the side of the road. Even then, the road is such a hot mess we are looking over our shoulder trying to make sure we don't get hit by something else flying towards us! So, we never really relax or recover, and yet we get back on the road sooner than we probably should! For the most part, due to circumstances, and delays, we just keep plowing through every dot, big and small to the extent that we can tolerate the rough patches because we need to get to where we are going! Bottom line though is that after a while, we feel nothing and hear nothing. Let's face it, we haven't really seen anything but a blur for a long time...the whole experience is mind numbing! We have some great mind tools for this, they are called resistance, avoidance, and ignorance. If that doesn't work, we start self-medicating among other self-preservation techniques! We started with band aides to cover the little cuts and bruises we get along the way, but eventually we are so distracted that that we can't even stay in our lane anymore. That's when we break out the heavier "medicine". After using some of that medicine, that's when the cop pulls you over and you are REALLY in trouble. Hopefully that is the least of your worries, and an ambulance wasn't required because something even worse happened, to you or anyone else! That's life on the road, from the mind perspective. Prepared, and balanced? NO, probably not well equipped at all. Definitely not balanced. More likely we are in a state of bewilderment, obtuseness, incomprehension, ignorance, maybe completely numbed out or just overwhelmed and essentially blind because of it! Not to mention what the "medicine" might be doing to us. Needless to say, we need some more effective tools!

So, I know you stayed with me through this and are making the necessary correlations, the dots are thoughts and patterns of thoughts, some are bigger than others. Let's take it a step further though and really understand this dynamic within the mind. We need to be able to SEE and KNOW where the edges are, and which thoughts are more "EDGY" than others because these are the ones carrying the weight! If the mind is chock full of dots, we can't really discern where the edges are by sight at all. The edges are just a mish mosh; they blend together. It is unclear where one ends and the next begins! At this point, we have NO CHOICE, so we plow through them. As in the cobblestone example, this just creates chaos, the mind chatter is loud, overwhelming even, so we can't hear effectively either! The net result of this is that we can't see with clarity and all we hear is NOISE which gets louder and louder, so we numb ourselves out or play games amongst our "selves" which occupy us with adequate distractions so that one way or another we can't FEEL anything either! The whole mind is full of edges, they are everywhere, its unavoidable...so we just take our lumps and move on. In fact, we do it faster and faster! That's what everyone else does, right? Oh well, shrug. Sigh. Just keep running... You could argue that this is why a lot of people seem to be edgy all the time, not to mention exhausted! It's no wonder why we self-medicate!

This is a problem at way more than just at the surface level! Do you see it? We are missing the lessons by driving right through them, over them or around them! Not only that, but it is also damaging the vehicle (ME!)! We are NOT pausing to SEE anything, no less process something! The dots are coming at us so fast and there is so much going on that the uncertainty factor is palpable! The unknown is a dark place for the mind! This is NOT FUN! If we are living in the darkness much of the time, if not all of the time, that's what brings out fear! Since the dots are thoughts, and we need to be over there, not only do we not want to deal with the dots between here and there, but we also don't have TIME! So, we avoid them, drive over them, bury them with a new one, we suppress them or "medicate" them, or use distraction techniques such as TV, social media, and other coping mechanisms. We try to ignore them, but they just keep coming, I mean the road is paved with them! They are everywhere and we can't make sense of any of it! What does this sound like? STRESS! Yep, completely, 100%! Seems like everyone is stressed, even the ones that don't seem to be doing anything! What's that all about? Well, go back a few pages. You have no clue what their last few miles looked like! Step into their shoes. Understand now? If not, just understand that there are MILLIONS of people going down this same road, doing the best they can to make sense of it all, and on top of all of that, just maybe they lost their pet, dog, cat, mother, father, spouse, friend, child, or someone / something else that was important to them. Maybe they have an illness they are dealing with, or something even worse? Does it really make the situation better if you or I mistreat them, yell at them, or even beat them up under our own breath while we are going down the road? Who does this help / hurt? There is a better way! It begins with the understanding that we are doing these things to our "selves" in our own minds!

So, what's the solution? SEE IT HAPPENING! If you want to help yourself, or the world, start by cleaning house! Stop closing your eyes to it, open them instead! Do your best to keep them open, IN THE MOMENT, and make some changes! By cleaning house, even just a little bit, we should be able to see and hear a little bit better, right? That's really important because the edges are where you and I need to be extremely diligent and pay attention! We MUST calm the mind to the point where we are more "balanced". When balanced we can more effectively use our SKILL. So, what does this mean, in the real world? The house that needs cleaning is our own. The MIND! Sweep up some of these dots and do something with them! Maybe the circular file. (sarcasm) LOL

Awareness and focus will not only show you where the dots are, but it will actually highlight for you where these edges are with much more clarity and precision! It's like seeing with ultra-clear magnified vision! Once they are "known", SEEN, and well defined for us, we have a mental reference point as to where we have drawn the lines, and we understand that coming into various situations (THE MOMENT). With this understanding and careful observation over time, a heightened awareness and focus allow us to see when these "selves" are getting close to an edge! The edges are good thought / bad thought, good emotion / bad emotion, good feeling / bad feeling, good situation / bad situation, as perceived by the perceiver. The me, and my preferences, fears, desires, wants, don't want, etc.! In fact, as we see this stuff, we may even be able to SEE where we can erase some lines! But how? Well first, slow down to a point at which you can see, hear, and feel! Once you do that, THEN you can take the next step to process, and understand. Once processed and understood, YOU, IN THE MOMENT, can remove a dot from the road here and there and smooth it out. What did that do in a sea of dots? Ever so slightly, just a teensee weensee iddy biddy little bit, that smooths out the road ahead. If we do this consistently, over a period of time, we remove more and more dots, the road becomes a lot smoother, and it is a lot easier to see the bumps. Not only that, but the manhole covers, potholes and larger cobblestones stand out like a sore thumb. We can see them coming way ahead of time! Each time, rather than plowing right over and through them, we take THE MOMENT to understand, process, and remove another dot, and smooth it out. We are paving the way to a super experience. While it may take a little while to smooth it out completely, there is a light at the end of the tunnel, and we know EXACTLY what paves that road! Knowledge truly is power. Once you understand, you understand, it is only a matter of TIME! What happens next is incredible, YOU STOP WASTING IT! Instead of driving around the potholes, you take the TIME, IN THAT MOMENT, to SEE it, fill it in, smooth it out...so that the next time we come down this road (similar experience) there is no longer a pothole there to begin with, ITS GONE! The MOMENT is where this all happens.

Peace vs NOT Peace is the net result of when our lenses are not seeing clearly or not knowing where the edges are! LOTS of scenarios could create this problem. Our lenses could be looking at bad information, be out of balance, be way off kilter, too drilled down, too zoomed out, etc.! The lenses are these vantage points as the "selves"! They don't realize that black and white both exist because they are stuck in one vs the other, so overwhelmed that they can't see the edges with precision, the edges are unrecognizable, inconsistent, or even jagged with random sharp edges! At a minimum, in any of these scenarios we can't see as effectively! Why? Because the edges are not defined, unclear. We don't know where they are, when they are coming up, there are too many, they cut in and out too much, they were moved, or blurry and as a result we are completely off balance and don't know which way to look! The human mind does NOT like uncertainty, and when there is a lot of it, well, let's just say that "peace of mind" is not a high probability! This is the result of living IN the mind amongst these selves' vs above the mind where we can SEE the selves with clarity!

In this symbol, there is a little white in black, and a little black in white, and they are interwoven together with very CLEAR EDGES! There is not a lot of uncertainty here, we can see the edges and we know exactly where they are! The MIND doesn't see things this way. It either has so much black and white intermixed together like a big bowl of black & white soup that it's just a hot mess OR it gets stuck in one vs the other and doesn't know where the lines are! That's when we get really blinded and can't see the forest for the trees. We get stuck in black and can't see white or stuck in white and can't see black. The mind takes both sides, or gets lost & confused in the maze, but we don't see it. That is precisely why we get blindsided; we don't know where one ends and where the other begins. We have virtual blinders on! You must know that they both exist and SEE IT. To see it, you must be above it, know the edges, understand where they are and why, and then smile, with awareness and a slight smirk. LOL. YOU can't be deceived anymore! Black and white both exist, YOU are seeing them with clarity, understanding them, and LOVING THEM BOTH because they are teaching you something about your "selves"! Loving them both is the equivalent of removing a dot, and smoothing out the road ahead, and as a matter of fact, behind us as well, there's no longer a bump, a hole, or pain point there!

That's easy right? Well, maybe for some things, but maybe not so much for others, so let's dig deeper. As we progress down this road, it will become easier to see these edges, right? That means we are going to be developing new ideas about these edges, especially since we will be seeing them all that much clearer and sooner now. We can take this to the next level and if we let it, it can make us even MORE edgy! Do we see this happen at all? Uh Ooooh...Yeah, that's not good right? HAH! Nope, that means we had a slight misunderstanding because that is NOT the goal. The point of this understanding is to make us LESS EDGY, so let's look at this properly. As we approach an edge, we may notice fear kicking in, or excitement, or glee, or giddiness...even THRILL, any and all feelings and emotions are a possibility. THIS IS WHAT WE WANT! Unfortunately, that's not the way the mind sees it! So, as a result, this is what can turn us HARD one way or the other, particularly if we are edgy! That is a **"RE"** action! Think BALANCE. If we are off balance, one way or the other. So, if we are off balance one way, let's say on the negative side, we would tend to be MORE resistant and shut things down, even "good" stuff that actually makes sense under "normal" circumstances! If we are off balance on the "opposing" side, the positive, we might be too accepting, and not see something "bad" or warning signs. Balance keeps us neutral, and unbiased which allows us to SEE, HEAR and FEEL much clearer, more accurately!

If these are dots then, let's expand on that perspective. What happens when we approach an edge? From the negative side, we can turn the other way, resist it, avoid it, and we use many other "coping" mechanisms! The fact is, we just can't take one more thing, no matter what it is! ALL of these are RE-actions, and they are all from the "selves" vs a NEW ACTION from the higher "SELF"! The alternative to the negative side of the RE-action, is the positive over enthusiastic version. That is when we are OVER EXCITED, with blind optimism, throwing caution to the wind, and we might run towards one or the other so fast that we tune everything else out and miss essential details that would otherwise warn us of danger! That's not balance either! In both cases, a lesson is going to be coming, and it will be an eye opener! NO, that's not us anymore. <u>Let's open our eyes NOW vs later so that we can remain balanced</u>! Better vision, higher vision, better vantage point, with understanding. Awareness, that all-encompassing field vision, with a focus and energized attention to detail as well...USING the SKILL! With eyes wide open we see the stuff that weighs us down, steers us, turns us, and we see why, how much, where and we even know when, AHEAD OF TIME! We see it coming!

You must, and you will see these early warning signs in an unfolding event as an opportunity vs resisting or avoiding it! In fact, this is <u>THE</u> opportunity we have been waiting for and a KEY moment is on the horizon! With the SKILL, we see it developing as the lesson is unfolding, we know it is coming and then we are on ALERT for it! This is a clue, a WAKE-UP call, to activate our awareness, turn it on high and pay attention! One of the selves is about to show its face! We are about to get an introduction and MEET IT to see how it wants to RE-act. That's why we need to know where the edges are, so that we see these early clues, and as a result we are on alert and ready for the lesson! We see the whole thing developing very early in the process, so we don't miss the opportunity! Once we see the emotion, we can't be satisfied with just seeing the emotion, we need to look UNDERNEATH the emotion. That's where the lesson is! What EXACTLY caused this stir, the twinge? That is an edge! Look under the surface, dig a little deeper, find the lesson, understand it, process it and take another step forward!

That next step forward is into the moment, without the "self" that just wanted to RE-act as you for you...the one that got stirred! The higher "SELF", with awareness, caught the lower self with its hand in the cookie jar and it didn't let it steal the cookie! (The moment). It's my cookie, my moment! Don't take my dam cookie. I want to live my life, ME...not you, my former lower unskilled self! So, with compassion, empathy and understanding, YOU as the higher "SELF" LET IT GO! That lower, unskilled self was just replaced. New YOU is now present, awake and aware IN THE MOMENT taking NEW ACTION!!

This all makes sense, right? So back to the question, why is this easier for some things vs others? Some things turn us much harder than others. They are way more important to us. We weigh things differently. In some cases, this is with a lot of weight, we are "attached" and the mind RE-acts with much more FORCE because of it. Have you ever heard the advice, don't force it? When you force things, stuff breaks! Well, this can be true for the mind and it's gearing too! So, I want to talk about that next.

For fun, and to break it up for a minute, check out the song **"Where is the Edge"**[36], by **Within Temptation**! The song, the way that I hear it...reminds me to SEE and UNDERSTAND where these edges are WITHIN! Pretty cool song. There are little edges, big edges, and sometimes ginormous edges! Some we have avoided or been unconscious of for years and so they are colossal! Some we see fairly readily, yet we force our way through them or around them anyway. Force strains things, muscling our way through is often hazardous to our health, sometimes wealth! Pay attention to situations where force is an option. This is a time where we need to wake up with awareness and see the ways in which we are reacting. Often times, there is a choice that we are bypassing, or missing...are we present enough to see it? Where is this edge? Let's stop here to consider force a little more thoroughly as it relates to these edges within!

**FORCE:** Certainly, another beneficial angle to consider, so let's examine this aspect of thinking from the mind perspective. In other words, how do we actually do the thinking? Are we trying to fit a square peg in a round hole? Are we forcing black where white would actually make more sense? Are we forcing white where black would actually make more sense? Did anyone consider gray, or orange? Am I locked in to one mind perspective, when another might be more beneficial? Do I have a balanced perspective or is it overweight to one side? Look at it like a see saw! The more we weigh one alternative, the more the scale tips to that side! Black & white are the extreme and that's why they are used for examples like this. The cool thing is that they are good contrasting colors, easily seen at the edges, but in the MIND that can create a problem! In the mind, polarity can create distress because we don't understand the game OR impermanence. We tend to want one thing vs another, we want it NOW, and in fact we want MORE of it or ALL of it and we want to keep it FOREVER! So, the mind goes from balanced to wanting, which is a preference to one vs the other and kind of leaning to one side. Then possibly we progress to NEEDING which is a DEMAND or heavily weighted to one side, and then onwards to a MUST HAVE! Not only must I have it, but then I must have more of it...and then sometimes with all that momentum, we get super excited, we go freaking bat shit crazy, and just forget you and everyone else, I want it ALL! Hmmm, sounds to me like there is a lesson or two here!

Do you see how this can escalate? I went from a casual enjoyable balanced experience to a little bit more of an edgy scenario with some elbowing and positioning to get what I want and then to get a little bit more of it (Gluttony/Selfishness), to outright NEED and then GREED! This particular lesson stems from at least one fairly substantial overarching lesson. What's the lesson? LACK. We live in an ABUNDANT universe; however, we are approaching it from a LACK and LIMITATION mentality! Where is your attention? Where is your energy going? What is the focus? LACK! Not only do I want mine, but I also want yours too because there isn't enough to go around! That is "scarcity" or a lack mentality and we are taking it to an extreme!

What happens is a MIND issue! With understanding we can change the "Attitude problem"! So, where's the problem? We get locked in to thinking in terms of polarities or dualities, black/white, Hot/Cold, Dark/Light, Always/Never, good/bad, want/don't want, my team/your team, me/you, enough/not enough, etc. Black and white thinking is the mind when it thinks in extremes like this. In the mind, this dichotomy can become a very powerful mechanism, an all or nothing extreme mentality, and a major TRIGGER!! This means that in this situation, at this time, to this mind, and this version of "self", the opposite is really BAD!!!! Here we are at resistance or avoidance again...a bump / hole / fork in the road! The "selves" WITHIN either resist the edge or avoid it all together, sometimes just to stay comfortable! When polar opposites become a NEED to have one vs the other, it just doesn't work! Roadblocks go up, we turn away, BLINK, and then we missed the opportunity, again! It happens that fast! You must be ready for it to see it. In the mind, it creates major resistance to the opposite! Resistance = the law of attraction working against you and the "self" is the "you" or becomes the "you" in that moment you blinked, the higher YOU, higher "SELF" was taken out! Nothing changes here, lessons are missed! NEW CHOICE is unavailable. We were NOT PRESENT!

Understanding is different, which removes the resistance and ALLOWS presence! PRESENCE SEES! Black and white both exist, and in fact there are an infinite number of shades of gray! Similarly, we can perceive cold as simply varying degrees of heat, or a lack of heat, right? Darkness is really just varying degrees of light or LACK of it. Bad, is only varying degrees of good, or LACK of it! If there is an abundance of light, darkness progressively goes away, right? An abundance of good, well...where's bad? If there's an abundance of heat, then where is cold? The idea here is that we always have a choice in how we SEE things and what we choose to focus on EXPANDS! We can choose to think from any mindset we choose to, choose wisely, right?! One of these vantage points, with understanding, is to choose abundance vs limitation thinking. We can do that relative to just about anything! Glass half full, glass half empty. We can think in terms of balanced or unbalanced too, comfort, peace, or any other alternative. With awareness we have choice and can prioritize! Which one do you want to expand? Understand the mind, and how it THINKS! By understanding the mind and how it operates, we can choose abundance thinking and / or just simply better thoughts. In addition, we choose to not re-create the resistance that invites fear and these other negative mindsets to our doorstep. If they aren't there, we can't accidentally let them in! This means LETTING THEM GO, in a previous moment or this one! If we let them go, they don't show up at the door and ring the bell to distract us! We are FREE...from them! YOU have that power, don't force things, WAKE UP, and FREE your "self"! Start to pay more attention to the road you are on with awareness, so that as you proceed down it, you repair and replace the miscellaneous cobblestones that don't look or feel so good, understand why they are causing a stir, and smooth out the road ahead and behind you. The net result of this is that your attention is not drawn there anymore! If your attention is not drawn as forcefully to the past or future, (less and smaller dots) it is easier to maintain your presence!

With awareness, and our highly acute skill, we have understanding, and NOW we have CHOICE. "Need to have" mentality goes away, right?! In fact, do we really have to fear the opposite? NO, because we get it, both are fine, we just have preference vs need! No battle = No conflict. No conflict = NO RESISTANCE. No resistance = what? NO FEAR! To the unaware mind, these battles are happening constantly behind the scenes, under the surface, and so we miss the lessons that are **present**ed to us because we are asleep at the wheel, unaware! This battleground can get ferocious as the lesson gets escalated, which is each time we miss the lesson before it. The universe, OUR UNIVERSE, in an effort to get through to us, speaks LOUDER when we miss lessons! (Call it karma, magnetism, or whatever else) That means bigger dots are getting thrown in the road, OURS! We generally don't see it in the early stages though because the lines are unclear, or the attitude problem has not advanced far enough yet. (They are still small dots) The stone being thrown into the water in the hurricane is not large enough to create waves big enough that we notice, YET!! Small ripples are easy enough to deal with. Hurricane force wind, rain, and the waves it creates cause damage, destruction and leave scars! Scars & internal bruising bring us to the past in FEAR and the other negative emotions! It is a vicious cycle that can escalate to a RIP tide with large fierce waves. Break the cycle, turn the tide, NOW! Deal with the small dots so that they don't become large dots!

We can be above this chatter early on and watch the battle as it is going on! SEE what each side is trying to do, with awareness and self-observation! By doing so, we get the lesson, step above and stay above these various players, "the selves" and RELEASE THEM! They may no longer deserve to be in the game if they cannot see beyond their "self" created walls! Let them go.

We probably don't need anything from these "selves"! You decide. With SKILL, we SEE, and we UNDERSTAND the games these various "selves" are playing, and where the lines are being drawn. We see it all the time. The selves are set against themselves, at the edges, and yet they don't even see it. They are caught up in their limited little worlds, and they don't see it, or a way out... and it is draining OUR precious energy as a result! They are so entrenched in their little battles they don't see the WAR and the result it is having on us. The "selves" within create all this resistance to each other and it is based on polarities. See it from above as this virtual tug of war is going on within and how it is happening across these "self" created lines / walls / edges they build. They conflict with each other. The battle is within and believe it or not it's called INNER CONFLICT! Brilliant. Two or more different "selves" with a difference of opinion. Where are they drawing these virtual lines?

**With this insight, awareness, and PRESENCE, we can SEE IT and get the lesson when it is available, NOW!** NOW, we just need to BE watching for it and know when it's coming. When is that going to be? When we are approaching one of these edges. We watch our little selves at the edges, so we as the higher SELF don't get EDGY! Higher "SELF" being alerted to the possible lesson coming, awake and aware, arrives to the moment in balance and GETS IT! We know EXACTLY when to pay attention so that we can release these non-serving selves. When? NOW...at the edges! **Where is the edge?** Where are YOUR edges? If you haven't made the necessary correlation, the edges are where your triggers are...so you are seeing them BEFORE they trigger you! These are areas where we have run into things, and we are running into them again. Here we have scars, internal bruising, heartache, pain points, don't want "stuff" and situations we would rather not be in, just plain resistance! In some cases, if you aren't seeing as effectively just yet, you will FEEL them coming first, which is the clue to open your eyes TO see it coming! Awake and aware! Ready... it is like seeing the future. I'd venture to say that with this level of foresight, you wouldn't need hindsight! Hindsight is 20/20, right? If you don't need that then how good is your presence vision? Get PRESENT with PRESENCE!

Did you ever see someone in a very difficult (to everyone else) situation with that grin on their face as if nothing could disturb their peace of mind? WHY? Did you ever stop to ask, or even think about it? I'll tell you why. THEY DON'T NEED ANYTHING, not from you or the situation! The interesting thing is that we proceed through life thinking that either this is better than that, or that is better than this and either way, WE MUST HAVE IT. It is a black / white thing in the mind, not racially speaking, but as described above! It is a mind perspective that in all situations, we (as the mind) WANT one thing vs. another. What's the way out? Don't NEED anything! If we don't need anything, what's there to STRESS about?

So, what happens when you NEED something and what's the problem with that? It's a mind dynamic. What happens is the mind gets ultra-dialed in to JUST HAVING THAT, and ONLY THAT vs the other! At this point, it is no longer a want...it is a NEED! This is NOT a balanced perspective; all the cards are on ONE SIDE! The mind toggle is 100% flipped. Ever see someone "FLIP OUT"? That's why! If it doesn't happen their way, oh boy...pain ahead, look out! Think about it this way: If I NEED something from someone OR some situation, what happens if I don't get it from them or the situation? Do I have any power/balance in that situation? Other than crying, stomping my feet, complaining, and making a scene. Joking of course. If I were to PREFER something from that situation, or person, would that be more balanced? If I were to need NOTHING from that person or situation...would that be more balanced?

What we are seeing with our awareness skill is where the mind is actually drawing these lines for our "selves", and that essentially defines peace vs NOT peace for us at that time. We don't need to listen to that "self", did you ever consider saying NO to that thought? Or at least stopping long enough to evaluate whether that is a valid line / edge? This is LIMITING US to that perspective and tainting our eyes so we can't see anything else. There IS a CHOICE here, at a minimum, pause to question it, otherwise WE ARE BLIND to any other alternatives! It doesn't exist and can't exist; we are drawing a haphazard line in the sand, and we will not cross it... We DO NOT WANT THAT! It cannot happen, or else! Where does one end and the other begin? Until we wake up and see this, the balance gets disrupted a LOT and in the case of 1000 dots we don't even know why. There is no balance! We have no clue where the lines are while we are TRAPPED WITHIN the mind and these perspectives. Not only that, the "selves" actually move the line on us because they think we aren't paying attention. They think we won't notice, and of course, they know best, or at least better than you! (sarcasm). As long as they are in control of YOUR mind, they are right! You have no control at all... It's the wild west in there! You and I need to be wise and alert to these EGO games and EGO tricks. With this insight and oversight, by observing it over and over again, the lines become more and more clear. We can even see when they try to move the line, which is kind of funny because it usually means they were wrong about something and trying to save face! LOL.

Anyway, knowing where the lines are REMOVES UNCERTAINTY because we can observe all of this happening, with awareness of it happening! Just to be sure we are on the same page here, where is all of this happening? Yep, you got it...WITHIN! The end result is that we realize we can smile no matter what happens, and we also recognize when and why we are off balance very quickly. We see how, when, where, and even how much as well as which "self" created the disruption! More often than not it is a mistake, and a simple lesson! Bottom line, we can be happy no matter what, it is a choice in how we relate to that thing. More good news is that by the very nature of this new relationship, it TAKES THE STRESS OUT of a lot of situations as you intensify your focus and heighten your awareness! That means you get more out of each day, and not only that you feel better and have more energy! This alone is something to build on!

You do realize that this is also about your personal magnetism, right? Where is the weight? What has the power? Do you? What is my personal magnet magnetizing? What am I attracting into my life? Let's backtrack a bit. If we absolutely MUST have black, and then white comes, we are met with disappointment, right? If we must have white and black happens, we are also met with disappointment. What we come to realize is that there is always going to be black and white, and if we are OK with either, we can keep smiling. In fact, even better, because we are NOT attached to one or the other (NEED), there is no magnetism to its opposite. Again, if we absolutely must have one vs the other, then fear of the opposite "the need" becomes a magnet for it, and the fear will win more often than not, you will get what you fear, particularly if it is heightened. It is the nature of thought, what you focus on expands! Your focus is on the fear, which means you will get what you fear! Remove the stigma, or attachment to the result. (THE NEED!) YOU can be OK with either, but first you must be able to SEE THEM BOTH and where the focus and attention is! That, in my opinion, is the meaning and usefulness of this symbol!

With understanding, and awareness, you remove the fear. When you remove the fear, you remove the magnet, meaning you are no longer attracting the opposite of what you want, you are ALLOWING WHAT YOU WANT.

## ALLOW WHAT YOU WANT!

Your personal magnetism is getting a huge boost! It seems so ridiculous to even talk about it that way, because most people will say...well of course, I will allow what I want. The fact is though, when they are attached to it, and let's say that a negative state follows if it doesn't happen, then you can be sure that it was the fear of the opposite that brought that result. FEAR WON. You can't RESIST or focus on what you don't want and GET what you want. It doesn't work! There is a lesson that was missed, and this is a prescription for understanding, a path through the woods! In order to make your way through this overgrown forest, you are going to need to get the lessons, understand them, and cut down some trees. The trees are the thoughts and patterns of thoughts that no longer serve you! CUT THEM DOWN in the moment!

RUSH has a cool song that seems to be about this, the way that I hear it anyway, "The Trees"[37]. That's the name of the song, believe it or not, and this song kind of helped me to understand this perspective. Thanks to Neil, Alex, and Geddy! Look up the song online. The way that I see and hear it is that the forest is your mind, the trees are your thoughts. Think about it from this perspective and have fun with this one. Bottom line, get rid of the old dead wood (The thoughts and programs that no longer serve you)! It's not helping you make effective decisions...and maybe, just maybe it is clogging up the machine! This is NOT a color thing, it is about thought, the MIND! In the street analogy, it is removing or repairing the cobblestones IN THE MOMENT and ensuring that they are truly processed and smoothed out so that the road ahead and behind is no longer causing us an issue and diverting our attention!

And from a different Neale: **Neale Donald Walsch**[38], he said it this way in an email to me:

**"On this day of your life
Doug, I believe God wants you to know...**

**...that yearning for a new way will not produce it.**
**Only ending the old way can do that.**
**You cannot hold onto the old all the while**
**declaring that you want something new.**
**The old will defy the new;**
**the old will deny the new;**
**the old will decry the new.**
**There is only one way to bring in the new.**
**You must *make room* for it."**

How do you do this? ...answer, you don't, unless you are **AWARE** that it is happening. Work on being in the moment, work on paying attention to WHO is making the decisions within your mind and why! Drill down and FOCUS! Is it YOU, or some former version of you? Is it an imposter, one of the "selves" posing as you? Is it some ideal, or a projection that expects and needs a certain outcome, or is it YOU, 100% present and completely balanced, OK with whatever happens? Are you attached, or unattached to something? HOW MUCH SO? **Awareness is key! With awareness we can make room for the NEW! In fact, you can BE new!** Remove some dots (Make room for it) in the moment and empower your higher "SELF" with NEWNESS!!

There is a level of mind that "THINKS"...see it for what IT is. That level of mind is NOT YOU! YOU must be above that level of thinking so that this NEW version of "SELF", higher YOU, can see the battles being waged by these lower "selves". From this higher vantage point, your mind and what's going on in there is clearly visible...LOOK WITHIN!! The edges are now seen, and that alone is huge! You are now the over seer of the mind. This higher "YOU" can watch the battle in the mind as two completely opposite opinions bicker back and forth across these edges! The little "selves" within the mind, while trapped within their self-created walls think they are you and that you are both of the bickerers, you are NOT...they are just positionalities within you. They want to BE you and they want to STAY you. It is this higher "YOU", higher "SELF" that I am speaking about that must STEP UP out of the mind and SEE them from this level. Seeing allows you to step into the moment to RE**PRESENT**, as YOU...the real YOU! In doing so, with empathy and consideration, YOU release these lower "selves" and their non serving positionalities at the gate to NOW! Concentrate, energize, focus, wake up, and ALLOW THE PRESENT YOU into the moment, THE REAL YOU, the BEST YOU!

And on that note, **Guy Finley**, in his email says it this way:

## "KEY LESSON:

### *Jump Off the Pain Train*

**The gradual realization that you're engaged in a conversation with a level of mind that's set against itself...is the same as being released from *its* pain."**

The answer to life's "problems" starts with <u>understanding</u>! Seeing with this heightened and energized awareness educates, explains, clarifies, and shines a light in the dark! That light enables us to see more clearly where we are directing our attention and focus within that awareness, more acutely. This shows us what is expanding and also what is limiting within us as we experience life on the leading edge of thought. It is the various parts of our "selves" that make up this intricate inner gearing that we are NOW able to see with extremely detailed clarity, in the moment, as they are highlighted / spotlighted for seeing with these new eyes. Inner vision. It is that inner cognizance that essentially opens the door to see new choices as we pause to assess the validity of our own inner mechanics.

Many spiritual teachers speak of doing some internal "weeding" of our inner garden, the mind! If the mind has been unattended for a while (we are asleep / unaware / unconscious) that may require a more serious effort. While we are not paying attention, we allow the branches of these weeds to become larger and a little more established, which can be problematic. Then it requires bigger tools, and more effort. At that point, the branches that we have let grow require a more serious "pruning"...maybe even a chainsaw! At times it may require a little more precision too, as these weeds can work themselves into the smallest corners and grow in seemingly infertile ground that is tough to gain access to! While getting at these roots may require some diligent and focused digging, they need to be uncovered to be cut out, else they will come back in no time at all! In this case, a sharper more honed instrument may be more effective in exposing the root. It's like shining a bright light in the shadows! Consider the mind as if it were a garden where some thoughts might be considered flowers, fruits, or vegetables and others are clearly weeds to be cut out! It's harder to tell the difference at night, or in the shade! AWARENESS SEES ALL! It is a powerful discernment and mind cultivation tool, and it is certainly up to the task. Put it to the test, it will deliver! Given enough energy, it offers us a choice in which "stuff" we want to fertilize, and of course, what we would prefer to remove from our inner garden all together. While some weeds are easily uprooted as they are small and undeveloped, many have grown too large to pull out by the root, so we must start by pruning. Realizing that whatever we focus on expands, we now see where our focus has been, as revealed by what that has produced in our existing life garden, so we change our focus, and plant new seeds. We also see where thoughts and patterns of thought have become mechanical, or robotic and we question the programming and logic behind these automated responses to life so that we no longer automatically plant these bad seeds by RE-acting to life on auto-pilot. Where things had been automatic, or accidental, awareness offers us CHOICE where only moments prior, we were blind and deaf, or these options were not readily seen, available, or heard because they were obscured by unconsciousness. This can happen in fractions of a second! PRESENCE, awareness, **IN**sight and understanding offer us new choices. In waking up and choosing newness, we break our own molds and establish new skills that enable powerful experiential field vision internally and externally. Surveying this new landscape with our heightened awareness gives us an amazing witnessing perspective with which we can observe and learn, and choose new thoughts.

By CHOOSING new thoughts with our focus and attention, we are adding the virtual fertilizer they need. That allows that NEW thought to grow NEW roots and those roots feed further new thoughts, new growth. Those thoughts reproduce and form more just like them and then new leaves and branches grow as a result. The choice becomes; do you want more branches, leaves, flowers and fruit or more weeds? With understanding, we see where it starts, at the root, tuber, rhizome or stolon. It is just above or often times underneath the surface of the ground where these root runners spread and sprout new growth, leaves and then branches! The mind is no different. What we allow to take root and fertilize grows new and stronger roots, which expand, spread, and sprout out in new ways. We must be watchful to SEE what is germinating, at their beginning, which can be the source of the "problem"! With a constant and conscious nurturing and cultivating process, awareness tends the garden as the higher "SELF"! It all starts small, but the seeds we sow grow, and depending on how much we fertilize them, they can grow quite quickly! We need to BE AWARE of what we fertilize with our attention! In fact, our inner garden can become quite a mess if we do not attend to it for a while. Attend your mind, not stuck within it though, above it, watchful, wide awake and aware of what's going on WITHIN it. See what has sprouted from it first though, that's your life, right now! Then see it as it is sprouting, as you are living it, as it is becoming your life. Then see it BEFORE it sprouts, as thoughts are developing, but BEFORE they germinate into your life. It is as if you see the virtual weed before it even breaks the surface, and you just don't allow it to emerge into your life anymore. Weeds are prolific, if you hadn't noticed them or done some gardening in a while, they are fast. We need to be faster! While we are looking over here, in our virtual garden, they pop up over there! It is crazy, they pop up overnight, or where / when we were not aware...IN THE DARKNESS. Time to shine the light on them, the light of our awareness!

I know in the south, we need to put down pre emergent on our lawns 3 to 4 times a year...and it seems like it is necessary to apply it more often if it rains a lot! If we miss an application, or lack awareness (use an inferior product / lack energy, awareness, or focus) the weeds seem to flourish, seemingly from out of nowhere! Awareness is like pre emergent, for thoughts! It isn't 100%, sometimes we need to follow up with some weeding here and there, but it's a whole lot easier if we just stay conscious, awake, and aware as much as possible! Keep that pre emergent applied. That means presence, awareness supplied with energy from above in the moment! This is how the weeds below the surface of the mind can be seen before they sprout into our lives. While the light of awareness is fully on and engaged, the weeds stand no chance!

So, as this higher version of "SELF" we attend to the mind, with awareness and a new higher level of consciousness. First, we see these lower "selves" and their thoughts, and then with awareness and presence we bring them together, we have a conscious communion of sorts amongst these selves, a virtual meeting of the minds of these internal "selves". It's like a strategy session, within. But we are not in it, we are above it...as this virtual meeting coordinator, as the RULER, or director of thought. From this more inquisitive knowledge seeking perspective, we are learning, and taking it all in. In doing so, we gain new understanding from watching these selves. We NOW know these various "selves" and what they produce. We see what they want as they want it, as they produce it. The higher "SELF" has basically HEARD all sides, SEEN all sides, and FELT all sides internally. Instead of being attached to one perspective or another, the unbiased observer perspective as higher "SELF" is the position which we see FROM that enables choice! Then, with CHOICE, we can even take it one step further and add an abundance mentality to it or fertilize it with highly attentive focus and precision application. Brilliant, miraculous growth!! The infinite, by nature is not limited, it is UN-LIMITED! We need to wake up and SEE where we are limiting ourselves by one perspective or another and / or by thinking from a lack / limited / or automated perspectives, and then UN-limit the self! We do this with awareness, and PRESENCE! You have the key. It is an internal game, look WITHIN! Try to see where these little selves are drawing these lines and where that may be limiting you!?! **These are the EDGES!**

Make sense? Weeds grow, FAST!

**WEEDS** = Worry, doubt, fear, negativity, frowns, bad attitudes, lack, limitation, non-forgiveness, basically anything that's not LOVE.

What we focus on expands, so we have choices to make! Do we CHOOSE to live in a mindset of abundance or lack? Do we choose peace, or war? A battleground within, or understanding from above? What we choose with our attention expands, so we need to choose what we want to expand, and we need to do it quickly, in the moment, with presence! Who, WITHIN is choosing? Are YOU choosing? In other words, are you present to choose, wide awake and aware? See the choices as they are made, and then do some weeding and trimming! Monitor the chooser! There are some mighty oaks and maples that are all grown up, with strong roots too. They may need to fall along with some pines and spruces! These represent bad mental routines, bad habits of thought, poor thoughts in general and specifically, attitudes, and themes of thoughts. This means ill-advised choosers / choices (The "selves"!). With understanding, we learn that magnetism, or creating something new in our lives is not about BLAMING the tree, or the forest for that matter. That means the situation, people involved or even the "selves" that got you into that forest. It is an understanding that first we must SEE IT, and then we must LET IT GO, all of it...and become NEW! That requires acting new, from this new version of me the best me...in the moment! I can only do that with PRESENCE, NOW! I can be a new chooser the moment I decide to wake up and BE PRESENT. CHOICE is available in the moment, but I must be there to make it.

What if we CHOOSE love, we let LOVE sprout and grow, and then fertilize it? What if LOVE were our foundational ROOT? Answers would pop up everywhere, right? Would they be different answers? Isn't love supposed to be the answer? Why not feed it and allow it to take root, within!?!

**LESSON KEY: Work to SEE and understand the edges that are being drawn within! What are they, when do they show up, and precisely where are these edges?**

How do I know when I am approaching one? Is it a feeling, an emotion? Something I see or hear? What state does this evoke in me? Is it clear, do I understand what it is telling me? What does it mean to ME, is it even about me? What was my RE-action? Is there a lesson here? Is it about my preferences, or have they developed into NEEDS? Where does the darkness begin, and where is the light? Is this LIMITING? How so? Is it one of these "selves" that is affecting my vision and hearing, specifically which one, and WHY?! This lesson key is more interactive. I want to point you to a few songs, because, in my opinion, they really do a great job of showing this process of discovery in a fun way! This process is the necessary "work" to master the skill. The only person that can do this work is YOU! It's not difficult work, but it does take effort, focus, diligence, and energy, with awareness! Here are a few songs that in my opinion, explain this process. They are, at a minimum, entertaining ways to reinforce this perspective. Understanding is key! Be watchful, particularly at the "edges", or when you get edgy! This is a discovery process.

**Within Temptation**: **"Where is the edge"**[39]? The lyrics in this song are very powerful, take a moment and look them up! It asks some very specific questions. Please understand this perspective and see it in your mind, explore these vantage points, and answer the questions for yourself! How does this relate to you in your life? SUPER song, among many from this talented band. Remember that it doesn't have to always be dark emotion either, we can be blinded by optimism just the same! Remember the symbol at the beginning of the chapter. Pay very close attention at the edges! Extreme vantage points tend to blind us, one way or another...where are they, and how might this be relative, possibly LIMITING?

**Visions of Atlantis**, **"Master the hurricane"**[40]. Really cool song. My perspective is that in the grand scheme of things, life happens. Situationally, that might mean that first you have peace and balance, then for whatever reason, your peaceful world comes undone, the darkness sets in, or peace is threatened one way or another. Then, with awareness, you ask yourself some really important questions, like: What are my triggers? What is causing the pain, crying, tears? (Maybe it is an edge?) This whole song goes from PEACE, through the hurricane, and back to PEACE...It's brilliant! Masterfully done :) My take is that this process of discovery is how you master the hurricane. Super perspectives to consider! Can this higher YOU learn to master the hurricane? Challenge your SELF. Look up the last line in the song. Can you be that force? That could be YOU, the higher YOU, or higher "SELF"! Cherish your PEACE and BALANCE, protect it, that's your CORE happiness, IMHO. Watch the thoughts and the little "selves" that try to steal that from YOU, taking you "off balance"! It starts at the corner of your mouth, right at the "edge" where it goes from up, to down...smile to frown! That's how YOU master your SELF! Don't let it happen! Lots of insights in this song, have a listen! Your CORE happiness is at stake. YOU must be the MASTER, don't let these little selves or anything else take you down. Amazing song, I am quite sure you can get a lot more from this song by listening! Do some exploring.

Soccer analogy: YOU are the Goalie, don't let these little selves get their little thoughts past you! PROTECT THE NET, the moment, NOW! Do not let them in to the moment, BE PRESENT, leave them at the gate! The gate is the goal line.

Make a save, <u>SAVE</u> your "SELF" the higher SELF that is! Challenge these lower self-perspectives. BE the master!

**Disturbed**: **"The Light"**[41]. This is a process of discovery, watching the mind! Some really powerful lyrics in this song, and an amazing delivery as well, compliments to the band, please look them up! Listen to this song in detail and look up the lyrics. This just reminds me of some powerful lessons as I listen to it, that's why I point these songs out. Hopefully you gain an insight or two by listening. Very cool lyrics!

The truth is most definitely available and waiting for you to find it, hear it, see it, feel it! Don't let these little "selves" take you out of the moment, by FEAR or whatever other means. They will make you turn or distract you if you are unaware! Be WATCHFUL, pay attention! Watch these shadow / lower selves! This is NOT to succumb to them, but to UNDERSTAND these "selves", the darkness and / or limitations that they bring. Awareness allows you to SEE what they do as you are able to look them in the face! As you do things from this oversight perspective, it brings them into the light of awareness. With further exploration, and FOCUS, it reveals the thoughts and feelings that are tucked away UNDERNEATH the emotion of them! You see them for what they are, top to bottom, not just at a surface level, and so you really do understand them. As a result, YOU get the lesson, and then the next time, YOU are ready, so YOU SEE THEM before they RE-act! <u>WITHIN</u> are the answers, **LOOK WITHIN!** Let the darkness, or these false / lower "selves" bring you to the lessons, let them show you something! LEARN from them.

**BIG THANKS to these bands for their talents and perspectives!**

# THE OVER-SEER

## GETTING IN THE ZONE III

OVERSIGHT, OVERSEEING, KEEPING A keen, discerning eye on the mind as the commander of thought. This is the supervisory perspective from above the mind, watching the mind, that I believe is the key of all keys. This is the vantage point that allows this skill to be used most effectively! How do you get there? RELEASE the old versions of you (the little "selves") that didn't make it there before, or couldn't stay there, LET THEM GO, let it go...the former self! Forgive it and let it go, immediately!! The newer version of you has a better shot at it...and keep trying. The more energy and focus you can muster up the better you will fare. Failure is the best option; you must fail forward fast, and BE WATCHFUL as you are doing it, living life. The more you fail to get to the moment, the faster you learn what took YOU out, as long as you do it with awareness. You cannot blindly just fail repeatedly, you must do it with awareness, effort, and intention. FOCUS! It is the awareness and **PRESENCE** from this overseer perspective that opens you up to the lessons. The lessons allow the new you to emerge the next time around, meaning...YOU MUST STEP UP TO THE PLATE AGAIN! Growth just occurred assuming you got the lesson, so now it is about waiting like a tiger to pounce, for that life situation to occur again, to use the skill you just gained from the lesson you just learned.

So, here's the process as a baseball analogy: Swing miss, LEARN. Oops, I wasn't quite fast enough again. Swing, miss, LEARN the same lesson... Swing, miss...curve ball, didn't see that coming, LEARN... GOT IT, Swing Ooh, I saw it a little clearer that time, fouled it off, LEARN, GOT IT. Take a deep breath, FOCUS... Get ready, mentally prepared, stable, balanced, swing, BOOOM, single! Yay, got on base, now we're talking! OK, ready for the next lesson, step forward... Swing MISS, LEARN! Over and over again. It's a process. Each time, a NEW SELF steps up to the plate, having learned something, and better for it! In the beginning it's a bit of a grind, and progress may seem a little slow at times, however, you can't move forward (get a hit) if you won't come out of the dugout! You MUST step up to the plate, and that begins with the understanding that swinging and missing is a part of the game. In order to swing and miss, first I must get in the batter's box! In order to get in the batter's box, first I need to STEP UP out of the dugout... What it comes down to is the fact that the game is being played on the cutting edge of NOW, THE MOMENT. We aren't even in the game a lot of the time! Over time it is going to get easier, you will become faster, and your eyes will see clearer! After a while, and a bit of practice using this new SKILL, YOU are going to be seeing so clearly that you are knocking them out of the park, CONSISTENTLY! BATTER UP! Are you going to take a swing or just stand there? Do it NOW! That might mean first getting out of the parking lot, then into the stadium, locker room, then into the dugout, onto the field, then into the batter's box. Play ball! It takes practice, and maybe a little bit of courage / faith. You get the point, it is a process, and that effort is worth it, because once you are there, THEN you have CHOICE, in the moment, as to whether or not to swing! You can't swing from the parking lot, or the bleachers. As **Jackie Robinson** said:

## "Life is not a spectator sport"[42]

My take, you have to engage, get in the game!

Please understand that this is not insinuating that you must be engaged, and running full on, 1000 miles an hour, every day, all day, and never rest. Quite the opposite actually, more than likely, that means a bit more balanced, and stable! This perspective will bring your entire life into focus, from the knitty gritty to the 10,000 ft perspective, all at the same time. I will say though that once it is understood, you will want to be engaged, because it is FUN! The more situational things life brings at you, the more you learn, so as you might expect by changing your lenses at the eye Dr. you just see things differently, clearer! Along with that comes more balance and more PEACE simply from the vantage point alone, not to mention all the lessons which are progressively adding "understanding" which just amplifies the gains. Overseer is a place where your life stream can be flowing really fast, or slow, and yet the "frame of mind" and orientation is unchanged, balanced, unwavering and unshakable.

There is a cool video online that really takes this baseball perspective and provides a wonderful example of it. This is chock full of lessons about being PRESENT in the moment NOW, TRUST, FAITH, FOCUS, errors and even how to respond to them! Take 11 minutes and watch the video or look up **Evan Longoria**'s mental emphasis on YouTube[43] if you can't click the link. Thanks Evan!

https://www.youtube.com/watch?v=eCH4zelZFNk[44]

This is a great coaching video and perspective! It has some amazing advice that is relevant to far more than baseball! So, pay attention to the similarities in the comments by Evan, his teammates, and coaches! I really got a kick out of the **Dr. Ken Rivizza**[45] comments in the middle where he talks about being comfortable being uncomfortable. That's super important to understand. Growth doesn't feel comfortable. Growth requires us to push on the edges. When we realize and understand completely that the reason why we feel the discomfort is because we are pushing on the edges of our comfort zone, it is seen in a different light. The discomfort is just an indicator that we need to heighten our senses and focus even harder because now we have identified an edge. We are at it! We are about to enter into the unknown and this is where growth occurs. We should be excited, not fearful, it's an opportunity! GET READY.

Bottom line, this is a NEW experience, and because we have prepared, we are ready...more ready than EVER BEFORE! With a full understanding that we have never, not once, ever been in this exact moment, we also understand that we will fail, periodically. In fact, we will fail a lot...just don't dwell on it, GROW, release it, LET IT GO 100% and move on! Step out of the batter's box for a second if you have to, catch a breath... get your mind right, and just KNOW that YOU MUST step up to the plate again! Get ready! Stepping up to the plate for you and I might be a different scene than a batter's box, and regardless of what the scene or situation might be, it means BEING IN THE MOMENT! So, GET READY! Wake up...alert, focused and ready to take a swing as that may relate to your life. As you start getting on base more regularly, (Seeing results) you are going to be "tempted" to steal a base, skip a lesson, move too fast, too soon, or lose your focus! (Miss a moment). That means that you are going to get called out periodically. (Something bad happens). Just learn the lesson so that next time you can be FASTER! (Get to the moment)!

Please understand that this is not just a baseball analogy! This is all super relevant to how we approach life. This is a methodology, a prescription for how YOU can ARRIVE to, and BE IN every moment in YOUR LIFE! It's a SKILL, and YOU must work on the skill. It is essential in getting to the moment where the lessons are available, and you have to be in the game and take a swing to get them, GET IN THE GAME! Step up to the plate, focus, and SWING, again and again...at the good pitches when it makes sense! With awareness you will see some really good ones, and by all means knock them out of the park. Equally important though is to let some go right on by, they don't deserve your attention!

## The game is played IN THE MOMENT, YOU MUST GET THERE!

If you fail, try again, just GET TO THE MOMENT! Work at this skill to SEE with awareness, focus and CLARITY, NOW!

Once you detach from the former you' s, the positionalities, the chains that tie you to the past and imaginings that lure you to the future, the new YOU can arrive and IS available in this MOMENT, NOW and FREE! FREEDOM is from those "selves". Freedom comes with releasing them and their limits! They are magnets that keep you coming back to these limited states of mind that distract you, and/or simply don't work, yet these "selves" try and bring you to them over and over again! It's like a broken record, replaying that old music... and it is that old "self" that does it! FREE up some space, release it, clear the cache, release the pitch, eliminate the magnets, play a NEW TUNE! A new at bat is coming, and it's coming up SOON, grab a new bat, a better one! Make your new "SELF" available, FREE to make a NEW ACTION! Get in a new groove, one that plays better music! Better yet just SHOW UP TO NOW! No groove required, make your own new music!

Some call that old stuff coming back to us karma. Like as in get rid of your karma. In the same vein, I have also heard the statement "Empty your cup". It's all relevant! That certainly makes sense if you think about it properly, from a magnetism perspective, or as in RELEASE THAT LAST PITCH! By doing so, that pitch is no longer stored in the database and clogging up the mind with something that either limited what you could do, or it didn't work period! No sense carrying that forward, right? This also eliminates the potential for it to be a magnet, we cannot focus on something that isn't there. Attention can't go there, it's GONE! So naturally this has a way of quieting the MIND! We swing and miss a lot in life, LET IT GO! Eliminate some of that unnecessary baggage you are carrying around in the mind. In fact, that is what meditation is all about...watching the mind and reducing the clutter, IMHO! It's just doing this process in a controlled environment, so that we can practice the skill. If we can't do it in a controlled environment, then how can we expect to do it when the "stuff" hits the fan? We can't and that is why we need practice, so we are ready for life as it comes at us faster every day!

In both scenarios it means being watchful from this overseer perspective. The difference is really just the adrenaline that is created in the moment when one of life's battles presents itself, when something is on the line so to speak, or we are at an edge! That is when we really need the skill to take us to the next level, and with practice it knows when the heat is on, it just felt something kick up a notch. So, when that happens, it is ONNNN, and so NOW, it takes the extra energy that was just created, and USES IT to amplify the SKILL! It's like they are feeding each other. Great teammates that are just in sync! Awareness SEES and gets you there, then the SKILL takes the energy and channels it! So, rather than going to the negative, or the distractor factor, which is a possible error situation without the skill, it uses the energy as a BOOSTER. Like your car slamming the gas pedal, with ROCKET FUEL, but instead of the throttle going only to speed, it distributes it to EVERYTHING! It dials in the awareness, gearing, focus, sight, hearing, skill, precision, and finally execution in the moment! It literally PUSHES you into the ZONE where everything is heightened. The odd thing is that it seems like time actually slows down vs speeding up. The added focus and amplified skill then SEE with new eyes and HEAR with new ears...like slow motion. It's like you are a meta human or something, with powers...its very dramatic! Hard to explain, but with this new ability, in the zone, with heightened skill and every detail accentuated, the whole scene is like a 3D Ultra High-DEF image highlighting every last detail frame by frame, and the EDGES almost POP off the screen! That is the competition view, that's what happens in the zone! In meditation, or contemplation, we are learning to deal with a slightly lower level of energy to sort of track it and watch it as the mind is processing. The benefit of this, if not blatantly obvious, is so that when we do get into the competition situation and SOMETHING IS ON THE LINE, the adrenaline and energy that gets sent through the system doesn't overwhelm it! When the system gets overwhelmed, that is when stuff breaks, the ball gets dropped, we fall on our face, or mistakes happen! We are training for the main event. The problem is that no one ever told us the main event is happening EVERY MOMENT OF EVERY DAY!

Recognize and be watchful of how powerful your awareness is getting, and of course that it is GAME ON, every moment! With "training" (working on your skills), awareness can take in a MASSIVE amount of information, if given enough energy, and this continues to grow. That is why energy is a really important thing to understand and manage, you'll need it! This is also why it takes practice to get into the zone and stay there! Your mind is an extremely valuable TOOL! In baseball, you don't just show up in the middle of the season, you arrive at Spring

TRAINING to work on your skills when the season is not on the line! In sports, you train 90% of the time, just for game time. Why should the mind be treated with any less diligence? You need skills. Life is a game. The MIND skills need to be tested and optimized. You also have to be able to manage the surge that adrenaline kicks up. That amount of energy, from a system perspective needs to be distributed properly. If certain parts are not built strong enough, or the skill is not 100%, well then, the weakest link breaks. As it relates to energy and the skill, that's the mind, body, focus, attention, awareness... sight, hearing, all of it, EVERYTHING combined! It is a coordinated effort. What is doing the coordinating? THE MIND! Who is managing the mind? YOU ARE! So, you better get ready, cause here it comes, the next moment is always right there, and now it is here, and it is Game ONNNN again! BOOOM! Gone, there it went... did you catch the wave? Did you swing? Overseer, is the tiger, ever PRESENT and watching...READY. OK, life: Bring it ON!

When we fail to get to the moment, because the system got tripped / overwhelmed or even just distracted...remember one word, a very important one. Release, Release, Release...Let it go! FREEDOM from that last pitch, that last at bat, or that last whatever we try and fail at is an opportunity to get the lesson, understand, and move on! With less clutter and baggage in the mind processor, particularly with stuff that didn't work, it is adding capacity so that you can ALLOW it to be filled with NEW stuff, NEW ACTIONS that have a better shot at it! Remember, like attracts like, so be wise as to what you store in there...it's a magnet! That's why you let the bad stuff go as soon as possible. This way you are not bogged down by all that "bad" knowledge / experience...it's like clearing the cache folder, it also frees up the needed space for your MIND to hear and see, NOW!! Your "processor" tends to work a little better! The problem is that human nature, the EGO, doesn't want to empty our cup no matter what's in it, or how full it may be, with good or bad!!!

The EGO is cunning, and fast, and those former versions of self don't want to be released, yet it is those versions of self that MUST be released for growth to occur. Being FREE from these "selves" ALLOWS access to the ZONE in the moment. All the other times we were attached to the past or projecting towards the future. It is ok to dream, it is fine to have goals, it is fine to want. It is only when you are dependent on that thing, that situation, that result, to make you happy that they become the fear that resists, the fear that prevents! The NEED is what creates resistance to the opposite of what you want. By not letting go of a negative result when it happens, it can become a magnet! Because that version of self was not released, it has the potential to revisit and make the same mistake again! He / She, that version of "self" is still lurking around in the shadows of the mind, you didn't let it go! That shadow self is "in the darkness" of the mind, and it can jump out and haunt you! No joke, it literally jumps into the moment out of nowhere it seems. That is what I refer to as these "RE-actions". They happen fast, and that's why YOU, as overseer need to be faster! When we arrive as that version of "self" the next time, it makes the same mistakes! Overseer doesn't allow it. If YOU let that "self" respond, it will automatically and consistently bring you the same or similar results because that's what it knows! We don't want that same result, we want to be NEW and be NEW, over, and over growing into better and better versions of "SELF". The higher "SELF" is no longer stuck in the trenches of the lower mind that binds us to that level of "THINKING"! We have literally stepped up, out and above the mind and are operating, functioning, and performing at a whole new level. Overseer (higher "SELF") can see that mind and the little selves operating in real time...it's quite amazing! From this vantage point YOU can see the clutter, and by doing so, you are seeing the mind / EGO as it processes...as well as all the games they play! You are the CEO of the whole operation, in touch with, aware and overseeing every aspect of it!

This is the path to WISDOM! You are literally shining the light in the darkness. Once the light is on, it's on! They can't hide anymore. From above, you can see the selves, their shadows and all their shenanigans going on! This is how you see where the EGO blind spots are and then they no longer blind you...but it's a process. It doesn't happen overnight, it requires effort! Don't be afraid to ask for help. There is actually a prayer for this, by **Reinhold Niebuhr**. See below. There are quite a few versions of it that I have seen, all of which are good in my opinion.

Here is the one I have heard most often:

**"God Grant Me the SERENITY to
accept the things I cannot change,
COURAGE
To change the things I CAN,
and WISDOM
To know the difference!"[46]**

WISDOM is gained each time you step into the moment as the watcher, from this overseer perspective...and **LOOK WITHIN!!!!**

To revisit one concept, it is human nature to seek comfort, and safety...basic needs. It is quite another to retreat gradually into a state of crippling fear, or even mild fear for that a matter. If we put up with mild fear, it will GROW, and that fear will eventually become debilitating, either from a mental standpoint, emotional or physical, or all of the above. The problem here is that it takes less and less and less to break down the system, or it just won't engage anymore because it has become intolerant of the pain. The "self" will not step up to the wall, no less over it, or through it, and so it can't see a way out. It just sees the ceiling as another wall, and so the walls seem insurmountable...too big, too thick, and the ceiling is getting lower too. What happens in life is we tend to try to push it back or go around fear, as well as other obstacles, and resistance / avoidance is not a solution. It just makes us even less tolerant the next time it comes around. Our comfort zone gets smaller and smaller. The next wall appears to be closer, and thicker even though it is essentially the same dam wall! So, it turns us sooner and sooner, and when we turn, we just end up bumping into another wall. To compound the problem, we truly don't understand the obstacle and why we are turning. We never take the time to really look at it in the eyes, so to speak. **Jaie Hart** wrote about it, and I believe it was in her blog too:

## "The obstacle IS THE PATH"[47]

She told me in an email a while back, essentially, to make friends with your anxieties! That was my interpretation. She probably said it better! So smart, how else to understand them than to shake their hand so to speak and investigate? Do yourself a favor, Look up Jaie Hart! Thank you, Jaie! This perspective really challenged the way that I looked at my own growth, and I very much appreciate the email and the TIP! Jaie explains things in unique ways that are very insightful.

As you know, I really dissect things. This was no different, so I asked myself, how do I make friends with my anxieties? In my mind, that correlated to friend = anxiety. But to me, fear was never my friend. In fact, I hated it, pushed it away, tried to bury it, ignore it, suppress it, etc. All the things I am telling you NOT to do, I did em! It doesn't work! LOL. It was the source of my issue, fear...fear was the source of all my fears, wait what? I think I heard someone say something like that, yep!

***"First of all, let me assert my firm belief that the only thing we have to fear is fear itself."***
**-Franklin D. Roosevelt[48]**

WHAT THE HECK? I had to really think about this HARD! So, I did...and so it is. They are BOTH right! Holey Moley, so what does that mean? OK, this is really cool, let me break it down for you!

Whatever the issue is, UNDERSTAND IT. To understand it, you have to kind take the top off, or open it up, see the parts & gearing, look underneath the surface, or through it! That's why I say look behind the emotion! How do you look behind or "through" something, if that something is an obstacle? Obstacle, by the nature of it either stops us, or detours us, but do we ever really fully assess the obstacle itself? So, I am looking at my life, the obstacles, and in this case FEAR specifically. I am starting to make correlations. I am placing the components in various order and playing with the different puzzle pieces. I think to myself hmmm, if something is my obstacle and the obstacle is my anxiety, and anxiety is my friend, then the summary is:

### Obstacle=Anxiety=Friend
### Or
### FEAR = FRIEND

WAAAAAAIT, Nooooooh, fear is not my friend! This can't be true, it makes no sense, I wanted to put that little slash onto the = sign, so it said UNEQUAL!

But I didn't, there had to be something in this that I wasn't seeing. I thought, let me back into this thing and look at it from a different angle because I most definitely did NOT want for fear to be my path. I passed a lot of math classes and solved a lot of problems and that is essentially what that equation was leading me to believe. Obstacle = path = anxiety = FEAR = FRIEND all breaks down to the final unequivocal and undeniable answer: I had to make friends with FEAR!

Initial reaction to this is. Don't talk to me, I have nothing to say to you. Talking to myself. LOL. I didn't even want to look at fear, fear was the enemy! So, naturally, I went at it from the other angle. Avoidance, right? The mind ...uggggh. OK, then, what do I know about friends? No, better yet, what about BEST FRIENDS? I like them! I am VERY fortunate to have some REALLY GOOD friends, BEST FRIENDS! Very appreciative for that. First, I know my friends pretty well, and I know my best friends really well, and they know me, really well! On occasion, we have looked each other in the eyes and talked. Eye to eye, heart to heart. Good, deep conversations. Call it "growing up" or whatever, it helps you to understand things about yourself that you may not have known previously or were somewhat unaware of. Because they are your friends, you are able to open up, and listen, own up to things, feelings, situations, and much more! To a shy guy, that is huge!

Just to get me to talk as a kid was a challenge for my mom. So, needless to say, I really appreciate my friends!

The crux of the matter is back to the original lesson, if you want to know an obstacle really well, make friends with it first! Get to know it. When we first meet someone, it takes a while to really get to know them, right? I mean sometimes you get that fast friend's scenario, but not always. That means, in reality, spending time with them, and going through lots of things together. It is the same for an obstacle. You can't take it at face value and just go the way it tells you to go, do what it tells you to do, unchecked! NO, you must look deeper, spend some time with it, KNOW IT, look at it straight in the eyes from time to time, the eyes don't lie! Minimum, pause to consider that it may be steering you wrong! Do you trust everyone you meet straight away? Some stranger tells you at the gas station to go over there, my buddy has something for you! Yeah, right pal. I am sure they do, but it probably isn't good! Did you ever have a friend, that really wasn't your friend, although it seemed like they were. The obstacle in front of you is actually the opposite. The obstacle kind of IS your BEST friend, with a caveat or two, of course! You don't go "through" your best friends, use them, abuse them, etc. Yes, I get that. Ok, back to the lesson. This "obstacle" best friend is trying to teach you something about yourself, FOR YOUR OWN GOOD, but you won't listen! Our best friends know us better than we know ourselves sometimes, don't they? LISTEN! Great, now I have to listen to fear too, wonderful. YES, the obstacle will challenge you, just like your best friend should, if they truly are your best friend! Best friends make us think about stuff, we have meaningful conversations about personal stuff we don't necessarily talk about with everyone else. They challenge us, and our thinking. That's a good thing, they care about us.

So, when approaching a mind obstacle, fear, in this example. Don't be tempted by the first RE-action the mind suggests...namely, to TURN, even if just for a moment, look at it. Not talking about REAL fear, like a fast-moving train approaching, that is get out of the way fear, and its real, MOVE! I am talking about mind roadblocks, as hypothetical emotional comfort zone type obstacles...illusory fear. Let me explain further. So, an emotion kicks up due to an obstacle, whatever that might be, don't close your eyes, don't turn away. Rather than that, say hello, shake its hypothetical hand in your mind, greet it, and just look at it and shut up to listen and watch what happens. It's not gonna shut up in the mind, it will engage you with thoughts, feelings and emotions, and images too...don't be satisfied with these, don't turn away. Your BEST FRIEND brought this up for a reason, so that you could see something (about one of these "selves")! Good news, these "walls" (emotions/feelings/the obstacles) that are being thrown up in front of you have some transparency to them. If you really look hard enough at them and listen carefully, there will be a lesson in it, but you have to dig a little behind the illusions / imagery / chatter / feelings this "self" is throwing at you. You have to work through, see through that surface level stuff that initially tempts you to turn. Don't turn, keep staring it down, ask it some pointed questions, dissect it, look deep through the entire illusion, the story. It is trying to tell you and sell you something. Make it justify its existence but be skeptical! Look at it as if it were something fictional, or fabricated, or maybe an advertisement pitch and it wants your money! You must KNOW and truly understand before you make a commitment. These obstacles need to be seen for what they are, a mirage, or a lie, but in order to get there we need to see the whole thing in order to see if it is "worthy", or not! The bottom line is that these "selves" paint some glorious and horrific pictures on the mind screen. Some are really good and very enticing, and some are so ridiculously bad... scary bad, and what does that do to us? It takes us to the extremes, and they both blind us which takes us out of the moment! It will hit you visually, audibly, or emotionally, or all of the above. You have to see through it, don't believe the hype, or at a minimum, question its authenticity! You need to be able to manage that initial "SURGE" of energy, and channel it...so that you can push through this, INTO the moment, and stay present! The problem is that when we get stuck in that vantage point within the mind, rather than above it, we can't see it. The obstacle turns us, grabs us, and then it is "in there". It has us in its grip so to speak, our mind in that state is literally "occupied" by it and can't see a way out. Why? Because we, are quite literally, "out of our mind". We got taken over by it. Calm down, take a big breath, and get back to your post as overseer! Breathe!!!! Awareness / presence is required here.

Another way to look at it might be that It's like that proverbial 3rd wheel that your best friend tries to warn you about because they are up to no good, but you don't see it until you see it. The obstacle is their issue (the 3rd wheel), not YOURS, but they keep telling you to stop, turn around, go the other way...with them! When the obstacle shows up, they grab your arm, and say, come on, come with me, let's go this way (avoidance/resistance)! I am not saying, don't go, but instead because your BEST friend just warned you about them, you start being a little more skeptical, and watchful. You still want to trust, but your best friend is your best friend, they must have said it for a reason! So, over time you learn about this new 3rd wheel and their "issues" (the obstacle), what drives them to do the things they do by watching them and seeing what they do! Not because you want to investigate your new friend, that's not the point, that's in the caveat category. This is not malicious. What do you do when you have a friend though? You spend a TON of time with them because you love them, trust them, and enjoy their company. As a result of that, you see what they do in ALL SITUATIONS, and you know them really well! Often times, you know what they are going to do before they do it, and WHY they do it!! You can spot a fake smile, fake laugh, a devious "tone", a situation where the action does not match the words they are saying! In other words, and to turn it INWARDS on our "self", a false RE-action! Something is not quite right here. The point is by watching, you see them, and not only do you see them... you REALLY SEE THEM. In fact, you KNOW them extremely WELL! When you finally do, "wake up", you know what makes them tick, and that is a whole different level of "knowing". Quite honestly, I really thought that was my friend, but they have some issues. LOL Remember, I am talking about my "selves" here WITHIN! It is a comical and enlightening perspective once you change the lens and see things this way.

So, ultimately, what ends up happening is YOU SEE what is driving them to "TURN", and when it tries to turn you! (resistance / avoidance). Once seen, with the understanding that these strategies do not work and PRESENCE is required here, we wake up and pay attention!! As we stay present, with diligence, focus, and a little bit of endurance, the real issue is revealed, brought out into the light. I know the obstacle now inside and out! What I personally found out was that originally, I knew NOTHING about fear. By staring it in the face, it revealed itself, and so it was, a mirage that looks very real and feels very real! Admittedly, looks real, feels real, so what was I missing? The mirage part, the lie. It's an illusion. All the cards were on the table, but it was a BLUFF, and I called it out! Once seen, it can't be unseen, it changes the game!

I needed to understand it at a deeper level, really KNOW IT, something was being lost in translation, missed! The equation was not adding up to FEAR = FRIEND. There is a reason this keeps coming up, there is a lesson in it, what am I missing? Remember, this is supposed to be my best friend, this obstacle. It would not keep showing up on my doorstep if there wasn't something here for me to understand and process. So, now, I must stay present and look just a little longer and try to understand what this obstacle is trying to tell me? When does it show up, how, what does it do to me, or I should say FOR ME?! OMG, that's it, I get it now, it is my best friend! I thought it was the enemy, but Nooooh! It's NOT. I misunderstood what it was trying to tell me, show me and GIVE ME! My best friend was trying to give me the gift of all gifts, understanding...and I finally got it. I understood. Let me explain this a little more thoroughly because it's huge! This is a key of keys if you can really wrap your head around it.

When I NEED it, my best friend shows up, and "it" (fear) is THERE FOR ME! It has my back. It is TOTALLY looking out for me. Every freaking time, without fail. Now that's a BEST FRIEND! Whenever this thing shows up in front of me,

BAM, there it is...how does it know I needed it? It's like a 6th sense or something. Amazing. Not only that though, but when it shows up, it helps me! C'mon, seriously, how? It gives me the energy I need to jack up my awareness, skills, and every ounce of perception I have to conquer the "beast", my obstacle! Oh, I am amped and ready now, where is it? Where's the beast? The beast is the obstacle. In this case, the beast was me, or inside of me, WITHIN! I just didn't know it. I was the problem all along... I had to conquer my "self"! It took my best friend (FEAR), whom I had just met, to make an introduction, and then we had somewhat of an intervention, now, we are BESTIES! Yeah, right. Fear introduced me to FEAR! The whole thing collapsed, fell in on itself... very funny right?! Actually, it is very educational! What did I learn? The original lesson, only now I didn't just get the lesson at the surface level, I UNDERSTOOD! That translated to: Make friends with your anxieties, they give you the energy you need to confront your anxieties, but then you must confront them, arrive in the moment, and ACT!

In other words:

## Fear gives you the energy to conquer fear!

Emotion gives you energy, it is how you interpret and USE that energy that makes all the difference. Here again we have a lost in translation issue...so, don't let it steer you wrong. USE THE ENERGY! The skill will help you distribute it properly, and then you have to be willing to take the risk to GROW! Step up to the plate. Don't "shy away from it"! GET TO THE GATE! Once you are there, at the gate, and see it, take that next step into the moment. Wide awake, energized, fully aware, and watch what happens. When the SKILL uses the energy properly, the ENERGY pushes you into the zone where you can achieve things you never dreamed of! In the zone, all that weight, all that garbage goes out the window, and all of a sudden, extremely heightened concentration, focus on a whole new level... the world just LIGHTS UP! Like whooooosh, all quiet, calm, this peaceful and ultra-dialed in FOCUS, like you've never seen before! YOU have to take the step, leave that "self" at the gate along with all the garbage it was telling you, it was a lie, a bluff, and you called it out! The mirage, you walked right through it. On the other side, the possibilities are seemingly ENDLESS! Some lessons are just like rocket fuel, they just catapult you to and through "space" that was formerly an "atmosphere" you just couldn't get through without this overseer perspective! The energy just wasn't being used properly. It lacked "direction"!

Look at it this way, from a storyline perspective which is really true, the way it plays out in the mind. You have to be motivated, there has to be a reason to get to the other side, something to incentivize you to do this thing, whatever it is, a driving factor. Money, security, peace, love, whatever. Let's call it a pot of gold, for arguments sake, but it could be anything of "VALUE", to you. Put that in the pot, and that's your gold! You have to get through something to get it, and that something may be a little uncomfortable! Job interview, or a date brings on the "jitters", some "nerves" as an example! Let's face it, you have to muster the "nerve" to DO IT, and first you have to get there to get through it, and that's when its game time! What's the motivating factor though? What is, and where is the pot of GOLD for you? Did you ever really think about it? Think!

OK, in this story, the pot is at the end of the rainbow! Oh boy, here we go. I feel some eyes rolling. LOL. I am serious though; this is a very real example! Why? WHEN does the rainbow form? AFTER the storm, of course! What does that mean? I have to walk through the storm, ENDURE it, the "nerves", just long enough, to get through this storm! Notice I said walk, not RUN, so you can be watchful! EYES WIDE OPEN! Bad thunderstorms come and go really fast, right? You can handle a little rain and noise...In the end, the sky opens up, the rain stops, and BAMMMMM, it's like a whole NEW DAY! The sun appears, and a beautiful, peaceful, and remarkable rainbow appears! The moment is like that. You have to stay with it just long enough and endure some really negative and very deceptive "self-talk" to get there sometimes, and your rainbow awaits on the other side of that thunderstorm! Follow that, with presence to your pot of GOLD, whatever that might represent to you! It's on the other side of the gate. A new day for you! YOU CAN open the gate and walk through, but who or what is it that is keeping you from getting to, and then through the gate? What "self", when and how? What is it saying, or doing? What feeling is this bringing up inside? Why? Is it just a cover emotion, a distraction? What is it covering? Is it keeping me from what I want? Does it steer me away or close the gate? That's what you need to see, on the edge of NOW, that's where they turn you! Always darkest, right before dawn. If that self happens to be in the past, which often times they are, don't be tempted to turn around. Remember, the rainbow is in front of you and the SUN is behind you, if you turn around it will blind you! STAY PRESENT, the light is all around you NOW, the darkness is GONE, storm is over, see this moment through, NOW!!!!

Wake up and SEE these intro's being made. These selves make introductions all the time, to your other "selves"! Make sure you see them first, and then take the next step to try and understand what it is trying to show you. It is weird, I know, but it is like the "selves" ring the front doorbell, and then for some reason you look out the back door. OR it rings and then it goes and hides so when you get to the door you can't see it. Either way, the emotion of it took you out of the moment so you can't SEE the "self" that rang the bell, the little prankster. You have to stay present and look harder, its right there, but you aren't seeing it. Seeing from this new vantage point will allow you to see this whole process as it unfolds. It is about being the overseer of the whole charade, unemotional and unattached, fully awake, aware, and PRESENT! Once you see it, you can BE IT! Congratulations, YOU got the job, YOU are NOW, IT!! CEO:

## Chief Executive Overseer!

Sounds WONDERFUL, when & where do I start? Well, you already know when, right? NOW. From the mind perspective though, where can you do this from inside this house of walls? You can't, that's the point! You can't see it from that vantage point because you are too deep in it! That is why you must step ABOVE it and watch from that elevated overseer perspective!

Example time! Chuckle...Have you ever watched a fly trying to get out a window, and it just keeps banging its face into the window from every angle? Did you ever think, dang, what a dumb ass? Sorry, after this, you will more than likely have to open the window for the fly. The fact is, you see something that fly can't see and you can help it, if you can catch it and point it in the right direction! As the overseer of your mind, relative to the "selves", you have that same ability, if you can catch it in the moment. (The RE-actions) You can see the fly banging its face on the window, because that is you as one of the selves! The lower "self" (the fly) can't see the glass! YOU CAN with this higher "SELF" perspective, as the overseer, but you have to be manning your post as the overseer to catch it! Your best friend is trying to get through to you so that YOU can see the glass and stop hurting yourself, and then maybe open the window! If you don't teach it so that it UNDERSTANDS though, it is going to do the same darned thing the next time it comes into this room! So, you literally have to SHOW IT the window, teach it this limiting factor, before opening it up! That is the "processing" portion of the lesson. Very important!

## "Give a man a fish, and you feed him for a day, TEACH a man to fish and you feed him for a lifetime" Proverb

Good stuff right?! Once the lesson is truly learned, it is UNDERSTOOD! Understanding carries through to the rest of your life, in EVERYTHING you do!

OK, I can hear you saying, I think I get that, but how do I really get there...to understanding? Like, what's the actual mind solution? That seems to be a far cry since I can't even seem to get out of my own head. Yes, YOU CAN! **YOU** CAN DO IT, as the higher "SELF" from the overseer perspective. The "self", as in the little you, not so much. It's the "self" that keeps you there. **YOU** as the higher "SELF" can watch the mind as it is processing like this though. It is a vantage point issue.

Let me ask you this: Is life keeping something from you? In other words, you want something, and you can see it in your mind's eye, out that virtual window, but the universe is not yielding. This thing, or situation, whatever it is just won't show up, arrive. What stands between you and it? What represents the glass you keep bumping in to? My guess is something is there. It may be something you don't want to or won't do, or something you don't want to give up. In your core of cores, there is an internal component that is just not quite right, or missing to really EXPAND INTO that person or that life which includes that thing. It may be relative to your comfort zone, and something MUST change to allow it in, or magnetize it for it to materialize. So here are the questions to ask, relative to "why": Am I expanding or contracting? Am I getting stronger or weaker. Am I testing the limits of my comfort zone, or am a resistant to do so? Why? What is the risk? Embarrassment, failure? Pain? What is it? In order for growth to occur we must make room for it or expand into it. We must see limitations and remove them, or the self-created box we put ourselves in. This often requires personal expansion. In other words, un-limit that "self"! Sounds easy enough when you put it like that, but I know, I get it, we need a methodology to do so. If it were that easy, we'd have done it already!

I propose that you look at it like this, relative to our comfort zone. In this example, the room is us, and it is getting smaller and smaller, right? And maybe the ceiling is closing in too...at this point, you are still in the room and feeling a little tense, maybe claustrophobic, PRESSURE, the heat is on! Something needs to CHANGE to alleviate this "situation"! LOOK UP, HARD, and focus. Visualize this. There is a door on the ceiling, and there is a staircase, OPEN YOUR MIND, and walk up the stairs in the mind and step up out of it. NOW, this room (your mind) has a glass ceiling, YOU can see right through it...but walk to the back of the room and look down. Now YOU are above and behind the mind, YOU can see all the gears turning, as well as what the fly (little you) is seeing out the front window. (Your eyes) For whatever reason it just keeps bouncing and bouncing and bouncing off the glass.... boom, boom, boom. Dam, what is that freaking thing doing, is it stupid? Different perspective, right? Now you can see the gears turning, what its thinking/seeing/bumping into! Makes you want to go let it out right? That's us, we need to let our "selves" out! FREE yourself, free your mind...get out and PLAY, new perspective offers new choices!

So, we watch these little selves and what they do from this perspective as the overseer. Seeing what they do, what they are bumping into, how they think (RE-act), where they turn, and all their shenanigans. What you'll ultimately see is that the wall that looked like a wall from within that room wasn't a wall at all, in fact, from above you can see that it was a complete illusion, or in this case, the fly was bumping into the glass window. Your friend was right and so you walk right through it (the illusion) or open the window. Maybe a little hesitant at first, but after seeing the illusion for what it is, with eyes wide open, you trusted your friend, and it was worth it! Don't look back for the wall, it isn't there anymore, pay attention, and take another step forwards, and keep watching in this manner! Appreciate your friend, be thankful for their insight! BTW, don't jump out a window thinking you are a fly, or can fly that was just an analogy! It is not that we should attempt to fly, but that we can achieve something we thought we could not, with freedom from that limited view, but first we must see it and believe it. In order to do that we must see what is stopping us, our "selves", and the illusion, the glass! Once we fully understand the situation, the obstacle, and the path forward, we see things in a whole new light! That is understanding, and you just can't unsee it, once seen! Everything changes.

You (Your spiritual higher "SELF") will bring you to the obstacles (the lessons) over and over again until you cannot go around it ...you must go through it. We RESIST THIS! When, where? At the edges! Unfortunately, if you don't see the edge, and understand how to process and get through it in the early stages of noticing it, the obstacle gets bigger....and harder to go through. We put ourselves back in the box! The mental RUTS can become like giant craters, and it seems daunting to climb out.... but it is really just another thought creating a mountain over a molehill .... Moral of that story is why wait? DO IT NOW! Is one illusion bigger than another or is it simply ME as a particular version of "self" and the way that "I" as that self is seeing / thinking about it? If I "wake up", realize and SEE that it is an illusion, big or small, the whole thing goes away the instant I see it as an illusion! It is like turning off the projector, or in the example above, opening the window! Now I am FREE at a BASE mind screen...unaffected by the illusion that had been cast upon it by that former self! I can create a BRAND-NEW LIFE, un-limited by that self and the illusion! It starts NOW, and NOW, and NOW!

Uncovering these hidden unconscious "selves", and UN-limiting them, takes investigation, which requires awareness! These "selves" can not only steal our lives in the form of time and decisions, but they can also steal ENERGY and PEACE!

Play the song **"Tom Sawyer"**[49] by **RUSH** and listen to the lyrics, it is super cool! As we progress through life, we MUST WAKE UP and see all the games Ole Tom plays! As we do, we come to the realization that we are making decisions unconsciously, from the vantage point of these former selves, patterned thinking, and all the different positionalities that want us to STAY comfortable (the same)! When reacting to life from these "selves", we are NOT in that moment, and therefore, we are incapable of making a **NEW** decision to move forward with our lives. In that moment, we are allowing an older version of us access to the moment to decide for us. It is old me / former me, blindly choosing for me **AS** me (unconsciously). When we FINALLY see it happen, awake and aware, it is most definitely a wakeup call! It is more than likely because we are fed up with the patterns of THINKING that bring on poor results and/or produce the same patterns in our lives as a result of what is happening behind the scenes in the mind, OUTSIDE OF OUR AWARENESS! The wakeup call is this amazing realization / understanding that the only way to correct this is sort of AT that level of that kind of thinking, but not from within the thoughts themselves and trapped by them or alongside them, we can't see it from there! We MUST RISE UP and elevate above them and WATCH the mind! This is the OVER SEER perspective! From this perspective, we can SEE these little EGO "selves" and the games they play! As the overseer, we step out of the "self" created box.

We must look at the process from above these selves, unaffected by them, and unemotional about them...which is a different vantage point that allows us to see things as they are happening as the witness of them happening!

As overseer, relative to the mind, it is like watching a stream or river from above it, like we are standing on a bridge watching the water flow right on by! Safe, and unaffected.

## "Bridge over troubled water"
## Simon and Garfunkel[50]

See the song lyrics for this one too! As a mind analogy, it's like literally watching the mind gears as they are turning, FLOWING! Overseer is the bridge from which we watch thoughts flow by in the mind stream. To see the mind from this perspective is very powerful, especially if you are in a FLOW state! From the bridge we are truly unaffected, the water (thought) doesn't really touch us, we can just watch and SEE! If we want to reach down and play in the water, we can, and then we can see how it affects the stream / river!

As it moves through, over, and around the various rocks, patterns of rocks, and the larger boulders and rock formations, we watch! The rocks and formations are in the MIND. Now we SEE where we won't yield...it's our beliefs and where we stand our ground, won't budge! As we watch, we can see the thoughts and re-actions as we approach and move through these obstacles, and mind "blockages" because we can see how the current changes, and we change, or we don't! We can also see the amount of force that's pushing against these obstacles, where they are, how firmly they are planted, how attached they are just to stay there in that spot! Is it worth it, is that effort productive? This is a path to WISDOM! What an education!

We must outgrow the mechanisms that drive us to blindly do the things we blindly do, and we do that with awareness of it by seeing it in our "selves" from above, as it is happening, as we are reacting to life in real time, in the moment. Once you produce a "ME", or an "I" that can see this as it happens, you can and will outgrow your limitations! You will walk right through them with wisdom and understanding! Unless you do this, you will continue to produce the same or similar results, and often times that means you feel stuck, in patterns, in situations that resemble ones you have been in before, meeting and being "FOOLED" by similar type people, the "selves", and / or situations because you were not aware enough to see through them to the truth. Fact is, there are a whole host of other things that are outside our awareness, gradually we begin to see but it takes effort, focus, ENERGY and AWARENESS! It's tough to see it when we are in the river vs above it. We must RISE UP!

STEP UP! STEP ABOVE thought, and watch. Work on being aware, in this moment, NOW! Every moment of every day is a moment to choose hap-piness, choose a smile, choose a pleasing thought above one that forces us into self-defeating behaviors, negative non-productive attitudes, and demeanors. Why choose in any moment to be anything other than a happy version of you, isn't that your favorite place to be? I mean seriously, if you had a choice, what would you choose, happy me or unhappy me? Smile or a frown? REALIZE that in every moment of every day, <u>YOU HAVE THAT CHOICE</u>! Step out of the box that created the frown. The box is "self" created.

You have that CHOICE...YOU just need to see these "selves", the thieves of thought, the imposters that want you to stay IN the box. They want to take you over for what they are, and they want to be in the box. They are the "selves"! Your own former thoughts POSING as you, in your mind...and they are deceiving you to remain in THAT STATE it produces...no more! They are stealing your life and your energy; are you ok with this? If not then, what are you going to do about it?

Don't be like the cowardly lion, be the KING of the Forest! Be the king of your mind, the **Over-SEER**!

Don't be like the **"Dumb driven cattle"**[51] that **Longfellow** talks about in **A Psalm of life "Be a HERO IN THE STRIFE"**[52] as he says! The hero is not to other people, although it can be, it is to your SELF!!!! Once you become a HERO to your "SELF", you can be a hero to others as well. I believe that Longfellow is saying the same thing as what I have been saying, in different words. Check out the poem, it is really good. Here is an excerpt from the Poem:

> **"Trust no Future, howe'er pleasant!**
> **Let the dead Past bury its dead!**
> **Act, act in the living Present!**
> **Heart within, and God o'erhead!"**
> **-Henry Wadsworth Longfellow**[53]

In other words, watch your MIND...do not be BLINDED by some idealistic future, however pleasant that might look on the mind screen. And similarly, don't be blinded by your past. **ACT IN THIS MOMENT**, in the living present (NOW...NOW and NOW). Pay attention, with awareness, you will see IN YOUR HEART, and with your NEW eyes, in THIS MOMENT, what the right choice is. It isn't necessarily the same as the last time trust me, no better yet, see for your SELF ...every situation is different. This is the ultimate description of being in the ZONE! YOU step up and step into the moment and RE**PRESENT**... with WISDOM, PRESENCE! **"Act, IN THE LIVING PRESENT!"**[54] NOWWWW!!!!! Just as **Longfellow** instructs!

**LESSON KEY:** ACT vs RE-act! This means by the nature of it, that YOU MUST TAKE ACTION!

When you are asleep at the wheel though, you get RE-actions from the "selves" and more of the same in your life! Wake up, pay attention, energize the over SEER, and BE ready for the moment with awareness and then in the moment, you are present to CHOOSE to take a NEW ACTION! Again, this is the SKILL and with it YOU have the opportunity, IN THE ZONE, to make a new choice, take a new action! That is the difference between re-action, and ACTION! One is NEW! Don't be blinded by the "selves", you now have CHOICE!

There is another neat song that kind of goes with this idea. **RUSH, "Marathon"**[55]. As with all these songs, what I hear and what the band intended may not be the same, so that's my disclaimer! Summary, of the Doug notes version. Through all the trials, and tests, and challenges, and errors. BE WATCHFUL, as you get distracted, blinded in some cases, overloaded, over-stressed, overworked, during the CLIMB, pay super close attention with aware-ness. Understand that there is always going to be another peak in front of you and be WATCHFUL as you take each step! There's no free ride, it takes effort. It takes time, opportunities, errors, endurance, energy, and balance! In other words, you have to get the lessons! You can accomplish a lot, over time, just be persistent, awake, and aware. It is truly a marathon, as the song seems to imply.  Amazing song and lyrics, this is my abbreviated summary version, as I hear it, to make it easier to understand relative to this book and how I personally look at it. Check out the song too because the whole song and lyrics are even more powerful, the delivery is awesome, IMHO! Practice, so your meters don't overload! Listen to some RUSH, its great stuff!

# DREAM

## GETTING IN THE ZONE IV

T HIS IS RELATIVE TO envisioning one's future vs the dreaming we may do at night while sleeping. Just clarifying which version of dreaming we are talking about here. Now that we have stepped out of the box, the sky is the limit, right? How cool. Exciting! Please understand that it is not a race, it's a marathon, as described in the previous lesson key and the highlighted song. You'll need to manage your energy and hopefully enjoy the journey! Otherwise, you'll burn it up too fast. Also, please don't read into this material and confuse it with not having goals or dreams and just allowing whatever to occur in your life out of laziness, complacency, or a fear of moving forward. That's not what I mean by "allowing"! I don't mean to tolerate, endure, or just put up with it in the interest of "peace" internally. The point is to be at peace WHILE moving forward to the extent that you can do this! So, what I do mean is really, take that step, wide awake & aware, and truly move forward, without resistance, avoidance, or ignorance! There is a BIG difference. Eyes wide open! BY ALL MEANS...DREAM, dream BIG, and reach for the stars, make goals, but don't be blinded by them. In fact, **RUSH** has a song that seems to speak to this as well, it is called **"MISSION"**[56]. It's really good! Check it out.

Our mission, the way I see it, is to take the step, and while we do, as we do, LISTEN, WATCH, SEE, FEEL and HEAR what the mind tries to do, say, where it tries to lead you, or mislead you, and limit you, the reasons it comes up with to tell you to turn, or not to, the roadblocks, excuses, and images it throws at you on the mind screen! The whole thing is geared to show you something about yourself, or more specifically, the MIND, WITHIN! So, while reaching, and reaching over and over again, just PAY ATTENTION for GOD's sake, do your best to be awake and aware in every moment, and watch your thoughts. By doing this, you will be brought to and through many lessons! Each is a steppingstone to the next, forever, and ever. Daunting it may seem at first. It's NOT...it becomes a game, and it becomes more and more FUN. You approach every moment with a sort of whimsical gleam and a smirk on your face in some cases, knowing what you now know! Chuckling inside...maybe even out loud! It is actually entertaining to watch the mind and laugh at it! It truly is a comedy show, I laugh at myself quite often. LOL. The essence of this is that YOU really do see and hear on a whole new level. It is amusing, and more importantly, it keeps things a little more lighthearted. It is a better frame of mind. The mind WANTS, watch it wanting! Notice when it tries to steal your peace, your smile! Have some FUN with this. Imagine taking that step forward JOYFULLY, with a GIGANTIC smile on your face! Lose the tension, and weight...life is supposed to be FUN!? LIGHTEN UP!

Now that you understand this perspective really well, let's take a look at these same insights from a more spiritual perspective. DREAM, the theme of this chapter, is essentially wanting right? It is just kicked up a notch, like amped up thoughts. What do we do when we WANT, like this? We think more thoughts about that thing, more often, and maybe with more emphasis, and focus too! We draw pretty imaginary pictures, landscapes, and scenarios in our minds. It's like a little mind projector in there playing short clips of dreamy movies, showing us images to match, and they all really appeal to us. So ideal situations, people, things, or whatever it is can come really into focus on our mind screen, wishful thinking, right? Didn't I just describe DESIRE? I mean, these tend to be really pointed thoughts, right? You might even call them prayers in certain situations. Some people actually take it to the next level and call that their vision board, or visualizing and spend time envisioning it, for real! This can be really powerful, if done properly. I actually put mine into a PowerPoint presentation, I know shocker right. Along the same lines, in some cases, the same thing is considered to be prayer, right? I mean, a lot of people officially take time out of their day and use it to pray, in many ways, not only to envision the future...but to practice peace, and balance, and search for answers, among other things, too. In this instance, I want to focus on the envisioning type of prayer, because that brings prayer into the realm of topics we would tend to consider when we want things to go a certain way in our lives. Isn't prayer one of the tenets of religion, and a common practice? Certainly, something to examine, like I like to do relative to DREAMING.

So, if desire is a consideration, and it is relative to prayer, wouldn't the opposite also be true? In other words, do people always pray in the affirmative? Do they take the positive approach and ask for what they want, or the negative and ask to NOT have what they don't want, or say "make it go away"? Prayer is extremely relevant to thought, and in fact, it matters how it's done! Make it go away as a thought is resistance, right? So, if thoughts are prayers, or prayers are thoughts, then they are happening all day long, every moment of every day. We just don't think of it that way! This is particularly germane to dreaming, remember, I am a dreamer! So, by dreaming, am I not praying really hard? And often, right? So, if I am doing it often, and with intent...like hard, then I had better be doing it right. My license plate when we lived in Virginia was DREEEM, so let's talk about this in depth. It's a pretty powerful perspective and I want you to understand it!

The great spiritual masters have given some accomplished instructions, and they are similar in a lot of ways, although they came in different times, conditions, and context. Slightly different angles and "spin", different stories, and what not, but overall, I think it's really interesting that the core messages are very much alike. If you really take the time to drill down on it and try to ascertain what they are trying to say...as if it were an instruction manual, it is quite productive, but who has time for that? So much to read, and so little time! The sheer quantity of content alone is mind-boggling, not to mention you have to be able to understand context, and potentially decode language disparities as well. Oh, and pile on the fact that a bunch of it comes in stories, or parables that can be lengthy and hard to understand and translate to reality in the here and now. Well, thankfully I had some time. So, this is my shorter decoded version! Remember that underlying theme I wanted you to see, well that seems to be true for this as well. While I can't say that I have studied every aspect of every religion or spiritual philosophy, I have looked at a lot, and in detail, as you might expect of me! The underlying themes are really powerful! So, this is coming through to you. I offer you lots of perspectives and insights, and I encourage you to always challenge your "selves" and how they think! Remember that while these might be my stories, its about YOU, and that means seeing how that might relate to your life.

As this relates to prayer, and as with other examples, I want to give you a quick story from my life, because it is real, it happened, it is very relevant and a great Illustration of how understanding this stuff can make a huge difference in today's world, the one we are in NOW! I want for you to SEE IT for yourself though, not my story, yours!!! I want for you to not only see it as a philosophy or strategy, but I want you to see it work, and then you know how, why, and when it worked so that you can do it again. That's understanding! I think that old saying is really true, when the student is ready, the teacher appears. It is debatable where and when this originated, as well as by whom? I honestly don't know, but I can show you that this is absolutely 100% true! I saw it as a quote this way as well, which makes sense to me.

## "When the student is ready, the teacher will appear. When the student is truly ready...the teacher will disappear"[57]

My interpretation: When the student gets it, and is ready, the eyes and ears open, and the lessons start to be seen and heard, but sporadically at first. When the student really gets it, the eyes and ears are WIDE OPEN, and then the teacher is no longer needed! The student understands, completely! It is internalized, and it becomes Second nature. The student KNOWS where to look and what to listen for, and basically how to do it, so they do it themselves. Quite honestly, they don't miss much, if anything after a lot of practice! Isn't this true of some people more so than others? Hopefully YOU, NOW with this skill! Some people just seem wise though, like my mother, hah, makes me laugh! I could never get anything past her. I swear she could hear me three rooms over!! I was like, I was whispering for crying out loud, how did you hear that? She knew what to listen for because I was "up to something", or my sister was, HAHA!! That is the perspective I want you to have when you are looking at your mind, WITHIN! So, to the point, on the spiritual side of things. Do you know what your mind is up to, and what to listen for, what to see or be on the lookout for? Are you ready to? Have you been paying attention? You could probably explain it to me by now but let's see it explained in a more spiritual theme.

You know how Jesus said that the people could not see and could not hear the parables? My take on that is that the student wasn't ready! So, this is something we should definitely look at! I have a story...Oh boy, I am laughing again...sorry. It's just fun to explain it.

It needs an intro though. So, let me start by saying that I know a lot of people pray, try to be good, do good and I applaud them for that! ME TOO! I pray for people all the time. In fact, the world seems to need it because let's face it, bad things still happen! So, what happens if we don't get what we want? Then we pray harder, right? But do we change the way we pray? I challenge you to consider that maybe harder prayer, in the same manner, doesn't work any better if we are simply doing it wrong to begin with. Sorry, again, to be so bold and blunt... but maybe our methodology needs an upgrade? Maybe we need a more scientific approach. Remember, I tear things apart and really dissect them, prayer was no different for me. I tore it apart, and assessed it, from as many angles as I could come up with! The net result is that I am not bashing prayer. In fact, I know prayer works! I really do, I have seen it work a lot in some rather AMAZING ways! Some, hardly even believable. Some, I don't even quite know how it happened, I only know the thoughts/prayers that preceded it. I hesitate to even explain some of them because they would be unbelievable for a lot of people. So, I'll keep it toned down. I see it working all the time though, in normal everyday things too.

All I am saying here is that in all the literature, and with all the wonderful information out there, classes, teaching and preaching with some amazing messages, from amazing people, where does it say how to pray? Aside from the Lord's prayer, which we will talk about, I promise! Of course, I want to know really specifically, in a comprehensive way, that is understandable and yields results! I am not talking about just having a positive attitude, which is fine, and great, and helps. I want specifics. Not talking about just the words, but also what is going through the mind as the prayer is being prayed. EVERY LAST DETAIL! If you were taught how to pray properly, and it works for you, I applaud the teacher, the philosophy, and I applaud you too! If we were never taught how though, through no fault of our own, or the teachers before us, because they were never taught either...then are we to just assume we are doing it right? Hmmmm, well, you know what they say about assume right? It makes an ASS out of U and ME. So, let's not do that.

Instead, let's say, for the sake of argument, that we were sick that day and we just completely missed school. We never got the lesson on how to pray; we missed it all together. We know now for sure that we missed the lesson, and while we know what it was about, there is no textbook... so we try to teach it to ourselves. Then, we approach it a little bit differently, right? Kind of forced into a trial-and-error type deal. If the way we are doing it isn't yielding results, then we tear it down to build it back up, hopefully better this time. We go back through it in our minds to see what we may have missed. It's a different perspective. Do you see? We are not assuming we got the lesson already and know what we are doing. That's just a way to approach it, anyway. Obviously, if you got the lesson, and you are doing it, and it's working then by all means, keep doing what you are doing! If not, maybe we could consider that prayer is a technique, a mental strategy, or methodology and tweak it a little bit to see if that changes the game at all, or the results?! I know that some prayers are really geared for one thing vs another, but if we don't understand what that prayer is saying, or showing us then how does that help us? Maybe our delivery is wrong. I get that persistence is good, and patience is a virtue, but think about it. If something isn't working, then there has to be a reason, right? Is it possible that something got lost in translation somewhere along the line? I mean, some of these messages have been passed along for a very long time. I am not saying that ALL prayers should be answered or will be answered, for that matter. BUT. Let me postulate that prayer is no different than what we have been talking about all along here. Are prayers mental thoughts, even if said aloud? I think so! So, everything we have just explained about thought is also relevant to prayer. OMG! YEAH!

Consider this. The MIND and AWARENESS, especially that overarching ALL SEEING awareness is really powerful right? How does that relate to prayer? Isn't every action and thought we take/think a part of that? In that same vein then, isn't every thought I think a virtual prayer? I mean, how is a basic thought different than when I formally sit or kneel or pray "officially"? Did I say it differently in my MIND? Did I use a different voice? By classifying this thought as a prayer and that one as just a thought, did that change anything? How is it different than the other 50,000 thoughts that went through my mind today? More emphasis maybe? Like PLEEEEEEESE.... PLEASE! Seriously, where is that thought? Does it have any more power? I either want something to be fixed from the past, or I am BEGGING for something in the future. Yes, or no? Which one is it? How badly do I want it, how badly do I want to avoid it, how much emphasis am I putting on it? Like, am I saying it with authority? Like a LION, or a mouse?

So, this is going to make you think here, but what happens if we are not present to think the thought that we thought we thought? Was that thought actually a prayer or not? Did that thought have any chance of being "heard", by GOD, the universe, or whomever / whatever you wish to pray to? Bottom line, in my opinion, every thought is a prayer...in one way or another, so I want to talk about that in various ways. Consider "presence" as it relates to prayer, as well as the TENSE and EMPHASIS with which that prayer is being delivered. Was the prayer postulated as a "PAST", "FUTURE", or a "PRESENT"? On top of that, what was going on in the mind as that prayer was delivered? Where was the imagery, pictures on the mind screen? WHEN were they? Please think about this in detail. (visualizing) Don't blaze through this, it is incredibly important.

Consider these examples and where the mind is. These are possible "Formal" thoughts / prayers, and postulating what the mind is doing, and where it is! Pay very close attention as you PRAY and / or THINK! This is your internal universe here, which affects the external! Whether you are awake and aware, or NOT, the universe is always paying attention. Remember, the law of attraction doesn't stop, it's always working! So, in an effort to absorb this powerful vantage point, play around with these examples a little bit as if it were a blueprint for construction relative to your life. You are the engineer, and it is your job to make sure that the architect hasn't cut any corners. This thought / prayer MUST BE structurally sound to yield optimal results! After all, we want our house to be safe and sound when we build it, right? Let's build a thought / prayer with the same consideration! The whole shebang begins with thought, and thoughts are prayers, or prayers are thoughts...so this is of the utmost importance, the BEGINNING, if you will!! So, let's start from the beginning.

## PRAYERS = THOUGHTS
## THOUGHTS = PRAYERS

EXAMPLES:

1. Thought type: negative: "I wish that hadn't happened." **(Past)** Prayer: GOD, fix this thing that just occurred. **(Past)** MIND: Going back over the imagery and details of what just happened in the past, contextually. **(Past)**

2. Thought type: positive: "I hope that this happens soon." **(Future)**. Prayer: GOD, please give me this thing/situation/achievement/award/win/whatever it is that you want but has yet to be delivered, wishfully. **(Future)** MIND: Picturing some glorious imagery which is in the future, contextually. **(Future)**

3. NO Thought, just presence: neutral: **(NOW)** I am wide awake, fully aware, and PRESENT! **(NOW)**. Prayer: GOD, please help with some instructions, what can I do right **NOW**? MIND: Blank slate, focusing, tuning in, open to receive, watching, listening, prepared to ACT! **(NOW)**!

See any difference? Which of these scenarios is likely to yield results right now? Why? Where is my focus? Is it "out there" or "In here"? Where have we been told the answers are? WITHIN, right? So, was that thought a projection, or the opposite? Where was the placement, in the past, future, or present? Do any of these scenarios work better than the next? Let's take a look to see!

In scenario 1, I just put myself in the past. Well, that doesn't work! We already know that. I can't change the past; I already missed the lesson. I was not present! It was something bad that occurred so what is the emphasis and pattern? In this case, negative with increasingly more emphasis depending on the urgency level or the weight / importance given to the prayer. More importantly, the focus is on what I don't want, which equals what? RESISTANCE/AVOIDANCE! Let it go, get back to now, with PRESENCE and do something that will move you in the direction of what you DO WANT!! Change your mind. With 1 caveat, wake up, be present and LISTEN first. Then ACT! It starts with thought, think a new thought, a positive one! This instantly changes the focus, attention, and direction of the underlying theme! Maybe that's to pick up the phone, call the person you just had a blowout with, apologize, ask forgiveness, or forgive them and / or do your best to resolve whatever just occurred in a positive way. If it can't be resolved, LET IT GO! Needless to say, if I stay in the past, nothing changes. There's lots more to learn here but let's keep it simple for now. Consider that there is always the possibility to think similar thoughts after restructuring them as a positive vs negative! Sometimes that may take some practice and correcting oneself for a period of time before this becomes a "habit". Constructive, affirming thoughts are preferred, so be watchful! Listen, and be open, aware, answers will come! Thankfulness and appreciation can also be "prayed" and / or added, the focus is then building on whatever positivity can be mustered in that moment, even the smallest scrap of gratefulness will be like adding fertilizer! Like attracts like and then it expands, we must start where we can and build on it. Think about how that might go differently. Turn that frown upside down, and that begins with a better thought, NOW!

In scenario #2, I just put myself in the future. Well, that doesn't work either! We already know this too. I was not present in my mind! Is this any better than what we have discussed previously? Not only am I not PRESENT, but my mind is literally PUSHING that image, that situation, whatever it is, out into the future. That's what I am SEEING on my mind screen, a future! Is that where I want it to stay? NO, but that is where it will stay! IN THE FUTURE! If your mind puts it in the future, by habit, whether by thought or prayer, what is your mind telling the universe, GOD, or whomever / whatever you pray to? It is in the future, that's what the mind believes, namely, that it is in the future. Great, then what did that thought / prayer accomplish? NOTHING, not in the NOW anyway! The future doesn't exist yet. You could be screaming at the top of your lungs, which is actually even worse, why? Because that emphasis cements it in your mind, in the future! If you want to talk about a belief that is a really strong belief, pay attention to how loud it is said, or how much force it was delivered with! So, that glorious future, as pretty as it may be, is where in your mind? It is still a FUTURE, not a PRESENT! To your mind, it doesn't exist yet, except in the future. You have very successfully convinced your mind, with conviction, that the image it just projected onto the mind screen is in the future! Can you see the problem here? It is a technique issue! The MIND DOESN'T BELIEVE that it exists TODAY! NOW! This is a TRUST, FAITH, BELIEF problem, which all stems from the genesis, intention, focus, tense placement, delivery, structure, and emphasis of the thought! That thought is a PRAYER, it's just a poorly constructed one. This is FIXABLE! YAY.

We have to wake up and see what just happened here! In fact, you did accomplish something, and the prayer was answered. The mind with faith, projected it in the future, and it REALLY believed it, with conviction! That is almost wonderful, but it missed the mark, and here is how: It did a "good" affirming thought, it believed it to be in the future, and it accomplished all aspects, so, it is still there, in the future! Good news, the prayer was answered, 100%. Congratulations! Happy now? (Sarcasm, sorry) You should be, because NOW you have the answer, a solution. FLIP the prayer, it's primarily a tense issue, but delivery and emphasis matter too! It sounds like a riddle, but it is NOT! Look at the anatomy of the thought, and pattern. Structure matters, belief matters, tense matters, delivery matters, emphasis matters. It is all relevant! Maybe the easiest way to look at it would be CONstructive vs DEstructive is a new beginning...that starts when? NOW! Right now, I am constructing a NEW life, which begins with a new thought, every moment! Do you believe in that thought? What was the thought? How much emphasis did you place in it, or on it? Was it regarding yesterday or tomorrow? What it boils down to is trust, which is the underlying "theme" at a CORE level, and then faith and ultimately BELIEF! Add emphasis, with a FEELING of gratitude, and you have the makings of a really powerful mindset! That's a powerful prayer!

Jesus even spoke of this faith / belief problem, and we will get more into that with many inspirational quotes and a lot more examples. If you dig a little, the solution is implied...but kind of only at a surface level, and not really spelled out in my opinion. Hearing a parable is different than UNDERSTANDING a parable, and what it is telling you to DO...like an action plan!

Let me explain how I came to this realization, though. I do understand that some of this may seem farfetched, or seem storyline "ish", but what I am about to tell you is 100% true. All of it! The reason I bring it up and explain it in such detail is because I really did have a moment of inspiration, for lack of a better description. So, I want to tell you that story and then the rest of this book is designed to answer to and explain in much more detail the application of #3, as well as give you a workable comprehensive plan if you haven't fully assimilated it yet. I have more solutions and angles to this prayer epiphany! YAY! You already know it's a trust, faith, belief, tense, and emphasis issue, but I'll expand on that too! To start, here's the story that goes with it!

Many moons ago, ha-ha, kidding, but seriously, it was a bunch of years ago. Trying to keep things lighthearted because for context, this is from a period of time where I was spiraling downward, so to speak. Things in my life were getting progressively worse. It wasn't pretty. So, I had been praying, I had been "trying", really HARD, and yet my prayers were not being heard or answered. At least that is what I thought at that time. I didn't understand yet what I just explained prior to this story. So, what did I do? I got frustrated, ANGRY, and I complained a lot, under my breath of course, remember I am shy ...but then eventually I vocalized it to GOD! In fact, I was FURIOUS! It takes a lot to make me mad, I mean, I have a really high threshold for pain, and I am extremely tolerant, even back then! So, with all this new "philosophy", thinking about thinking, and trying to apply all of that book knowledge...I was exploring and testing new things, and while doing so, making every effort to hear, and see things differently. I had gone from a life where everything was working really well, to something that was an extreme opposite. I mean, it felt like almost nothing was working so I was trying to do something about it, actively! So, from a mindset perspective that meant I was trying to see what the differences were, WITHIN! Like, what was I doing wrong? Something had to be "off", but I didn't feel like a whole lot had changed in my overall mindset, not enough to justify such a drastic turn for the worse anyway. I had a few more psychological bruises, from life beating me up, but thankfully, I still had my wife, my dog, my family, friends, and moral support. I tried to maintain a positive attitude, because I knew that was important, but it didn't seem to be helping. There was an undertone of negativity, and my results were so consistently negative that it was somewhat overwhelming. In that state, it is as if you are just waiting for the next thing to go wrong, so you pretty much just expect it. Even though you try to put on that positive face, the "tone" is basically a mindset where you are just waiting for the other shoe to drop. We know what that mindset yields right? Nothing good! I didn't really vocalize my "issues" to anyone though, and I continued to suffer. The problem was that I was almost maxed out. I wasn't truly processing anything. Anger, not "processed", not understood, and redirected internally is the equivalent of BUILDING frustration, right? That energy has to go somewhere! The fact is, I just kept burying it, over and over again. Over time, that makes for a massive buildup of frustration and emotional baggage. ("ignore"-ance). Eventually, there just isn't enough room anymore, it has to find an outlet. In this case, instead of beating myself up, or burying it, I finally let it out and vocalized it, to GOD...and I mean LOUD. This had been building for years, so I blew a gasket. There may have even been steam coming out of my ears, not quite sure. Thankfully, I was all alone, so no one saw me lose my "cool"! I was super mad for my circumstances, and what was going on in my life, however I was not directing that anger at GOD, it was different. My complaint was VERY POINTED, and the complaint was postulated in the form of a question and then a very powerful statement, with a massive amount of feeling and emotion. The thought / question was: How am I supposed to help others if YOU won't help ME? It wasn't all about me...something changed in the way I was looking at things, and I did understand it a little. But nothing in my life was changing. So that was the basis for the argument. Oh Yeah, and it was an argument! A heated one! Here is what I ultimately ended up saying, and remember, I was super ANGRY. I said, basically YELLED... "I can't ****ING HEAR YOU...SPEAK LOUDER!" With massive amounts of energy, crazy high emotion, and tears running down my face, I was BEGGING, not for him to hear me but for me to be able to hear HIM! The student was ready!

Important to note here that the lead up to this event was all my own fault and this is a beneficial clarification. I was listening, but I couldn't HEAR! My eyes were open, but I could not SEE! Let me explain why though, so that you can fully digest this very real example! I had been bottling up my feelings and emotions for years and years. (suffering) I honestly didn't know what they were there for. So, I just ignored them, repressed them, buried them, avoided them, and so by habit, I had quite literally shut my eyes and ears OFF in some cases, and in others, my filters were set way too high! As a result, I couldn't hear or see very important details, and I couldn't feel anything. I was numb to it all, frozen, impenetrable! In that state, I was not receptive at all, nothing more could get in, I was FULL...and so I was missing critical information, and a lot of lessons! They were basically just deflecting right off me because I was in DEFENSE mode, that was my underlying theme! I have always been a really positive person; however, because of this mindset/mode I was in, I was getting less than desirable results. This had been going on for quite a while too. Even though I would put on a fake smile, and intermittently gather the courage to try to go on offense, that would of course yield more punishment, because of the state I was in. It was like reaching out for the cookie, full well knowing your hand was going to get smacked, HARD. No cookie, and more pain! Sooner or later, this had to come out in one way or another because I was eating the pain, for breakfast, lunch, and dinner! Quite literally, too, I had gained a lot of weight. Other than that, though, It didn't come out in outwardly negative ways overall, mainly because of my nature. I just took it, or took it out on myself in self-defeating behaviors, distraction and avoidance techniques which just postpones the lesson again. What happens when you miss lessons? They come back a little more forcefully the next time. So, I was, quite simply, setting myself up for failure, and more pain. Sooner or later, you get that final straw scenario. This eruption was the result of all the postponed lessons, and pretty much an isolated incident, lucky for me! The volcano had been rumbling for a long time prior though, and thankfully, by the grace of God, it was a productive conclusion rather than continuation!

Ever since that day, my mind has been different, everything changed. I can even tell you about the dream I had that night, where GOD was talking to me with a giant gold megaphone. Dramatic, yep. I get it, you may not even believe me, but that is the God's honest truth. It happened. I have to look up the exact details of the dream from my journal, it was pretty cool. Ever since that day, it is as if I can see with new eyes and hear with new ears. It seemed as if the filters were all tweaked, enhanced, tuned in even. NOW, I see and hear messages and lessons in virtually EVERYTHING! Why? I implore you to really see this. After all the pain, all the failed efforts and all the frustration, **the student was finally ready to listen, SEE, HEAR, and FEEL!** See with different eyes and hear with different ears, and no longer numb. I bottomed out, throwing my hands in the air... I knew that I didn't know, and so I asked and pleaded for help! I asked very specifically, to be shown something so that I could perceive! I said, SHOW ME, TELL ME, somehow, some way, in a way that I can hear or see. It was a full-on conversation. My intention with the words I was saying was as follows: You know me, everything about me. You may be speaking, but I can't hear you! <u>SPEAK TO ME</u>, not only that <u>PLEEEEEEAAASE</u> <u>SPEAK UP, LOUDER</u> <u>and in a way that I can hear you or SHOW ME!</u> I truly wanted and needed to understand what I was doing wrong. It brings tears to my eyes as I write this because it was a major turning point for me! Up until that day, I had not had enough pain yet, I wasn't ripe, wasn't ready, didn't want to hear it, see it, or feel it. The student wasn't ready up until then! I tend to take things to the extremes, I think my wife, Joelle would agree. That can be good and bad. In this case it was somewhat climactic.

The purpose of me telling you this is not to suggest that pain works, not at all! The objective is to emphasize emphatically that the pain, and suffering in particular, is not necessary if the lesson is learned. What I was shown is that I was getting the lessons, they were right in front of me ALL ALONG, I just wasn't hearing or seeing them properly, if at all...so they sped right on by! A lot of missed opportunities and much more. I was mostly just postponing the lessons, but I did not know that at the time! My device wasn't tuned right. ME! My ears were a bit off, and my vision was certainly not 20/20, and that was feeding into my mind which was processing all of that bad information! If the information going in is bad, not "TRUE", what comes out the other end is also bad. I could see it in the result, my life, and my reactions to it! Could I hear, yes! Could I see, yes! Pretty well actually, by ordinary standards! So, what was the issue? I was filtering out a massive amount of information, data...it wasn't getting in, I had tuned it out! So, what changed was ME, HOW I saw, and HOW I heard! My vantage point changed too, like where I was seeing FROM, and how I listened changed as well, which in turn affected what I REALLY saw and heard. I was praying all along, all day long, in everything I did, said, and thought...but I had it all wrong, or a lot of it wrong! Minimum, my methodology was flawed, and I was asleep at the wheel most of the time! Once I woke up, and realized what I was doing wrong, I stopped what I was doing, and started doing things differently, to the extent that I knew how to at that point! It has made all the difference!

There is a learning curve to it, so, I don't want you to have to go through the extensive trial and error phase that I went through. That can be somewhat painful. How about we skip that part and get to the good stuff? Sorry, NO CAN DO... you are going to need to work through your "stuff"! It's unavoidable, but GOOD NEWS, with understanding it makes it a lot less painful and probably a lot faster too! What I am saying is that working through the "stuff" brings up the baggage that needs to be processed. Initially, that may be perceived as pain, however, in the processing of it, or getting the lesson, it is different. The pain doesn't convert to suffering, it converts to understanding. This is not a play on words, it's REAL! The result is truly a lesson learned, and DIGESTED, and that is HUGE! Different outlook, different spin, different "attitude"! FUNdamentals: the underlying theme just changed! With that very small seemingly insignificant tweak, you took the up ramp instead of the down ramp, if that makes sense. You FUNdamentally changed your life, and you continue to do so one step at a time! On top of that, it happens FAST, instantly each time a lesson is assimilated = another step forward!! The key is open eyes and ears! Seeing with eyes that can see, and hearing with ears that can hear, and then integrating the feelings that go along with the inputs is also important. They don't always show up as a group, or in the same order, angle, magnitude, weight, etc. so that's where the overseer comes in to ensure that you can get the lessons and process them in an appropriate and timely manner, with a productive mindset, NOW!

Ah, to "tune" the eyes and ears, and even emotions into the music, what a fun concept! To hear this FUN perspective in a song, check out **RUSH, "The Spirit of the Radio"**[58]. Seems to me that this speaks extremely well to this ability to tune the radio in a very illuminating way, assuming of course that you dissect and hear the song the way I do. It mentions freedom as a kind of noble concept, the way I hear it... If the radio were us, we just need some fine tuning! The machine may just be a little off, frequency wise. What happens if you are tuned in to the wrong channel, or maybe in between stations on the old radio dial? There was, at a minimum, a little static, right? It's either not going to come through clearly, or at all! Let's say, for clarity, the message comes through one channel, but the machine was tuned to another. As an example, the machine was drilled down on sight, but the message came through as an audible. OR The machine was tuned into to hearing, but the message came through as a feeling. That's called being blindsided. We get too dialed in, or too dialed out! That is the advantage to the overseer perspective, with awareness, it sees ALL of it! One of the cool things about this song is that it references the wavelength as timeless! Can you imagine getting messages on that wavelength? Check out the song, it's really cool! The song is brilliant, and really captures the essence of being in the moment, with eyes that can see, ears that can hear, and with awareness that is even tuned into the emotion of it. It's truly electrifying, experientially! I believe that the lyrical version is pretty powerfully delivered in the song, so look it up, see what you hear!?! I think that there is so much data streaming through this machine that the antenna is literally glowing from the heat of it, so cool!! You have to be deliberately tuning it out to not see it, feel it, or hear it...its powerful, like the megaphone is being heard above all the normal voices one way or another. Awareness SEES ALL! Like I say, once you see it, you can't unsee it... It's in your face. In some cases, quite honestly, it feels like a curse, and you almost want to go back to being NUMB at times, but for obvious reasons that is not chosen as an option! Been there, done that. No thank you. The presence vision is unavoidable though once the overseer perspective is solidified! You see the "selves" and their sales pitches from all angles! If you are in sales then you know all the tricks, gimmicks, and techniques. The EGO is less likely to get something past you because you are wise to its methodologies, disguises, and games! It is most certainly clever though, so the vantage point, and tuning is KEY!

As an example, once you've received a lesson, and let's say that you didn't really GET IT wholly, and / or maybe it hits you from a different angle, so you didn't process it 100%, then the next time it shows up you become like, oh darn, I did that again didn't I? I didn't see it soon enough. I missed it initially, but then I saw that I missed it. It is seen, in the beginning sometimes after the fact, but each time it is seen, heard, or felt just a little bit faster. The beautiful thing is when you can truly tune in like that, and SEE...it is quite amazing, like night and day, pun intended! It ALLOWS, and it is a fascinating, positive, inspired way to live life. On top of that, it is a vantage point from which you can keep a keen eye out for the salesmen, "the selves"! When you can see them coming, with all their bells and whistles on, well then you have a finely tuned machine! You will SEE, HEAR, and FEEL in the timeless MOMENT of NOW with exceptional clarity! Like seeing miles ahead...VISION, and from a safe harbor, so to speak, like a guarded and protected vantage point, unwavering! With the overseer championing every effort, and a CORE stability, there is an underlying cheerful optimism, an enthu-siastic NOWlook, along with the fact that the "selves" can't get away with their shenanigans anymore. This is an actual recipe for "success". Understanding is the key ingredient here. Understanding = lessons received = less suffering, less pain, and a progressively more positive outlook, NOW ("NOWtlook", I made that up, makes sense to me) one step at a time!!

Let me pause to make a really key point before moving on. SUPER IMPOR-
TANT to understand this, relative to seeing and hearing. The "selves", when
they take us over, are re-setting the filters on OUR mind, our eyes, our ears,
and our overall perception, including the emotions!!! They are the source of the
problem! That affects our ability to perceive, take in information, and ensure
that the data is PURE, CLEAN, UNFILTERED! We can only do that if we
are PRESENT, with awareness and have the ability to focus from this detached
perspective. Using the SKILL, NOW! That should clear things up for you if you
haven't already made that connection. That is why we can't see and can't hear
properly when the "selves" are in control of the mind, because we are not receiving
all the information that is available IN THE MOMENT! A lot of the data, if
not all of the data is getting filtered out by these selves. Once they reset YOUR
filters, you are done! All your efforts to this point are out the window, muted.
Why? Because you just changed the radio station, YOU are no longer dialed in,
present, they are in control, using THEIR filters. YOU are not present to receive
the timeless GIFT, information, lessons! So, again, flip the scene, YOU STAY
PRESENT, then THEY have no control. YOU use YOUR PRESENCE to tune
in, listen, hear, see and feel! When we can arrive in the moment, without the selves
affecting our vision and hearing, what happens is we can finally see with new eyes
and hear with new ears! UNFILTERED / UNBIASED / UNTAINTED! We get
the information, we get the lessons, we get the TRUTH! The truth will set you
FREE!

So, moving on. From a more spiritual perspective: methodologies and mind
strategies that work! Call it prayer, thought, dreaming, envisioning, visualizing,
setting goals with a divine partner. I don't really care what you call it, or who
you choose to pray to, just keep dreaming, and don't be blinded by them! Pay
attention and do your best to be wide awake and aware! Watch your thoughts
VERY carefully and LISTEN! The fact is that we are praying all day long every
day! So, pay attention to what you are praying for. Watch your thoughts and,
oh...one more thing, BE THANKFUL! First, get the lesson and be thankful for
the lessons that are shown to you! Second, when you are "officially praying", like
the envisioning type, with emphasis, be thankful that it is DONE! Being thankful
that it is DONE changes where it is in TIME! So, in the instance of dreaming,
or envisioning, it is no longer a projection into the future. It is DONE already,
NOW, in other words, in your mind/prayer it is in the PRESENT/PAST. There's
always a caveat, right? It is one of very few times I would suggest that you use the
past. Why is this important? Because if it is in the past, it happened, its real, its
DONE. I am envisioning my future, as if it is a past, NOW and being thankful
for it...so it is "delivered"!

Think about this. If I just thought about something I WANT, in my future, but then I reached out and in the mind picture, I spun it around and put it in the past, as if it has already happened, and then on top of that I am THANK-FUL for it with every ounce of my BEING, NOW, what just happened? At what level is belief? 100%. To the extent that you can get your mind to believe it, it is TRUE! That is the reason for giving thanks or being appreciative. If you can do this with ENERGY, FEELING, and EMOTION.... with the imagery that matches, put it in the past and BE THANKFUL for it. What does that do in your mind? It makes it believable! It must have already happened if you are being thankful for it. The appreciation factor MUST be real though. When I take timeout to do this, and I imagine something that I want, there will be tears of JOY running down my face! I can literally FEEL as if that thing, event or whatever it is, happened. True gratitude. On top of that, I do it as often as I can muster the strength, energy, and drive that level of emotion. The mind must surely believe it if there are tears of joy! That is the emphasis factor. If you were never taught how to "visualize", that is how!

Some people instruct to envision in the present, I believe it is more powerful the way I have described, mainly because for me, it makes it more real. I think that there is a fine line here, so you may want to play with it a little bit. See what works for you! Oh, and BTW, once you see it, as if it has already happened. NOW is always a good time to go to work and make it happen in the real world! Just sayin.... we live in an abundant universe, thankfully! Now you can allow it to show up in your life, quite naturally. YOU KNOW IT! "Make it happen" are a few catch phrases I hear a lot, which are good! I would prefer more of a go to work and "allow" it to flow into your life. Semantics, right? My take is that there is a fine line between forcing things, which implies PRESSURE, and operating from more of an overseer and orchestrator perspective. Which sounds more enjoyable and less stressful? I envision a mindset perspective that is action oriented, yet stable, poised, balanced and very much in harmony with its environment. At EASE, PEACEFUL, FLOW! Add an appreciation factor, and you are GOLDEN! The point is, take ACTION, ACT vs RE-act! When things go your way, be thankful. When things don't go your way, be thankful, you just got a lesson!

That brings up this passage below, so we can now appreciate the meaning, significance, and importance of it:

*"Rejoice ALWAYS, pray without ceasing, give thanks in all circum-stances,*

### *for this is the will of God in Jesus Christ for you".*
### -Thessalonians 5:16-18[59]

When you are GIVEN something, BE THANKFUL! There is always more to a story, right? Don't glaze over life, DIG IN and quite honestly enjoy it! Isn't being appreciative, and thankful FUN? I totally LOVE giving people thanks for how amazing they are, how they've helped me, and it's NOT FAKE! It makes ME feel good that they are in my life, and it makes THEM feel good for being appreciated! That's a WIN-WIN! Oh yeah, and what is the byproduct of that? What we focus on expands right? So, by the nature of it, if I take the time and really focus on it, really put EMPHASIS on it, won't it expand? BEING thankful, and I mean REALLY THANKFUL means MORE to be thankful for, call it selfish...but it is the truth! Like attracts like...be thankful, mean it, and you will be given more to be thankful for!

Relative to the quote above, we agree that prayers are thoughts, right? What's the problem with that? Uh Oh, that means I AM praying without ceasing, all day long! HOLY ****. Maybe this doesn't surprise you at this point, which is great. When that finally hit me though, my wheels really started spinning. OMG, OMG! Once again, I was asking the question, but kind of shutting out the an-swer. I was asking, "How the heck am I supposed to pray all day long?" Thinking and thinking and thinking about it. I can't freaking do that, I am busy. I don't have the time to pray all day long. Seriously, again, kind of throwing my hands in the air. And then, all of a sudden, I realized. Wait a minute, I AM praying all day long. DING, DING, DING, DINGGGGG. Let's just say another light bulb turned on.

Where does that leave us? It takes us right back to the fact that we become blinded by our THINKING, or we don't get the full picture! We are not PRESENT! Awwwwww crap, It's ON ME! DAMMMIT, I just wanted someone to fix it for me, I didn't want to have to do it myself! HAH! Another wake up call, I had to take responsibility! This was much more serious than I thought. Oh, and what about those "bad" thoughts? I better get myself some new goalie mitts and catch those darn things! Not that I am an evil person or something, not at all, just knowing this kind of paints a little different picture in your mind. All kinds of silliness surges down through the mind stream! Yikes. LOL

Key distinction here, just to be as clear as day: "I" as the Higher "SELF" am differ-ent than the lower "selves". Higher SELF is the one with the skills! It is our lower "selves" that get in the way. When we act as the "selves" we get in our own way. Too much clutter in the mind, most of which IS the "selves"! Too many captains trying to right the ship, insurrection, rambunctiousness and even foolishness. No daydreaming either, if you are going to do it, do it right! The lessons are right in front of us, but we don't see them because we are too distracted, or looking in the wrong direction, and our ears are clogged! We are either preoccupied, frozen in fear, wearing rose colored glasses towards the future or trapped by some menacing thought from the past. These are examples of when we are literally BLIND to the moment, and incapable of hearing and seeing properly. It happens all the time! We are incapable of growth because while we are blind, in that lightning strike of a moment, we cannot see what needs to be seen, and we cannot hear what needs to be heard! We have bad information, because we are NOT present to do the hearing or do the seeing! Former me or future me, as the lower "self" has stepped in and made a choice for me, and inevitably, in that moment some version of my little "selves" that are battling it out in the mind has won. THIS TIME. Do not reach back and BLAME that former self, rather, understand that that version of self was INCAPABLE of anything else. FORGIVE IT, and by all means do it with the understanding on why! Why, because #1 it couldn't hear or see right due to its filters, it was looking at an illusion, and/or it was in the past or future. And #2 without forgiving it, you will carry it forward to the next moment and that version of self will step in and make that very same decision, that very same choice the next time and you will have lost the moment again, and again growth cannot occur. SO, IT BUILDS UP, it accumulates! Why? Because we are missing the lessons! **Growth ONLY occurs in the moment** and we were not there, **we were not present!** These lessons, these "understandings" are written all through the various religions, and also distorted in all kinds of ways, but this is the TRUTH. This is how you can step above that level of mind and HEAR as Jesus did, SEE as he did...but it takes effort and concentration, and most of all PRESENCE with AWARENESS. Without it, we are just dumb driven cattle... walking the same paths, as they do...trudging them over and over again. Does that sound like fun, running into the same walls and ceilings over and over again? These paths in the mind become worn, as we trudge them, over and over...and it becomes our comfort zone. Is that YOU? Didn't think so.

The readings really make you think though. Such as this one:

*John 14:12 "Very truly I tell you,*
*whoever believes in me will do the works I have been doing,*
*and they will do even greater things than these,*
*because I am going to the father"*[60]

Why on earth would Jesus say this if it were not true? Doesn't this make you ask some serious questions? For instance, where am I drawing limits? He did some incredible things! How?

These are the questions, and understandings that got ME fired up, and that in turn gave me the energy I needed to move through the chart from Chapter 10. Emotion packs energy, don't avoid it, ignore it, or bury it, USE IT...and be sure to use it in a positive way, as described! Going back to that original diagram, whenever you "NEED" a certain thing, or result, or whatever to feel good, or be happy, that need can prevent a flow state. The need is a requirement, meaning the alternative, or it's opposite is completely unacceptable. That dynamic in the mind creates resistance at the "edge" of that alternative which is the equivalent of FEAR. Resistance is persistence, what we resist persists...and this is why! FEAR will attract what it is focused on, even if it is in our unconscious...in fact, particularly when it is in our unconscious! **Jesus** said specifically:

## "RESIST NOT EVIL"[61]

Again, why did he say this? It is a VERY powerful message, once truly understood. If you really take the time to investigate, it makes perfect sense. Resistance, conscious or unconscious, is still resistance! Resistance = a magnet! That is why we need to increase our awareness, so it is not in our unconscious anymore and can't magnetize us to what we don't want! So, instead of flip flopping between arousal and control, which pushes us into a flow state, we are flip flopping between anxiety and worry. (Low skill / high challenge on the chart) Why would that be true if we think we have the skill? We may think, or even know what to do, but be incapable because the anxiety and worry will not allow the skill level to show up in us to demonstrate it in the moment. If its unconscious, we don't even see it and if we don't see it, we don't get the opportunity to correct it. (We are not present) Even though we may be very close to having that level of skill, the SKILL needs to evolve from the focus on worry/fear (negative outcome, negative visualization, the mind in fear = RESISTANCE) to a state of FLOW or very close to it. This is where we are able to stay present, awake, and aware in the positive expectancy quadrants / states...ALLOWING...as the over SEER / higher "SELF", in the ZONE! That's where we are ACTING AS the CEO using the skill. We can SEE, unfiltered, and more balanced, and when we see the resistance, we can let it go! DONE! No more magnet!

Resist not evil isn't just some general recommendation, nor is it incomprehensible like a parable. It's not just a good idea to consider lackadaisically, or sometimes when we think it matters. That just isn't going to get it done. Once again, this is one of those things that comes into play with just about everything, if not EVERYTHING! I think back to what I thought about this statement when I was younger. I basically blew it off because it just didn't make sense, I didn't understand what it was that was being advised or what to do with it. I was like, yeah right, whatever, and of course went about my business! At the surface level, resist not evil doesn't seem to make whole lot of sense, until dissected. At least it didn't to me years ago! I had to dig deeper, back up, and really think about it, the nuts, and bolts, to understand how impactful it is.  Where actual progress is made is when we really do understand the logic behind this brilliant advice at a deeper level, then it becomes actionable! Eliminating resistance as a mind pattern with awareness is a literal prescription that removes DIS-ease and restores balance! It is guidance at the highest level that truly gets to the root of the problem! The reason it is so important is that the disease is in the MIND and how <u>IT</u> is reacting to life!  Poor patterns of thought, poor processing, vantage point issues, lack of awareness, lack of balance, and finally, lack of PRESENCE! Once understood, we will literally INVITE situations where we have been resistant in order to see how, when, where, and how much the resistance is affecting us so that we can be cured, or "delivered from" its nasty consequences (Evil), quite naturally. Once seen, and understood, resistance can be LET GO! It has to be seen first though. Once seen, it's like an intracranial operation done with awareness...to release it! We can see it coming and walk right through it. It vanishes like a mirage.

The brain in an anxious state cannot perform at that higher level though, it is im possible...the energy, or the "selves" overload the system! From this lower mindset the resistance can't be seen, the mind apparatus from a functional standpoint shuts down. It's like an invisible mutiny within that overwhelms us, and whoosh, in a flash, our attractor factor is negated! The processor gets jammed, or the circuits gets tripped, and we get taken out of the moment! Funny, that it is right at the <u>gate</u> to NOW, we are taken out, neg<u>ated</u>...kind of a play on words, but very real! It's very much like we missed the virtual detour sign inside the mind, and we unknowingly just took the detour out of habit or unawareness!  Our programming got in our own way. We were supposed to be awake to see that virtual sign, and "proceed with caution" energized by it, so that we could grow through the moment. The problem here is that the detour sign was not seen, recognized, and basically "considered" with awareness...so it wasn't able to be used as a catalyst. We were unavailable to be guided by it, to perform, momentarily. The unfortunate result in these scenarios is that the energy overwhelms the system instead of optimizing it and maximizing it. The immaculate perception didn't happen! We take the detour, shut down, or the mind shuts down, and the FLOW is interrupted. It can happen in a flash! That is, ultimately, when you get the deer in the headlights, freezing, dropping the ball, choking under pressure, errors, and ultimately failure to attain the desired result. The brain in an anxious state operates from a completely different place, the mind has basically been seized! Once that toggle is flipped, we go into "fight or flight" mode via the "detour". The processor is essentially shut down and we are no longer in "control" of thought or the peripherals which the mind controls! We are no longer our highest "SELF"! People say that all the time, right? I don't know what happened, I wasn't myself! I don't know why I did that, said that, reacted that way! Easily understood really. They were "out of their mind", momentarily, GET BACK IN THERE, with PRESENCE! When emotions get involved, the mind is vulnerable, it often gets hijacked more easily. So, it is in these times that we must be ever vigilant, and AWARE!

Higher "SELF" control, especially in moments like this is easier said than done, right? It's not going to happen from a lazy unattended mind, I promise you that! We have to be able to manage that massive influx of energy, adrenaline and focus HARD to stay present. These are the moments where we may feel the energy creeping in, maybe anxiety, or even full-on fear. Often times there can be a mix of positive and negative energy too, so it is tougher to decipher. It's basically like the energy needs to be used to process the energy, but there are times where it comes in so fast, with so much oomph that it catches us off guard too. Positive and negative. Either way, we can't do it from overwhelm! The energy must be processed, channeled, and made available. It is in these exact times that we must amplify our skill to stay present and see this moment through, with every ounce of awareness we can muster, watching the mind from every angle as we step forward and THROUGH that event / situation / resistance! That takes practice, to regulate this incoming energy, NOT TURN, not shut down, not avoid it, or deflect it. With extreme focus, awareness synthesizes all of the available energy, and then integrates and optimizes that energy for use. With practice, and an unwavering bedrock of attention, the marriage with energy pushes us into a FLOW state where that energy is optimized, maximized, and used with precision and expertise! When we are in a flow state, or even close to it, we are staying in the more positive expectancy quadrants which include arousal (Energy), relaxation, control, and then FLOW.

Stop here and think about this for a moment though. Arousal, and relaxation don't ordinarily go together, do they? In other words, arousal means a heightened senses, more energy, which in a lot of cases will make us TENSE UP! This is that critical juncture we must RISE UP, sometimes WAKE UP, and maintain control to see the moment through with presence. Instead of tensing up we see that tendency arising within us and instead of allowing that energy to "RESIST", and turn us, we use it to AMPLIFY OUR PRESENCE!

ENERGY MUST BE USED effectively, or we will more likely be ABUSED by it. Resistance, as an energetic reaction, will invite what we don't want. That often means more pain, and even more resistance, which is what creates the cycles. With awareness we can eliminate this magnet and see it through to a better result. That is mighty change, robust lessons learned, and commanding power gained!

When you reach the flow state, that is PRESENCE! Awareness channels that energy and focus to give us that final push into FLOW, The ZONE where we "ALLOW" without attachment, without resistance. Resistance attracts the opposite result because first it trips our circuits and then because it took us out of the moment, it generates an automated response, from the "selves". So rather than a jammed processor and no decision, or a jammed circuit and an automated response from the selves with a magnet that is headed towards the opposite of what we want, our mind is now PRESENT and ABLE to process in the moment! Said differently, without all that "weight on our shoulders" so to speak, carrying our past with us into the present via the "selves", which also flips the toggle, we are once again FREE to choose, free to perform at higher levels, from a better version of "SELF" not limited by previous thoughts, previous "selves" and what they may have done previously. The patterned mind is developing a "NEW GROOVE" so to speak and not following the same beaten path, like dumb driven cattle. We have CHOICE. When the toggle is flipped, or the circuit is jammed we do not have choice. The mind is locked up. The gate is latched, the moment is unavailable. Presence can't happen. With this new insight, and our highly developed skill, it is like the best of all worlds, complete and utter relaxation in an energetic and highly focused state. What does your body and / or mind do when it really focuses and drills in on something? Did it "tense up"? In football, as a receiver, that's the equivalent of "stone hands" and dropping the ball. As coach, it is a "delay of game" penalty or calling the wrong play. At work, with a deadline, this is the equivalent of "STRESS". With this perspective, it is that proverbial deep breath, sigh and a big breathe out...a peaceful, relaxed focus, with skill, and precision. YOU GOT THIS! FEEL it, KNOW it, LIVE IT! Talking about it isn't good enough, you must BE IT!

I know I have said this before, but I am trying to convey it in different ways, so it is understandable. Once again, you can be intense, you can WANT to WIN and you can GO FOR IT, all day long every day. Just pay attention to where you are operating from. Are you "stressed"? WHY? Change the thought, the underlying "TONE", to a more positive relaxed and open "expectancy" frame of mind as an example! Make sure YOU are in that STATE, using the skill, and present to make the choices! It matters that you pay attention to what is going on "out there", sure it does, but it is also important to pay attention to what is going on "IN HERE", inside you, in your mind, in your heart of hearts as all of that is happening "out there". To put it one more way, and this may be a stretch for some people, if you are in the bottom & left quadrants, you are more or less OUT OF TOUCH! It is virtually impossible for you to act in your own best interest. Your brain is essentially disconnected from your heart and what matters to you. Snap out of it, get up, do something, and make a mistake...laugh at yourself, it will be healthy! As I said, I laugh at myself a lot these days...maybe that's strange, I get reminded of these lessons, and it is productive! It's better than the other alternatives, too, like not getting the lessons. LOL Small situations, it is easier to manage the presence, and the energy....so sometimes that is why people say baby steps. Sometimes if you bite off more than you can chew it puts you right back in the box, in fear, but with understanding and practice it gets easier!

I know that the whole baby steps scenario does not sound very encouraging...for sure, I get it. I prefer to be positive too...but I bring it up for a reason, because I have been there! Uh Oh, story time. ha-ha! I wrote it out the day it happened. Good news though, I already told you the story. Remember the slow-motion trade? I knew what to do but was incapable of doing it. I was so fearful of the alternative that all I could do is attract what I didn't want. In fact, I saw it happen in real time, right in front of my own eyes, with awareness, all the way up to right before the thief (old me) jumped in and made the decision as me for me. It happened without the REAL ME having the capability to override that thought/decision! It happened like a lightning bolt, in slow motion, time almost stood still, and there went the moment...THAT MOMENT was a turning point for me. I SAW IT as it happened!!!! It told me and even showed me what happened, in that moment, because I was actually 100% present to see it and then I watched it happen again and again, it was very odd, it was as if time was slowing down for me to see this phenomenon! I knew and I could even SEE why it happened and from that moment on, I knew I had to change course. Total eye opener for sure...and I was in AWE, I had identified the problem, and it was ME! At that time, there was a part of me that was really angry at myself, which converted to feelings like: disgusted, frustrated, and annoyed! What's that? Resistance...uggggh! Someone still had some learning to do.

What I didn't know at that time was that it was the beginning of a pretty lengthy process of discovery...or baby steps. Had I only known then what I know now, the learning process would have been a lot smoother and easier, probably a lot shorter too. I saw the issue, and I was determined to eliminate this limiting factor within me! I saw it, but at first, I didn't really know what to do about it. What I did do was take the next step to learn, and slowly but surely, with a lot of effort, I turned over stone by stone, and each revealed a new insight! At first it wasn't a whole lot of fun, in fact, it was painful to work through it...and IT WAS WORTH IT! Not all lessons are right at the surface, sometimes you have to dig a little, and in this case, I had to do a lot of digging to get to the core of the problem. I knew it was ME, but I had to really understand it at my CORE! On top of that, I needed to be FREE from it.

**"You will never be FREE until you free yourself from the prison of your own false thoughts!"**
**-Phillip Arnold[62]**

**"Men are not prisoners of fate, but only prisoners of their own minds"**
**-Franklin D. Roosevelt[63]**

OK, quiz time. ha-ha. Playing of course, but seriously, what does this in us...what limits us, and resists or avoids these needed changes? What is it that creates and then reinforces the walls that imprison us? More importantly, how do we break FREE? I did figure that out over time...while painful, it was the UNDERSTANDING that I needed! It is the EGO, and what is the ego but these false "selves" I refer to repeatedly! The discovery was that over and over again, I was the problem, and I saw it! I was now conscious of the fact that I was unconsciously allowing these "selves" to run my life, unmonitored and unsupervised. LOL. But really not funny, because "I" was the problem! I was consistently "RE-acting" as the "selves" vs making a new decision and taking a new ACTION.  Once SEEN, I couldn't unsee it...and these "selves" were a TRUE education! It was as if a whole new game had just started, I was seeing through new eyes, stuff I had never seen before, stuff I was BLIND to previously! WOW, what an eyeful...what I saw was mind boggling! Not only did I see stuff I never saw before but I heard things too, it was as if I had ears that just got new filters and they were filtering out all the "noise", the garbage! My life took a major turn, it was like a new life, and again, I literally began to see lessons in EVERYTHING! Not only in myself, and the lessons I was missing previously, but outside too... Billboards, license plates, songs, lyrics, movies, signs, literature, emails, books, stuff people said just hit me differently. I could go on and on. It was like the whole world just lit up.

Bottom line, we are doing it to ourselves, we create the prison bars, walls, and limits...but we don't see it while it is contained / disguised in these storylines. The EGO has these "self" driven attachments / programs & motives, and they are contained within these stories, and it cherishes them!

### The "cherishing" of and / or BELIEF IN these various storylines is what gives them the power to turn you!

This makes for some fairly substantial EDGES! That's the weight, that's the "rub", and the EGO sells these stories with very saleable mind imagery, because it knows our triggers, IT IS OUR TRIGGERS...and so we buy in! SUCKER-RRRRR! Didn't see the detour sign, did you? HAHA! We get caught up in the story and these storylines become entrenched in the mind gearing, so things can't change. We can't change because deep down at the core level, we don't want to, as the "selves". The EGO does not want its stories to change! Its desire is to continue being the "you" in the same story, good or bad, doesn't matter to the EGO! The little "selves" are always jockeying for control, to become and STAY "you" and that becomes the blinding factor I keep mentioning. It doesn't even have to be true if the mind is bought into it! Like an imaginary wall, it's the virtual detour sign. We go right up to it and turn, even though it's not really there! Regardless, if true, or false, good, or bad, it wants to keep the story going, and that story is a wall in the house of you, an EDGE! Telling yourself the same old stories adds some pretty paint, some decorative molding, and maybe even some nice artwork! At the end of the day, we grow to really like that darn wall even if it is a LIE and the wall is an eyesore! We may have told ourselves the same garbage so many times that we now believe in that crap! Change is fearful for the EGO and when we are acting through EGO, as the "selves" we avoid it or resist it. I saw that happening REAL TIME! I was literally getting in my own way!

Fast forward 8 years or so from that initial moment of insight, and a lot of "processing", here I was contemplating the moment that changed everything...and my thoughts at that juncture:

1. **NO LONGER SEEK CERTAINTY, safety and security are overrated and will never come to pass without TRUST, trust is LOVE in the moment.**

2. **Step into a willingness to NOT KNOW. To not "CONTROL". Stay Balanced!**

3. **FUNDAMENTAL TRUST allows wisdom (Higher**

"SELF"/GOD/LOVE) to be present...undistorted by FEAR and DESIRE!

4. Profound evolutionary capacity exists in the moment... not in the future or the past... Change only happens NOW, and NOW...and NOW!

5. LIVE from a consciousness of possibility, or amaze-ment...awe...ABUNDANCE vs LIMITATION, each will bring its likeness to your life, your choice!

6. Comfort zones are for people that are FEARFUL, FEAR brings what is feared into your life...don't succumb to fear...be amazed at life instead!

7. Accept uncertainty with open arms, welcome it, thrive in it find JOY in it...and watch the world change right in front of your eyes.

8. Instead of watching your lower "self" tell the same sob stories, "POOR ME"[64] and allowing it, learn the lesson that enabled that sob story to exist in the first place, the energy patterns that drive it... ("poor me" is one among other energy dynamics that are explained in The Celestine prophecy, by James Redfield)

9. Watch the EGO change its mind, every time a decision is made. That's NOT YOU! WAKE UP!

10. Black and white both exist. SEE, understand, and LOVE them both!

AND THE BONUS #11:

### You cannot be who you were, and who you intend to be at the same time!

The student was ready, and he learned some incredibly valuable lessons in that 8 year span...still learning and sharing them, as much as I can! So, lets talk about how it can go a lot better for you, and how you can get the lessons without the extended tour through pain, or at least by minimizing it! The short version is, SEE THE DETOURS...and go straight instead! The extended tour through pain is what happens when you take each detour. Sounds simple enough, right? The mind will create endless detours. The detours take us away from growth. We need to become NEW, each and every moment. The EGO doesn't want that! The lower "selves" don't want that, so they resist it, by default! What does this mean? It means that we need to see and even FEEL the fear / resistance and instead of taking the recommended detour that the mind suggests, take the next step forward, THROUGH IT. Take the RISK, the risk is to grow through this moment and become new. New means BEING NEW, being this higher and best SELF that you've never been before. This is the NEW YOU! It requires stepping into the unknown for just a hot second...can you do that? C'mon, its just 1 second, you got this!

In order to BECOME and BECOME...and BECOME... **GET IN THE MO-MENT**, it is the only place to advance from an unbiased / impartial observer perspective and be NEW! It is the only place where **YOU CAN BE GUIDED!** Seriously, read that again until you really GET IT! The Universe, GOD, or whatever you personally want to call it, your higher "SELF", Jesus...the still small voice, **it guides IN THE MOMENT**...It is your job to get there to receive that guidance. In fact, I came up with an acronym for myself that helped me to think about this properly. GGITM: God Guides In The MOMENT...or GO GET EM, go git em! Kind of a fun and encouraging way to think about it anyway. Feel free to use it if you like! I feel like it is just that little push, to get me going, puts the wind at my back with a great attitude! Use it to make that next step forward, into the moment!

The alternative, of course, is to NOT be in the moment. I can assure you that if your mind is in the past or future you will be just as **Jesus** described. You have ears but cannot hear, eyes but cannot see!

> **This is why I speak to them in parables, because seeing they do not see,**
> **and hearing they do not hear, nor do they understand!"[65]**

FEAR and DESIRE and the stronger emotions will take you over every time, turning off the logical part of the mind, taking you OUT OF THE MOMENT where you will be blind, deaf, and controlled by previous versions of self, prior programming, and incapable of "EVOLVING". GROWTH, or evolution ...CHANGE...takes place in the moment, else you will be blinded by your "selves", the ones that are patterned and want to remain you. They are the EGO's stories, coming to pass, digging in and wanting their comfort zones. They want things to stay the same, even if they are BAD...believe it or not. Call it karma, magnetism, the law of attraction, whatever...the longer you stay in your self-created prisons the more energy it requires to tear down the bigger walls you created. The moral of the story is don't build the walls to begin with!

## PAST=comfort zone, patterned thinking, biases, your stories, programming= EGO driven, and can be FEAR BASED!

## FUTURE= whatever you let in your imagination... projections of your stories, outcomes, DESIRE=Trying to "CONTROL"=EGO driven and includes overexcitement as well as the FEAR of the opposite!

Once we define either of these and become attached to the amazing picture and the imagery that we just drew for ourselves in our mind, the EGO grabs it, plants it, fertilizes it, waters it, shines it up, decorates it and lets it have full control to grow crazy strong roots...IN OUR MIND! What happens next? It becomes a big OAK TREE, and we love it! I can't get rid of that gorgeous tree, look at it, its beautiful! In fact, don't even think about trimming it. Change is difficult for the EGO, it doesn't like it, not at all, even if your tree is a pathetic looking overgrown monstrosity! Resisting and avoiding change is one of the EGO's favorite pass times! It passes time by taking you on detours, distractions, and endless shenanigans! Did you ever consider that the mind is not the friend you think it is? I should actually clarify that to say that the lower "selves" in the mind, may not be the friends you think they are. In fact, the mind is just the processor, so garbage in garbage out, right, the ego selves just aren't feeding it good data! Situationally, they may even fertilize or FEED the weeds...

**LESSON KEY: DREAM...and while doing so...question the motives of the mind(ego selves) THOUGHT!**

Is what this is telling me to do in my best interest, or not? Is this going to move me in the direction of my dreams, or am I stepping sideways or even backwards? I must take the step, I get that. NOW I am going to concentrate, pay attention, and make sure I know where it is taking me! Is this a distraction, a detour, or a productive and beneficial thought / action? Should I listen to it, or should I come up with a better more positive idea? Where did this thought even come from, holy moley, did I just think that? It might be an eye opener here and there! Just watch! Oh, and lookout for the kick back the mind (EGO) gives you. It is truly entertaining for a while, but then you realize... wait, I am supposed to be learning something here. LOL. So, then you get more serious and look for the lesson in it, behind it! For this lesson key, there are several songs that come to mind that are very relevant:

**RUSH, "Mission"**[66]. This song basically says to me; DREAM and BE WATCH-FUL...just as I have been describing, this is just a fun way to hear it in a song. Check out the lyrics again, they are very insightful, there is much to be learned from this song! Once you are well into the "mission" then listen to **"Second Nature"**, another **RUSH** song, it will be much more easily understood. Second nature is melancholy, the understanding of it all is kind of a different "tone"! One of the segments in the song is really telling, it talks about too many rapids and too many captains. That is, in my opinion, referring to the lower selves. Really powerful lyrics! The "selves" feed their own flames, and we let them, until we don't! Check out the song for FUN!

**Within Temptation "Entertain You"**[67]. Really funny song and video. Watch the video! My take is that It is truly a brilliant depiction of the disguises the EGO wears to try to fool you, and it is totally played out in the video and lyrics! That's what I see anyway. So cool, I applaud the band, this is amazing, and it makes me laugh! Pay close attention again to the lyrics too, super powerful to understand the EGO and its mind "games"! As life goes on, the stakes do get higher, and sometimes that means the EGO has to experience some pain, for the greater good. The higher "SELF" sees this, and as it implies in the song, YOUR FREEDOM IS AT STAKE! Once you see from this perspective, YOUR FREEDOM will be undefeated too! So, let's talk more in depth about FREEDOM!

# FREEDOM

## GETTING IN THE ZONE V

W ITH THE CONSTANT FLOW of data in our world which seems to come at us faster every day, we are challenged with information overflow. I know, as if all that wasn't enough, right? Here we go piling on one more thing. It's a real issue, so it is important for us to manage this data flow so that it is not bogging down the system. (Our mind) When we get really drilled down on the details, it can become a bit overwhelming to process everything that's going on, because it's coming at us so fast! We can often fail to see the bigger picture OR focus on details when this happens, especially if we are juggling a lot of different things. In order to maintain more of a "field awareness" AND relaxed focus, try to keep a constant connection to this higher "SELF" vantage point as the over SEER! This oversight perspective allows you to act as a virtual traffic director above the mind, as the "CEO", with a super powerful highly optimized filtration and energy management system! The filter that I am talking about is not only the data itself though, but also of the "selves"! They want to direct your attention towards different things, and then once they captivate you, you are locked into processing that data, or engaged in a side battle between them. This is a very important distinction because this skill allows you to cut the data feed off at the source. This is the same skill you are mastering, and it is within from above if that makes sense. It gets better and better as you let go of the "stuff" that no longer serves you! This is a great way to create more freedom and remove the "stress" associated with data overload by managing it a little bit more assertively! It sounds like it would be more stressful, but it actually has quite the opposite effect and brings about more of a calm, focus...like energized, tranquil, observation even while performing tasks! It's hard to put it in words, but here is a bird's eye view of the way I see that from the overseer perspective.

**Bird's Eye View, as overseer:**

1. It enables YOU to SEE where the selves WANT to direct your attention "Out there", and YOU can choose whether to allow that or not. This alone will eliminate a lot of needless and unproductive distractions which saves you time and energy straight away! In addition, by CHOOSING to prioritize, and not engage with distractions, whatever they might be, it minimizes peripheral data inflow "in here" which naturally optimizes the processing, which also gains you TIME!

2. Directing your FOCUS is highly relevant to and optimizes task performance / task management by distributing energy towards the skills that are needed in that moment. This allows the data processor to process and perform efficiently, with optimal power, focus and energy. Tasks get done faster in a relaxed manner without residual inefficiencies that would normally bog you down and add stress, so this naturally has a calming, commanding effect! You feel more in control of your SELF!

3. The SKILL enhances the tuning IN and FOCUSING, while it is also managing the energy distribution and peripherals! Full on SELF COMMAND. Envision a car moving forwards, but you also have side and rear cams as well as one hovering about 20 ft above the car like a tracking drone, so you can see the whole road. The details are totally dialed in, while the SELF has not disconnected from AWARENESS. So, you have a multi focus lens with a peripheral filter as well, and a protection GUIDE! This also has a calming effect because we can see the whole picture, KNOW that all is well, and we are not missing something! ALL GOOD!

4. As all of this is going on "out there", the other part of the skill is managing the view "in here", WITHIN. The selves are all jockeying for CONTROL. YOU are overseeing everything they do, and what they want to do, all of it! This requires real time scanning and highly attuned radar for all types of programs that these selves want to run towards and away from...some are good, some bad. Some are just plain malicious, and some corrupt too. In addition, they get sidetracked, and want to project stuff onto the mind screen, which would ordinarily take you out of the moment, this is monitored very meticulously. So, this oversight acts as a distraction prohibitor, virus protection, and it also has an eye out for other suspicious programs. We are VERY selective with what we ALLOW in this state and by eliminating these diversions, attention is

channeled and maintained in the NOW! This tends to keep you out of trouble, and things running smoothly!

5. Lastly, the skill has some automated warning lights to monitor the internals in real time, and alerts set up so that the system knows when to reset the filters or do a reboot.

    a. If something flips a switch.

    b. If a circuit gets tripped.

    c. The system went off course and is stuck in the past.

    d. The system went off course and is stuck in the future.

    e. The system is desperately low on energy, in danger of a shut down.

    f. The Skill was inadvertently turned off or ran out of energy.

    g. The system is over optimistic.

    h. The system is being over critical, like analysis paralysis.

    i. The system is over pessimistic.

    j. There are thousands of alert and warning lights, these are just a few.

That's my basic model. I am sure we could come up with thousands of additional functions, but you get the jist! I wish it had a "How many miles left" indicator, like on my car. Hahahaha. In all seriousness though, just like your computer, the more processing power you have, the faster and better your machine will work! Consider this your data and energy management system, be vigilant and watchful WIDE AWAKE, AWARE, and PRESENT!! There are most definitely some software programs running that you'll want to "uninstall" once you SEE them, and what they do, or what they want to do!

Be deliberate! On top of managing and filtering current information as detailed above, try to prioritize based on YOUR LIFE, needs & "stuff", NOW. Make a conscious effort to release or LET GO of both the past and the future in particular, to the extent that you can.  This will free up MUCH needed space. Stand above them and watch as the virtual storylines play out in the mind and notice the "tense". This virtual movie theatre in the mind is kind of running in the background a lot of the time and hogging up space as well as processing power. Notice also that this will draw up emotions, possibly tension, sadness, "stress", fear, relative to what's being broadcast on the mind screen, again chewing up energy. This can be going on as you are trying to process new information too, so it bogs you down which translates to more time lost on the same chore, and errors. The mind movies can be truly entertaining as depicted in the video from the lesson in the last chapter, so they will grab your attention from time to time. Pay attention, when you do get sidetracked like this, as to where your mind is being taken, past or future? Note trends, and themes, and how long it takes for you to regain your focus! Also notice the lost energy, and bodily reactions to it. As you gauge and prioritize what is important, and what's just "NOISE", it will allow you to RELEASE and LET GO of more and more "stuff" that is just not necessary. This includes information, scripts, themes, software programs, and "apps"! A lot of it is senseless, not necessary, and simply a distraction, so it can be eliminated. This will be a progressive and ongoing self-maintenance operation that is constantly optimizing your skills, as well as managing energy use & preservation! Some patterns and programs are a little more difficult to completely let go, but over time it is freeing up more and more needed space as well as optimizing the current systems! Bottom line, we sample a lot of software, and a lot of it doesn't work. Its high time we just let it go and uninstall it to free up some bandwidth. Lastly, we employ the old data dump! We carry a lot of useless information around, we see it and let it go more easily. Cleaning out the mind closets, from our old "hoarder" days will also free up an incredible amount of space! It's amazing how much "stuff" we accumulate after living in one place for a while, yikes! Doesn't it feel good to purge? How good do you feel after decluttering your home, room, cleaning out your closet, car, or garage? Another cool thing is once you clean it out, you want to keep it clean! After all of that, shazaam, bright and cheery, with massive processing power...a beautiful shiny and clean NEW YOU! YOU are maximizing space to optimize and energize your SKILLS app, which will run more efficiently as a result! As the skill develops, the process itself becomes more efficient too, it is constantly happening in the NOW, so each and every moment is a progressive optimization real time!

What's left after a lot of processing, in the moment, is a quiet, finely tuned & hallowed mind unattached to previous failures, stumbling blocks, and unconcerned whether the future works out the way one might like it to. It's like a breath of fresh air! This is possibly your first opportunity in a while to actually be present to enjoy your life, with some PEACE OF MIND for just a moment, regardless of what is currently taking place. Take a really deep breath and ENJOY IT! I would venture to say that this is freedom, you might even call it FREE WILL or happiness! Feel it, and ANCHOR THAT FEELING! Freeing your mind is truly liberating, everything feels better!!!! It lightens the load, and it honestly makes you feel like you are carrying less weight around! Your CORE is lighter, and brighter as a result. It is easier to just smile for no reason! It seems like there's less weight on the sides of your lips. You are going to be smiling so much that people will think you are up to something, I am not kidding. Sometimes, I'll think of something, like a cool lesson because I just saw something and so I literally chuckle out loud. If someone just happened to be standing there, in a store or something, you get some interesting "looks"! LOL, I guess they probably think I am NUTS! The fact is, I just noticed or saw something that reminded me of a lesson or something insightful, and it made me smile with appreciation for having just been shown that lesson again. Did you happen to notice something with this statement though? I said lesson, and chuckle...not lesson and PAIN!

As you continue to develop this SKILL, YOU will notice more and more things, some you know already which reinforces the lesson, and some you never noticed before, as they bubble up to the surface of the mind to be "processed". With presence and awareness, you will have the ability and choice to able to hold onto them or process and let them go. At this stage, your skill and discretion are getting much more powerful! Using this SELF COMMAND allows you to focus on what is truly important to you and gives you the calm confidence to move forward. In fact, it gets you excited to take that next step. So, you tend to stop wasting time in deliberations, and procrastination.

Finally, with all this FREEDOM you have just created, and without all the distractions, YOU are primed and ready. You are in a position to make a really important connection if you haven't done so already. Take this very influential, and emotional step very deliberately though! STOP, maybe even close your eyes for a minute to LISTEN, deeply, to your core...and connect to your HEART! This may take some time and effort, particularly if you have ever been "heart-broken", so a minute may be an hour or even a day, week, or month. That needs to be "processed", so that the connection can be established, or re-established! There is or was a connection here, at one time, and if it is shut down, the system is missing / filtering out critical information. This is an important and necessary integration, so do your best! This will get easier over time, so don't worry if you have difficulty with this in the beginning. The progression of this working model is building trust, and this does not need to be forced, nor can it be, it will happen quite naturally.

From this point forward, just keep a little mind sticky note or something on your "To do" itinerary to try to make and maintain this connection periodically throughout your day. The intention with this is to ensure we are in touch with our CORE priorities, as well as FEELING, and add this BASE connection to our skillset, permanently! First, make the connection, then work on the always part! Once this is initiated, then it can be calibrated over time. The difference is a move from SKILL power to WILL POWER. The difference being that one is connected to your heart, the other is not! This will enhance your ability to notice first, and then monitor and fine tune the emotional circuits. Without willpower, and oversight, these can get overloaded very quickly, which affects EVERYTHING, and we just can't have that! They are responsible for many different emotional interpretations & feelings and can leak into the other mind zones which would affect your ability to interpret and process other data. So, it is extremely important to understand the heart dynamics as they relate to the rest of the system. We don't want to be blowing any fuses, or tripping breakers, but rather maintaining a serene composure that absorbs that surge of energy periodically and distributes it effectively, and appropriately to where it is needed!

Finally, when you are energized, awake and aware in the FLOW state, with a clear FREE MIND, acting as the over SEER, your skillset will NOW include a heart and mind that are communicating all the time, and further enhanced while you are IN THE ZONE! The complete oversight and management of the mind, as I am describing, is often termed "mindfulness" in current spiritual philosophy. By tying that into the heart it is giving you the complete picture of your thoughts, theme, and tone as well as your emotional and energetic state PRESENTLY! Your task is to constantly, NOW, attune the machine! Make, maintain, and manage all the connections! Unruffled and imperturbable...quiet confidence, or sometimes described as: "calm, cool, and collected"! If you are following the progression here, we first freed up the will, creating FREE WILL, and then we gave it power, WILLPOWER!

Pay attention as the CEO! The EGO, based on current input, tries to push, and pull you into the past and future. Just watch, from this sort of elevated / unattached vantage point with PRESENCE! YOU have the capability and freedom NOW to decide, to choose, is that something that I want to focus on right this moment? Is it important? Is there a lesson in it? What was the driver? Where did it come from, heart, mind, sight, hearing? What was the exact thought or feeling? Was this a past me, or even something that was put in there by a teacher, a parent, a sibling, or someone else? Am I seeing a sales pitch here? By seeing it for what it is, from its creation, you are seeing it early enough so that you can also see the EGO stories that are attached to it! So, as a result, you are slowly uncovering the drives, the motives, the various attachments that coincide with these storylines and where it originated from, what clues were given! Along with this come the realizations of what those attachments bring along with them, the FEAR of not having this or that, or of that storyline / that comfort zone changing, perhaps ENDING?! In essence, that is the fear of losing what you do have, even if it isn't much! Didn't the Bible say that in so many different ways? From those with little, more will be taken...and to those that have a lot, more will be given. And THIS IS WHY! In essence, we are observing / witnessing thoughts rather than being caught up in them! It is a detached witness perspective. Once we can experience life from this overseer perspective as the observer, this unattached perspective allows us to remain somewhat unaffected...it's almost like having shock absorbers as you are driving down the road because even though we see and experience the bumps, they no longer have the impact they would have otherwise. We are involved, able to engage fully, and yet we are in a much more neutral and commanding stance, so we are much more capable in the driver's seat. We are in charge, less affected by distractions, and able to steer more effectively as a result.

This is an elevated self-governing vantage point that operates from a detached, more unaffiliated, unaffected perspective. We can literally see our "selves" getting out of our own way! It's like a managerial point of view that takes it all in, and then with all the information available, sees things through as needed, "ALLOWING" life to unfold naturally as the "OVER SEER". On top of that, it's from a more peaceful demeanor, which is even better! NOW, we are FREE. Free from the "selves", such as overweighted thoughts, overweighted emotions, and unaffected by what the mind tends to think is more or less significant situationally! Notable considerations, however, FREE from these past & future selves. Life is less sticky. In other words, the negative stuff doesn't stick on us and stay there anymore, we don't drag it around. It isn't that we don't fully experience the "stuff", quite the opposite, it allows us to completely experience life, and by doing so, nothing is missed. The key element here is that the "bad" stuff doesn't latch on, like a parasite, and hitch a ride for the rest of our life. We are FREE, by CHOICE on what we choose to focus on, NOW! Presence is unattached, FREE. Free from the past, free from the future and free from the "selves"!

In my opinion, the best song that I've heard that describes this "freedom" was done by Whitney Houston. What an AMAZING artist, I mean, what a voice and presence! I still play her singing of the Star-Spangled Banner, one of the most amazing renditions I have heard. Play the video from that Super Bowl. Talk about a moment, Holey Moley! Seriously, Look it up. Thank You Whitney, rest in peace.

I know that the United States represents freedom for a lot of folks, that's not exactly the song I was referring to though, as powerful, and influential as that may be for a lot of people. Check out the lyrics and listen to the song **"One moment in time"**[68], by **Whitney Houston**. It is a really cool and powerful reflection of this dynamic in the MIND! I am not sure if this is exactly what she meant by it, but it sure seems powerful to me. She surely seized a moment at the Super Bowl singing the National Anthem! The Lyrics seem pretty clear assuming you went and looked them up. Thank you, Whitney, for delivering such a powerful message :)

My take is that FREEDOM is a state that follows after all of the work! It comes when we FINALLY have the faith and confidence to take the next step because of it! We have done the work, and we have paid the price of working through ALL these painful errors, and lessons! We have paid attention to the battles going on in our own minds, thought vs. thought, and worked through them. With understanding, we realize that these problems and challenges are not solved by an opposing thought at that level, and we are NOW elevating above these conflicting thoughts. Our SKILL now includes STEPPING UP and BEING above ALL opposing thoughts all together. We are seeing the battle with clarity for what it is, and with presence we are leaving these thoughts behind at the doorway to NOW. At that point, by passing through that very narrow gate, we are FREE and WITH FREEDOM, we step into THE ZONE, the TIMELESS moment of NOW!!!! That's PRESENCE! Freedom truly defined.

If we miss it, which we will...OFTEN, take a pause, immediately, or as quickly as possible, rewind it and replay it as described in the **RUSH** song **"Vital Signs"**[69], Please look this song up, it is an amazing song that describes this process extraordinarily well, in my opinion! The warm memory chip, the way I look at it, is our MIND. We need to rewind and replay the moment that just passed in order to look at it from different perspectives, and to see what was happening in the mind if we missed something, missed the moment. GO BACK, while the chip (mind) is still warm, while we still remember, to figure out what happened, who was there and how were we taken out of that moment, WHY? NOT TO BE CRITICAL! It is to SEE that something triggered us, or got us sidetracked and maybe caused an emotion, and that emotion or whatever it was that distracted me for just a fraction of a second. In that second, in that moment, "I" was NO LONGER FREE!

What actually happened was you were taken over, distracted, by sight, sound, situation or caught up in or by an emotion or a thought / storyline...and it TRIGGERED a "RE-action" in you!! A virtual flash of lightening hit, it caught your eye, ear, or an emotion, and it blinded you for just a hot second, and then you MISSED THE MOMENT while your mind was elsewhere. An "illusion" (former you or future you) stepped in...and BAM, "IT" (the "self") became you, RE-acted as you, and in that flash took your CHOICE ability away as you missed the moment. We need to WATCH where we didn't quite measure up, didn't quite meet the moment the way we intended to. Replay that moment and figure out what happened. WHO DUNNIT!?! Ask the question, what have you done "self"? Which one of you is responsible and why'd you do it? Look back at it. Again, this is NOT to be critical of the you that you just were a few seconds ago and blame it or anything else... it is to LEARN!!!! YOU MUST BE FREE TO CHOOSE, FREEDOM IS KEY! Seeing that you were not free opens the door to understanding, and the lesson is learned.

Learn, understand, grow. This is super important. <u>What took you out of the moment?</u> Do it right after, so that you can see exactly what happened else it will happen again next time you are in that situation! What happened is you got in the way of YOU. You have to SEE IT though, so replay that moment and SEE IT, so that this higher YOU can get the lesson, else it'll happen again the next time the heat is on! Interject what could have happened, by looking at it from different angles, by making a different choice, taking a different ACTION, instead of re-acting in the same old way, you can BE a new YOU! A new action is possible for you. Again, please DO NOT be critical of the choice, DO NOT be over emotional about failing, DO IT because you want the lesson! Levelheaded, emotions in check, without "attachment". You must do this and keep doing it over and over again until you get the lesson. With persistence you will get it! Once the lesson is retrieved, absorbed, understood & processed, return to NOW and maintain your presence there, ready, and **WILL**ing, with free will, and will power!

That requires a lot of energy and stamina to do it consistently! YOU absolutely 100% NEED to guard your ENERGY because you really do NEED every ounce you can muster! Energy is the fuel that is required to be consistent with the application of this skill, because a tired mind is incapable, it makes MISTAKES! A tired mind has poor vision and hearing, the filters don't work, at least not as well! The skill basically stalls out or is MUTED because the tank ran out of gas! YOU need the tank to be full and the SKILL to be firing on all cylinders so that you can SEE and HEAR with CLARITY! You should be seeing this now, at a minimum after the fact. An indecisive, or tired mind, will flip flop around, changing its mind back n forth and is often incapable of making effective decisions. Too many little selves and not enough energy to monitor them! Often times a tired mind can have a bad attitude that is harder to shake too. On top of that, it is wishy washy, back and forth it goes in dreamland, in the false, not "TRUTH", often chasing its own tail, indecisive. Shape shifting or transforming is one of the EGO's specialties. This type of mind grabs onto one "self" vantage point to go this way, only to hop onto another "self" coat tails a moment later and reverse course. With energy, and focus, we can remain above it with awareness, and so these selves have no control, their shenanigans do not affect the higher "SELF"!

To me, it is about removing the MIND obstacles to SEE and HEAR while understanding that we can't go around them, they must be processed and LET GO! My take is that GOD is available, every second of every day. GGITM. God guides in the moment. We cannot hear or see the guidance that is available if we have not learned how to, or we lack the energy and expertise to get there and do it consistently! We miss the moment. For some people, it might be that no one has even explained this properly so that they can understand what is required, or how to do it! It's truly not their fault. Once understood, this is extremely powerful. Somewhere along the line, someone has to explain it in terms and ways that are digestible, understandable, and ACTIONABLE! That's why I wanted to share this with my family and ultimately you too!

This information is really consistent with what the various Religions are actually attempting to say, and by going through this process, we are building a really solid foundation. It is paving the way forward so that we know that our ongoing action plan is truly rock solid. Each step is building on the one before it which is further solidifying our foundation! Even with missteps, understanding is adding STRENGTH to the CORE of this foundation, and the steps we take educate us even further as we take them! We are taking the old structure, tearing it down piece by piece so that we can build it up, stronger with more up to date code, and hurricane strength components! This process feeds faith.

The structure is OUR HOUSE, and it is a house chock full of beliefs! Sometimes we need to take it back to the sub floor, or maybe even the beams to see the errors that were made in building that "room"! Now we know where to find them, HOW to find them, uncover them, EXPOSE THEM to the "light"! We see where these beliefs may be off base and know how to challenge their authenticity! With SKILL, we SEE the times where they get in the way of our faith and how that may not be supporting us in THAT ROOM and so we rebuild the house room by room!

## Faith grows as you LET GO of limiting beliefs, not gain more!

It is a process of analyzing how our rooms were built, all the garbage that has collected in them, whether that stuff support us, and if doesn't, why? This will eliminate a lot of beliefs that simply don't hold up to the "light" test! As a result, it is quieting the mind, removing distractions, endless chatter, the various versions of self, the false beliefs and programming that go with them. It is THEM that want to STEAL our life from us (EGO, false selves, our "demons"). Building a faith based "house" is about **NOT <u>RE-acting</u>** from those "LIMITED" versions of self and **ALLOWING GOD** into the moment so that we can **ACT** from a totally unbiased and UN-limited perspective. We can be in any room, at anytime, anywhere, and KNOW the truth, instantly. That is extremely powerful! Quite honestly, and quite simply this is the process of allowing unconditional LOVE access to the moment. In the moment that we do that, we BECOME the best version of ourselves, and Heaven meets Earth right here and NOW! In this MOMENT! YES, it is that **"One moment in TIME"**[70] **Whitney Houston** sung about, IMHO! Fact is, the moment is ETERNAL, ultimately timeless! At the end of the day, the truth doesn't set you free because I told you "About a truth", it is SEEING THE TRUTH for yourself that sets you FREE. YOU MUST SEE IT!

Did you ever think about why they say GOD is Love, and LOVE IS THE ANSWER? Ponder that, we will revisit this quite a bit!

**<u>LESSON KEY:</u> SEE where and when you are NOT FREE to choose! Why? Because the truth will set you FREE!**

It is important to observe when we make choices that do not seem to be in alignment with who we've become! As we grow, that means based on LOVE. In the beginning, we just need to make better choices and when we don't, we need to see that there was a better choice available, but for whatever reason that choice didn't happen! We seem to know better and yet a "bad" choice was still made, whether it be in error, or quite simply a better choice was available and yet we just didn't see it or take it. Said differently, who we intended to be didn't quite make it through the gate to the moment where a less than stellar decision was made instead. Here are a few clues as to when a decision was possibly made by one of these more limited versions of "self". There are gazillions of these, it seems, this is just a small sample:

1. When you decided and don't quite remember making the decision clearly.

2. In hindsight it would have been made better a different way that was fairly obvious had you been paying attention.

3. You actually knew a better choice was available and yet still chose differently.

4. The choice didn't serve you or anyone else for that matter.

5. There was a better choice available, you simply didn't see it at the time.

6. You couldn't decide and delayed so long that a choice was made for you!

7. You were tired, hungry, angry, jealous, overzealous, or any other adjective. describing a state in you that prevented you from making a good decision.

8. An emotion or thought brought on a state in you that "inspired" a poor decision.

9. Fatigue, whether mental or physical, a lack of energy eliminated discretion.

10. TOP DOG: Any choice NOT inspired by LOVE in one way or another!

Remember, Love is the answer! Please understand that this list is not to be used as a mind method geared towards BLAME. We already know that doesn't work and is actually counterproductive; this is geared to LEARN! We must learn when we are being taken over by these false selves and when they make decisions on our behalf because we were not present. In these situations, we are limiting ourselves to what we were, and by NOT showing up to REPRESENT as the NEW ME, You & I miss the opportunity to make a new choice and take a new ACTION vs re-action! All this means is that in order to get the lesson, we must understand who and why we were taken over a moment ago, which caused me to miss the lesson, so that enables me to go back and grab the lesson now or get the lesson more fully the next time it resurfaces, or both! When we understand that this freedom, we are talking about, is from self-imposed limitations, we become more diligent and inspired to get the lesson and grow from it!! With understanding, we have the power to set our "selves" FREE! In fact, we WILL it to happen, we invite it to happen, like a kid on Christmas eve, anticipating the joy ahead!

The spiritual equivalent of this lesson key is just as Jesus instructed his disciples, so please think about this for a minute!

**"If you obey my teaching, you are really my disciples.**
**Then you will know the truth, and the truth will set you free"**
**Jesus, from John 8: 31-32[71]**

Do you see this? Think about it. You just saw the truth of that situation, a moment ago, right? Who did it set free? THE FORMER "you", the lower "self" that's who: "I" freed my lower "self"! The next time this situation presents itself, which it will, <u>you will be free to choose differently</u>! Free from what? The limitation of that version of "self". That self just got that limitation removed and is now UN-limited by it. Why? Because you just got the lesson, now you are FREE from that more limited self! You just freed yourself and are now UN-limited! Over and over and over again, Un-limit the "self". Over time this progression is like a snowball rolling downhill....think about all the limitations you will have grown out of after a little while. Isn't that effort worth it? NO PAIN, NO GAIN is actually false when it comes to the mind. Pain, truth be told, is optional. While we do see and maybe even feel pain when we miss lessons, the suffering part of pain is most definitely optional, from a mental standpoint.

Once you see this, and you know you blew it in a certain situation, you'll be begging for that situation to present itself again in your life so you can see it through this time! Sometimes that means you need to wait quite a while though. MAKE SURE YOU GET THE LESSON, and learn it well, so that when it does present itself again, you are READY!

To hear this message in a song. Check out **Visions of Atlantis**, **"A life of our own"**[72]. It is a fun way to hear it in a storyline fashion, IMHO. Brilliant lyrics! Once again, I can't promise this is what the band was trying to convey, and this is obviously my own interpretation, the way I see it / hear it. My take is that we all have a virtual beast within, if not many! There is also the potential for "darkness" within, so to speak, or the false "selves" as I refer to them. Life is about conquering our "demons", and / or shadow selves! Once this beast is seen, known, and we know we can handle it because we got the lesson...we actually invite it back. Once we know a truth about ourselves, it can't hurt us anymore, we don't let it! The monsters (demons, false "selves", caveman, etc.) have no power over us anymore. The Truth will set you free! That is how we gain a life of our own...<u>NO DOUBT</u>! Check out the song and band, very cool! Once we see one of these false selves take us over, and we miss a moment, we will be inviting it back in order to release it once and for all. This is basically to verify that we "understand". Its essentially digesting and proving to oneself that the lesson was learned and putting it behind us for good...being FREE from it!

## The TRUTH will set you FREE by seeing where and when you were NOT FREE!

The alternative to the song above, where they actually got the lesson, is another brilliant depiction of the whole mind operation when we don't get the lesson or choose to avoid / ignore it. Check out the song by **RUSH, "Natural Science"**[73]. Once again, the way that I hear this is my opinion, as an explanation of a process, how we can get the lessons, and what happens when we don't. Have a listen and see what you hear! If we leave a trail of lessons behind, and life goes on as it was, that means nothing changes right?! We must be honest with our "selves", but first we must SEE them and the lessons they bring, by taking that quantum leap into the MOMENT! Once you SEE where you are NOT FREE, or where you are limiting yourself, your universe has the capability to expand. By arriving to the moment, you can get the lessons and then instead of life going on as it has been, without changing, change is NOW possible! Getting the lessons ALLOWS expansion. That's my take!

The process of expansion, receiving lessons, and growing through them requires faith. The reason it requires faith is because it REQUIRES stepping into the unknown, momentarily, which is outside of our comfort zone. We can't do that without trusting that a favorable outcome is possible, if not probable. So, lets discuss faith in a much more detailed manner.

# A Chance To Explore Your Limitless Potential With Doug Giesler

South Carolina, USA
From the desk of Doug Giesler

Dear Friend,

I hope that by this point in the book, I CAN call you a friend *(just one I haven't met yet or maybe I have).*

If you're reading this, I believe you're someone who's ready to break free from self-imposed limitations and step into a life of boundless possibility.

Congratulations on taking the first step towards unlimiting your mind!

How would you like to explore what your "Limitless Potential" could truly be? That's right, even if you're already achieving great things, there's an even more extraordinary version of you waiting to emerge.

I invite a select group of individuals each month to join me on The UNLimit Breakthrough Call. This is your chance to look beyond the horizon and discover what life has in store for you when you remove the barriers holding you back.

Space is limited, so please visit the link below and enter your contact information to reserve your spot:

**BeTheInstrument.com/breakthrough**

Don't worry if you don't get invited this month. You can enter your name every month for a chance to participate. (Only ONE entry per month will be registered, and slots reset on the 1st)

For approximately 1 hour, you'll have the opportunity to work with me on:

★ *Identifying and challenging your self-imposed limits*
★ *Developing a heightened state of presence and awareness*
★ *Learning to make conscious choices that propel you towards your goals*
★ *Mastering the art of learning from mistakes without emotional attachment*
★ *Balancing your past, present, and future perspectives for optimal growth*
★ *Creating a personal blueprint for unlimiting your mind or whatever is personally imporant to you right now...*

This isn't just another call – it's going to be a true breakthrough for your personal evolution. Together, we'll explore the edges of your comfort zone and discover the extraordinary potential that lies just beyond.

Are you ready to unleash your limitless self? Join me on The UNLimit Breakthrough Call and let's break through those barriers together!

**BeTheInstrument.com/breakthrough**

Remember, the only true limits are the ones we choose to believe in. What limit will you shatter today?

Warmly,
Doug Giesler

**P.S.** *Don't let another day slip by trapped in your own limitations. The clock is ticking, and every moment you hesitate is another moment lost to mediocrity. Claim your spot on The UNLimit Launchpad Call now and start your journey to unlimited success!*

# WHAT IS FAITH I

## GETTING IN THE ZONE VI

I N THE MIDDLE OF the last Chapter, I mentioned that with this skill, we finally have the faith and confidence to move forward, take that next step. What exactly does that mean though, to have faith? I mean at a core level, deep seated faith, not just at a surface level. We hear that recommendation over and over again, right? It is passed along by almost everyone, somewhat generically. It's a good word, and it truly is a positively spirited idea. It is also worthy once it is truly understood, but from a more detailed MIND perspective, what exactly does that mean within the gearing, to have faith? I mean, other than to just have a generally positive attitude. That's good, and productive, but not what I am talking about. We hear that and we are like, yeah- yeah, whatever! I have heard that 1000 times before, right? You can almost feel the response without even looking, an internal shaking of one's head, with little to no beneficial uplifting effect as it was intended.

Have faith is almost like the universal response to everything, and it loses its meaning when delivered or heard that way. People just blow it off and they don't think it is worth the effort to even say it or hear it when it is used in a hollow, more superficial manner like that. Seriously, that is how it can be perceived as well. We can see that in the faces, tones, and demeanors that receive the message, regardless of the many different routine ways in which it is delivered. One dimensional flat delivery and limited absorption of the true meaning of "have faith" is not going to get it done. So, let's look at both sides of that statement, how it can be said, received, perceived, and "taken", whether it is absorbed, and useful, and / or when it is falling on deaf ears, "out there", as well as "in here" within! In doing so, it will help us to understand faith more deeply as we see it operate internally over time.

We will arrive at a more useful way to look at it, see it, hear it, and potentially, as a result, it will help us use it to help our "selves" as well as deliver that message in ways that are truly uplifting and beneficial to others as well. This means, with practice, understanding and using the tool ourselves, it actually does help us internally! By using it repeatedly in our lives with consistency & awareness, we are able to grasp the concepts more intimately, maybe masterfully! This is the level of understanding we need in order to enlighten those around us as to how they too can use this skill more productively. It is no longer just a word; it is a knowing that is being delivered and shared. It is invigorating, energizing, and quite a blessing to be able and willing to help people in this way, particularly the folks that are close to us. These tend to be the people we would like to help the most! As a result of knowing this experientially, when the word is spoken, we and they have deep KNOWING that it is useful, and beneficial, and the true meaning behind it. Everyone wins!

Until then though, before it is understood at that deeper level, we have some challenges to get through. This is a very complex topic. It may seem to be a simple word, but in my opinion, there is much more to it than a general attitude. Because faith is a requirement in so many situational, as well as mind type scenarios, it is going to take some time to explore this in more detail. Situationally, "Have faith" must be delivered in a way that it can be understood, integrated, and used which often requires more empathy & consideration. Typically, that means a more personal involvement, and "digging" in order to truly understand, just as it does with the "selves" within. With investigation, the lessons are underneath the face values or surface emotions. However, digging is not always possible, or wanted, when dealing with someone "out there", particularly if it is someone that we don't know all that well! We would not even know where to begin. Fact is, we do not know how they see, hear, and interpret incoming data because we all do it differently. In addition, when numb, or resistant from having been beaten up by life, or the "selves" within, the words can often fall on deaf ears, or eyes that cannot see, for example, and so they ultimately do not have the power that is needed to provide that lift to guide as it is intended to do and should. Have faith, or faith, when used as just a word, or as advice in some ways can often have a certain "tone" to it. Whether it be condescending, or otherwise, perception wise it can hit in ways that are less than useful. The perception can be that it is just BS, as an example, when people just don't believe in it. Alternatively, they may have lost it momentarily as a result of some chaos in their lives. That may mean temporarily, to some degree, or they have completely lost it. It can be perceived in other ways too, like that it is being used as a catch phrase, as a way to offload responsibility, or even to avoid being too involved, to keep one's distance, safety!

There are a lot of less than productive ways that this statement or word can be perceived that are less than optimal from the receiving end. What does that mean on the giving end? The delicate effort to help, but not "pry" into another person's business can be difficult, and there can be a tendency to want to avoid it because of these intricacies! Attitudes and EGO's get involved. Human nature right, often times that means we try to avoid confrontation, or just speak the words and get out of dodge, so to speak. It's not that the intent is not genuine, people often do want to help. The point is that there is "risk" in getting involved, in more ways than you might imagine. We live in a complex world; some folk's lives are much more complicated than others. It's not just our delicate feelings that may be affected, but it requires time, effort, energy, and much more sometimes! Let's be honest, the thought will occur in many ways, at many times, in different ways to let it go and leave it alone. I need my time and energy for my own "stuff"! I have my own issues to deal with, or something to that effect.

Certainly, in the wrong situation, or with the wrong tone, even an innocent "look" on someone's face can be perceived as malicious. The attempt to "advise", or help can be violently rejected in some cases, where EGO's get involved, and in heated situations. It is often ill advised to try to interject in this environment, certain situations are just better left alone until the stigma is gone, so to speak. Even though we may have a deep understanding and be able to explain an amazing vantage point that would help instantly the way we understand it, it just won't be heard, no less absorbed. Pick your battles, right? Good advice, we would think. In less dramatic fashion, it may simply be that "have faith" advice, or attempt to help is not digested, understood and "available" to the person that is advised to "have the faith" so it is considered a waste of time and energy. That might even mean that the effort just isn't made, which is sad! Fact is, we don't know if there will be another opportunity like this, particularly like this soon...so as always, presence is imperative. It's always a "game time decision", and the clock is ticking!

We must always be ready for what the moment NEEDS vs. what we want out of it. A casual nonchalant verbal "have faith" statement is often just not enough. Not saying it or anything at all isn't good either...so where does that leave us? I mean, either way it feels like we gave up on the other person involved, for whatever reason. That may arguably be a very valid reason too. Bottom line, giving up on someone because they just can't hear or understand doesn't feel good at all, because in essence that means they will continue to suffer, or struggle, and we know it... whether that be now, or later. Have you ever given up on your "self"? How does that feel? A lot of times, because these people are close to us, we need to watch it happen too which is equally painful, maybe more so. We could have provided a solution, but we held it in, because the last time we got our head chopped off, so to speak. Not good, that's not LOVE, nor is it an understanding of the word, faith! I find that these situations can often be revisited very quickly, before the thought is lost, and yet after the tensions have cooled slightly. It is very similar to revisiting a situational thing with a version of "self" within, that needed to learn a lesson, but may have missed it. In fact, it is very much the same! Having faith is very powerful, we know it, and we see it everywhere!

To expand on that concept a little, we are not here to be enablers, internally or "out there"! That doesn't mean we have to interject ourselves into everything out there or every situation either. That is one example where the confrontational aspect of it may turn us in the moment, and we just avoid it all together. It's tough, yes, I get it. Sometimes, it is possible, and warranted.... others, not so much. How does that work within though, to choose avoidance and not get a lesson? How does it work to choose by default to have faith in the negative vs the positive? Not so good, right? My take is that when we truly see something, we see it for a reason. Take that however you wish. It is either for us, or them...maybe both! I believe that we are all here to help one another, as well as our "selves"! The best way to learn is to teach our "selves", and then of course, we can share an experiential KNOWING! Keep in mind that this doesn't mean to JUDGE, it is intended to help when situationally, it makes sense. This can put us into very delicate situations though.

Everyone has a lower version of "self" right? That could mean a lot of things. It could be bad habits, or bad mental thought patterns. We understand now, that truly affects everything! That could mean within, or "out there". Either way, they ultimately hurt the individual and bringing it into the light of day may hurt us! It certainly will if it is within and we do not acknowledge it, right? Seems to me that once we understand something, it is the wish of the universe, or the powers that be for us to share that insight. Assuming the intent is genuinely aimed to help, and the delivery is with empathy and love, I would think it would be received with appreciation. However, that isn't always the case. Mind your own business is one of the attitudes that will inevitably come back at us. Unfortunate, but true...what is that? Resistance!

Just remember the way our EGO, and our "selves" respond in similar situations, and that sometimes these lessons don't really hit home until well after the dust settles. If someone doesn't truly understand what it means, when receiving this type of advice, "Have faith" might sound like blah blah blah...and it could almost be annoying. Right? Can you see this? In the wrong frame of mind, or in a situation where it is truly not understood in a way that is useful, it would be like putting salt in a wound, especially while tensions are high. First, unless highly diluted, salt crystals have very sharp edges...such as approaching things without empathy, or tough love for instance. It might even sting a little because it re-opens the wound, increasing the pain vs what was intended to be helpful. That's when you get the more confrontational re-actions, like get out of my face, get off my back, leave me alone, or a worse response...regardless of how genuinely we want to help. This can be true for the people really close to us as well. These experiences can set us back a little bit from time to time when the advice is not wanted, resisted, or even avoided...if not thrown back in our faces in an attempt to hurt, because they can't stand the pain of the truth. This understanding allows us to absorb it, and not reflect it back out into the world, it ends at us, period end of sentence. It's GONE at that point!

We have to revert back to empathy, and love. Understanding cannot be forced. What can be done though is having the presence of mind to call that person shortly thereafter, maybe an hour or two later, and sort of check in. At that point we can evaluate whether it might be the right time to discuss it in more detail. That is often the time when we get an apology, which opens the door to make a suggestion. "Oh, you know, _____ I meant to say earlier..." That opportunity may or may not be available, you will know! Just offering up some ideas and methodologies that work. We all need a positive uplifting spirited boost from time to time, be willing to be that person. These situations are opportunities to step up and make the world a better place because it is ever so slightly a little brighter for someone else! You have given them a boost, just when they needed it most! Not that you are doing it for yourself, but that LOVE will come back to you in spades. What you put out into your universe comes back in multiples! Do it for THEM though, that is the only way to understand the situation so completely that a valid loving response is generated! That comes from WITHIN you, with PRESENCE!

I remember a time or two when I was the receiver of such a gift. It doesn't even have to be the words, "have faith", either. It can be as simple as a look and embrace in someone's eyes that really shows a deep understanding, almost like a virtual hug and nod, when a true hug is not absolutely necessary, appropriate, or possible. It could be an action, or even just a true genuine hug of reassurance, and an offer of availability. There are always opportunities. Quickly, because it's making my eyes wet again just thinking about it, I want to show you a few examples...ones from my life that I have really appreciated because they transported me, changed me, in a moment and brightened my world.

The first one is when I was in the airport in Tennessee. My wife called me and told me that she just had to put our first dog Ranger down. He was my best friend, other than Joelle, I mean I loved that dog so much. He was my first real pet, so I am sure that you can imagine my response. I was torn apart internally. My heart was broken, and I was all alone, amongst thousands of people! I don't know whether the people that comforted me that day were angels sent by GOD himself, or just two amazing people that noticed an opportunity and understood what was needed. I was in major pain, tears were streaming down my face, and I was just in a blank stare looking out at the planes when this amazing couple came over and sat on both sides of me and put their hands on my shoulders to inquire what was wrong? They truly had no idea what they were walking into. BRAVE SOULS! I explained in very few words because I couldn't really speak words very well, that I had just lost my dog, and I couldn't stop crying. As I blurted out the words, they basically sandwich hugged me, and it wasn't just for a moment. It was the most amazing embrace that was so loving and compassionate that I have been forever grateful. While it didn't change what had happened, it was EXACTLY what was needed in that moment. I was empty, and they truly filled me with love in that embrace. It said, have faith, better days will come, and it delivered me from that hollow place. I felt it and have appreciated it ever since. Presence offers us opportunities to truly help and provide support for others, as well as ourselves.

Secondly, I had another situation where I was the receiver of almost that same sandwich hug nearly 17 years later after losing my dog Kappi. Two amazing clients of mine, Bruce, and Cindy, also dog lovers, hugged me so graciously that we all cried together! They knew the situation, and in fact, they had just lost one of their dogs too only a short time ago. I believe we had a mutual heartbeat for a moment. I for them, and them for me! Amazing, and of course, so appreciated! It brightened my world, and as a result I was able to take that home and tell my wife about it. While it didn't change what had happened, it changed us, and maybe ever so slightly, it filled a void within our hearts with love and kindness. People can be amazing, BE AMAZING for someone else, it'll make them, and YOU feel better, if not GREAT!!

So back to the point, sorry for the detour. Be mindful and maintain a balanced perspective, to the best of your ability! Presence offers opportunities to use faith in order to help the "selves", as well as others...and remember the funny stuff! It is helpful. The thing is, with keen reflection, like a parallel relativity, we see this same stuff within, in our "selves" as well, right? Kickback, resistance, avoidance, and even some animosity from time to time as we get lessons we may not want to hear! Do we give up on our "selves"? NO, we persist, sometimes begrudgingly! A different angle, tone, or situational reference may explain the insight in a way that is more productive. "Tough love" is almost always a last resort, as it is rarely as useful as it seems it should be, and often feels needed! Sometimes that means a 3rd party reference might be beneficial, an example from someone else's life that has worked. This makes it less personal because otherwise it might seem accusation oriented, and / or "pointed", which can mean people can't see it because there are feelings involved and / or they are too close to it. It has already overwhelmed their system. Reframing it can offload the tone, or pressure, situationally so they can see it from a different perspective! A "sales" objection handling methodology I learned when I was very young in my sales career is a wonderful tool. It is called **"Feel, felt, found"** and it goes like this. The empathetic side of us says, I often feel that way, or I understand how you FEEL, which is the ice breaker. It shows empathy, and care. Then, with their approval, or an implied NOD of yes, we proceed with explaining it in a way that has affected someone else we know, and you show them and explain the way that they FELT. This shows them that they are not alone in feeling this way. It also establishes trust that we actually know what we are talking about, having been there, and that leads us into providing the solution. Lastly, as a way of explaining the understanding, since they are now listening, you convey what you have FOUND. The mental strategy employed to get through the situation, in this case, a deep understanding of how faith is useful and beneficial. That is conveyed by saying, I have found that in this situation, the following has proven beneficial...FEEL, FELT, FOUND! Use it, internally and externally!

Another way to truly change the direction of the sinking ship so to speak, is to lighten the load, with humor. I find myself in "uncomfortable" situations like this quite often, where the tension amongst people is palpable, so I understand how you might feel, I feel a little anxious myself in these situations. As a result, I use this methodology a lot, mainly because I have felt that it is wildly successful and FUN. You see, I have used this in many situations, and I have found that _____. Do you get it? I just did it again. So, what have I found, as an example you can use? Here's one:

I like to think of it this way, which makes me laugh, and the laugh helps all by itself, it's like an instant attitude adjustment! A whole internal or even external room ambiance change can occur in an instant using this technique, but there is a risk, it might feel and even be extremely awkward! You have to be quick, and almost literally BLURT IT OUT, kind of loud...so you will know rather quickly if it worked! Imagine you are hearing this through a loudspeaker system, on a plane, with a little static. Use your imagination here and keep in mind that this could be big ME talking to little me, the selves, or me talking to my best friend, wife, family member, or anyone else for that matter. It's actually quite fun, and that's the way it is intended to be delivered. It goes like this, with a somewhat amplified and deeper tone of voice, hands cupped and curled in a "O" shape near your mouth one in front of the other as if blowing a trumpet, or speaking through a megaphone, say:

**"*This is your pilot speaking, we are experiencing some turbulence here, please buckle your seat belt, the next few miles are going to be a little ROUGH while we are searching for some more stable air*"**

Ha-ha! Look around for the response. It's like a breath of fresh air...I can't help but laugh, I am sorry if you think it is stupid. I think it's hilarious. Tension can be relieved with humor, and then logic prevails, more often than not. Level heads are certainly more coachable, in my experience. That applies internally and externally!

It is actually very funny how a lesson can hit us and really be meaningful, seconds, hours, days and even weeks or years later. Have you flown recently? Keep this example in your back pocket for the next time tensions are climbing. You may like it as it acts as a pressure release. If nothing else, use it internally, or for a nice little chuckle! Either way it opens the door to be the mediator, which makes you a true leader, from this point forward, as higher "SELF" overseeing within, or a leader amongst your peers "out there"! Interjecting a laugh or smile, with fun sort of playful mockery, a joke, or a weird funny facial expression can often have amazing effects. My dad used to do this to my sister when we were younger, and it would almost unfailingly make her laugh and get her instantly out of a foul state! We could literally see her holding back the laughter, face all red and all, even though she wanted to "pout"! Then we would all just bust out cracking up. Pressure relieved, OK, let's move on. Good job Dadaroo! The heated moments are most definitely not as much fun right, I mean, for heaven's sake, we are truly just trying to help, only to get our hand slapped, or ego bruised, if we let it! It is wonderful to have a "GO TO" in order to snap us out of a poor "state"!

We can just as easily get fired up within as we can dealing with stuff and people "out there"! Obviously, when we are the receiver in that foul state, whether we attempt to help ourselves, or someone else tries to help us, we are not seeing or getting ANY lesson in that less than stellar state of mind as long as we stay there. If we, or one of the "selves" is stuck in one of those rotten moods, for example, we might even say to ourselves under our breath, "Yeah right, shut the heck up", or worse, while licking our wounds. Not good right? That could be directed at our "selves" amongst the selves internally, or the little selves directed towards the higher "SELF" as an example, or some other "Authority"! Some dissention, resistance, even though it is seen and understood as we progress...sometimes that means the dust has to settle for a minute, or longer before we are receptive to a more productive line of thinking and an attitude adjustment! We almost have to slap our own wrist, or use one of these other playful ideas, if only to wake us out of our temporary slumber and spark a bit of energy to climb ever so slightly up that proverbial ladder, where the air might be a little less turbulent. Inspiring a laugh or changing the tone / tune can do this! Forcing a smile in a situation where it takes digging deep to grab one can turn that frown upside down a little easier and faster! From here, the message can be heard, felt, or seen from a more elevated, aware perspective. Instantly, more receptive. We typically know what works for our "selves", and possibly the people that are close to us as well, so we can be super ridiculously persistent, and maybe even push a little to ensure that the message is heard or seen. That doesn't necessarily work all that well when the advice is pushed on someone else though, out there....so we do need to be sensible, and present!

When "have faith" is being directed towards someone else "out there", even gently, with love, it is not universally accepted nor is it absorbed and understood! Be prepared and alert too because the reactions can be at the extreme ends of the spectrum. The quiet version of that is that in some cases, it can be very subtle, almost imperceptible. With eyes wide open, this can often be a good gauge as to how it has been received. That might mean silently, and the only clue we get is in the minor facial changes, like a minor eye roll for instance. Be observant of bodily responses and reactions, they tell a story, and sometimes they are the only clues we get, so pay attention! (This includes our own face, and the way we are holding the body when dealing with the "selves", so look in the proverbial mirror, often!) In the end, and from a more strategic perspective, we need to understand, NOW, in the moment, like as in frame by frame, how it works, so that we can use it and believe in it, NOW vs later as well as to know whether it is being used properly, our state of receptivity, if you will! We need to understand it so well that we can explain it to the "selves", as well as those that we love so that it is actually helpful "in here" as well as "out there"! Like second nature. EASY! It will eliminate some of those less than stellar responses too. Thank goodness. YES!!!! We need the lesson, and we need it to be useful sooner, as stated, NOW...BEFORE things get heated! By then it's too late. There is no later anyway. As a matter of fact, it has to play out at that point, right? The lesson, the understanding, the KNOWING what faith is and how to use it, from a bottom-line perspective truly has to happen, NOW! So, FAITH is especially important when we are down, low on energy, or truly need a break, something to go our way! Important is an understatement, right? Crucial, or imperative is probably more accurate! From that standpoint, it needs to be integrated, and available within instantly! Sometimes, all it takes is that one small step in the right direction, and everything changes, but if things continue to break down instead of up, the downward spiral can escalate very quickly! So, let's break it down, so we can build it up! FAITH is available, and faith can be used, NOW!

I want definite ways to get to that state of mind instantaneously though, so that we can move to that more productive frame of mind quicker, in a flash, like almost as if by snapping our fingers we are just taken there, because we know how it works that well. In particular, like as in VERY specifically, comprehended, understood, absorbed and available for use, NOW! So, what are the ways we can we use it in times like these when we really need some more stable air quickly, or an environment where we need some solid footing to take that next step because it is happening, ready or not? We know we need to take it, and we are taking it, but that can create some distress, and this is EXACTLY the time when we need FAITH to provide that stability because we believe in it! That giant ROCK, the foundational one under the SOUL of our shoe, pun intended. Let's face it, it's a whole lot easier to have faith when we are in a good mood right? Optimistic, energetic, enthusiastic approaches tend to produce better attitudes for sure, and quite honestly, better results as well. So, let's talk about both. We can and should thoroughly dissect this FAITH thing with an open and positive frame of mind, and from different angles. I do want to take it down to that level, frame by frame! That's the best way to ensure a thorough understanding of it, and that it is available for use in the moment.

You will notice that a lot of these mind processes are actually happening beneath the surface, unconsciously, until they don't...that is until you become AWARE enough to see them happening real time, consciously. Your PRESENCE is what is required to see it. You see it because you have done the work to build your skills to SEE, HEAR, and FEEL, for yourself in a lot of NOW moments! By continuous effort, these skills are getting more and more efficient, powerful, and integrated, like a well-oiled machine! Faith is one of these skills, and we need to use it properly.

In using this ability to help ourselves, and seeing how it works, we will have many opportunities to help others as well, which is wonderful, once seen that way. While these opportunities may not be as obvious initially, that will change too. Everything we focus on expands right? In addition, while this vantage point kind of implies that we should help people, the EGO can play games with the mind in this regard too, as you might imagine and as discussed, a little bit so far anyway. In other words, that may not align with our more selfish desires situationally, which can push us into the negative feelings if we don't. Certainly, we don't want that right? We can't allow that to happen. In fact, there are entire books written about this subject and the havoc that buried feelings & emotions create in our overall health and wellness. This can show up in physical and emotional ways, or both, when we don't deal with them properly. Bottom line is when there are opportunities to help, help and be ever vigilant about watching these "selves" as you do! Pay attention in here as well as out there! You will hear all manner of complaints, resistance, it's a waste of time, why bother, save your breath, save your energy, among thousands of other re-actions!

There is another point to this interaction within the mind though, and it is important, that's why I am belaboring it. What we must realize and SEE is that our attitudes towards others is EXACTLY what our attitude is towards our "selves". This is something that I really encourage you to watch and see, very closely. It is also why I have detoured to explain it in various ways, so that you can and DO see both sides of it. This plays out on the world screen, as well as within our minds, like double vision! Often times, the world can be an amazing mirror, and we can see our reflection in it in all sorts of ways, our biases, our conditioned thinking, our slanted ways of seeing things based on our positionalities and programming. Until we truly wake up though we won't see it. We must wake up, open our eyes. This must be understood, and seen...EVERYWHERE, not only within our "selves". Be watchful.

Why is this so important? Because this expands and amplifies the ability to learn through our experiences. It creates more chances for learning, quite naturally. The lessons are truly everywhere, inexhaustible numbers of opportunities. As we are "doing" stuff and paying attention out there, we constantly need to be aware and conscious IN HERE as well, ever present, awake and aware. It happens both ways. While we are focused within, we have the potential to miss an amazing lesson "out there" as well. That is why we need to maintain that exceptional "BALANCE" in the way we position ourselves relative to the mind! When balanced, and present, we are gifted opportunities for learning countless times in a day, both in here and out there! This is why we hear the phrase "open your eyes" so often, it's like a spiritual type of eye that we must learn to see with in a different way, both ways, in and out broadly and acutely.  As our awareness, attention and skill improve in this regard, we see more and more of these opportunities for growth.  What this does in a fairly amazing way, depending on how much we are exposed to various situations and how large our magnets are, is it amplifies our ability to grow through experience at a more rapid pace! While we help others, we have the opportunity to grow WITH them by helping them. To me that's a WIN, WIN! The world can be an amazing teacher if we are truly paying attention, and helping other people can be very rewarding. The interesting thing is that once this is realized, we WANT to see it MORE, and we want to HELP more!

Caveat here, the JOY of GIVING is very rewarding, and worthwhile, but the alternative is that sometimes, it can be painful, as I have hinted at above. While we are anxious and excited to help, please remember that not everyone wants to be helped. Keep in mind that there are times that we are feeling low, down on energy, sick, angry, or whatever and an "emotion" or situation has us captivated. In a moment like that, we can see our "selves" as they refuse or fail to see legitimate help, or maybe shortly thereafter we see it and acknowledge it. It is possible that maybe we even apologize and accept the help moments later. We understand that it is because the EGO stepped in and would not allow it previously. That person had just "pissed me off", offended me, done something wrong, or I just wanted to feel bad, for whatever reason. The result was that I didn't want to, nor would I accept anything from him or her, or anyone like them, or even affiliated with them in any capacity, their family, friends or whomever else. This stuff happens, and we see it happen. There are many reasons why we refuse help, and lots of situations where the EGO can get in the way of us getting help, as well as us giving help!

So, having said that, be careful not to interject yourself into situations where your help is not wanted. It may be needed, but believe it or not, some people just do not want to be helped. While we may offer it up, and even try to deliver it in discreet ways, with gentleness and even kid gloves sometimes, the result is going to be an array of eye openers! A true spectrum of feedback is what we get, and of course, more lessons! Wonderful, yes, but sometimes these lessons can make you really step back or JUMP BACK in some cases. Don't be dependent on "control", or the result! It is at these junctures that we must admit and acknowledge that we have come to a point where we must retreat and let it go, feeling satisfied for having made a wholehearted effort. The statement that I think works best for me is something I heard at a sales meeting, and I apologize but I don't remember the man who said it, but it stuck with me. No matter how much I really wanted to help, and used every opportunity, with compassion, love, and tenderness to give it, they just haven't had enough pain yet. That is the understanding, while pain is not a requirement for learning, sometimes people just haven't had enough pain to wake them up out of their slumber. The virtual slap in the face wasn't enough, nor was our attempt to snap them out of it to show them something in order to help. The responsibility in this situational thing can no longer be ours. I would suggest that "try" in this case just flat out failed. At some point, people need to want to learn, and be open to it, and they just weren't ready yet. That is the reason for the statement. It makes perfect sense, and while it feels kind of mean, our help doesn't need to be accepted. We can't help someone that doesn't want to be helped. We can, with our amazing skills, be balanced and comfortable knowing that it was offered and rejected, just as easily as offered and accepted. It just feels a whole lot better when someone accepts the help and it helps them, and we see it help them. Obviously, that feels amazing which makes us want to do it more. In addition, it gets us through the situations and times where it is refused, because these are the ones that can be painful! There has to be something that would motivate us to take the risk to grow, right? Some things to consider as we encounter more and more opportunities.

For a shy person, as an example, this has a way of making the world a less dangerous place. In fact, it may even provide the impetus to step out of that shell from time to time, and it feels good! Trust me. Not just understanding but KNOWING changes things! In fact, it sparks a curiosity and a fascination with what might be perceived as quite ordinary things. (Chuckle!) It also has a way of literally explaining things to us as we experience them, in rather amazing ways. This is experiential and will be seen and integrated more quickly and efficiently as the skill grows. This growth on growth really compounds and as it does, the skill gains power. The integrations are no longer so laborsome, they just happen more and more naturally. As the higher SELF embraces this vantage point, effort can amp up as well. Change can feel like it is almost constant for extended periods as we absorb what life offers up and learning intensifies. Once again growth is taken to a new level, over and over again, which requires energy. Sometimes it means that we must take the time to truly SIT and rest to absorb the countless lessons that were perceived in a short period of time. Otherwise, the tendency is towards overwhelm, which has more of a negative effect if we push onwards too quickly. Given the time necessary to absorb and integrate, it amplifies the energetic response, and that spark creates a chain reaction which fires the heart within to do more! The world is truly seen with different eyes once tapped in, turned on and fired up. It lights up as we light up!

It's kind of funny, and cool, but when you just go ahead and DO THE RIGHT THING, you are gifted back what was given, but it isn't a one for one, it is like a ten to one, or more! Naturally you might think that I am speaking of "out there" right? Well, of course I am, but as I said in the previous paragraphs, it goes both ways. The world is a mirror, so you MUST and I mean MUST do the same for your SELF! Treat others as you wish to be treated works equally well if you reverse the view and look WITHIN. Please remember, as we grow, we are dealing with these "selves" more and more often, if not constantly. This is particularly important when dealing with one of the EGO selves that refuses to acknowledge ones "worth" or "worthiness". That's also why I say that when given an opportunity to help someone, help them...it will come back to you in amazing ways, some of which cannot even be fathomed or imagined. You will be amazed, and that amazement and appreciation will also contribute to the feeling of "worthiness". Funny how things like this work! By helping others, you actually get better at helping the "selves" overcome their hurdles. Often that means with KINDNESS and consideration, vs "tough love"! The kid gloves, sugar vs spice is usually a good idea. LOVE eventually wins out above all.

Another perfect example of this is when it comes to forgiveness. As a general attitude, people say that they forgive others, but they really don't, for the most part. At least that's not what I see in general. I am not being critical; trust me I get it. I am just as guilty when I am not present, if I am overtired, over hungry, or just not 100%. Human ≠ perfect. I do try my best though, and I try HARD! I am bringing it up for a reason, not as an accusation, or to make anyone feel bad, but to show the lesson in it... which is often missed. This is another one of those "out there" vs "in here" scenarios. I'll explain.

My Mom taught me this really cool tool. It's a simple way to assess things, like as in, whether or not someone "means it" or not! She said, and repeated this all the time:

## "Actions speak louder than words!"[74]

It tells a lot sometimes, and it is pretty darn accurate! Of course, as a kid, I didn't understand it, or how powerful the lesson was! In fact, I got tired of hearing it...and resisted it. What I heard was blah blah blah! I should have listened better. LOL. I hadn't had enough pain yet! First you have to see it in your "selves", as it relates to your own actions and reactions, and then you will see it in others as well. This is relative to pretty much everything, but in this case, I am focusing in on forgiveness and forgiving. It may be a surface level "let it be" attitude, or a "let it go and karma will get them". I can't tell you how many times I have heard that statement. What people tend to do though, it seems to me, is carry that with them by internalizing it, or by offloading it right away, in a negative way. One way or another, it EATS at them! They feel bad...and then sometimes they offload it and then swallow that bad feeling too, for a lifetime! Ever heard of a grudge? A lot of people just can't ever really let it go if they let it go at all. Again, I am not being critical, I am being HONEST, there is a difference. It is difficult, I agree! When someone "wrongs you", or makes you feel bad, it is sometimes extremely difficult to just let it go, straight away! Bad things happen, I don't disagree for a second. Depending of course on the severity of the "offense", or "intent"! What is needed, is the level of forgiveness that you will ultimately give yourself now for making errors over and over again, WHY? Because NOW, with this new understanding, you GET IT! It is a REQUIREMENT to move forward. I understand, and deliberately choose to process and LET IT GO!

> *"The fool doth think he is wise, but the wise man knows himself to be a fool"*
> **-William Shakespeare**[75]

This is why I refer to them as the little "selves" within us. They are fools, and when they take us over, they make mistakes! We just need to understand this and be alert to their stupidity! So, understanding the human situation within our "selves", and that we are all human, doesn't that make it a little more understandable as we look "out there"? If a spouse, or child, mother or father or someone you really LOVE a lot says or does something that disturbs you is it easier to forgive and forget? Do you immediately throw it back in their face and try to make them feel guilty or berate them for the way you feel because of their "action" or "word"? Do you internalize it so that you can throw it in their face later? How about if someone outside the family, or someone you don't love or care about does the same thing? Is it different? Are they any less or more human, "innocent", or are they not deserving of your forgiveness? Do they get a little forgiveness or maybe a lot, or do you complete the transaction with unconditional LOVE and total forgiveness 100%? Just understand that this is a serious matter, and this is one of those all or nothing things...you either did it or you didn't! Actions speak louder than words. If you didn't let it go, it will show up again. Whether you internalize it, or offload it onto someone you love, or someone else...you don't get the lesson! You will get it again. Pay attention to your own actions and words, particularly when they are not aligned! It is easy to see this in others, what I want for you to do is reverse the vision, and instead of looking OUT, LOOK IN! Now, as situations happen and you are the "guilty" one and made a mistake, maybe offended someone, or maybe you even deceived yourself! Can you get the lesson and let it go with forgiveness and "make it right" with your "self" and / or them? Maybe an apology is necessary. Either way, and emphatically I say: PLEASE, FORGIVE yourself! Let it go...just don't keep doing it! The reason I ask it this way though is because the tendency seems to be that if you don't let OTHER people off the hook, you are JUST AS CRITICAL of yourself, and if you don't forgive yourself you will internalize it, that is BAD! Internalizing things = PAIN, either now or later. It is usually measured. To the extent that you let others off the hook, you do the same for yourself. Or you don't, and that's really important to understand! If you don't let anyone else off the hook, do you also beat yourself up when you make an error? For how long? Point is, whether measured or not, it's not a contest, either way, you don't get the lesson!

The energy is not released, very important. We want the lesson, so we can let it go and move on, whether it is shown to us "in here" or "out there", so get the lesson. Forgiveness is a requirement! To be FREE from it you must LET IT GO! If you don't want freedom, then by all means, point the finger...and hold on tight, the lesson is going to circle right back around! Brace yourself.

Another way to look at this is to determine whether you tried to do something, or you actually did it. 98% in this case is not going to get it done. There is no state of trying. Actions speak louder than words! Either you did it, or you didn't. This is very relevant to forgiveness, so pay attention to your actions and words relative to it, situations, and people. FORGIVE 100%! Check out the words of **YODA**[76], in his instructions as the Jedi Master! Look it up or click the link if possible:

https://youtu.be/BQ4yd2W50No

Well said!

We the people, in general, are unconscious to certain things that blind us, and again, we are all different, ME included! I am not putting myself on a pedestal, I get blinded too from time to time, particularly when I am tired or hungry...or both! While we "try" to do the best we can, we are not present 100% of the time. That's just the reality of it. We are human, and we make mistakes when we are not present! So, anyway, having said that, we get blinded in different areas, situations, with certain people, and things, and that is based on our biases and programming. We see that within, when we are looking "in here". The compliment to that is that when we are looking "out there" so to speak, it would be THEIR biases and THEIR programming...so they cannot see, or let's say they just see the world a little differently than we do, and so they are also failing forward, making mistakes! We can see how that might happen and relate to it. We truly do understand, deeply.

As **Jesus** said:

## "Forgive them, for they know not what they do"[77]

Now we have a really deep understanding of why this is true, and needed, and why he said that! It's not just a good idea, or a noble goal, it is a requirement to move forward with our lives! When we are not awake, aware, and present, we literally do not know what we are doing, the "selves" choose. We are unconscious! We do it, they do it...and <u>ALL</u> must be forgiven to move forward! Let's be honest here, sometimes we can't see something within ourselves, we are just too close to it.

What happens then? The universe, or the powers that BE so to speak, whatever you want to refer to it as, it tries to show it to us through someone else, or in another way, LOUDER! Seriously, that's what happens...and it keeps getting louder, which should make it more obvious, but for many reasons we just keep right on missing it, until we don't miss it, we finally get the lesson! Once we do, we kind of wonder, how did I miss that for so long? What the heck, how was I so blind?

KARMA, if you really want to break it down to the essence of what it is in my opinion, is AUTOMATIC, just like this!! Non-forgiveness. It is the natural process of US bringing US back to the lesson, to the obstacles, by our own magnetism, needing certain LESSONS. So, we get brought back to them, or them to us... over and over and over again UNTIL WE GET THE LESSON! If we get the lesson, its done, gone, it doesn't have to come back unless it is only maybe marginally forgiven, let's say, less than 100%. We get the lesson 100% when we have finally had enough pain to FULLY let it go! It is our UNCONSCIOUS, under the surface of our minds "MAGNETS" bringing us situations and people so that we can learn and grow and LET IT GO!

## Learn and Grow, and Let it go!

In some cases, it is so that we can help others learn and grow too...it is a give and take. One way or another, we are going to get the lesson well enough at some point to LET IT GO 100%...eventually, why not NOW?! Once you get the lesson, pay it forward. Obviously, just like my mom tried to teach me when I was young, but I didn't get the lesson for a lot of years. You can't force it on people...they'll get it eventually, but you can lovingly, with empathy and kindness give them a nudge, a kind word, maybe even some guidance if they are open to it and willing to listen. My mom told me that one lesson when I was a kid, but it took me 30 years or so to get the lesson. Actions speak louder than words! Very insightful, looking IN and OUT!

You might say, well I don't want to help others...I don't want to be in the service industry. Heck, sometimes we don't even want to help ourselves because we are in such a poor state of mind! Isn't that accurate? Well, not everyone is intended to do the same thing, but whatever we are doing, we need to do it with awareness...and when we mess up, forgiveness. This applies to the "selves" as well as others! In other words, we need to understand the human condition, on a moment-to-moment basis as we are doing it. What gradually happens if we do it with awareness is that we learn the underlying themes, the storylines, the beliefs, motivations, programming, and whatever else drives us to do the things we do. More and more, we learn our motives, our passions, our drives...these things that make us tick. These ultimately break down to "Pleasure seeking" or "Pain avoidance" which is very basic...but when we break it down and see it happening in our own mind as it is happening in the moment, it shows us exactly HOW and WHEN we are being blinded and operating on autopilot. It shows us, with awareness, where we might have been wearing rose colored glasses (blinded by some future ideal) or we were doing the opposite. We entered the moment carrying some baggage from the past and the stigma, or emotion that was carried forward from it has influenced our ability to access the present moment because the emotion carried us away and we were NOT IN THAT MOMENT. Instead, we were in pain avoidance mode without realizing it...or whatever else took us out of the moment.

**"Tom Sawyer"**[78] who I refer to in that **RUSH** song is both, the way that I look at it. I always appreciated that song too, for that reason, it gave me a frame of reference in a way. It was something that I could relate to because for some reason the name kind of stuck with me. For me, he represented that element of mind (The "selves") that flip flops between pleasure seeking and pain avoidance. Like the proverbial angel on one shoulder and the devil on the other, and here we are in the middle. Smile/Frown, Good/Bad...back n forth, like a ping pong match and you are the net. In one moment, he's going to tell you that you are the king of the world, and then smack, the ball goes to the other side and the very next moment he'll be digging your grave! Talk about the devil's advocate, sheesh! LOL What you must do is wake up and see it happening, moment by moment and DON'T LET IT HAPPEN. Don't let Tom steal your life! WAKE UP!!!! From above, the ping pong match can be enjoyable, even entertaining to watch for a while...until you just end up telling them both to turn in their racquets. What if you are the net though? Not only is it confusing watching the ball speed back n forth, but sometimes you get hit right in the face with the ball! I know, my analogies are stupid sometimes, sorry. I just think they are fun ways to look at things. If I am right smack in the middle of the argument, at the same level, that's what happens. I get beat up, or exhausted, or both! We need to be above it, for that reason!

Without this ability, the skill we are building, we do not have the presence needed to make choices based on the truth because the truth is not available in the past/future and that's where we are! It is about "TIME", not where we are necessarily, but WHEN we are...and when we are there, in the past/future, we are LOCKED OUT of the moment, NOW. We are quite literally BLINDED by our "selves"...the little ego selves in our mind that we have yet to overcome! They have literally slammed the door (the gate) in our face and shut us out of the moment! Are you going to let that happen again and again? Presence is the ability, YOUR ABILITY, to be in the moment, the ETERNAL PRESENT! The Eternal present is the "NOW". NOTHING else is real, it a mere mirage created by falsities...LIES...essentially EGO generated illusions, generated because you ARE ASLEEP AT THE WHEEL! That is why I say it is a SKILL, because with practice, YOU can get better at it.

The question becomes, do you want to respond to life while seeing and hearing illusions that these "selves" are projecting onto your screen? ...or do you want to REALLY COMMIT to your life and to "BEING" present to see and hear the TRUTH? The truth is available in the NOW, and that is PRECISELY where the still small voice can be heard, and where we can SEE life unfolding moment by moment by moment. So, what exactly is the still small voice? I'll leave that up to you to put a label on if you wish to do so, call it higher guidance, the higher "SELF", Jesus, GOD, angels or whatever else. Other religions give it different names too, which is fine! Call it what you will, I say GGITM, God guides in the moment!

The interesting thing is that the moment is where it all happens, without access to it you are essentially cut off from it,,, from growth, cut off from that level of instruction! Just like the words in the Bible... you cannot hear, and you cannot see! Why though? Because you are NOT PRESENT, you are in one of two other places: future or past. GET PRESENT, GAIN PRESENCE, NOW! Work to become more AWARE...awareness will turn these light bulbs on for you, over and over again! With the ability NOW to access the moment, naturally we progress to higher states of living, of being. Can you imagine having such awareness that you could respond to any and every situation, moment to moment, with UNCONDITIONAL LOVE? I am going to lay it on the line here and say that THAT is the God response, and that we have the ability within every one of us to HEAR AND SEE the God response. We truly do have the ability to be "an instrument", but we need to hear and see from the truth, without preprogrammed biases and weighted influences from former and future "selves" that put illusions in our windows (eyes and ears), blur our vision, and amplify falsities in the mind so that we cannot see/hear the truth. The GOD response in and through US is not an option if we are not in the moment, (in the zone) awake and aware, because our programming (little selves) will get in the way! With faith and trust, it can be different, NOW...**YOU CAN BE THE INSTRUMENT!**

Conceptually, now we do understand how this is a possibility. We just need to work on the actual skill of DOING IT! Let's face it, we miss the mark a lot. So, let's talk more about the actual implementation of the skill from some other angles.

Faith is a key element, a very necessary one. As we dissect this it is becoming more and more accessible, so lets continue down the river!

YES, the River, and water in general seem to come up quite a bit, right?

I think it is interesting that a lot of artists speak, write or sing about "The RIVER". You see it more often than could be a coincidence in my opinion. **Esther Hicks** talked about going with the **"FLOW"**[79] of your stream. The message is very powerful. What I gained from it was an enhanced vantage point. The logic made sense to me, I was to compare thoughts in order to know if they were going upstream or downstream. She said this in various ways, over and over again, on her audio CD's as well as in the book referenced above. In order to determine if a thought is going with or against the stream though, what must we do? First we need to be awake and aware enough to ask the question! In other words, we need to be present to ourselves! Wake up, be aware, be CONSCIOUS! Once we wake up, we can then BE CONSCIOUS of not only the thoughts, but the state of the body, emotions, tension, ease, etc. That, in turn is "processed" in the moment with our skills. Once the net of all that is "understood", the translation shows us what that thought, or line of thinking, is aimed at...up or down! It could be the thought itself, or the underlying THEME of thoughts. I think that this offers a really cool vantage point and allows us to go with the flow more easily from a more analytical mind angle...as if asking HOW, exactly, can I do that? This is a way that works! It helps us kind of back up, and strategically dissect it to reposition things if needed, like mind "SPIN"! HOLD ON, PAUSE, let me get in the trenches here to make sure that my mind is right and all systems are GO. The machine is not bogged down, adjustments have been made, gears are not going to be grinding, I am at the ready, I am basically re "optimized" before proceeding! It is at that moment when we are prepared and ready that faith can be implemented.

See also, **Styx**, the band and their song **"Boat on the river"**[80]. This is a cool song talking about the river idea. My take is that with a major vantage point change, we can watch from a different perspective! As we watch life happening, we can be fully engaged, from this more elevated vantage point, above vs in the river! We can see the different levers that are being pushed and pulled within us, and then with understanding, the natural progression is to a more curious, educational, and empathetic demeanor vs a more erratic emotional status that can swing to both extremes. In essence, the result is that there is no more crying! Even crying can be watched, understood and then, it is as if instantly, the lesson is received and the crying just kind of stops. The reason for the pain isn't necessarily erased, but It's essentially the same thing really, with understanding there is no more pain associated with it! We can identify with the pain if we choose to, but it is seen as truly optional! Nothing can bother us from this overseer position, it is all SEEN, understood, and simply processed. More of a matter of fact type view... like Oh, yeah, I see that! That's really Interesting vs. OUCH that hurts, make it stop! Everything makes perfect sense, the lessons are learned, and we move onwards, all the better for the lesson. Another step forward. I want to note here that the song mentions time standing still. Doesn't that make you curious, wondering what they meant by that? You may want to explore that concept a little bit. As described in the previous paragraph, this pausing to "optimize" is something that can be very productive. I encourage you to think about it.

**Rush**, **"Time Stand Still"**[81]. This song, in my opinion, opens the door to really think about and explore TIME, in depth! Please do. They say that time is a human construct, right? What does that mean? I encourage you to ponder that and not just glaze over this section and this idea. If you don't understand what this means, take a time out here and really try to digest this concept of pausing time, freezing a moment. This could quite literally mean the difference between getting and digesting a lesson or missing it all together!! This is one of the songs that really jumped out at me back in the days when I was trading "in the zone" and that slow motion trade happened. I mean, seriously, what if you could really slow time down, in order to "catch" these lessons a little bit easier, faster? Wouldn't that make this process a lot easier? Well, I have to be honest, that DID happen for me, quite literally! If you really start to dissect the way that the mind processes, TIME can be seen in a different light, so to speak, as it is slipping by ridiculously fast! Each experience we meet, in the moment, is an opportunity to sort of capture a lesson. Unfortunately, the lessons are being missed quite often because in the heat of the moment, stuff happens so freaking fast, we just can't keep up. What happens is that we completely miss moments when our mental circuits get jammed, overloaded, or whatever else takes our attention away. We get distracted, and all it takes is one freaking BLINK, or that we are looking in the wrong direction. Any number of other scenarios can happen, and then we have the potential to miss a lesson! Our eyes go over there, and we miss something over here. I hear something, but I didn't hear it right to really capture the lesson, it wasn't loud enough, or it didn't hit me the way that I needed to hear it to "understand"! When I was trading, back in that timeframe of my life and learning this "stuff", I was literally asking for time to slow down so I could see these "opportunities" better, among other lessons! I wasn't doing drugs or anything, but as explained, when in the zone, it does feel as if time slows down. In addition, because of this insight, I was totally working on my eyes, ears, and senses to be able to see, hear and feel BETTER, quicker! Naturally though, I was not artificially trying to enhance the senses chemically, with the exception of caffeine to heighten my focus. Admittedly, coffee is something that has helped me stay focused longer! I WANTED the lessons, please show me, I begged! In fact, both of these songs mention time which is really cool. I want to explore these ideas!

What if time were to stand still just for a fraction of a second, while you got the lesson, before moving on. Could that happen? What exactly is this song talking about, pausing time, freezing moments? I really looked hard at this! My take is that this song, the way I look at it, is very similar to what I was asking GOD to do for me. I was basically begging him to speak louder, in a way that I could hear! I asked, PLEASE show me so that I can SEE! Look very closely at this song and the lyrics, doesn't it look similar to this request, in detail and theme? I kept missing stuff, opportunities, but I could see that I was missing them, I was seeing them only after the fact. So, I was basically begging, PLEASE slow it down so that I can see it, I can't see it at this point, it's going too fast. I would have to wait for that same scenario to happen again so I could see it faster the next time. So, either I would be faster, my mind would see it quicker, or time would move slower, so I could be faster.  Either way, conceptually, it is essentially the same idea. If time were to stand still though, like a frame-by-frame type scenario, I wouldn't miss anything, hypothetically of course. How could I unwind a wound? To me it seems to imply that we should be able to do this, but how?  Is that not the equivalent of learning a lesson so that there is no longer any pain associated with that lesson, as described in the previous song? See the similarities? How do you make a sensation or an impression stronger as it seems to request in this song? Am I not asking for the universe to SPEAK LOUDER so that I can hear, see, or feel it? Like please enhance my vision, hearing and senses...I am missing too much stuff, and I KNOW that I AM! Help me, I am begging you...help me see!  Please take a moment and explore this song in detail. The concepts that are being talked about are amazing, brilliant lyrics, IMHO. Time is a very interesting concept. Take this opportunity to step back and think about it for a moment relative to this song and watching the mind as it processes "stuff". Bottom line is that once the universe speaks up, in one way or another you will HEAR, SEE, or FEEL a lesson come through LOUD AND CLEAR, so to speak.  You truly do "GET IT"! You learn the lesson. Whenever that happens for you, then what happens next? You implement this new understanding in your life, it is processed, and then it's no longer holding you back. From another perspective though, and this is important: You can't IGNORE IT anymore either! You are no longer "innocent", so the next time you see it, you better see it good! LOL

So life is a river, right? Let's go back to the river idea. **RUSH** mentions the river in their song **"Tom Sawyer"**[82] from a different angle, IMHO! Look up the full lyrics, it is an amazing song, one of my favorites of all time actually! Oh yes, I have so many of those. Ha-ha. Many messages and meanings, I see, so many songs, so little time. (Chuckle, laugh, sigh...shaking my head, smirk!) If you don't already, you will know that face, and it will be yours if it isn't already. It happens when you gain or are reminded of an understanding! Anyway, I suggest you really look hard at this song too, it is so insightful. It may speak to you in different ways as sometimes songs can show you things in multiple ways, I think this is one of those songs! Another way that I look at this one is from the vantage point that I am literally ON THE PROWL, for lessons! Surely, we don't want to rent out our minds to the "selves", right? After all, they are the ones that are providing the lessons, so if they occupy that space, how am I to receive the lesson? I just want to be watchful for when they attempt to take me or my mind over! As long as I am seeing them from above vs IN the mind, at least I have a chance, assuming things aren't moving too quickly. The way I see it is that the mind is like a river, if it is raging along at a rapid pace, it is going to be a little more difficult to see what is contained within those RAPIDS. We have to figure out a way to slow it down, along with establishing a vantage point from which I can look within the river and see the rocks & sometimes boulders that are causing the water to be so turbulent. Being ABOVE IT, vs. IN IT is the beginning of that process, and it is a much more powerful position to observe from. We can SEE, HEAR and even FEEL with exceptional CLARITY as the river moves amongst and tries to go around these "obstacles", one way or another! That is where we can SEE the day's events happening from that overseer perspective, unafraid and unattached, just AWARE, observing! This is that vantage point ABOVE MIND, not stuck and trapped IN IT! From this vantage point, we are the proverbial TIGER waiting to pounce on its prey, the lessons are continuously provided, moment by moment... courtesy of the selves as they work their magic in the moment and do what they do, provide lessons! Over and over again, they bob and weave, as the EGO tries to push and pull the river. It is fascinating to watch a river, is it not? The EGO, once seen is equally entertaining with its remarkable maneuvers and its cunning manipulations! BE WATCHFUL...it is a true education.

The idea behind this being the instrument concept is that you must be aware enough to know that you are NOT being the instrument first! (Going against the FLOW!) I know that sounds rather obvious but knowing that you lack the ability to change the vantage point because you are essentially lost in thought is a key revelation! Fighting against a raging river is not only counterproductive, but it also takes a ton of ENERGY! Doing this makes the battle even MORE difficult because we lack the energy to use the skill! The river has drained it. Changing the perspective dis-empowers the little selves and EMPOWERS the higher "SELF"! That means powerful insights and an education that builds on itself in a seemingly parabolic fashion. It is also providing more resources exponentially as energy is preserved more rapidly with each lesson! Like that proverbial snowball rolling downhill. Its gaining speed and bulk. The higher "SELF" is gaining SPEED and SMARTS, a true education and SKILL that is useful and progressively beneficial not only to the person who gains this ability but everyone around them! It's something that they can't help but share, its just too good, and too much fun to not share. How can I possibly keep this to myself, it is insanely powerful, and I can't even imagine life without it. As I say, once seen, it can't be unseen, it just keeps getting better with practice and skill as you enhance your own abilities to maintain this presence. When people can't see though, it is frustrating to try to explain...that is why I belabor points sometimes, because I truly with all my heart want it to be understood, at a depth of understanding that is unequivocal!

Wasn't it **MOSES** that was able to **Part the SEA**[83]? I believe that to be symbolism also, whether a river or a Sea, **you must part the river of thought in the mind to be able to SEE and HEAR** more effectively, and that ability leads you to freedom, just as Moses led the way to freedom! The key is seeing the mind from a perspective that allows you to see where you are NOT FREE, and why! You have the keys, and the ability, use the skill...the vantage point that works for me is kind of elevated, and behind, like a bird's eye view. For me, that works...

If you really want to go down the rabbit hole, here are some more songs that seem to say the same things. Again, my opinion...what the people and bands meant may not be exactly what I hear! I have a very different way of looking at things sometimes. That said, I can show you a TON of songs from many bands that speak very powerful messages to me! What I hear may not be what they intended, so that's my disclaimer *** stars. I am simply offering a perspective, often times that is a different way to look at things!

My favorites to date have been Within Temptation, Evanescence, RUSH & The Scorpions, although more and more artists are starting to come on the scene with some amazing music with powerful lyrics now! I will reference them when possible and relevant. The cool thing that I am seeing is that this perspective seems to be showing up in more ways, more places, and in more people too. The world is waking up! That's encouraging, smile worthy!

Here are a few more songs to consider listening to if you are so inclined, and what I hear. I am not saying that this is the intent of the band, just what I hear:

**Scorpions**: **"Send me an Angel"**[84]. **Jaie Hart** showed me that **"The obstacle is the path"**[85]. The **Scorpions**, in this song **"Send Me An Angel"** seem to be saying something similar in their song. Take a listen when you have a moment! There appear to be a lot of messages, and symbolism in this song, so I encourage you to listen with an open mind, you may hear something I don't, or the band didn't even intend. Be aware of the thorns is one of the messages I hear! NOTE: It doesn't specifically say that, nor does it say go around them or avoid them. Quite the opposite actually! Ha-Ha. I had to ask myself like I do, well, WHY? And then of course, I go and look for answers! I encourage you to ask the same questions of yourself. I just assumed roses to be symbolic of something I might want. So, when you go after the things that you want, as this seems to be suggesting we do, whether that be roses or whatever else, are you aware enough, and paying close attention, with your eyes wide open? Of course, a rose is a very pretty flower, surely it is attractive, silky, and we give them to people in all kinds of life situations, for love, comfort, etc. The flower is an important thing, maybe symbolic? I mean, life is intended to be fun right? What is the counter thought, what are the thorns for you? Are you aware of them? Do you know where they are? Are you avoiding them? Do you even see them, feel them? When you do see the thorns, or bad stuff, what happens within you? When we can really see with open eyes and hear with open ears as the storms show up in our lives, it makes a huge difference. To me, it truly is the way out of the dark because the light of awareness is purposefully and consciously turned on, by choice and we are operating from a better vantage point. If I were to intentionally insert myself into a storm, to be sort of safe within the storm, but I could see what was going on from a better vantage point, where would that be? To me, it would be the eye, because that's the calm place in the center! Seems like a good place to be, to see, but why? From that vantage point the storm would literally be all around me, I could totally see EVERYTHING! That's what I WANT!!!! I need to see what's happening within as the storms show up in my life! Also, look up the morning star, it's VERY BRIGHT! Even in the darkest of night before the dawn, is shining it's light! A storm can make it really dark, so we need a light in that darkness. I surely hope you can use this light of awareness to find the door / gate I refer to so often. It requires TRUST and FAITH combined with the light of awareness! YOU MUST get to, and BE IN THE MOMENT as I have described because the alternative is that you are in the past or the future, and that essentially means, in the dark! Me weighing in here: Get to and through the door! It is right after the past, and right before the future: NOW...that razors edge in TIME or should I say outside of time? It is the separation between you and the promised land! FREEDOM is on the other side of the gate/door. Part the sea of thought right up to the gate and monitor the gate! The "selves" are only a step behind, and you are faster now, you MUST be, to have choice! That's my take anyway. Lots of heart in this song, the delivery is amazing! BTW, is a hurricane a storm? Does this remind you of another song I mentioned by Visions of Atlantis?

**Scorpions**: **"Winds of Change"**[86]. This is truly an AMAZING song, one of my all-time favorites. I have listened to this song over and over again and thought about it a lot. I have painted a lot of pictures in my mind, and really tried to imagine what this meant. My compliments to the band, I love this song. My opinion may be different than the bands intent here, as far as what it means. I am not making any claims, just offering up some thoughts relative to what I hear and what it means to me, and why I love it so much. It reminds me of important lessons in a fun and descriptive way. Take it for what it's worth, to me that is a perspective and a very powerful one, at that! Seems to me that there is a lot of symbolism again, assuming you can see / hear what I do? I am not saying it is or isn't, but if it were symbolic, I'd have to ask what is the symbolism? Of course, then I'd have to answer the question. I can only do that for ME, so here is my take on this song. It makes me REALLY THINK!!!!!

What does a soldier represent to me? They fight for what they want, change, possibly freedom. What is a river? To me it is symbolic of the mind. The Moscva is a river that runs through the central part of Moscow. What is a guitar, or balalaika? A balalaika is an older guitar, an older instrument, to keep it simple. If I were going to say something with an instrument, how would I do that? From a different angle, I ask more simply, how, when, and from where can I BE the INSTRUMENT?! Is the instrument ME? Just a hypothetical. The only place where change happens is in the moment, right? NOW! That is why it is important that we figure out a way to get there!

So, to put the pieces together in my hypothetical world, you'll really need to put on your envisioning capabilities. If this is relative to the mind and the mind is a place, where would the best place to learn about my mind, this City, or this place be? How about Central Park? Makes sense to me! Gorky Park is right in the middle of Moscow. So, if I wanted to learn about it, the people there would surely tell me, maybe even show me about this place! Pay attention to details and THEME, just like when watching the mind! Let's take a walk through this park and follow the river...should be FUN!

My take is that I am the instrument trying to read or hear the music that is to be played in this hypothetical world! There is a river, and a street that goes through this place, which always makes me think about the MIND and thoughts, themes and watching from above it. The future is coming, tomorrow's illusion is on the mind screen. As I walk down the street or float down this river, I am SEEING from the central part of my mind (Central Park) as the overseer, seeing literally everything from this amazing vantage point. I am watching ALL that is going on from this fun perspective, this wonderful, dreamy place in the park! As I see my thoughts of the future, I also see the worn patterned thinking which puts me in the past, my memories, TIME! Who occupies the future and / or the past as far as space goes in the mind? The "selves" right"? And what do the selves do? They fight for what they want, like soldiers. They want to stay and continue to be ME! The selves (Silly, naïve, uneducated children in some cases) are in the future and the past, but where is the answer, where does change take place? We know this one. In the MOMENT, right? When we leave the selves behind at the gate, then we have access to the moment because we are not stuck in that thing called time! The lyrics are amazing in this song, full of hope, and possible change in my opinion, truly brilliant. They seem to reference TIME relative to future/past and really bring it together by ringing the FREEDOM BELL in the MOMENT! Peace of mind, so COOL! Have a listen when feasible. Change takes place in the moment, when we arrive there because that is the only place where choice is possible. We must listen and HEAR. We must look and SEE. Where does the wind of change put us? Where does it take us? Where does it blow?

I suggest that it take you to the moment. I encourage you to arrive there with eyes wide open, and ears with which you can listen and hear with exceptional clarity, as well as senses that are dialed up and tuned in to feel with every ounce of your being! It makes all the difference! With this skill, I hope that you are ringing your freedom bell, NOW, BEING in the moment, to hear and see!

Notable, the reference to time and / or where he is asking to be!? Did you notice? On the edge of darkness, and a magical place! The change in vantage point has to do with where we are in time. My take is that if we find a way to get to the moment, we can ring that freedom bell, it is our FREEDOM that's at stake, as discussed previously. By waking up, with PRESENCE, we gain peace of mind because we can finally SEE and HEAR from that new perspective, free from the "selves". Freedom offers CHOICE, to choose a new direction, not one that is dictated by a mind that is stuck, frozen, or operating from patterns and programs! That perspective is THE SKILL we have been working on...and quite possibly, that just may be the wind of change if the opportunity is seized! Just what we needed, right when we needed it! The MOMENT we arrive in to NOW! Seize the moment! VERY POWERFUL lyrics, they seem to lead us right to the door! With our freedom we can <u>ALLOW</u>... <u>we can be an instrument</u>, which changes all the "TIME". The way I see / hear it, is that maybe the balalaika is YOU and I, the guitar is the more advanced instrument or the guidance for the instrument. One way or another, I need to find a way to BE the instrument, NOW!! Without growth, and learning, or getting the lessons provided... we are a more primitive instrument, and the music may not sound very good! Ha-ha. We just need to be tuned a bit to be able to play better music. That means being able to hear and see the guidance and then we would be able to CHOOSE to play a different tune, a GOOD ONE!! GOD is showing the way in the moment, we need to tune our instrument, the BODY / MIND! (We can be The GOD response)! We can **BE THE INSTRUMENT**! That's what I hear. Find the door...

There are plenty more songs I can refer you to, from all of these bands, and more... I will probably have to write a list at some point and explain what I hear if it is something that is of interest. They have so many great songs and albums that I can't write them all out here, maybe I will on the blog. I used to do this for myself when I had more time so that when I listened these songs, they would have more meaning to me and would remind me of the insight I gained from dissecting it for myself. If you would like to see this, let me know! Music has helped me to and through my own understandings, and to sing a new tune so to speak. I am not a singer, not by any stretch, not even in the shower. LOL. I am very thankful to these bands, and these people I mention for that reason though, they are and I really appreciate their talents! For me, music and listening to the lyrics in particular paints a picture with words and sounds. The mind hears messages, and it is a way for me to be learning and absorbing / revisiting lessons as I am driving down the road hearing these songs, as an example. I love that! I listen to music as a sort of "study" or teaching mechanism because for me it is helpful, and I enjoy it. Not only is the music exceptional, but it is also an opportunity to learn, process, grasp and understand these concepts in another way, all while being entertained at the same time! That's a win-win! These are truly amazing, and TALENTED bands, from the musical instruments, and the way that they are played and organized, to the singing of the songs. Tone, speed, delivery, it all comes together so beautifully! Even the titles to their albums can be a clue as to what they are trying to convey! Their music is a gift to the world! As I say, these are my personal vantage points, I make no claims to what the bands intent was or is on any of this stuff. This is just what I hear, and I work very hard to assimilate as much as I can from everything I see and hear... If I hear something within a song and don't immediately understand what they are trying to deliver or convey, sometimes I'll replay it a bunch or if I am in a position to do so, I'll pull up the video to see if that offers any additional insights. I am always looking for a new aha moment! At a minimum, music inspires a lot of chuckles and grins, even a smirk or two and once in a while I hear something new in a song that I have heard a bunch of times! Kind of like reading an educational book, you learn more the second or third time you read it than the first! I hope that you gain a perspective or two from listening and / or watching. The way that I tend to listen to songs is to try to discern who the singer is speaking to, singing to, or singing about? Some of the "darker", pointed, or angry type songs can seem to be about the alter ego and its shenanigans vs singing as if vocalizing a "tone" or message to a lover or a friend, or someone else for instance. So, I encourage you to listen with this more discerning ear to potentially get a different meaning to the songs than to just accept what the surface level vocals tend to be leaning towards. Often there may be more substance to them, in my opinion. Possibilities are endless of course. Ego self to ego self, Higher SELF to ego self, ego self to higher SELF, all the internal "drivers" of thought...and of course, all the various "out there" possibilities as well. Have fun with this. Let it lead you wherever it leads, hopefully that means to a new level of freedom!

As **Guy Finley** put it in his book **"The Courage to be FREE"**:

**"This level of awareness sees what is real and what is not. Its power to command challenging moments derives from its complete innocence. Higher consciousness doesn't "try" to control events, because its timeless nature is already a partner in guiding creation itself, so what has it to fear? And <u>the more we place ourselves in the presence of this indwelling light</u>, the more <u>we will see</u> small miracles take place before our very eyes. Quiet command over all that unfolds becomes as effortless for us as it is for <u>the spreading light</u> of dawn to chase away morning shadows. An upwelling confidence in the secret goodness of life replaces conflict and self-doubt. After all, how can we fail to find the fearless life we seek when reality itself points the way!"[87]**

The **Science of Mind Magazine** has some great instructions as well, please see below from July 2017! SUPER POWERFUL! Thanks to **Reverend Karen S. Wylie**! She wrote the daily guide below. The magazine provides a wonderful daily guide for each day that my wife and I love to read, the authors and guides are amazing! This one from Karen is super! At the top of the page, she even provides another valuable quote:

**"Every person, all the events of your life are there because you have drawn them there. What you choose to do with them is up to you."
-Richard Bach[88]**

**"There is nothing that happens in your life that is not an opportunity for great learning. There is life happening and then there is**

the spiritual truth in each and every situation. In that perfection is the process of our inner evolution. When you can begin to see your life from that spiritual perspective, you will experience heaven on earth. In that, you will find your joy and your salvation. We are given opportunity after opportunity to reveal the truth of our being.

It is for you to understand that nothing happens as a punishment, but rather <u>a LESSON</u>! It is our birthright that <u>we should learn and grow</u> from life. It doesn't matter the circumstance; look for the spiritual truth. <u>Look for the light behind every bit of darkness</u>. <u>We are here to learn and grow and become</u>. There are no accidents. When we <u>realize that everything happens for our spiritual growth</u>, we can ask: "What can I possibly learn from this?" "What possible good is in this situation?" To remember our true identity as Divine Spirit, this is the human walk, the human experience—to find God in all things. How Grateful I am to be on this sacred journey of self-discovery with you! Let us thank God and joyfully welcome our own becoming! AFFIRMATION: Today, I move to a new place in consciousness. <u>I release old limiting ideas and turn to new ways of being</u>. I ALLOW the great revelation to begin!"[89]

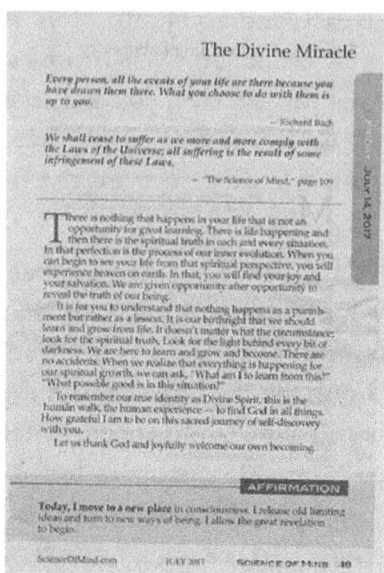

From **Science of Mind Magazine, August 2017, Daily guides,** it states:

## <u>"KNOW we are one with the only power that is"</u>[90]

...how many times have we heard that? Yet no one ever seems to explain how to get into this zone. How to BE THAT? These folks are gracious enough to explain it. So awesome! Here is an added hint = as Jesus did, with 100% trust and 100% faith. IN THE MOMENT! Was he UN-limited?

Here is another one, check this out, from **Reverend Dr. Ron Fox**, in **Science of Mind Magazine**. He explains the perspective that I am talking about too. Reprinted below as well:

**"Ernest Holmes writes that the hardest thing we have to do is learn to <u>TRUST THE UNIVERSE</u>. We like to dabble—to pray and pull our words back to see if our prayer is taking hold. What we NEED to do is <u>KNOW</u> we are one with the only power that is. <u>The great example for us is Jesus</u>. He had no question that spirit responded to him the way that he wished it to. It responded because <u>he never doubted</u>. And the great message for us is <u>when we can develop a belief like that, the universe will respond to us in kind!</u>"[91]**

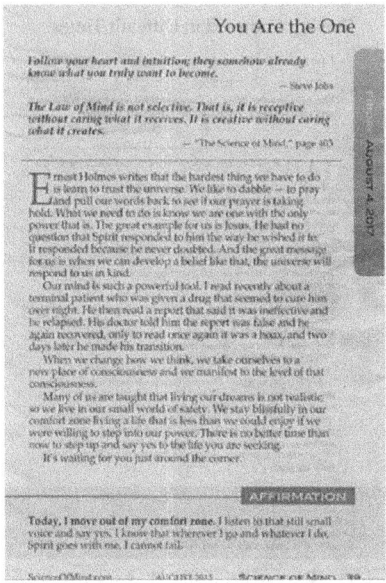

Listen to the wisdom of the advice in the guide above! Notice WHEN he recommends that YOU should step into your power! Of course, it's NOW! **"There is no better time than NOW to step up and say yes to the life you are seeking"**!!! So, TRUE, and a wonderful affirmation too: **"Today I move out of my comfort zone. I listen to that still small voice and say yes. I know that wherever I go and whatever I do, Spirit goes with me. I cannot fail"**[92]!!! That is faith! Thank You **Reverend Dr. Ron**. Well said! Today is NOW!

**Jesus** also said in similar fashion that it is done unto you as you believe!

### "GO, it shall be done for you as you have believed"[93]

Can we believe like that? When? Can we "BECOME" the GOD response? We come to each moment, do we not? Do we actually see it through though? Do we actually arrive in the moment, that precise moment of NOW? Are we actually getting there? Pay attention, pay very close attention, with laser focus, massive amounts of awareness, HUGE amounts of energy...NOW, and NOW ...and NOW! With these new eyes, with these new ears...in the exact moment of NOW, without being distracted by our "selves", we can see and hear the TRUTH, and then, and only <u>THEN</u>, we can BECOME! That is when we step into our POWER!

Said slightly differently, when I say, I AM _____ or I AM _____. The moment we fill in the blank, we become THAT, in the MIND, and from that microsecond forward we are <u>LIMITED</u> to being that version of "self". THAT is exactly what keeps us from the moment, locked out by time. ON THE WAVE, at the very moment it is crashing forwards, that microsecond, between the past and the future is when the false self (former you / future you) steps into the moment, BECOMES you, and ACTS IT OUT as you for you and STEALS IT! That version of "self" is LIMITED. Un-LIMIT it! First you must SEE IT limit you! Then you must arrive in the moment to CHOOSE differently.

See that Instead of you ALLOWING the GOD response, you became limited by something else that former you or future you was ATTACHED to and THAT is unfortunately the response that happened in the moment. (that's the EGO re-action / response)! With 100% trust, 100% faith, and 100% awareness IN THE ZONE, IN THE NOW moment, we can get out of our own way, become a better version of our SELF, and ALLOW the GOD response. With choice, the GOD response is an opportunity for a NEW ACTION, vs a re-action. Instead of our own patterned LIMITED MIND slipping in and making the choices for us we are BECOMING NEW. It happens in a lightning strike of a fraction of a second, and without being there, precisely at that moment, we are unable to make a better choice. Change can only occur NOW! LOVE is only available NOW! UNCONDITIONAL LOVE, in my opinion, is the GOD response, but when is that choice available? Can that choice be available through us? How? Answer: YES, NOW!

**From another spiritual philosophy, an amazing book "I am THAT"[94], by Nisargadatta Maharaj[95]:**

"Absolute perfection is here and now, not in some future, near or far.
**The secret is in action—here and now.**
It is your behavior that blinds you to yourself.
Disregard whatever you think yourself to be and act as if you were absolutely perfect
—whatever your idea of perfection may be.
All you need is courage."
**-Nisargadatta Maharaj**

I'll add, and AWARENESS! IMHO

"As you watch your mind, you discover your self as the watcher. When you stand motionless, only watching, you discover your self as the light behind the watcher. The source of light is dark, unknown is the source of knowledge. That source alone is. Go back to that source and abide there.

"I Am That"—pg 188"

### Nisargadatta Maharaj[96]

CAN YOU BE THAT!?! Didn't they call Jesus the light of the world? How bright was that? How bright is your light? Can you see it? Be it? Share it? Is it Limited, or have you UN-limited it? What is the status of your dimmer? What % light is getting through? How do you know? As an analogy, check your dimmer switch at the gate! Was your mental circuit breaker "tripped" by a trigger? If so, nothing was getting through, NO LIGHT even got to the dimmer! You gave away all your power! Now check the dimmer, are YOU letting the light through? Is there power to the switch? How do you know? As the light, is energy moving through you? Have you BECOME IT? How? First you must be the watcher and SEE, then you are the watcher and HEAR too! After a while you SEE and HEAR and KNOW because the instructions are crystal clear! You have become the light, think about it, you don't need to know "ABOUT" something if you are it! Jesus was an example of a SUPREMELY bright light...the light of the world. So again, I ask you, how bright can you let your light shine? Where and when do you want to start? How? NOW of course! You discover your "SELF" as the watcher, with AWARENESS! You literally have to practice this skill and make every effort to arrive in the moment... over and over again. This may be more difficult than you might imagine. Seriously, it is a challenge, I get it, so keep making that effort! From a mental, emotional, energetic, and awareness standpoint... putting all the elements together requires a massive amount of focus! That level of focus requires a TON of energy, and from an operational standpoint...unfortunately, you can't really see it through at first. It is HARD, so you fail, and you fail a lot in the beginning! It seems like every now and then though, it happens, you get there, and you see it through!

Once it happens, and you do see it through, you realize that most of the time you are NOT capable, NOT present, NOT aware, and NOT making it to the moment! While you are behind the wave of thought so to speak, or not in the moment, the best version of "I", me / you... the little "self" is not making it to the critical juncture and decision (NOW)! It is still on the other side of the gate, shut out by time! The MIND circuit breaker cut it off at the breaker box! It is when YOU are finally capable of arriving IN THE MOMENT to see and hear with awareness as The higher "SELF" ...then and only then....IT, THAT...whatever you want to refer to it as, will meet you there! You will see, with TRUST and FAITH, in that MOMENT! In that moment, the choice is available! YOU can ALLOW the GOD response to occur through you. From inside "THE ZONE", in that moment... You BECOME the best version of YOU. As **Nisargadatta Maharaj** states, **"I AM THAT"**[97]! Again, that is a great book :)

**Ernest Holmes** says it in a similar fashion below. Here are a few of my favorites:

*"The Great spiritual geniuses, whether it was Moses, Buddha, Plato, Socrates, Jesus, or Emerson...have taught man to <u>look within</u> himself to find God"* [98]

*"I cleanse the windows of my mind, that it may become a mirror reflecting inspiration from the most High. I do this, not with strenuous effort, but through quiet contemplation, through gently reaching and affirming an inward recognition. I know exactly what to do in every situation. There is an inspiration within me which governs every act, every thought, with certainty, with conviction and in peace."*[99]

*"All limitations are SELF IMPOSED"*[100]

*"<u>Peace comes from the absence of FEAR, from a consciousness of TRUST, from a deep, underlying FAITH</u> in the absolute goodness and mercy, the final integrity of the universe in which we live, and of every cause to which we give our thought, our time, and our attention."*[101]

So NOW we know that to get into the ZONE, it requires <u>FAITH</u>, right? Let's dig deeper!

In the first sentence of Emerson's "The Over-Soul" he states:

**"There is a difference between one and another hour of life, in their authority and subsequent effect. <u>Our faith comes in moments</u>; our vice is habitual"[102]**

## BRILLIANT!

As human beings, we build patterns, and those patterns become us...that's a HABIT! It is the known, or what I refer to as our "programming", and often times a comfort zone. To the extent that we have a learned response to anything, that learned response, or software "program", will represent us in the moment until we learn to step into the moment without the "support" of the habitual or "unconscious" self that wants to represent or react for us in that moment. (As the "selves" vs higher "SELF") **That requires FAITH**, to step out on a limb and BE NEW! Being new means being consciously in the UN-KNOWN vs the known. This means uncertainty, and possibly being uncomfortable, momentarily!

So, Is this good or bad? Well, both really. In the situations where learned skills are necessary, such as repetitive trade skills, life skills, routine everyday tasks etc. I'd say good, so we don't mess them up much! However, the ability to act on new information, and BE NEW, in the moment is something that the mind is generally incapable of doing consistently! Why is this? In its design, it is programmed to STOP, research, and RE-act. This is how it works, and it all happens in a FLASH, I mean really fast! So fast, in fact, that it is mostly invisible to the mind that is asleep (lost in thought), or unaware. So here is what the mind does, it arrives at the doorway to NOW and it:

1. Stops time, momentarily...while it "thinks"! (Based on its own positionality, reference point, vantage point, KNOWLEDGE)

2. Researches, while on pause, to find the closest match to the current "input" (information, situation, etc.). Just be careful here though because it could be a similar situational thing, a similar person that looks like this person so that you match them with someone or something that you knew "like that" in the past...and this is why we can instantly like, or not trust, not like someone and never have met them before. It can also be intuition, so be just careful here! The point is the "MIND" is gathering information from the PAST, so that it can use that information as a basis to RE-act as it did the last time from what it "Knows"! It is just searching the mind database for the best alternative. So, on to step 3.

3. Using the information that it just gathered in a fraction of a second in

step 2...The MIND will RE-act. RE- means acting from a previous version of our "selves", knowledge. A memory is stepping into the moment to act as if it were us. Again, this RE-sponse is based on a biased vantage point FROM THE PAST, perception in this case is NOT reality! It is a curve fit solution based on previous decisions that is expected to work in this one.

## Faith, is relative to our ability to wake up from our psychic sleep and to be present...NOW.

WHY? Because GOD lives in the eternal present! God is omni**present** and omnipotent right?! Trustworthy? I would think so, I challenge you to take a chance and see...and you MUST arrive in the moment to find out! That is why faith is required...and also why we must know what faith is! Unfortunately, our habitual nature is to flip flop between the past and the future, depending on which one we are focused on, and which is carrying the weight of that moment. Our prior selves want to step up and react from our past, or programming(knowledge). Our future selves, our projections, which don't exist yet, also want to step up and act on our behalf and based on their vision in the future. Depending on where our focus and energy is, that's which version of our "self" will arrive at the gate. You SEE the problem with this right? In both cases, we are seeing an illusion, a virtual projection onto the mind screen of that past/future!

In most situations, this does not present a problem, especially when life is "easy". Life is "easy" when we are in the same or similar situations and the "pattern" can respond and that doesn't cause an issue! It is when we live life to the fullest and challenge our "selves" to do better, to overachieve, in new ways, putting us in new situations...or life throws us a curve ball, so to speak. That requires us to be NEW, and we are not accustomed to doing this! That is also when we run into resistance that turns us. We are in unfamiliar territory, and that may be uncomfortable. In the moment (just before the moment) it turns us from being in the moment to either past me, or future me, searching for solutions. In both cases, IT doesn't have an answer, AND we are not present! Let's further dissect this and repeat that there is no state of trying. **Marshall Sylver**[103] showed me this as a pretty cool demonstration in his course. He basically put a pencil in his hand and instructed someone to pick it up. The point was that either you picked it up, or you didn't. This was an example he showed on his video presentation, in his course. So TRUE!

It is the same with presence. You are either present, or you are not. If you are not present you are living from, either the past you or future you. Unfortunately, this is driven by the same emotional baggage and storylines that comes with them. So, for instance, if you are in the past and driven by the past you will enter situations in which you experienced something, either good, bad, or indifferent, but most times if we are carrying it forward it has some kind of charge to it, such as previous pain, and / or a stigma with it, possibly with a fear of a bad result. Similarly, if you are in the future and entering a situation where you have never been before, you may be anxious, or fearful, that it may not turn out as desired...which also may be relative to your previous track record. So, what your mind does, is it creates an ideal, and then becomes attached to that "illusion". So, your mind flip flops from past to future. Again, depending on what is carrying the weight, and where your attention goes, so goes your focus, and energy...so that will determine WHO (what version of self vs "SELF") arrives or doesn't arrive in the moment to make the decision!

**FAITH is going to be dependent on your ability to TRUST!** What are you trusting though? Are you trusting your "self", GOD, the ether, the probabilities? Let me break it down to components, it may help. Let us say that maybe in the case of "faith" there is a state of trying, for kicks and giggles. To the extent you can "try" to remain present will be the equivalent to your "FAITH"...and remember that faith represents your ability to TRUST, and TRUST converts to "LOVE" and unconditional love is GOD, right? It's like a super-fast metamorphosis.

So, a situation presents itself that has an emotional component to it, you have been there before with a negative result, or positive, doesn't matter...regardless it is a very important event to future you. For whatever reason, this event has a stigma attached to it. Therefore, you are either somewhat, or VERY "attached" to the result. That means baggage, right?

With various degrees of "attachment" lets propose some scenarios. When you are not really attached to the result, your ability to be present is amplified tremendously. In other words, presence in unemotional situations is easier. Less baggage, and minimal energy to manage. We are more than capable of handling the energy involved here, so overwhelm is certainly not an issue. So, past you, and future you are less likely to intrude on your moment and BECOME you for that moment. In this scenario, you are not really "attached" to the result, and therefore are able to TRUST in a reasonable outcome... "whatever happens...happens" is your mindset. (a state of detachment) In these scenarios, we ordinarily get a reasonable outcome, do we not? That is because potentially, as an example... 1-20% of you may still be in the past, and maybe 5% is hoping a certain thing happens, but you are then 75% or more unattached or primarily present! We basically trusted in a reasonable outcome, something good would happen, and it did!

Let's introduce a different scenario with a more weighted and "attached" situational and "personal" BIAS. In other words, you really want one thing to happen vs another. Again, as an example, there may be 30% of you that is thinking through past examples, it remembers previous versions of yourself and the associated successes and failures. There is another 60% of you that is projecting this imaginary "good" result, and the "you" that is necessary to make that result happen. This leaves only 10% of you to be present...with "faith". That is NOT a whole lot of manifesting capacity. In fact, you have reduced your ability to focus and decide IN THE MOMENT drastically because your processor is nearly maxed out.

Unfortunately, if that situation does not occur exactly as your mind projected it, you will be very much like a deer in the headlights, because the future you is here in this moment, and future you did not project this, so future you has no idea what to do. While past you and future you have been scanning the mind for a similar situation like this, they are eating up a huge amount of bandwidth, 90% of it! They are projecting their videos for how things were OR ought to be so they can re-act accordingly...the moment has passed, and a decision was made either for you or by you, but it wasn't you that made the decision.

It was either made by:

1. The situation

2. Past you

3. Future you

YOU dropped the ball; YOU were not present! So, you either had the situation answer to the situation, a former self stepped in and acted the same as the last time it was in a similar situation, or future you guessed and that was your RE-sponse. In each of these scenarios, YOU were not even in the moment! (i.e., you were blinded by your "selves").

Let's face it, we get caught up in the past and future a LOT! The "task" at hand doesn't even need to be a difficult task. Even in small seemingly meaningless tasks this can happen, such as picking up the salt, or pepper...or something out of the refrigerator. If our mind is elsewhere, do we drop things? If the mind was not "occupied", is it really difficult to grab the ketchup without dropping it on the floor? NO, the mind was temporarily not present. This is stuff that happens when the mind gets sidetracked. Did you ever really drill down on where the mind was that moment that you dropped something? What was it "thinking"? It was more than likely in a projection...mind imagery vs present. That mind imagery is where? Typically, it is past/future oriented, or envisioning something on the mind screen, but not here, NOW! Daydreaming, or whatever else! A momentary blip, and boom, spilled milk or an exploding bottle of ketchup! If this happens performing routine tasks, imagine if there is a life situation, or a competitive / demanding situation and something is really on the line, with ENERGY, and more DATA throttling in! How much more bandwidth is required performing a complex task, in a fast-moving environment, and how quickly can this type of scenario happen? Life happens fast, a snap of the fingers and the moment is gone...it would not take but a fraction of a second and we will have missed it. That is why the statement, narrow is the gate. It's not a gate per se, it is a time slot, essentially NOW!

Trust emanates from faith, which enables and empowers it. It enables by open-ing the door giving it access to NOW, the moment! It empowers by giving it FULL access, all alone, without the "selves". It has eliminated the distraction. The "selves" would have taken us on a detour, out of the moment, distracted, elsewhere in TIME! We essentially gave this higher version of "SELF" ALL of the power vs none of the power. Without faith and trust, the moment was inaccessible, NOW, it is. I'd certainly call that empowered. Take the selves out of the picture with awareness and skill, add faith and trust, and you have a pretty solid game plan!

Let's introduce a third scenario, you have paid attention, and with a lot of hard work, YOU have GROWN tremendously. With your enhanced SKILLS, you have become better and better at meeting the moment as the moment occurs. Years and years have passed, and you have become brilliant at TRUSTING and "allowing"! What does this mean? It means that you have grown to understand that whatever situation you are brought to, you are bigger than, and the answer will arrive in that moment to assist you(trust)! You are completely and unwa-veringly NOT attached to the outcome (future you), and you have completely forgotten about or released the past (past you, no regrets, no baggage)! In this scenario, you are Zero percent limited by the past versions of "you" because they have been slowly and surely RELEASED in favor of growth and learning in the moment! In other words, our older more limited selves have been seen, understood, and LET GO in previous present moments! We have seen and know all their tricks! LOL. Releasing them is what allows you to ACT as the higher "SELF", the BEST SELF in this moment! These former versions of you have been "integrated" / updated with new information, and the new software that is more optimized deletes the old. You are gaining NEW skills moment by moment and current methodologies that are necessary relative to THIS particular challenge, which helps. This essentially UN-limits the YOU, increases the trust factor, amplifies faith, and maximizes YOUR ability to be present this time. NOW!

As you aim for success in whatever it is you are dreaming of achieving, you have grown to accept that whatever situational information arrives in the moment will be met by a YOU that is able and qualified to ACT in your own best interest NOW (trust). While I (you) don't necessarily have all the informational components, nor have we been in this exact scenario, whatever this moment brings, the "I" will be awake, aware, and PRESENT to get the guidance needed to make the best decision. THIS IS FAITH. When you have released the past and all the little selves that have the potential to affect an outcome, you have ZERO situational biases pulling you to the past. Likewise, if you are unattached to the result because you have learned that ANY result is OK...you have ZERO situational bias pulling you into to the future. In this scenario your ability (hypothetically) to remain present and TRUST, and to have FAITH is 100%. In this situation you have the opportunity to BECOME the best version of YOU! YOU are capable of being the instrument!

What is the instrument in the moment? What is the answer? Isn't it LOVE? If you become LOVE, it is never wrong! Without the selves stepping in front of you at the gate, and without your "baggage", YOU can trust, you can "allow" and you can BE PRESENT, NOW! GOD meets YOU in the moment to ACT. Your focus is FLAWLESS, your faith is <u>unwavering</u>, and your ability to act in your own and others' best interest is PERFECT. YOU are presence! YOU ARE THAT! Love is the answer.

### What does that make YOU? LOVE, YOU became it!

Becoming faith and love is relative to your ability to TRUST and be present. They all go together. GOD lives in the NOW, in the eternal PRESENT, that's why presence is needed...and that is where / when you can BECOME the best version of your highest SELF. That is where / when you can **ALLOW**. As an example, remember that "YOU" that you wanted to be? The one you INTEND to be. Reminder, it's that one that brings tears to your eyes when you see a projection of your potential self in life, a movie, or someone you admire. That is where / when YOU CAN GROW into that version of YOU, the one that you have not quite become yet! That is where you can ACT in a way that is TRUE to yourself, and not make the same mistakes over and over again. That is when and where GOD is truly on your side and the ability to "SEE" and "HEAR" is guiding YOU instantly because finally YOU are in the moment to actually hear and see the guidance! This is timeless guidance; it is NOW and NOW and NOW! Complete Love and Complete faith are always available, however, you must meet the moment to receive the guidance and BECOME IT!

Stated a different way, if you are 10% present, and 90% asleep at the wheel; you are losing 90% of your ability to hear and see the guidance that is available in the moment. Your faith in GOD, in "SELF", or in the universe, whatever... to help you in this moment is a mere 10%! 10% is not unconditional, is it? In fact, if you really think about it from the other side of this equation, that will mean 90% LIMITED! Yikes, that doesn't sound favorable, does it?

If you are 50% asleep at the wheel, and 50% present your chances are increasing dramatically to "TRUST", have faith, and ACT on the guidance you receive. BUT there are problems with 50%...it's basically a coin toss! What will you HEAR and SEE? There is a good portion of the time that what you hear or see will be the wrong side of the coin, especially with all that mind chatter going on to distract you! Why? Because the little "you" that meets the moment is a hypothetical version of you, a projection by past or future you, which is bringing an illusion into the present and acting on it vs what is really here in this moment. Past you brought a past situational response to a similar situation and just made the same decision, or future you projected a scenario and decided based its decision on a guess what might work. Think about all the cross currents too, all the mind chatter and the bandwidth that it's eating up! These decisions are all based on an illusion, a projection on the mind screen, do you see this?

As an alternative, what if the higher "YOU" ACTS on the information received in the moment without the involvement of these past / future "selves". That would mean we are more available, present, awake and aware and REAL guidance would have a chance to reach us. We could decide NOW, based on current REAL information, right? That's a "REAL TIME" ACTION, and it is that higher "SELF" within YOU that must show up to take it!!!! ACTION vs RE-action!

As you increase TRUST in your "SELF" or the "UNIVERSE", or "GOD" your faith increases! GOOD NEWS...your ability to meet the moment and BE in the moment is also amplified. Therefore, when you gradually quiet the mind, and the number of "selves" making suggestions, or voices in your head are fewer and fewer, the "NOISE" level goes down. Don't you think that the likelihood you hear the correct voice (See / hear the truth) is amplified as well? When 45 people are speaking in the same room (your mind), at the same time, what do you hear? It's a mish mosh right? Its hard to make sense of it. Exaggeration, yes, I get it, but seriously, don't you think that without carrying all that baggage, hearing that "Still Small Voice" is going to be a lot easier? In fact, because you will experience this ability and learn to trust this ability, your faith will also naturally increase.

Continuing with the example. As you eliminate more and more programming and reduce the "NOISE" level, as well as the need to attach yourself to the outcomes in each situation, you expand your presence even more. Faith grows as a result. Your FAITH becomes more "trusting" as you enhance the skill. They are basically feeding one another, like a turbo compressing them through those final few stages just prior to the gate! One is fuel, the other oxygen. Your faith is increasingly being injected into the engine by YOU with your skill. TRUST and FAITH are adding fuel to the fire! Your ability to stay present is being amplified as a result. With more presence you are not flip flopping back and forth from the past to the future eating up bandwidth, so that added presence is adding even more fuel to fire, its purer, and responds even better to the added faith, so they both expand, building on each other. This is where you have to channel the energy and focus, HARD to manage from the overseer post because of the uptick in energy being thrust through the system!!! This is a massive amount of energy, it needs to be distributed appropriately, and that converts to MORE SKILL. When your skill level is increasing to where it is climbing into higher and higher percentages of the time, YOU, as the higher "SELF" are being present more and more, then YOU begin to hear and see the truth more as well (still small voice), which ADDS even more FAITH. This has a compounding effect. As you attain 60---70---80 and even higher percentages of "presence", with AWARENESS, your FAITH increases in like kind, and as you approach the edge of NOW, FAITH and TRUST are basically building on each other really super-duper fast, like a snowball rolling down a giant hill, but remember this is a FIRE, combustion! More fuel and more oxygen being highly compressed and burned IN THE MOMENT! The cool thing is that the natural faith building process is feeding the fire, which is feeding ITSELF....because you need more and more energy to get you there, into the moment! Finally, they combine to give you a final push, like a quantum leap into NOW as these thrust you through the gate and BOOOM, like a final flash, and HERE YOU ARE, NOW! PRESENCE.

It's like this ridiculously fast chain reaction, trust, faith, presence...BOOM! The moment explodes with OPPORTUNITY! The opportunity offers a new choice, and the moment is infinite, which means what? It is not limited. I would suggest that means UNLIMITED! Endless opportunity, how does that sound?

If you want a fun visual of parting with a former self that no longer serves us, lets back up a fraction of a second...and replay that as a variation of a song I heard recently. It goes like this, in my words, but check out the song below too, it's really cool. My words: Blah Blah Blah, and then, faith and trust are feeding the fire and right at the narrow gate, super compressed, squeeeeeezing juuust small enough to fit in the gate and BOOOOOM, a massive supernova as it blows those last few "selves" to smithereens AT THE GATE, and this final explosion pushes YOU through the narrow gate, all alone, no baggage, one solitary SELF arrives in NOW! How fun was that? You are the only one that makes it through the gate! You really "processed" those former selves. HAH! Woo-hoo. When you arrive IN THE MOMENT, YOU BECOME PRESENCE. Your processing power / speed has increased dramatically as well. YOU are FREE to BECOME! You have the power, with guidance and no distractions! Choose wisely :)

Credit to **Within Temptation** again for the song. It was their song that put that visual in my mind to share with you, so thanks to them, I really enjoyed it. CHUCKLE! Song reference, **"Supernova"**[104]! What a fun way to process a lesson, part with a former "self" that we have grown out of and become NEW as we arrive to the moment! Nice fireworks display to celebrate :) That doesn't actually happen, well, it kind of does, and it's a fun visual...

**With FOCUS, AWARENESS & ENERGY, YOU are gifted even more FAITH AND GUIDANCE in the moment of NOW! In that moment, YOU and your abilities are amplified with 100% CLARITY, and YOU can HEAR and SEE the guidance NOW available.** Your processor NOW has ZERO distractions! The interesting thing that you'll undoubtedly see, is that faith becomes love in the moment to the extent that it shows up through us and LOVE answers. When faith becomes 100%, it represents unconditional LOVE, and anything that is met with unconditional LOVE is met with exactly what it needs in that moment! Let's just say that the choice is there, whether or not YOU make it is something you'll need to pay attention to!

Check out this Johnny Nash song below as a lesson recap. While this may not be exactly what he was referring to, it is a super perspective, and I love the positive nature of the song! It is also a nice reminder of what happens when you take on this overseer perspective. Once you do, you can see the obstacles, and see the darkness within, with awareness and new eyes so to speak! By seeing them with your new skills, you can remove them, or let them fall away quite naturally. As a result, you can see much more clearly, and then go right ahead and have an absolutely beautiful sunny day as depicted in the song! What a great song to exemplify this perspective and use as a reminder to STAY PRESENT as the overseer. Thank you, Johnny!

### "I can see clearly now"
### -Johnny Nash[105]

Seeing clearly gives you CHOICE! Faith & trust get you there, LOVE can answer, but you have to CHOOSE IT! You choose it with PRESENCE by BECOMING IT! Be the instrument.

Having said that, let's assess the faith and belief factor from a different angle because this is really important! It can be seen in so many biblical statements, in different ways, depending on bible version. The one that immediately comes to mind is this one: To those that have, more shall be given...and to those that have not, they will lose what little they have.

**Mathew 13:12** says it this way:

### "For whoever has, to him more will be given, and he will have abundance; but whoever does not have, even what he has will be taken away from him."[106]

This can be problematic for a lot of people, mainly because it is not understood. I always want things to be fair for people, and that doesn't seem fair. So, WHY is this true?

A lot of people seem to think, well, if I am "GOOD" I should get rewarded...like MORE, not less! But it doesn't seem to work that way, does it? Sometimes, yes, but other times, not so much...so there must be a caveat, right? So, let's talk about that. If you don't get it from the above, it has to do with faith, but in a slightly different context. The basic answer is that it isn't necessarily based on "merit", per se, but it CAN BE, so yes, caveat indeed. In this case it is based on our BELIEF in merit, which is what? In a different frame of reference, it is essentially what we are having faith in, what we are believing we are entitled to, or "deserve", so to speak at a deeper level! It is a certain "worthiness", or lack of it. A deep embedded unconscious belief, OR karma if looking at it from a different spiritual philosophy. So, Let's dissect it.

For those that "have not"...they have patterned beliefs that are programmed, and within. If you are not conscious, not present, not awake, and NOT aware, then what are you? <u>Unconscious</u>! So, when you are unconscious, or asleep at the wheel, remember that your core beliefs are driving what occurs in your life, NOT YOU! Because you are unconscious, (not in the moment) your beliefs are in the past and future and aligned with the little "selves", and THEIR STORIES. They (as you) will step into every situation and respond to that situation as if it was a past or future as the "selves". (Your stories) Therefore, that "<u>have not</u>" personality or "self" is programmed to, believes in, and has FAITH in "have not" at a core level! When the situation presents itself, as it will, and since you are unconscious, you RE-act from the programmed selves (vs. the REAL SELF...the NEW YOU) the programmed RE-action is going be aligned with "have not" and so what little you have shall be taken from you.... until you make a decision to WAKE UP!!!! Without waking up, you are on autopilot, nothing changes! You wake up with SKILL when YOU can muster the strength, energy, and where-with-all to ARRIVE in the moment with focus, awareness, faith, trust, and PRESENCE! That is where a NEW choice is available to the HIGHER YOU, the one that is NOT aligned with LACK, or have not! This NEW YOU with awareness and presence can CHOOSE abundance, as an example, or CHOOSE to "feel deserving" if you believe in a more merit-based system! In that world, you will have moved from "not worthy", to "WORTHY" from a mind and belief / faith perspective! Semantics, really. The point is, with presence, CHOICE is available to CHOOSE a better thought which affects our results. Law of attraction, what we focus on expands, right? We are CONCIOUSLY CHOOSING what to focus on.

Relative to feeling "worthy", and to appreciate their purpose. Aren't the 10 commandments designed to make us feel more worthy? It's like a top ten list. Do all that, and you should, at a minimum, feel a little better about your "self"! Wouldn't that be in essence, treating others as we expect and want to be treated? Do we not feel a little bit more deserving? We feel a little bit better, have a little more self-esteem. Not that it puts a chip on your shoulder or anything, we can simply value our "selves" and feel good. That is the religious version of a merit-based system. Integrity, Morality, all that "stuff" contributes to that feeling of and belief in worthiness. That is of course assuming you are conscious enough to have CHOICE and make the right ones! That is the difference between having beliefs and being able to honor them, it means waking up, being in the NOW! Consciousness, PRESENCE! If you are NOT conscious to make "good" choices and are therefore unable to follow the commandments for example, then where does that put you? What happens if you lie, cheat, steal, etc.? Remorse, regret, guilt = no fun. All the negative emotions. Do you feel good about yourself? Worthy? In addition, WHERE are these emotions? IN THE PAST! It amplifies our unconsciousness and then we miss the next moment too, because we are looking back to the past, and again we miss the lessons...which compounds it! It cycles on and on until we wake up! Until we wake up, the negative cycles just repeat. So, in essence that means that the "have not", in the merit-based system, is getting what they believe they deserve...at their CORE! Why though? It simply comes back to the fact that they are unconscious. Unconscious responses and RE-actions are going to be aligned with your core beliefs. In this case, your core beliefs are NOT WORTHY, they believe in "have not"! So, is that fair? You actually might argue that it is. Did karma come back and bite them or did they simply get what they believe they deserved, and/or what they had faith in? Arguably, they got what they had faith in.

So, let's look at the other side of the equation, to those that "HAVE" more shall be given! Yes, indeed, we see it all the time! Let's be honest, some people just seem lucky right? Stuff just falls in their lap it seems, over and over. I get it, really, I do...did you ever wonder though, WHY? I mean, seriously, why is that? Is there any jealousy or animosity here? Can you say "trigger", uh oh, time to do some digging!! Ok, so either way, let's dissect this too. Haves: please understand that they are also programmed, and have beliefs, we all do, right? We are human. But, contrary to the previous example, now those CORE beliefs are in "having". Their "selves" believe in the abundance idea, and they are aligned with "MORE". The interesting thing is that even though they can often be asleep at the wheel, their programmed responses can still be reasonably successful. (In the eyes of the world) The fact is that they TRUST in abundance, they have "FAITH" in having...and so their choices are going to be biased and aligned with more because at their core, they believe in it...and so they are given more! EVEN if unconscious. Makes perfect sense, right? They are also getting what they have faith in.

Put another way, those that have not are programmed and their software is geared to have not. It is possible that they are fearful, or don't feel worthy for whatever reason, and that could be due to any number of negative patterns. Moses gave us 10 of them! Regardless, their beliefs are aligned with NOT having! Their true faith is in not having. Where attention goes, energy flows right?! If you are not paying attention, energy will flow to your pre-programmed beliefs. Have not's have beliefs that allow them to have not. Haves have pre-programmed beliefs that allow them to HAVE! In some cases, haves are thankful and appreciative for what they have, that attitude of gratitude amplifies it, it is a programmed response to having, and so it is expected! If it is expected, it is more apt to come even if that person is asleep at the wheel and they are unconscious. Belief and faith build on one another and they are only DELIVERING what is believed in, and what that person has faith in. Said another way... if you think you can or you think you can't, you are right! Fact is, we are delivered, every moment of every day...EXACTLY what we believe in.

Beliefs drive the equation! If you want to change your life, WAKE UP, hop in the driver's seat, and take hold of the wheel. Be watchful and realize what or WHO is making the decisions in your life, NOW! These former "selves", their programming, and their choices might not be aligned with your glorious imagery of the future! When you do this consistently, over and over again, you begin to override their pre-programmed responses in favor of your "SELF" and higher guidance. In doing so you override the negative cycles, the recurring patterns, and ALLOW a different YOU to bring different results. This is because you are INTENTIONALLY redirecting your focus IN THE MOMENT to have faith in something different, your TRUST is INTENTIONALLY placed in your NEW version of "SELF" in this moment, and your ability to ACT from the guidance you receive! You have great power in INTENT, but it needs to be intent that is unattached...untainted, that is a part of the skill. You CAN arrive to NOW with intent that is untarnished, you really can. That version of YOU has faith and trusts in "SELF", "GOD" or the "Universe" and arrives in the moment to receive the guidance to ACT in the moment! Do this and YOU will know the TRUTH and your actions will be according to TRUTH...and you will be AMAZED at life!

Intent carrying baggage, such as a fear of failure, guilt, remorse, regret will fail. Even though you may visualize a wonderful outcome, your intent is tarnished by an attachment (negative association, negative charge, FEAR) and that attachment will drive the "you" that is attached into the current moment. That you will make the decision in the moment (Instead of the real YOU) and the decision will be driven by where your attention is. In this case since you are driven by fear, the fear is going to drive you to WHAT IS FEARED, and you will get your feared result rather than what you "wanted"! Wanting something while fearing the alternative doesn't work to get you what you want, it works to get you what you DON'T WANT because that is what you have faith in, by default! In the merit-based system that is what you believe you deserve. When the fear of the alternative is greater than the faith in the desired, fear wins! Your attention, your focus, your vantage point must change!!!!

You must break the cycle of fear in your life and the only way to do that is by understanding the selves that drive that fear, as well as the other emotions. You do that by being present to your "selves" and watching them as they react for you over and over again in situation after situation PRESENTLY, NOW. As you do this, and as you start to understand the old versions of "you" that need updated software, the opportunity will present itself for you to release these patterns...by

CHOICE! As YOU release more and more of these "old you" patterns, as you release more and more of these little "selves", you "empty your cup"!

## As you empty your cup of the baggage, you simply allow FAITH to fill it up.

As more programming is released, more faith enters, as more faith enters, more TRUST arrives, as more trust is allowed in, LOVE can arrive in each moment. As YOU begin to HEAR and SEE with clarity, even more faith comes. As even more faith comes, better decisions result, LOVE grows...as better decisions result from your ability to see and hear the guidance available in the moment, more faith grows. And to those that have...more shall be given! FAITH: to those that have... more shall be given. FAITH! Faith literally builds on itself like a snowball rolling downhill which builds up the trust factor. It feeds on itself, gaining strength, and giving us the intestinal fortitude to take that next step!

HAVE FAITH! Focus and really drill down on it, pay attention, and SEE it as often as you can muster the energy...faith, faith, faith, faith! I cannot say this with any more emphasis or any more emphatically, but I'd like to, so in ultra-BOLD, please hear this:

## Whatever I am focused on IS what I am having faith IN!

Whatever it is, it will expand! Focus on LACK, then LACK will expand, focus on ABUNDANCE and ABUNDANCE will expand! Don't focus on anything at all and flip a coin! If you are unconscious though, just know that the probabilities will favor your core patterns and overall magnetism! The odds favor the house, so if your house is filled with core beliefs that are all negative, find the door! Sorry, that's just the reality of it and it is relevant to everything you do, in all areas of life! You don't have a choice until you arrive IN THE MOMENT to CHOOSE! Take care of your "SELF" and choose wisely! The door is right after yesterday, and right before tomorrow. Right after the past, and before the future. **With faith you can get there, trust opens the door, presence walks through, there YOU HAVE CHOICE! NOW!**

## MAKE BETTER CHOICES, live in the NOW.

If you want more in your life then FEEL more deserving, worthy! It totally builds on itself...

We live in an abundant universe! KNOW THIS, THINK THIS, LIVE THIS...it takes practice, and conscious aware PRESENCE! What you have faith in IS being demonstrated in your life right now. If you think you deserve better, then BELIEVE you deserve better. Make the choices that are aligned with it. If that means doing good deeds to "earn it", then do good deeds! You MUST have FAITH, TRUST and BELIEVE!

**The most powerful form of prayer is to believe in something BEFORE IT HAPPENS, AS IF it has already happened. That is faith!** If you truly believe that you are not worthy, then you will be fighting an uphill battle! Lose the guilt, remorse, or whatever the negativity is. Please, please, please understand this, it is in the past, process it, understand that it was a former self that made that decision, basically a former life before waking up! The fact of the matter is that bad choices are made unconsciously, unaware... FORGIVE IT!!!! You have to let it go, and just do your absolute best to be present next time so it doesn't happen again! Not letting it go is no good, in fact, very BAD! It's like holding on to "GUILT" as an example, and in particular. It causes all kinds of negativity, in the mind AND body simply by holding onto it. It is POISON to the mind and body! Now you know why! LET IT GO!!!!!

If you do have pain, look up **Louise Hay**, what a wonderful resource!

## "You can heal your life".[107]

Do whatever it takes to wake up and BE WORTHY enough to BELIEVE IT and have faith in it! Have faith, think faith, live faith. Faith demonstrates what was believed in a moment ago! That is your current life. Think on that.

If you are a believer, why did Jesus die for our sins? The simple answer is above, to make a "sinner" FEEL WORTHY again. It eliminated the requirement for "suffering". It is difficult if not almost impossible for people that have done really bad things to forgive themselves. Carrying that forward is almost unbearable and the mental RUT, and physical ailments that ordinarily follow as a result can make life extremely difficult. Fact is, that is what we believe we deserve, so we punish ourselves. Consciously, and unconsciously. With understanding, it is FORGIVEN, no matter what. Jesus basically cleaned the slate, for lack of a better way to put it. No longer is it on you to do it. He said, I'll do it FOR YOU! You must believe, IT IS DONE, because it is. He even said so.

## "GO; it shall be done for you as you have believed"
### -Mathew 8:13[108]

In order to DEMONSTRATE a new pattern, for example, in someone's life, what must happen? Faith and belief in something different must happen. Right? Where does this start? WITHIN! **Faith is WITHIN!** Faith DEMONSTRATED, is demonstrated by the ACTION we just took. Was the ACTION you just took an ACTION, or a RE-action? It was generated from within, either way, do you see? WE MUST arrive IN the moment to **REPRESENT** as our "SELF", higher SELF that is!!! If you allow the former "selves" to run your life, what change is possible? What do the former selves believe in? Look at your life, that's what they believed in, up to today's date, a moment ago! Are you ready to believe in something different? Maybe have faith in something different? How? You know the answer already, NOW!

I want to show this to you in someone else's words too, maybe it will help. This is from **Ralph Waldo Emerson** in his essay **"The Over-Soul"**[109]. I will just refer to him as **"Emerson"** from here on out for ease! I love this, He says we don't even represent ourselves! Check it out:

"A man is the facade of a temple wherein all wisdom and all good abide. What we commonly call man, the eating, drinking, planting, counting **man, does not, as we know him, represent himself**, but **misrepresents himself**. Him we do not respect, but the soul, whose organ he is, **would he let it appear through his action**, would make our knees bend. When it breathes through his intellect, **it is genius**; when it breathes through his will, **it is virtue**; **when it flows** through his affection, **it is love**."[110]

More **Emerson**:

"Ineffable is the union of man and God in every **act** of the soul. The simplest person, who in his integrity worships God, becomes God; yet for ever and ever the influx of this better and universal self is **new and unsearchable**. It inspires awe and astonishment. How dear, how soothing to man, arises the idea of God, peopling the lonely place, effacing the scars of our mistakes and disappointments! When we have broken our god of tradition, and ceased from our god of rhetoric, then **may God fire the heart with his presence**. It is the doubling of the heart itself, nay, **the infinite enlargement of the heart** with a **power of growth to a new infinity on every side. It inspires in man an infallible trust**. He has not the conviction, but the sight, that the best is the true, and may in that thought easily dismiss all particular uncertainties and fears, and adjourn to the sure revelation of time, the solution of his private riddles. He is sure that his welfare is dear to the heart of being. **In the __presence__** of law to his mind, he is overflowed with a **__reliance__** so universal, that it sweeps away all cherished hopes and the most stable projects of mortal condition in its flood. **He believes** that he cannot escape from his good. The things that are really for thee gravitate to thee."[111]

More **Emerson**:

"You are running to seek your friend. Let your feet run, but your mind need not. If you do not find him, will you not acquiesce that it is best you should not find him? for there is a power, which, as it is in you, is in him also, and could therefore very well bring you together, if it were for the best. You are preparing with eagerness to go and render a service to which your talent and your taste invite you, the love of men and the hope of fame. Has it not occurred to you, that you have no right to go, unless you are equally willing to be prevented from going?"[112]

In other words UNATTACHED to the outcome! What is reliance? TRUST, right? What exactly is he describing here? An infallible trust is FAITH, in my opinion. Like as in error free, unfailing, faultless, PERFECT! How perfect can it be, maybe infinitely perfect? What would that describe, THE TRUTH? The truth is the only thing that I could think of that would be forever perfect. This is amazing stuff...the whole text from Oversoul is incredible, check out the links provided! I just inserted a few of the more powerful statements. In my opinion, the references to presence, GOD, time, and space...trust, faith...it is all the same as what I am describing above. It explains how you are to be the "watcher", and how that allows you to "see and hear" (in the moment) and also the nature of the relationship with GOD! Quite cool really, take the time to understand it! Emerson really helped me grasp this idea, and this understanding.

HERE is a little more **EMERSON** that I think is really powerful:

"Of this pure nature every man is at some time sensible. Language cannot paint it with his colors. It is too subtle. It is undefinable, unmeasurable, but we know that it pervades and contains us. We know that all spiritual being is in man. A wise old proverb says, "**God comes to see us without bell**"; that is, as **there is no screen or ceiling between our heads and the infinite heavens,** so is there no bar or wall in the soul where man, the effect, ceases, and God, the cause, begins. The walls are taken away. We lie open on one side to the deeps of spiritual nature, to the attributes of God. Justice we see and know, Love, Freedom, Power. These natures no man ever got above, but they tower over us, and most **in the moment** when **our interests tempt us** to wound them."[113]

Our perceptions/biases **"our interests tempt us"**. Is this not a specific instruction to look WITHIN? Within what? Within Temptation! More specifically we are to look within the temptation to RE-act from the "selves" and as the "selves" instead of BEING NEW and UN-limited! We must SEE these self-created walls, limitations...and take them DOWN, UN-LIMIT them! This is HOW to do it! IN THE MOMENT!

WITHIN TEMPTATION is also the name of the band I reference so much, coincidence? I think not! Within temptation is where the lesson is! You can be tempted, and then don't RE-act from the "selves", DO ACT from the higher "SELF"! With conscious awareness and presence, CHOICE is available.

More **EMERSON**:

"**The sovereignty of this nature** whereof we speak **is made known by its independency of those limitations** which circumscribe us on every hand. The soul circumscribes all things. As I have said, **it contradicts all experience**. In like manner **it abolishes time and space. The influence of the senses has, in most men, overpowered the mind** to that degree, that the walls of time and space have come to look real and insurmountable; and to speak with levity of these limits is, in the world, the sign of insanity. Yet time and space are but inverse measures of the force of the soul. The spirit sports with time"

"Can crowd eternity into an hour, or stretch an hour to eternity."[114]

Sovereignty is what? Dominion... SUPREME POWER! It also seems to imply that maybe we should look at time with a little different lens? When we do, we can see that we essentially get locked out of the moment. With awareness, we can see it happen. We must increase our awareness to the point where we can see it happen. Seeing it happen is key, the eye opener.

Check this out too, from a different essay: **Emerson "Spiritual Laws"** In this Essay, he says:

"**The lesson** is forcibly taught by these observations, that our life might be much easier and simpler than we make it; that the world might be a happier place than it is; that there is no need of struggles, convulsions, and despairs, of the wringing of the hands and the gnashing of the teeth; that we miscreate our own evils. We interfere with the optimism of nature; for, **whenever we get this**

**vantage-ground of the past, or of a wiser mind in the present, we are able to discern that we are begirt with laws which execute themselves**."[115]

These are the "LAWS" I am speaking of...and explaining! The instructions are written a little differently by **Emerson**, how cool right? **Emerson** goes on to say a lot more so let's break some of it down:

"...A little consideration of what takes place around us every day would show us, that a higher law than that of our will regulates events; that our painful labors are unnecessary, and fruitless; that **only in our easy, simple, spontaneous action are we strong**, and by contenting ourselves with obedience we become divine.

**Belief and love**, -- a believing love will relieve us of a vast load of care. O my brothers, **God exists**. There is a soul at the centre of nature, and over the will of every man, so that none of us can wrong the universe. It has so infused its strong enchantment into nature, that we prosper when we accept its advice, and when we struggle to wound its creatures, our hands are glued to our sides, or they beat our own breasts. **The whole course of things goes to teach us faith**. We need only obey. **There is guidance for each of us**, and **by lowly listening we shall hear the right word**."[116]

The right words are only available to us in the NOW, the moment. The moment is infinite, eternal...the future and the past do not exist. Heaven is at hand, it is NOW. GOD exists NOW! The more appropriate question is where are you? Even better question is WHEN are you? If you can BE present...you can experience GOD, you can get the guidance, with faith and trust! If you can only move from the past to the future, you are skipping over your presents (presence)! FAITH is not something to be believed in, as if some future result, some future outcome, some future thing...**FAITH is a SKILL**, an ability...and only comes with practice and effort... NOW!

It's nice to hear it in someone else's words...it reinforces the lesson keys, so here is a little more **Emerson** from the Essay: **"Self Reliance"**:

"The relations of the soul to the divine spirit are so pure, that it is profane to seek to interpose helps. It must be that when **God speaketh** he should communicate, not one thing, but all things; should fill the world with his voice; should scatter forth light, nature, time, souls, **from the centre of the present thought**; and new date and new create the whole. **Whenever a mind is simple, and receives a divine wisdom**, old things pass away, -- means, teachers, texts, temples fall; **it lives now, and absorbs past and future into the present hour**. All things are made sacred by relation to it, -- one as much as another. All things are dissolved to their centre by their cause, and, in the universal miracle, petty and particular miracles disappear. If, therefore, a man claims to know and speak of God, and carries you backward to the phraseology of some old mouldered nation in another country, in another world, believe him not. Is the acorn better than the oak which is its fulness and completion? Is the parent better than the child into whom he has cast his ripened being? Whence, then, this worship of the past? The centuries are conspirators against the sanity and authority of the soul. **Time and space are but physiological colors which the eye makes,** but **the soul is light; where it is, is day; where it was, is night; and <u>history is an impertinence and an injury, if it be anything more than a cheerful apologue or parable of my being and becoming</u>**."[117]

In the instance where we can gain the lesson, <u>history is a parable</u>, my history...when I use it PROPERLY, to look back quickly to a moment ago, just long enough to get the lesson, grow, and then BECOME NEW...so that the next time, I SEE IT! I AM BECOMING NEW, that is a cheerful way to look at the past vs BLAME or any of the negative emotions, don't you think? A little more productive? It even explains that if we use it for more than that it is inappropriate, and it INJURES US! Use it for BEING and BECOMING! It is a LESSON, nothing more, please get the lesson and BE NEW! It sure seems as if Emerson is saying the same thing here, in different words. I love that it seems to be reinforcing the lessons we have been looking at so thoroughly!

"Man is timid and apologetic; he is no longer upright; he dares not say 'I think,' 'I am,' but quotes some saint or sage. He is ashamed before the blade of grass or the blowing rose. These roses under my window make no reference to former roses or to better ones; they are for what they are; **they exist with God to-day. There is no time to them**. There is simply the rose; it is perfect in every moment of its existence. Before a leaf-bud has burst, its whole life acts; in the full-blown flower there is no more; in the leafless root there is no less. Its nature is satisfied, and it satisfies nature, in all moments alike. **<u>But man postpones or remembers; he does not live in the present, but with reverted eye laments the past, or, heedless of the riches that surround him, stands on tiptoe to foresee the future. He cannot be happy and strong until he too lives with nature in the present, above time</u>**."[118]

One paragraph later, again **EMERSON**:

"And now at last the highest truth on this subject remains unsaid; probably cannot be said; for all that we say is the far-off remembering of the intuition. That thought, by what I can now nearest approach to say it, is this. When good is near you, when you have life in yourself, it is not by any known or accustomed way; you shall not discern the foot-prints of any other; you shall not see the face of man; you shall not hear any name; ---- **the way, the thought, the good, shall be wholly strange and new. It shall exclude example and experience**. You take the way from man, not to man. All persons that ever existed are its forgotten ministers. **Fear and hope are alike beneath it**. There is somewhat low even in hope. In the hour of vision, there is nothing that can be called gratitude, nor properly joy. **The soul raised over passion beholds identity and eternal causation, perceives the self-existence of Truth and Right, and calms itself with knowing that all things go well**."[119]

**THAT IS FAITH!** Ralph Waldo Emerson was an amazing writer, thank you for this AMAZING text!!!!

Faith practiced becomes trust and LOVE, Love unconditional = GOD! GOD is in the present moment eternally...Heaven is NOW! NOW is timeless, eternal. You, with courage, trust and persistence, can arrive there with GOD...but only with FAITH! GOD is timeless... GOD is NOW! (OMNIPRESENT)

Omnipresent means present everywhere, at all times! It is my opinion that with awareness we can get the clues that are given anywhere, anyway, anyhow, but that requires us to be awake and aware and tapped in so to speak. That means when we try to revert to the past, and / or disconnect...we get a jolt, a tap on the shoulder, a hint to WAKE UP. That push alerts us or clues us in to GET PRESENT. Who did that? The same applies to the future. It's one thing to dream up some amazing future, but in the same manner, we get a signal, a twinge, a snap of the fingers so to speak to get back to NOW, as that is where choices need to be made to "make it happen"! Wake up, get the guidance...it is invaluable!

Freedom is a choice; you can be bound by the limitation of the past and/or future by your subscription to it. Or YOU can be NEW, and FREE from those limitations with GOD presently. It is your choice. Bondage is "self" given; freedom is higher "SELF" / GOD given when you TRUST that it is available!

### WITH FAITH & TRUST, YOU arrive IN the moment! The MOMENT is where CHOICE is available.

Let me give you an example of how this process in the mind works, as it steals your freedom, so that you can be alert to it, and the various ways it can happen. This should help you get better at being FREE vs letting that happen to you! Understanding is a very powerful tool to have on your side...so have a look at it from this unique perspective. It is fairly extensive, and very thorough...kind of funny too, so let yourself play with it a little bit and expand on the thought process visually in the mind. Relate this to your life and substitute in some of your passengers as you see fit. It will make it more powerful for you.

This is my BUS DRIVER analogy, as I compare it to the MIND. Please use your imagination here, it will help you to really take in the story and its meaning! You are supposed to be the bus driver...

# WHAT IS FAITH II

# GETTING IN THE ZONE VII

## The "Faith" BUS DRIVER:

P ICTURE THIS. YOU, ACTING AS the higher "SELF" are driving the faith bus, BIG rolling sign on the front and it says "**FAITH BUS**" in BOLD letters! This hypothetical bus is loaded up with a full load of passengers that all have different ideas of what faith means, and of course all kinds of destinations in mind. In fact, some of these passengers want to go backwards, and some want to go forwards. Some want to go left and some right. Below is a description of what is going on in the bus, and what these passengers are doing to "YOU" as the driver: It's primarily an A / B scenario...with a potential wild card C scenario as well. The essence of it though is that the passengers are either from the past, or the future. This represents places you have been, and places that you INTEND to go. The passengers think you are going to get them where they want to go.

On the left and right side of the bus is a string that the passengers can pull to get your attention as the bus driver. The passengers from the past are all on the left side of the bus, and the passengers of the future are on the right side of the bus:

1. The PAST passengers keep pulling the string wanting you to turn around and make a U-Turn. They think about and see the imagery in their windows, and it reminds them of something in the past. They keep pulling their string wanting you to THINK of and FROM that very worthy past and the perspectives that past generated! It might be from a moment ago, a few days ago or a few decades ago! There was a destination that really made an impact on them one way or another

and they THINK that they are still there, and that the mind strategies / directions that were created THEN still work today! The problem with these folks is they have no discretion, and it doesn't matter if that strategy / experience / impact was good or bad, they still want to go there because it's the only thing they know! They have old paper handwritten notes and map printouts that are so worn they have holes in them. Some didn't even print right from the early internet days or have water wear from spilling drinks, rainy weather, and miscellaneous food stains as well. Some of these maps are from many years ago and are drawn/printed with varying degrees of "updates" too. That said, from different print years, they each have different roads. They don't even SEE the new roads that were built since that map was created because they are still looking at these old maps! They tend to want to go revisit places that had an impact on them, good or bad, and many of these places are no longer on the newer map, they've been torn down and don't even exist anymore. In some cases, there's nothing there, and in other places something else was built in its place! Unfortunately, none of this is shown on their map, so they keep doing a double take wondering what's wrong with their map! Very confused, and a little overwhelmed. They can't quite figure out where we are, quite honestly. The problem is that they are still on the bus and have 1 or more fingers on the string! Each time there is a fork in the road, they are pulling on their string to get your attention. Depending on the weight and "impact" of that past, or the attachment to it, that will determine how hard that past passenger is pulling on that string and the harder they pull the louder the sound is amplified in your ears as the bus driver. Quite simply, it is distracting!

2. The FUTURE passengers on the right side of the bus all have different ideals, and they are a pretty vocal group. Many of their ideals are conflicting because these passengers' range in age from your current age to when you were much younger... maybe even past lifetimes if you subscribe to that "belief" system. Nevertheless, these future passengers all have GPS coordinates sort of plugged in and are watching to make sure you are on track and headed their way, towards their desired destination! BTW, some of their GPS coordinates are flat out WRONG! Anyway, each time a fork in the road comes up they are pulling the string and trying to get your attention to make you turn one way or another, so you stay on track. They have a schedule to meet, they NEED to be there at a certain time too, so they are a little edgy! Because of their timeline, they are under pressure, and in order to get to their place in time, they

need you to listen to them and do what they ask of you. TURN, or go straight, step on the gas, or hit the brakes they yell directions, all while pulling the string. The other problem with these passengers is that they are NEVER SATISFIED! There are a wide variety of these future passengers, to be sure...all with varying pitches and tones, some voices are deep and loud, and others are a little softer and even some squeaky ones! You know what happens to the squeaky wheel right? LOL Sorry, onwards... Some are feminine, others masculine, some dominating and others not so much. They are all just trying to spin the situation, so you listen to them, so that you steer one way or another! Some of them have very specific destinations in mind. These folks are so excited to get there that they are literally pulling your strings at every turn BEGGING for you to turn left or right to stay on track and on time. Then, of course, some of your favorite future passengers on the bus are so sweet and nice, super courteous and respectful, but they have no idea where they are going! They keep tugging on the string when there aren't even any turns coming up, asking "Are we there yet"? Can you say CLUELESS? Yep, some of these future selves pull the string for no reason!

3. OK, YES, there is a 3rd scenario, way more actually but let's keep this simple! You, as the bus driver, are watching the road! Eyes front, right? So, you can't see the passengers because you don't have eyes in the back of your head with the exception of glances from time to time in the "rear view mirror". These future and past passengers are talking back and forth amongst themselves in the past or future, and some are talking back and forth across the aisle as well. Some are pretty much friendly, and cordial. For the most part, these future and past passengers agree on how things were and how things "should be". They are having normal conversations, in a normal tone of voice, at normal volumes. Other passengers got seated next to someone they despise, and they absolutely cannot agree on where they are going. These folks are bickering amongst themselves mostly, but every now and then they are yelling at someone across the aisle too! These folks are creating a commotion because not only do they need to talk over and above the "normal" people having normal conversations, but they are also fired up, and NEED to be heard so they are talking louder to make sure their adversary hears them and their point. They can be pretty intimidating because they really want to get where they are going, and of course, sooner than later! These are not patient people, they have an agenda, and a timeline! On top of all that "NOISE", these future passengers are tracking their GPS

and if you missed their turn, they are telling their friends on the left side of the bus to pull their string too. If their friend on the left isn't paying attention, they start screaming across the aisle at whomever will listen, to tell them to pull their string. We have to go back. We missed a turn! HEEEYYYYYYYYYY!!!!!! Louder and louder, they get pretty ridiculous, obnoxious even!

So, that's the scenario. With a FULL BUS LOAD of these passengers, and all that going on, we have a variety of GPS coordinates and directions, some of which are wrong, and others that may have worked years ago but the road has changed or doesn't even exist anymore, what do we do? Also, I forgot to mention that as their bus driver, this is a long journey, and you need to periodically stop for gas and / or to rest. These passengers are from all different walks of life! During the day, as the road goes up and down and around the bends, they are seeing the scenery pass by and this is generating "triggers" because they THINK they know where they are(memories), or where they are going(projections)! That makes these folks pull YOUR bus strings over and over again, for different reasons. Other passengers just create noise, and grumble and groan! They criticize you under their breath, and sometimes just blurt out random insults, seemingly from nowhere because you are not listening and not going their way!

To say the least, imagine this scenario, you are tired, it's getting DARK, and you have a whole host of back seat drivers, but you can't see where you are going because one of your headlights is out, maybe BOTH! A lot of these passengers are getting frustrated with your driving and want to just take over the wheel. They are no longer content to just sit back and watch as the bus goes the wrong way, so they keep getting louder and louder telling you instructions or jockeying to take over the driving. No one agrees on who should drive, but they all want to because you are just not getting it done. You are no good, and no matter how amazing the scenery is, you have failed to get them where they want to be!

Somehow, some way, you manage to maintain the driver seat, despite all the battles going on amongst the passengers wanting to drive... It's been a long day and you are just plain tired. You can't really SEE all that well because not only is the sky now pitch black, but the weather has also taken a turn for the worse! The passengers keep pulling your strings and / or grabbing for your attention, spinning you around and so you can't keep your eyes on the road, even though you can't see it anyway, as much as you would like to. You can't HEAR effectively either because of all the noise and chatter! This is a recipe for disaster, all of these passengers are all still on the bus clamoring, no one ever gets off! You can hear all this murmuring going on, some are louder than others, but because it has become so loud you can't really make out what any of them are actually saying. That one passenger keeps blurting out random directions super loud and it scares the crap out of you, so you are completely on edge and basically FEARFUL because you don't know who to listen to, what they are saying, or if you are going to go off the road and hit a tree. It's also possible that someone else in the back is going to get scared, scream and / or just jolt you out of your seat for whatever reason they feel! Very unstable and erratic environment with a lot of uncertainty from moment to moment!

Each passenger from the past has a full set of images and emotions tied to destinations from the past and these past successes, failures, good moments and bad are triggered by the things they see out their "windows"! Likewise, each passenger from the future has future agendas and ideals and they are seeing through a much different set of windows! They are not even seeing the present landscape, which is really beautiful. They are missing the whole thing because they are so busy visualizing where they are going to be. Sometimes they settle down for a while, but in general, they are not very patient. They don't care where they are, they want to get to where they are going! Quite honestly, these folks want to drive but they have blinders on, and they can't even see where they are most of the time...so when the bus passes a cop with the flashing lights, it scares them and they yell out, scaring everyone, because it spooked them! They didn't see that coming!

So, in this situation, what kinds of things happen to us as we are the bus driver? ...hypothetically of course. Here are just a few scenarios that could present themselves:

1. Willingly, you get fed up, and just let someone else drive because they convinced you to.

2. One of the passengers takes the wheel because you get tired and sidetracked.

3. One of the passengers pulls you out of the seat and grabs the wheel.

4. You are forced to stop to refuel.

5. You get sidetracked by all the noise and don't know which way to turn.

6. Several people are pushing and pulling on the wheel, and you end up hitting the curb and damaging the tire.

7. The passengers get so loud and obnoxious, and you get so sidetracked

that you get in an accident.

8. You get so tired and so overwhelmed that you pull off to the side of the road to rest to try make sense of it all and come to a group decision on where they want to go.

9. You are convinced that something went wrong, and you make a u turn and start going backwards.

10. Add any other scenario relevant to your life!

OK, back to "bus" iness! Just realize, in our hypothetical world, lots of things can happen while you are the bus driver taking care of business. Keep in mind that when you are stopped to get fuel other stupid stuff happens. Many of the passengers hop in YOUR seat and imagine where they were or where they are going, even full well knowing they can't drive! They are plotting their agendas and trying to come up with a way to get you to go their way, one way or another. So, they play their games, and plot their strategies! (EGO tricks) The funny thing is, there's no gas in the tank, you are going NOWHERE because you have no gas (energy)to get there!

To the point: As the bus driver, YOU need to take and MAINTAIN CON-TROL! The passengers are unruly, misguided, and quite honestly out of hand! YOU need to reign them in and tell them all to QUIET DOWN! When FINAL-LY, these folks ALL UNDERSTAND that you have it all under control (faith and trust), THEY ACTUALLY DO IT! They quiet down, and even better, they quit PULLING YOUR STRINGS!

With all this QUIET, you can now HEAR the slightest little murmur from the passengers (the "selves"), and you JUST got done fueling up, cleaned your windshield, and can SEE very clearly ahead FOR MILES! YOU have just installed the latest software to the bus and now it is telling you ahead of time where the detours and speed traps are REAL TIME! CLARITY!!!!!

If you haven't fully made the connection, the passengers are the "selves" in the MIND, and these selves all have different "voices", each of which "pulls your strings" or "triggers you", in one way or another, some good, some bad! On top of the voices that are coming from our past and future selves, we have other "voices" that are generated from previous instructions, beliefs, teachers, parents, grandparents, siblings and all kinds of people and stuff that we have "bought into" over the years! They are all trying to get your attention, one way or another. You have to HUSH the crowd so to speak, QUIET the NOISE to make sense of it at all! The other problem is that you really like some of these passengers and some of their stories are very compelling! (attachments). After all, some of these represent authority figures in your life that are supposed to KNOW! Someone somewhere along the line made an impact on you for whatever reason, and each has their SPIN and "voice"! The EGO and its various friends combine to make up a very cunning machine doctor! The gearing of this machine, (your mind) is quite incredulous, and it is constantly swirling up lots of medicine in the form of stories to make you FEEL SOMETHING, good or bad! Again, it is a machine, and it has no discretion, it just keeps spitting out stories and agendas over and over again...all generated from the scenery! The problem is that the scenery is taking these passengers backwards or forwards to a place in time that doesn't exist NOW, and they are responding to that "ILLUSION" and PULLING YOUR STRINGS! These "selves" try to SELL their story and their agenda TO YOU, to get you to BUY INTO IT, to go their way, yet they all have different destinations in mind, and again, they are seeing an ILLUSION! Not only is what they see FALSE, and their agenda (beliefs) based on it, they are so conflicted that you literally cannot and will not please everyone, if you can please anyone! As you can see now, this is a real shit show! Sometimes, as the murmur level begins to elevate in volume again, with the same old people raising their voices, you just want to throw your hands up in the air and just yell SHUT UUUUUUP, SIT DOWN!

What's the answer? LOVE! Isn't love the answer? LOVE THEM ALL, with empathy, consideration, and UNDERSTANDING... HEAR THEM! The problem is that you can't hear them all at the same time, and that is why this is a process! One by one, over time and a lot of miles, through the ups and downs and curves in the road, in all the different types of weather and varying degrees of light and dark, LISTEN...as they try to grab your attention (pull your strings: triggers) and take over the steering wheel. JUST PRIOR to the moment, on the cutting edge of now, JUST BEFORE THEY GRAB THE WHEEL, hear their story and their agenda, tone the conversation down if you have to and deal with some of these unruly passenger's first! The goal here is to BE THE BUS DRIVER, not the BUST driver! If you don't gain control of this bus and its passengers, you are going to go bust! By hearing their messages, and GETTING THEIR LESSON, true or false...you can move forward with the appropriate "ACTION" vs RE-acting without thought, without "CHOICE", unaware and unconscious. If you are "asleep at the wheel" (NOT IN THE MOMENT) there's no telling what you might run into, or who might grab the wheel! The re-action will be from their agenda/programming that just came out of the "darkness" in the middle of the night and that RE-action may not be appropriate to the CURRENT road and Its turns which we can't see because we are asleep at the wheel anyway!!! By WAKING UP, fully aware with PRESENCE, you have quite literally shined the light in the darkness, on THAT belief system that was just activated WITHIN you (a passenger pulled your string)! FULLY AWAKE AND AWARE, NOW the "YOU" can elevate and evaluate whether that is valid "pull" or not, and either you still want to subscribe to that belief or make a NEW CHOICE to go in a NEW direction! As the bus driver, in the bus drivers' seat, with a clear windshield and a quiet bus, YOU HAVE the power of CHOICE! You can take this bus wherever YOU want to! You have the steering wheel and can hear the REAL TIME GUIDANCE that is fully updated presently! If you are asleep at the wheel, ANY ONE of these passengers can take over the steering wheel and take you anywhere they want, at any time and you will automatically be going their way! YOU had no choice; you were not in the driver's seat anymore.... Please remember that when these passengers RE-act, they are RE-acting from and to an ILLUSION! Over time, how successful can this truly be? Talk about a fried transmission, these passengers would be changing gears so fast your vehicle would be SHOT! Moral of that story is don't let them drive the bus! MAINTAIN YOUR SEAT! NOW! Your presence is required here!

At the end of a long road, YOU have STOPPED TIME, periodically in a massive amount of previous present moments, enough to get a fine education! YOU NOW have a TRUE UNDERSTANDING of what FAITH is, how it works, when it works and BELIEVE! With wisdom and presence, YOU can take NEW ACTIONS and BE NEW consistently with PRESENCE. Without the "selves", their attachments, false thoughts & stories, your vision, and hearing are PURE! CLARITY at last! With FOCUS, TRUST, FAITH, and PRESENCE... GOD is there, in the eternal NOW, YOU MERGE! LOVE is one of the available choices. With God & pure guidance, Love is unconditional, and this is where LOVE can call the shots and because we merged LOVE is the answer! YOU are THE INSTRUMENT, by CHOICE. YOU ARE LOVE and LOVE RESPONDS, that is when love truly is the answer!

## BE THE INSTRUMENT!

If you are still asking how? You have the answer, NOW! Now is always how...with LOVE!! This is the alternative to the philosophy that the EGO must DIE, I must kill the ego. The problem with that strategy is that when you tell these unruly passengers (the ego) to SHUTTTTT UP, they are angry, and they can get BALIGERANT! They are like that mole in the mole game; they just keep popping up randomly and you have to keep bopping their heads over and over again trying to keep them down! That's called RESISTANCE, the approach is flawed...it doesn't work!!! It is also a recipe for "ignore" ance (IGNORANCE)! When we ignore stuff and try to go around it, we become IGNORANT of the lesson that was supposed to provide us with understanding! With consideration, empathy, LOVE and understanding....you are gradually explaining to these "selves" that their shit doesn't work, NICELY! With UNDERSTANDING and a newfound respect for that education, and sloooowwwwly, over time, they ALL quietly and respectfully sit down in their seat and don't pop up much anymore, if at all...with the exception of a situation with a more powerful "trigger"! When that trigger happens, please understand that ignorance and resistance don't work, WAKE UP and get the lesson in the moment, NOW...and take the appropriate and NEW ACTION accordingly with PRESENCE! You are NOW FREE to CHOOSE, YOU have CHOICE! Choose wisely!

So, now that we know that conceptually, we need to arrive to the moment with faith, empathy, and consideration so that we can respond IN the moment with LOVE...how do we do that consistently with all the little "selves" running around in our heads trying to distract us and go their own way! Life "stuff" always seems to be getting in the way...well of course it is, as you can see, we bring it with us...a BUSLOAD! That's the baggage, we need to lighten the load! LOL.  In any case, the short answer is as instructed above, with a lot of energy, patience, and persistence! It is a process!

Where can we get some additional instruction from some insightful angles? I mean even **Jesus** said:

## "The spirit is willing, but the flesh is WEAK!"[120]

What did He mean by this? How do we get stronger "flesh"? Well, first...it's not so much the flesh, per se...as it is the mind! It needs some training to get out of its own way! It may even take some tough love! So, let's hear it with some new words and coaching!

See the Poem at the beginning of **Emerson**'s Essay on **Self Reliance**[121] with **John Fletcher**'s help, it tells exactly what to do, how cool this is:


**"Ne te quaesiveris extra.**
**Man is his own star; and the soul that can**
**Render an honest and a perfect man,**
**Commands all light, all influence, all fate;**

Nothing to him falls early or too late.
Our acts our angels are, or good or ill,
Our fatal shadows that walk by us still.


*Epilogue to Beaumont and Fletcher's Honest Man's Fortune*


Cast the bantling on the rocks,
Suckle him with the she-wolf's teat;
Wintered with the hawk and fox,
Power and speed be hands and feet."


Giving credit where due, please go to check these out and thank them for providing this amazing stuff for free on their website!

http://www.emersoncentral.com/selfreliance.htm

Emerson Self-Reliance is downloadable here:

https://emersoncentral.com/ebook/Self-Reliance.pdf

See my comments line by line. Of course, as always, this is my own interpretation/translation. Whether Emerson meant these exact words, is arguable, but he is not here to ask, unfortunately!

**"Ne te quaesiveris extra."**[122] (Latin; Stretch your arm no farther than your sleeve will reach. Translation: Do not look / seek outside yourself. Look WITHIN!)

**"Man is his own star; and the soul that can Render an honest and a perfect man"**[123] (When the soul delivers the man, and teaches it, causes it to BECOME perfect= live from SOUL or SPIRIT higher "SELF" vs. from the "selves") (Balanced. Empty cup... "delivered", open & ready to be GUIDED!)

**"Commands all light, all influence, all fate;"**[124] (it can receive perfect instruction, and he is the master of him "SELF" and his circumstances)

**"Nothing to him falls early or too late."**[125] (PRESENCE: "NOW" is always how = patience, understanding, balanced. He is always in the "NOW", so how could it be early or late? Early=past, late=future)

**"Our acts our angels are, or good or ill,"**[126] (Our acts, or <u>RE-actions</u> literally do speak louder than words...good or bad, they deliver our results! See how smart my mom was! They are our Angels because they teach us about our "selves" so we can LEARN and GROW! These are also the passengers on the bus, our angels TEACHING us)

**"Our fatal shadows that walk by us still."**[127] (about the shadows that still lurk WITHIN us, these are often referred to as shadow "selves", and they operate in the shadows of the mind, unbeknownst to us until we wake up and shine the light of awareness on them! In the shadows means "darkness", these are our EGO personalities we are either unconscious of, or we ignore / resist! If we are unconscious to them, well...GET conscious, WAKE UP!

### *Epilogue to Beaumont and Fletcher's Honest Man's Fortune*

**"Cast the bantling on the rocks,"**[128] (Throw the young child (lower "selves') to some tough love. These are the passengers that need your empathy, love, consideration, and understanding! Sometimes this will require an intervention! Tough love stings a little bit, and that's casting the "self" on the rocks. Giving it an education. Being honest with oneself.)

**"Suckle him with the she-wolf's teat;"**[129] (Wolves represent: Teaching skill, perseverance, endurance, strength, loyalty, success, thought, intelligence, pathfinders, intuition, learning. Wolves take every care to educate their young and are devoted! Who better to teach?)

**"Wintered with the hawk and fox,"**[130] (Hawk=Nobility, clarity, awareness, observer, the soul, truth, foresight, discrimination) (Fox= Cleverness, protection, intelligence, diplomacy, feminine magic, adaptability, discretion, integration and playfulness. This is combining AWARENESS as the observer and exceptional VISION, clever LOGIC to the Heart and LOVE, the soul side of the equation and integrating them all for a complete person! The FOX is cunning, cerebral, and fast, we need that mental agility to out fox... the fox, the EGO. First with the eyesight of the HAWK, we SEE IT, then with the mental agility of the FOX, we BEAT IT TO THE MOMENT, mental training at its best! "SELF" vs "self", higher vs lower!)

**"Power and speed be hands and feet."**[131] (Strength & GOD SPEED you'll need it in order to get you there...YOU MUST ARRIVE IN THE MOMENT! YOU MUST BE FAST, with the POWER of CHOICE!)

GOOD STUFF, RIGHT?

I want to reference **John Fletcher**'s **"An Honest Man's Fortune"**[132] because to me this is a very powerful statement, and for some reason it was not acknowledged. Check this out:

> **"Doth not experience teach us all we can**
> **To work ourselves into a glorious man**
> **Love's but an exhalation to best eyes**
> **The matters spent and then the fools fire dyes**
> **Were I LOVE, and could that bright star bring**
> **Increase to wealth, honor, and every thing."**

In simpler terms, if we SEE love (the choice) IN THE MOMENT, we can become it...and breathe it out in our experience, our RESULTS. And furthermore, WHEN WE SEE IT, **"That matters SPENT"**[133] and that old "self" that was not love, that little "self" that I was is GONE, SPENT, no longer ME. The inspiration and fire that was formerly me just died as I GREW out of it, with UNDERSTANDING, and LET IT GO! Since it no longer serves me... I have RISEN UP and BECOME NEW! That FOOL can no longer LIMIT this new ME! I am NEW, I AM NEW...I AM...I AM...new and new and new...dying to my former selves and growing out of them over and over and over and over again, faster and faster and faster and faster! You GET IT?!?!

Are YOU PUMPED? Excited to get this going?

OK, BREEEEAAAATHE!!! I know, it's FUN! So exciting! SIT DOWN, SHUT UP! LOL:) I am joking of course! (referring to the bus driver example) This is just a quick & hopefully funny reminder that you can also be blinded by excitement!

**LESSON KEY: BE CONSCIOUS, AWAKE, AWARE... PRESENT! HAVE FAITH!**

As much as you can muster the energy for it, and at every possible opportunity, with as much empathy, consideration, and LOVE, Let LOVE answer, Be the Instrument! When situations present themselves and something less than that responds to life, SEE IT! Understand what it was that took over so that the next time, it can't do that, you are wise to it. In this way, we are increasingly more ready to BE THE INSTRUMENT! Forever expanding, growing. I wrote this out for myself as follows to remind me of what that looks like in my mind:

Gaining

Required

KnOwledge

When

I show up to

Now....with

God!

That means presence, wide awake, aware and completely 100% dialed in! Receptive, balanced, and READY with unwavering faith to TRUST the guidance, and BE what is needed in the moment! Growing means ever readying this higher "SELF" to maintain this foundational steadfastness. Being immovable or unshakable mentally requires practice, confidence, FAITH and TRUST. This is how that is achieved, moment by moment by moment. Faster and Faster we become the instrument, better each time we show up to represent!

**rePRESENT**!

You can't do this if you are not present, NOW! Wake up, consciousness is required!

# SEEING WANTING

## GETTING IN THE ZONE VIII

A T SOME POINT, AFTER watching the mind for some time, questions are going to come up or get caught in the crossfire. You'll see them and then want to explore them a bit more thoroughly, this is GOOD! A lot of the time, that's just not possible during the day with our busy schedules, unless we actually make time for it! Let's face it, life is always demanding something from us, right? Make a note of the things you would like to ponder, or questions / vantage points and ideas that you want to explore. Why am I here? I have seen this situation before, why does this particular life situation, or this type of person / challenge keep revisiting me? Stuff like that. Make it a point to come back to them as soon as it is feasible for you. It is probably a good idea to just set some time aside here and there and just sit with them, maybe you can make that a particular time of day to "take a breath" or breather! Ponder these things, do some "processing", quite often there is a lesson in it! There is something to see, for sure, else it would not keep coming up. Maybe even try your hand at meditation if that intrigues you. You don't have to name it though if that rubs you the wrong way, or the selves resist it. Of course, they would resist it, or avoid it, right? They don't want to be seen!

This is an opportunity in a more controlled environment when things are not coming at you at lightning speeds to sort of slow it down and watch the mind, and THEM, as the mind is in "process" mode. JUST WATCH! This is NOT to solve the world's problems, it is to understand the processor, and HOW it is processing! This is to understand what it is processing as well, as in, the weight it is putting on things, YOU! Keen attentiveness as to how something "hits you", the weight, and impact, is valuable information. Understand! Seeing the selves wanting doesn't mean YOU have to BE wanting! That's the point of the position as CEO, you have CHOICE! What to focus on, what to "think", what to BE! Sometimes that means that you MUST be something / someone that is contrary to what the "selves" are demanding. That can be difficult if the selves are projecting enticing imagery on the mind screen. It can also mean, NOT being something or someone that you have grown accustomed to being but fully realize that this is just not "You" anymore. It is simply a self that you've grown out of and no longer want to be. Well, let me rephrase that because the little selves want to be it all day long, it is the higher "SELF" that knows and sees that it can't continue to be that in the name of growth, as an example! As I say, once seen, it really can't be unseen. That is why it can be seen as a blessing and a curse sometimes...because we, as the selves, really do want that proverbial cookie!

Seeing "wanting" is the title of the section, yes, but in reality, seeing from this vantage point is really overseeing everything that's going on in the mind! It is the opportunity to back up and know what the "selves" are doing, thinking, perceiving, "getting into", and then decide if you want to tag along, or cancel the engagement so to speak! The skill in the overseer position allows you to put the mind to work if you choose to vs the mind actually being in control of what you get to see, do, and experience! The mind will run you ragged if the table was turned, and it was left unsupervised! This is isolated ME TIME. It may not feel like isolated time though depending on how many of the "selves" show up. Life is a stage, and we are the actors. When we take the time to LOOK WITHIN, without the intention of doing anything specifically, it is quite informative to watch the various scenes play out in the mind, as the selves choreograph and play it out on the mind screen. From this perspective the actors can be seen first by paying close attention to who shows up, and of course, which ones show up more vocally and / or obnoxiously in some cases. Then once seen, we can pay attention to when and how they are seen, as well as why, their reasons for being there, because they always have a reason, a driver! They want things to go a certain way in the future, or revisit something from the past. These are the attachments we need to pay attention to. These selves can be watched and seen trying to steer things and of course, they will play their parts with YOU in the starring role! So this all plays out very innocently, if you don't really watch it carefully. They are attempting to pull your strings, some louder and harder than others. That might mean trying to get you to DO SOMETHING or show you something about a former self / future self as an example! It may take a little restraint to just sit quietly and watch but this can be extremely beneficial. Do it "in spite" of what those selves are telling you, particularly the ones that are telling you that this is a waste of time, you have more productive things to do! Just pay attention, it's fascinating and quite educational! The various roles and interplay amongst these various selves that step in to grab your attention can be observed and analyzed, and it can be a lot of fun. "Meaning" can often be deciphered, and insights gained from the different interactions if truly watched, broken down, embraced, and analyzed! It must be from a detached, empathetic, and somewhat compassionate perspective though. The selves will come at you, and / or each other from many angles. Consider acting as the chief investigator of this mind and the myriad of interactions, almost as if it is not even yours. It is more of an inquisitive, hands-off stance just kind of taking it in and watching whatever happens and making assessments.

It is super important to watch the mind when the pressure is ON and life is IN YOUR FACE, because these are the times where we tend to stumble, for whatever reason. Pressure, right? Sometimes we handle it better than others. We need to see when, why, where, and how this happens. Fact is, the faster our life comes at us, the more we will stumble, we need to see it with open eyes and ears. As we fail, from time to time, we note the situational dynamics. What happened, how, who was there, who within represented in that moment? The "selves" ultimately have to be accountable, and all of the situational components understood, so that we can learn! This is time we deliberately set aside to do this. While being in the moment is critical, it is equally worthy and beneficial to slow it down from time to time and revisit a scenario that maybe didn't go quite right and we are not sure why! Maybe we missed something, or we were not 100% at that moment. As a reminder, this is not to be critical, it is to learn, to see, to grab a lesson that we may have missed. Understanding is powerful.

In addition, "Practicing" when life is not demanding something from us tends to help us to maintain that anchored and unwavering (over SEER with non-attachment) vantage point when the HEAT IS ON! This is an effort to ensure that same mistake doesn't happen the next time! Remember that this is a skill and the more you can work on the skill, the better you'll get at it! One way or another, it's important to let the mind have some time to digest and contemplate stuff, "THINK" stuff out, and as it does this, the "YOU" actually STOPS being the thinker at that level, and YOU purposefully and deliberately elevate out of being the thinker and start watching the thinking a little more easily! Even in a controlled environment, being the watcher/overseer and maintaining this vantage point can be a challenge sometimes, so practice is going to be advantageous in more ways than you might imagine! Ultimately, this will help you build the skill. As you are trying to do this, pay attention to what else is demanding your attention. Notice the dominant themes, and the pushier "selves" that continuously show up...especially the challenging / demanding ones! Its these feisty "motivated" ones that are pushing the WANT buttons. Something behind that motivation is giving it the PUSH.  Keep tabs on these jokers!

This is especially important if what we are seeing in our current landscape ("life") is our vehicle winding through some jagged cliffs at a rapid pace in harsh weather with seemingly no guard rails vs driving down a straight country road on a bright sunny day! If you are going through a formidable stretch of road, it can be taxing on the body and mind! When life has you clinching the steering wheel, it tends to go into "trigger mode" a little more easily. When we are edgy, or tired, it really doesn't take much, if the mind isn't already set off situationally. That status can be caused by physical, mental, or emotional challenges, pure strain, a lack of endurance or a combination of things. This can send the system into "overload" sooner than it might have otherwise, under normal circumstances.  It's like our threshold or tolerance is lowered in more ways than one. Surely, something to pay attention to. The physical can certainly affect the mental, and the other way around as well. On top of that, emotions affect the whole ball of wax. Mental stamina and agility matters, and everything we do affects this, which correlate to real time performance using the skill! What we eat, our sleep patterns, our physical conditioning, EVERYTHING affects our intestinal fortitude, as well as the skill we need to perform!! My sister is a personal trainer and she helped me understand this. Thanks Donna!

If today is a physically challenging day, the "stress" on the physical apparatus counts a little more heavily and that may mean we have a little less to give at the end of the day from a mental standpoint. To a certain extent though, the physical will energize the system, if "trained", so that is warranted! As with all else, a balanced approach is likely best. I just know that when I was trying to get in shape physically, and also learn a ton of very detailed information, I ran out of steam a little quicker mentally. It places more demands on a system that is already taxed so to speak. Reading a book after a very demanding day, physically, mentally, or emotionally for instance, it's like good night! I can't keep my eyes open. HAH! The correlation here is that they all require ENERGY and pull from the same tank so to speak. That gives us more incentive to optimize our physical & mental systems, focus, endurance and ultimately the SKILL with which we live life in order to make sure we use that energy wisely and efficiently. It's also why we need a personal trainer, to get in shape so we have more energy to begin with, right Donna?

Bottom line, the mind doesn't do well when it is in "fight or flight" mode, and so the more we do to maintain an energized and balanced frame of mind, with endurance and composure, the better off we will be! If our environment is physically, mentally, and emotionally challenging 10 or more hours a day, then this "down time" is even more important! It might be significantly less for you, something to watch, for sure! Every day is different. Regardless of where your personal threshold is, we need some time to process and think through "stuff", and practice is a super idea. Make time as often as possible! If we don't carve it out, it doesn't happen. So keep in mind that one way to process is to look back at the day in order to re-SEE some of the things that happened. This can be very productive. Where and when were we able to maintain that overseer perspective and when/where and with whom were we not able, or should I say, not stable?! Sometimes this allows you to go back and get a lesson or two that you may have missed, because we were off balance or distracted at that time, for whatever reason. Needless to say, this is not to be critical, it is to retrieve a lesson or two!

With all of this new understanding and perspective though, let's go ahead and address the elephant in the room! One of the bigger questions that likely comes up is: Why does the mind seek, desire, "WANT" anything, EVERYTHING for that matter...what are the secret drivers of the things that are supposed to "bring happiness"? Does true happiness really exist in this human form? Looking at the mind, how it processes, how it "thinks" ...well, let's just say, valid question! The whole over SEER, watcher perspective is an eye opener, for sure, and watching helps...A LOT! My basic take is that it brings us to the lessons. That's the simple answer anyway. We are here for the lessons! GROWTH!

The more complicated answer to that question though, is that it is going to be VERY personal, absolutely, particularly in the beginning when it is a little more of a mish mosh with varying degrees of awareness! Remember, you are driving the FAITH bus. So, let's revisit that example really quick!

Caution: exaggeration, and drama to follow in this example. Ha-ha. In the beginning of the trip, as the faith bus driver, you aren't really familiar with all of the passengers...mainly because you haven't been driving (as the watcher) for long enough yet! You may have been driving, but not from this perspective, and remember there may be some unruly passengers to deal with. Let's face it, we are all here to get certain lessons! Some of these lessons may be harder to deal with than others because they've been postponed for so long. Depending on the road you are on, it may take a little while, and varying scenery and weather conditions (life situations) for these characters to come out of the woodwork and show their faces so that you can get acquainted and see the lesson they bring with them!

So, having said that, from the bus driver perspective, we can be trucking along at a good clip, making good time, and all is seemingly going well! The windshield is clean and clear, and just a second later, seemingly from out of nowhere a thunderstorm screams in. It gets dark, the rain pours down and it's hard to see again. You get blindsided by something in life. The passengers (The "selves") are in an uproar, it's the middle of the darn day, and you don't even know what happened! Quite an unruly crowd (in the bus / mind) all of a sudden. You are literally looking for the switch for the windshield wipers, (Trying to fix stuff, put band aids on) and while you were distracted you hit a curb or just went out of your lane! Boom, hit a bump in the road, so to speak. Life has a way of ensuring complacency is not an option. Ha-ha! Anyway, as you upgrade your vehicle, (your skills) to better prepare yourself with more functional hardware and software, the windshield wipers that you used to have to turn on manually now have an intermittent feature, which turns on and off automatically. (Your skills are improving) However, a lot of the time you forget where that switch is too, or you didn't engage it! (Were not aware, present, manning your post) As time goes on, YOU become better at finding the switch, or leave it engaged, although that requires more energy! This helps a lot, but that means you have to rest more often. With software updates though, it actually starts working better when you are energized and ready. In fact, the system is more efficient, so it burns less fuel which means that you can drive for longer stretches. (You can man your post for longer periods and stay aware as overseer!) As time goes on even further, and you upgrade your vehicle again and again, the windshield wipers go on as soon as it starts raining, automatically! In fact, you can even see pretty clearly in the rain. (Life situations) The wipers progressively speed up depending on how hard it's raining, and the headlights turn on automatically as well! This has a way of progressively enhancing your vision and hearing...the path, sort of lights up in all kinds of conditions as well as varying degrees of light! It's like the headlamps adjust as well, so it's always high "lighted" for you. Even in the darkest of night, the path is sort of lit up, so to speak. This is what it means to get out of the darkness, all of a sudden, we see the light, and the path ahead is clear as day! As we start to gain some stability, firmly planted in our driver seat as the OVERSEER, it seems as if less "stuff" hits the windshield, and when it does, it is manageable. The headlights seem to be on all the time!

In this situation, and under these circumstances, we can see the motivating factors that are affecting our "peace of mind" much more clearly. Fact is, the demands on the system, and the requirements for happiness become different along the way, and we are much more in tune with what, or WHO is wanting to drive it. The bottom line is that in our original bus driver example, no one ever got off the bus. It just seemed to add more and more passengers, and chaos! Remember the bus is our mind with all the selves in it. After installing the overseer functionality, we have lots of scenarios and situations that offer us opportunities to actually reverse this progressive retrograde and let passengers off the bus, so we do. This typically starts with the unruly ones! As we meet them, and after they reveal their lessons, they quietly exit the bus in an orderly and respectful manner! As overseer, it's OUR BUS, and the fact is, we just don't want them on the bus, nor do we want to put up with that behavior anymore. They taught, or received their lesson, had their "say" and their stay, and that was that! With empathy, consideration, and understanding, sensibility prevailed, and we said our goodbyes! Another step forward. In some cases that might have been a "good riddance" type feeling and a bit of a relief, quite honestly! Looking back for a second, we are a little surprised that we let them stay on the bus that long, ha-ha. Remember, I am talking about the "selves"! The EGO selves will most definitely hold on for a lot of miles, sometimes clinging to their seat! Their patterns, and behaviors, let's call it "stuff" can be somewhat addictive! Mental, physical, and emotional patterns can become anchored, or the "selves" are somewhat belted into the bus seat! If allowed to stay, no less "drive" by accident, these selves can become somewhat obsessed in ways. Got to monitor these enthusiasts, for sure...we might let them off the bus and then after a while we realize they hopped back on at a rest stop!! Bottom line, priorities change, and after a few more miles down the road what happens? We realize the mental, physical, or emotional energy demands of a particular undertaking that a "self" wants to engage in is just not worthy of our time and more importantly, the commitment of energy it requires. Consequently, we cannot allow that "self" to stay on the bus! So, we let them off, and don't allow them back on! Another ounce of energy preserved, and that energy is very useful, every day going forward. Our virtual gas tank gets MORE milage every day now.... tell me that's not a huge advantage! It may seem inconsequential but remember this is cumulative. Imagine letting 50 passengers off the bus. How far can you go now without all that weight on the bus? Less drag on the transmission, and a way more efficient machine! Not only can you get "up to speed" faster, but you can drive farther, and with more focus! It is safer, you are more agile, able to turn easier, and overall, just more dialed in! You actually get more done in a day and might even have a few more hours to do it, because you need less sleep! This is not recommended though, per Donna. We need our sleep! Just sayin. LOL.

Keep in mind that some passengers are tough to part with, some are easy to let go, certainly no two are the same, so there are periods of digestion, adjustments, and feelings that come up. Periods of melancholy, a taste of loneliness from time to time, and retrospectives, as if a friend or loved one has left us. It's real! These "selves" have often been on our bus for a long time, thick as thieves they are! It isn't easy to let go sometimes, and part ways, but the realizations come, that it is time.

These are parts of ourselves that we really identified with though, after all, that's why they are still on the bus when others are long gone! At long last, we are left with very few passengers, not a lot of voices, and not a lot of demands. As a bus, we are lighter, and it's actually brighter in here too, without all these passengers. In fact, there aren't a lot of "selves" left in this bus anymore that actually want to be "drivers", they mostly want to just watch, peaceful and content with whatever rolls on by. All dressed up with no place to go! Such an opportune moment, CHOICES! Assuming they stay on the bus, the remaining passengers are easy to see. In fact, we know them really well! Their "needs" are in the limelight, as are their mannerisms, games, idiosyncrasies, tricks, and overall psychology. The remaining characters are good, REAL GOOD! They know us, and they know us extremely well...just how to pull the right string...so they still "get us" from time to time! Sneaky little "devils"!

There is no question that we are all driven by different things, wants, "needs" and these drivers are mind driven, or "self" / EGO driven. Our minds and passengers are different, with different levers and strings, and lots of different "selves" pushing and pulling them. And then when you really back off enough to see it, the whole charade is SPIRIT driven, or from higher "SELF" (or a higher power if you prefer) bringing us to the "lessons" over and over again, or the lessons to us, right? Without going too far down that rabbit hole, let's just say that there may be an infinite number of "consciousness" levels for us to grow through, which means MANY TESTS!! That is why we need to stay in growth mode and practice. We can achieve a lot over time, for sure, and in order to do it, we must be consistently in growth mode.

The point in being the watcher (<u>OF</u> the mind rather than IN the mind) is to see the lessons and GET them, sooner than later which opens the door to another one! From this vantage point we can see the EGO "payoffs" before the RE - actions take place and pass the test! This perspective is established and maintained so that we can see the motivations, and the traps the mind (EGO) sets up for us. Why all the endless "tests"? Because we keep failing, we miss the lessons over and over again. If we don't truly UNDERSTAND the lesson, it keeps returning until we get it. At the end of the day, if you really pay attention, all of the wants and all of the needs, are empty. YES, I am sorry to say ...WANTING doesn't seem to want to go away. The EGO selves WANT! Let's just say that's a good news / bad news type deal. Wants and needs may give the ego a momentary thrill, a sense of rear-view mirror satisfaction, but it doesn't last, at least not forever. What's next, as a question, always seems to pop back in there, almost immediately, right? Always a higher mountain peak, so to speak, the next thing...DRIVENNESS, DESIRE gets old as a thing, after watching it in the form of many egoic adventures. That's obviously the bad news to some. Net, net, impermanence is a life lesson. The sooner you get it and understand it, the better off you'll be! So, yes, the bad news stings a little, lasting happiness is not in things or accomplishments due to impermanence.

What's the good news? The good news is that happiness IS definitely available! Base CORE happiness is WITHIN....it is INTERNAL, unaffected, and unattached to the daily roller coaster ride called life! Impermanence helps us to understand that the roller coaster ride is to be enjoyed, NOW. It's not about wanting, it's about BEING! BEING happiness affects us and everyone around us. Imagine not NEEDING anything to be truly happy, like it's not dependent on this or that. BEING HAPPY, period, end of sentence. NO NEEDS. EMPTY, fillable space. How about we just choose to fill it with LOVE? Wouldn't that, by the nature of it, allow us an expansive, seemingly endless capacity to just appreciate and LOVE LIFE along with everything and everyone in it? Just BEING here would be amazing right, no less BEING amongst our favorite people that are in it, NOW? That is CORE Happiness...maybe even JOY, PEACE. YOU decide. If you don't choose to enjoy being here NOW, then when will you?

### "It's NOT the destination, It's the JOURNEY!"
### -Ralph Waldo Emerson[134]

Enjoy the trip!

Speaking of love, check out this really FUN & positive song by **Lindsey Stirling**, featuring **Rivers Cuomo & Lecrae, "Don't let this feeling fade"**[135]. This makes me smile, thanks to you all! Lots of very powerful messages. Do it for the LOVE, ENJOY!

In fact, if you want or need some amazing music that is primarily without lyrics to keep your mind engaged and energized while working, or on the computer, check out Lindsey Stirling's channel. I really enjoy it, thank you Lindsey! It's amazing, and it is very uplifting musically, speed & tone wise and the way she mixes it up keeps it entertaining! It also has some inspirational messages when Lyrics are used. It's very well done; I am listening with appreciation right now as I write this!

Relative to presence, living in the NOW, how to do it and potentially enjoy it a little bit more easily & consistently, check out this quote / advice, below. I hear and see this one a good bit, and I like it a lot. It makes perfect sense to me. It offers us a pretty good starting point, certainly a vantage point that could help position us properly from a mind perspective! It's like a tool for the overseer.

*"Wear the world like a loose garment,*
*which touches us in a few places, and there lightly."*
**-St Francis of Assisi**[136]

This strategy allows us to maintain a level of detachment, as nothing is hitting us full force, and knocking us off kilter. "Life" and the world is not too tight, and yet we can feel it enough, and because our clothes are not too tight, we can enjoy the ride a little bit more and it is a little easier too, because we are not all constricted and uncomfortable! We can actually walk without the fear of splitting our clothes and exposing our "selves". LOL Funny, yes, but really take that in and think about it! How often do we respond to situations while the "mode" or the paradigm we are operating from is responding to life from a protection of a "self" mode, which is various versions of the EGO? That is the equivalent of resistance, or "ignore" ance right? It is re-acting, and that re-action is protecting the EGO and its existence, or what we HAVE...which goes back to haves and have nots, limitation vs abundance! That = STRESS! FEAR / PRIDE / VANITY and all the lesser emotions! Money, status, power, health, friends, relationships, things, situations, etc. All of these can contain the stories the ego cherishes right?

This is all playing into the same GAME! So, with all this understanding, SKILL, and a nice new set of loose-fitting clothes we are READY! From this less distracted and more comfortable vantage point, with better hearing and clearer vision we can just BE, a whole lot more PEACEFUL, RELAXED. Emotions in check! The unknown is a lot less intimidating, at a minimum, if not sought after and ultimately trusted. The "SELF" is a lot more DISCERNING, and with this highly developed SKILL we have CHOICE! With choice we are renewed, and renewed, and renewed...over and over again. We become NEW, every time we leave one of these "false selves" at the gate! This is what it means to be "BORN AGAIN"! Re-NEW!

*"Do not be conformed to this world, but BE TRANSFORMED*
*by the renewal of your MIND, that by testing you may discern*
*what is the will of GOD,*
*what is good and acceptable, and PERFECT!"*
**-Romans 12:2**[137]

Sure, go after the things and stuff you want to, but don't expect them to change your basic demeanor. If you expect that something ahead of you will bring you happiness, it will not, at least not permanently. Just SEE that this thing, goal, achievement, situation, whatever it is, is just another up in a roller coaster ride that always has ups and downs, the cycles of life, waves, and tides! Then, you are much more apt to appreciate the moments for what they are and have the ability to enjoy them. Believe it or not, you will actually appreciate the downs because YOU understand that the ups would not even feel as good without them! In fact, consequently, you are much more likely to get what you want because you will have eliminated the resistance to getting it, the fear of not having it... you know that story! HAH :)

These are all lessons in themselves, and each situation, each moment is an opportunity to see through the façade...see through the illusions, self-created, which give you that momentary up, or momentary down...and without the self-created "story", there remains a base happiness underneath all of that. That CORE base happiness, the SMILE you can create and maintain RIGHT now is unaffected by the mind's storylines! You have to see this... LOOK DEEP WITHIN, pry the door open and look behind the "story" that tells you to feel this way or to feel that way! NOW just pretend, just for a moment, that the story did NOT exist... pause, and put on a BIG SMILE, not a fake one, a REAL ONE, make it BIG...force it if you have to in this case, just for a second! Now go back to the story. You SEE? The story is MIND generated, just SEE IT...and then drop it and SEE that a smile is still possible WITHOUT the story! NOW, bring it back, now drop the storyline again...and see what feels better?! Which mode do you want to stay in? Story, or no story? LIMIT...no limit? Smile, no smile?

Now, stop to really think about this for a minute. Does this make sense?

## NOW... YOU HAVE CHOICE!

That alone feels better, right? You literally have the KEY to your own shackles, or prison gate, limitations, UNLOCK THE DOOR! It starts how? **WITH PRESENCE!** The door is right after yesterday, and right before tomorrow, that's the door, or "gate". In fact, it's not even locked, OPEN IT! It is in the here and NOW that you have CHOICE! The key is a perspective, an understanding.

Here is an example or two:

You want to stay in grief? I understand...it does take time to process sometimes, and everyone is different, each situation is unique. I agree with that, but how long do you want to stay in the pain now that you have seen and received the lesson it brought? The only thing left is to process it and move on. Take that step! It is quite literally one thought away.

You want to stay angry? I understand, bad stuff happens, but how long do you want to postpone the lesson, or stay with this anger now that you see it as a lesson? If you don't see anger as pain, or as a lesson, then you really should back up and look again! At some point, by watching, you SEE and UNDERSTAND that it is a CHOICE to stay in the pain, the mood, the "attitude", and YOU can leave it behind! How much pain can you endure? Is this the best use of that energy you are trying to manage? Once seen as a lesson, it is quite simply an understanding that moves us into processing mode which then ALLOWS that next step forward. Again, a smile is one simple thought away. Grabbing the lesson is to grow into that more ever-present smile that is more and more difficult to remove from your face!

Pain or mental suffering shows up in non-smiles, otherwise seen or felt as frowns, sadness, stern faces, anxiousness, fear, regret, disgust, remorse, etc. and by choosing these less than stellar demeanors you are churning and / or BURNING energy needlessly and unproductively. If your face is showing anything less than a smile, then it simply means a lesson has been delivered or is being made available to be received.  There is a choice, and one of them is to grab the lesson and move on! Whether this means anger, frustration, or some other less than stellar emotion. There is always a choice to stay in the pain or GROW out of it by grabbing the lesson and taking a step forward! Just one, that's all it takes...and then just keep that upward momentum going for just long enough for a smile to re-emerge!

How much pain do you want to endure? Do you realize it is self-inflicted by your choice to stay there with those thoughts in that storyline? It is absolutely 100% a choice and by choosing the pain, you stay there with it...it is a mind angle, a thought, or a line of thinking. You are refusing the lesson and choosing to stay the same, which means NOT GROWTH! Watch this happening, watch the choice...it is being made. Be above it, watch it, see it, and understand it. Then decide. How much more do you want to endure before making the critical and life changing choice to choose something different...NOW!? Do you want to stay HAPPY and SMILE? DO IT!  How? NOW!!!! It's a CHOICE!!!! Make a decision, a NEW ONE! Smile right NOW! CHOOSE a different thought and DO IT NOW!

Happiness just is...it doesn't come from something that is outside, although the mind would like to project all of the various scenarios that the "you" will be happy (in the future/past)! All the time it does this! And even if that scenario presents itself, as it likely will, you will be left with the same wanting you came into the experience with. That is the mind, the EGO, and that is why I like to refer to the mind as an "IT" vs a "me", it just makes it easier for me to gain clarity with non-attachment! It's less "personal"! Bottom line is that "**it**" (The mind/ego) will NEVER be "satisfied"! There will always be some unturned stone, some unmet desire, a higher peak, (Wanting) the next thing that will ultimately make **IT** happy. Pay attention, "it" say's things like this: "If I had this, or I did that...THEN, oh for sure THEN I will be happy. If only I had "Security", So much money that I could never spend it all, then I would be happy." (False self). If only I had a big juicy hamburger, chocolate bar, milkshake, candy bar, fast car, truck, house, partner... fill in the blank _____! The mind goes forwards in time as well as backwards in time just as well to fill it in. It WANTS, mainly it wants to feel good, watch it wanting! Bottom line is that regardless of what you put in the blank, it is an illusion on the mind screen. The "FEEL GOOD" visual. It is being projected there by the "selves", the IT. NOW, KNOWING THIS, from this new perspective, as the higher "SELF", with awareness... ABOVE the "IT", it is SEEN, in all its glory!! It is ego BAIT! The plain and simple truth is that it can't get away with this deception anymore as long as this new version of "I" is awake & aware, paying attention and PRESENT, as the overseer, watching!!!! Sometimes YOU may choose to give it what it wants, sometimes YOU may not, the point is **NOW**...**YOU HAVE CHOICE!** Don't let the mind deceive YOU with its endless shenanigans!

This is really quite easy and ultimately as simple as this, the summary version of it:

**Since you now have choice**
**Don't choose to stay in the pain!**
**SMILE BIG!**

With PRESENCE, the "I" is changing the vantage point from where we are seeing and hearing life as it is happening, so choose something different! Don't allow yourself to be deceived by the selves that are telling you to be miserable or whatever else has temporarily removed the smile! Whatever "IT" is projecting on the mind screen must be seen for what it is, an illusion, a LIE and it is this imagery / story that is bringing you down! Whatever that may be, whether it is things and / or accomplishments, or something else situationally maybe, they are not the ultimate answer. If those things worked for the "IT", (The mind and many "selves") then why do you see so many millionaires committing suicide, and or are ultimately miserable in their own skin? The reason is because they can become trapped in the mind amongst these selves, unconscious and unaware, and they don't see a way out! CHOICE is unavailable while we are unconscious, the IT has control <u>in and of the mind</u>. The virtual prison doors are locked!

From that vantage point, without awareness, trapped within the mind and its self-created walls, IT truly will never be satisfied, and IT really doesn't see it while IT is in control of the mind. The eyes and ears are unable to see / hear from this higher perspective! So, once the IT (lower mind) obtains that desired thing, then it either wants more of it, or fears losing that which IT obtained. Well, that didn't do it, maybe MORE will do it... LESS certainly won't, I have already been there! OR. It got white and black is still a potential, or it got black and white is still possible, Oh Nooooh..., same principle either way! It's a dynamic within the mind, and again, not racially speaking, it's a perspective, as explained previously...a way of looking at things! It is truly comical...and I am joking of course because once you see it, its hilarious watching the EGO try to play its mind tricks on you and get you to buy in! It's like the little you that you were years ago trying to fool higher current "YOU"! LITERALLY!!! SEEING from this higher perspective with discernment means that you cannot get away with your own shenanigans anymore! Higher "SELF" sees what lower self is up to and shuts IT down! You have become WISE to your "selves"! Stepping out of and above the mind as the watcher OF THE MIND is the vantage point that really helps to see this! Very powerful.

When I was younger, I used to get real upset when me or my team did not win, when I made a bad shot, or when I was not "right"! Truth be told, it doesn't matter...win or lose...it is truly being above winning and losing that allows you to just appreciate being in the game! CORE / BASE happiness is a lot more stable! It is above being right or wrong that one is able to see the minds storylines that would imply rightness or wrongness! Quite honestly, what is right for me, may not be right for you at all...and what is right for me this moment, in this situation, may be completely wrong in the next moment. The truth is NOT static! Also worth mentioning is that ALL MINDFRAMES are below it from this vantage point. They are SEEN and understood.

The ability to stand above the mind like this, and separate yourself from the thoughts themselves, or to step out of the raging river of thought is a talent. That talent is the key to your new HOUSE! This is where you LIVE from, this vantage point. It starts and progresses from your ability to stay there. At HOME, with a rock-solid foundation built on understanding, trust, and faith! It is your responsibility NOW, to change and maintain this new vantage point from where you live your life, to BEING THIS, the watcher, the EGO-less, and unwavering TRUTH hearer, TRUTH seer PRESENTLY and to skillfully BE AWARE as the watcher, energized and ready! The watcher is unattached to outcomes, unaffected by stories, and unbiased in action assuming the "YOU" can maintain that level of detachment and awareness. As the watcher, YOU will have the PRESENCE ability, that SKILL is a requirement, and the ability will grant YOU access to the NOW. Being in the NOW is completely different than RE-acting to life from storylines and illusions created by the mind to project scenarios in which you can be happy. YOU already ARE HAPPY! You don't NEED anything! All of those storylines are in the past or the future, just watch, YOU will see! That same mind (it) will turn on you the moment that the moment is gone, and it becomes taken over by a different storyline, a different "self" within the mind with a different agenda, or a different desire/fear. YOU will see "IT" with awareness, all these little selves battling it out in the mind, for dominance. It says, choose me, choose me, and my story! SALESMEN! BAIT! Ad pitch! Just watch while they try to divert your attention towards what THEY want, to satisfy their "self" and that attention diversion keeps you from the moment! The thief of the moment literally STEALS the base happiness you could experience NOW by interjecting it "self" between the YOU and the NOW! It happens in a flash, it's so fast that it is almost imperceptible. What is the tell tale sign though? Your smile disappears...that's what happens. This must be seen as a wake-up call.

These little selves are stealing your "NOW", and your life along with it! Their storyline or "attachment" is in the past or the future, and once you are captivated by and have "bought into" their story, that's where the minds focus is, so you get caught up in that whole web of deception, and it's a complete ILLUSION! The little "you" gets attached to the past or the future & the storyline that goes with it. In that flash of a moment, a literal blink of an eye, you are locked in the illusion, and out of the moment by time as the mind is focused elsewhere! BAM, you missed it again. It happens FAST, I mean REALLY fast! Pay very close attention!

Why is this? Now getting to the nitty-gritty. This is what the EGO does! It has endless games, strategies, and diversions. It is very cunning and extremely clever, has many tricks and disguises! Here is the thing though, they are all geared to preserve their "selves"! THEY DON'T WANT TO CHANGE! If you become wise to their games, and actually SEE THEM, they know that they DIE when you become re**NEW**ed or born again! They are no longer useful anymore, you don't need them, and surely, they don't want that! You would move on without them! How could you? (facetious) That is EXACTLY what you must do, and YOU have to see them to do it! Let them off the bus! When does this happen? The MOMENT YOU wake up and see it, YOU arrive on the razors edge of NOW and cut them off at the pass, right before they interject themselves in front of you to the moment of NOW! That exact moment is where that ego "self" ENDS. YOU STOPPED IT by being awake, aware, and PRESENT to your "SELF" as the watcher! You saw, you elevated, and you conquered that "self"! Not with a hammer, axe or saw...but with simple understanding, once SEEN, you can't unsee it...so you ready yourself for the next little "self" and the next and the next...and the processing begins to happen much more quickly! It is SEEN, understood, digested...and we are NEW! Being NEW, we SMILE!

The EGO in all of its various forms, shapes and sizes are the "selves"! They represent storylines and attachments; they are memories and projections! They are based on former selves & future selves and the associated stories one has told themselves for long enough to believe it. If you have bought into that storyline, and are experiencing life through that version of self, or paradigm, then you will undoubtedly be met with disappointment. Even in the achieving of a goal, the initial high is met with a NOW WHAT? The mind then goes back down through the despair or realization that that didn't do it either, the momentary high was still met with a falling off of the excitement, and the inevitable fall of mood to one of despair and helplessness...even hopelessness sometimes...as long as you stay in that storyline! Imagine being above that, ALL OF IT! You must be above that, and not susceptible to the "let down"! To do so ...YOU step out of your "selves" and their perspective which is IN THE MIND. YOU, as the higher "SELF", step up...elevate out of and BE ABOVE the MIND! Here and NOW, YOU are above that level of thought completely, and UNAFFECTED, or should I say un-infected by the EGO's "self" generated illusions!

Happiness is not in the future, and happiness is not in the past...happiness is in the eternal NOW and available with presence. Take this in for a moment:

**PRESENCE, with 100% faith and 100% LOVE cannot be unhappy because it is unattached to anything that could put it in that state!**

Unwavering presence. Think about that for a moment, from that vantage point, it is impossible not to be happy. CORE HAPPY is your essence, YOU are that! Once you WAKE UP and BE THAT, you take the wheel away from these little selves that would be something else! They no longer control "YOU"! YOU are literally above them! YOU are now the director of traffic above the mind and thought all together. These "selves" that drive the thoughts that happiness can be bought with any kind of THING, or attainment, do not have access to the moment anymore, YOU don't allow it! YOU are unaffected by them. From this higher SELF vantage point, these "selves" are basically considered imposters, they are not welcome here "within"! YOU SEE THEM, and no longer allow them to steal these moments from you, the REAL YOU! The ego has many shapes and forms, now YOU are seeing them as they cross your screen, and they cannot deceive you anymore! Maintain your PRESENCE above them, and unaffected by them! This will enhance your SKILLS even further!

The fact is that the mind cannot make the mind happy…happiness is always based on, or dependent on something, and that something can change or disappear in a heartbeat. (impermanence) In the world of mind, or ego, happiness is based on the existence of some condition, and conditions change. That is the fact. True happiness is not dependent on conditions! True happiness is that base, unwavering CORE "stillness" that is referred to so often in the various spiritual philosophies. That stillness is generated from this perspective, the higher "SELF" above the "selves" …the one that is DETACHED from the mind, elevates above it and NOW this NEW "YOU" can SEE and HEAR life happening from this vantage point. STRESS FREE! YOU can watch all the little selves running and jumping, first in glee and then in horror, sometimes in excitement and other times in turmoil / misery. Meanwhile, the higher "SELF" is STILL. It SEES, the waves are sometimes slow and gentle, and other times are violent and extreme. All the while, the higher "SELF" is unwavering, undaunted, and STILL. YES, it SEES the little selves and their attachments, and yet the CORE higher "SELF" is unaffected by the ride and the tide, uncompromising, and always present when it is IN THE ZONE, or in FLOW state!! This is how to get there…with PRESENCE!

## With presence, <u>YOU have CHOICE</u>!

Stay in a miserable thought, or don't! Stay in some level of emotional pain and live in the "dark" thought, or elevate…with choice, and choose to live in a different thought that is "light"er and brighter, with presence and LOVE. See the light, the TRUTH, the guidance, it is available as a choice, NOW! There is a light that is ever ready, and always available, all YOU need to do is turn it on! You turn it on by CHOOSING IT. **It's <u>YOUR LIGHT</u>**! You turn it on at WILL, and YOU make it brighter with WILL-POWER! Your will is powered by faith and trust. In fact, it's getting brighter and brighter every day, every moment! Truth be told: You are the light!

## <u>YOU ARE THE LIGHT OF THE WORLD!</u>

## <u>Go brighten it up!</u>

You are most definitely the light of YOUR world, now you have a choice as to how radiantly you want to shine!! Ever hear someone say, "you are GLOWING"?

That's YOU, and you will FEEL IT too! People will see it in you too, they'll notice because you'll be beaming, radiant! It's like you are plugged in, charged up, and primed and the inner light within you is shining right through your skin! Smiled up and READY! You'll be tapped in and turned on. BRING IT ON! NOW!

To the ability or extent that you can **TRUST** that your moments will be met with EXACTLY what you need in that moment represents your faithability. Not sure if that's a word, but it should be. Faithability is going to come down to your level of BELIEF. Belief is trusting that the "YOU" that arrives in the moment will be given exactly what YOU need in the moment. (See the Lord's prayer below, this is your "daily bread") That is another element of, or an extension of the SKILL that builds on itself as you do this over and over again. Faith builds on itself! Take that one step, and as you do, each moment becomes easier and easier as faith builds, and you are given EXACTLY what you need when it is needed. As you start to arrive without the EGO biases and EGO distractions, because NOW you KNOW you don't need them, your "CUP IS EMPTIED" and what happens is truly astonishing...it is filled up with a belief and a faith so strong that even the SELF is amazed. Like some kind of quantum entanglement just happened that includes faith, trust, and belief. Wonderstruck, the SELF sees faith become LOVE. When your faithability reaches 100%, this awe-inspiring quantum union happens, it represents 100% love, or unconditional LOVE. That transition into presence in the moment is YOU, becoming LOVE...and love responds. That presence is GOD given and eternal. NOW! Not only have YOU delivered, but YOU are delivered, as the prayer says below.

The Kingdom of Heaven is at hand the moment you allow it ...the moment you become present with GOD. YOU ARE THE INSTRUMENT, Be the instrument!

Doesn't the Lord's Prayer even instruct us to do this? VERY specifically too, and the instructions are pretty darn clear IMHO! In the Lord's prayer, aren't the following words instructions from Jesus, Mathew, and Luke. How exactly is "Thy will be done" going to be done if we don't do it? How do we do it apart from becoming it? Check this out:

**Mathew 6:9-13 and Luke 11:1-4:**
**"Thy kingdom come,**
**thy will be done,**
**on earth as it is in heaven"**[138]

How is that to happen if we don't become it? How are we to become the answer...and what is the answer? LOVE is the answer, right? We become LOVE.

Here is the whole prayer for your reference:

> **"Our Father, who art in heaven,**
> **hallowed be thy name,**
> **thy kingdom come,**
> **thy will be done,**
> **on earth as it is in heaven.**
> **<u>Give us this day</u> our daily bread.**
> **And forgive us our debts,**
> **as we forgive our debtors.**
> **And lead us not into temptation,**
> **but <u>deliver us</u> from evil.**
> **For thine is the kingdom,**
> **and the power, and the glory,**
> **forever. Amen."[139]**

May I be so bold as to interpret it further?

### **"This day"** = NOW!

The moment we arrive to NOW, we are GIVEN, or delivered our daily bread, the guidance we need! In addition, with presence, we are delivered from the "selves", they no longer affect us or have the capability to BLIND US, steer us wrong, get us sidetracked, the higher "SELF" is in the driver's seat, the lower selves were left behind at the gate! In essence, we are delivered from all forms of evil, some of which is that which the "selves" would have gotten us into! Therefore, and by the nature of this "DELIVERY", the higher more "learned" SELF is NEW. It is a rebirth of sorts. With this understanding, I went ahead and wrote this prayer out for myself in my journal so that I could understand and internalize the lesson better, in my own words. Everyone perceives words differently. Call it semantics, but for me, it takes this understanding to a new level, so I am offering it up to you, for perspective. Please take some time to really digest it, fully! Think this through. Remember this is not about me, I am not trying to offend GOD or the church, or rewrite the bible for heaven's sake, it is simply an explanation of how I think of it. I am doing my best to explain the vantage point to you in a way that you can truly grasp it, understand it, put it into practice and live it. I still speak the prayer the way it was written, for the record. The difference is that now it is not just a bunch of meaningless words. There is TRUE MEANING behind them, impactful, powerful understanding! This is actionable intelligence, enhanced skill with words that are convertible to ACTION! True action!

There is, in my opinion, a much grander vision to this prayer. It is much more than just a hollow prayer, this is to be lived, not just spoken haphazardly. I am simply trying to show you something, an angle, and within it is a powerful perspective that will allow you to do that. I wrote this out for my own ability to truly understand it at a deeper level in an attempt to do just that! It just helps me by coming back to it, as a reminder of the lesson too. Similar to the way songs and lyrics speak to me, maybe even in ways that differ from the band's intent. I know that GOD is LOVE, LOVE is the answer, and that I can always do better. I can't just "try", I must BE GOD's instrument to the best of my ability. In order to do that, I MUST arrive in the moment! Otherwise, that choice is not available. Without presence, being NEW is not an option. We are shut out by time. This prayer is a complete and comprehensive action plan, if you truly take the time to understand what it is saying! I hope this helps you to do just that, understand it, and then live it more fully with a gigantic smile on your face while doing it!

This is the way that I look at it and internalize the meaning of the LORDS PRAYER. It is what I believe it should say to make it more comprehensible, and actionable. Glory be to GOD! An interpretation, for lack of a better terminology, and of course for your benefit. Substitute me for you, in other words you be the me, the "I"!

Our father, my GOD, within me
I respect, honor, and love YOU, as I Love myself.
Show me, please, the kingdom here on earth, within me
Let me SEE your divine instruction with
Your infinite WISDOM and UNDERSTANDING, through MY eyes
So I may carry it through to completion!
Forgive my limitations and lack of understanding as I forgive others
And I forgive myself
Let me SEE in my mind through YOU
Let me recognize illusions and see through my own senses where they fail me
Rise me up and deliver me from them, and make me all powerful
Thank you, my Lord, my GOD; I appreciate all you have given me
I believe in YOU to ACT through ME,
Let me ACT with PASSION, in service to your will,
With full FAITH that YOUR WILL, will be done!

Glory to YOU!
AMEN.

NOW that is <u>WILL power</u>!

Whenever **YOU**, (the higher YOU) arrive in the moment, NOW, YOU GET the "DAILY BREAD". By getting to the moment, you are actually FREE and AVAILABLE to receive! Your cup is empty. Empty as far as a "cup" goes is just trying to explain something. We are not literally empty per se'. It is a way of saying neutral, impartial, unbiased, even keeled, balanced, unattached, non-attachment. Open and ready to receive instruction is the way that I interpret that. This is what it means to let go and let GOD. Let go of the "selves", their faulty vision and limitations, and let GOD fill you up with the "daily bread" and his infinite WISDOM! The daily bread is THE GUIDANCE we need in the moment, PRESENTLY, NOW to fill us up. We ask and maybe even pray for it, however when we do this, we are projecting in the past or future, as the "selves", and so we are literally "full of ourselves"! Nothing more can get in, there is no room for GOD. At the very EDGE of NOW, we quite literally edge God out (EGO) by being FULL. As we approach the moment, the "selves" inject themselves into the mind, or they are already in there! (The mind) At that moment, we are so full of ourselves that just in front of the gate, we get diverted. It's like a time-diversion mechanism, that when the self is full of itself, the gate closes, or switches the track....at that extreme last second... keeping us out of the moment right at that very edge of NOW. Ever see how the train track gets switched over and then the train goes whichever way the track is pointed. It is like that, but it is a real time deal...like instant, the speed is so fast it is almost imperceptible. This is why I have made such a strong emphasis on the "edges" in a previous chapter. It is at the edges where the EGO gets involved more heavily, every <u>TIME</u>, until we see it, and beat it there. <u>TIME</u>, literally a split-second, the blink of an eye locks us out of the moment. Instead of being diverted, or choosing to turn with the ego selves, at the gate, in that microsecond, we need to leave them at the gate. There is a virtual fork in the road. Like the virtual train switching tracks. This is the path we choose, right at the Edge of NOW! What I am suggesting is to LET GO and LET GOD help in that moment to CHOOSE the right path!

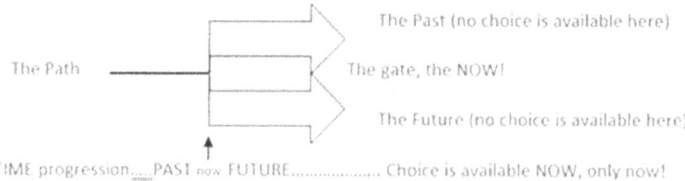

The Past (no choice is available here)

The Path    The gate, the NOW!

The Future (no choice is available here)

TIME progression....PAST now FUTURE................. Choice is available NOW, only now!

NOW is where the rubber meets the road. The choices that go to the past and the future are dead ends! The doorway to NOW is flipped, in that case. What happens in the diagram above is that the ego self, RE-acts! When it does this, the past ego self is "triggering it" to flip it left, or the future ego self is "triggering it" to flip it right, these lead to nowhere(illusions)! The GATE or the DOOR is available and accessible via the middle road, the middle track, straight forward...NO TURNING. The NOW, or that moment in time, is the narrow gate, which is STRAIGHT but it's a ridiculously tight squeeze! Razors edge, as described previously. Meanwhile, we are barreling full steam ahead. The only way through is to not be triggered, not distracted, and with mighty RESOLVE, stay present! Calm, balanced, UNWAVERING, foundational KNOWING and trusting where and when we need to be, NOW. Minute fractions of a nanosecond make all the difference here. Distraction is NOT an option. With unshakable FAITH and TRUST, we must be available and present to choose the narrow gate. With presence we are able to see it. We think we "know" the past. We also like to THINK we know the future...these are the alternatives. We can choose to run towards, or away from one or the other. (FEAR/DESIRE) It makes no difference, either way, we would be diverted at a crucial interchange. The problem at this point is that we only SEE two options, but NOW, wait. With presence there is a 3rd option that just revealed itself at a gate. Like an invisible stretch of tracks just appeared and is now visible, but very narrow. It is straight ahead, it is called "The unknown" To KNOW IT, you must squeeze through the gateway. It takes trust, and faith, and the where with all to take the step forward not "KNOWING" what is on the other side!

## God is available through the narrow gate, which leads to NOW!

You want to know GOD? God is available in the moment, but in order to fit through the gate we have to drop our baggage! That means the EGO "selves" and all their "stuff" as well as their slanted ways of seeing things. What we THINK we KNOW! OMG! The ego "selves" ARE the baggage, YES, and they are steering us astray, away...left and right, past/future, diverted away from the gate to NOW! By SEEING THEM and choosing to arrive to NOW without them, leaving them out, cutting them off at the pass so to speak and edging IN, by choice, the union is possible! GOD inspires us, powers us, and becomes the answer! We truly have the WILL and the POWER to respond to life and in life with unconditional LOVE with PERFECT INSTRUCTION! Our awareness of the presence of GOD within and OUR ability to BE THAT is a SKILL.... work on the skill, come back to NOW, GET TO NOW!

Visualize this "path", find the middle road, you must KNOW that it is there, and then YOU can BE in the moment. This is the way to BE the instrument! First you must be able to get there, and then you must be open to it, willingly. Leave the EGO biases and the false programming (the "false prophets") at the doorway to NOW...on the razors edge, EMPTY YOUR CUP at the gate...and SHOW UP to NOW with PRESENCE! The guidance will meet YOU there! Let FAITH fill you up and BECOME the answer! LOVE. Love is the answer here and NOW! There is no room for doubt...no room for baggage, it will not fit through the gate! All YOU need is LOVE. This is truly an inspired life, inspired by the "most high"! The highest WILL, the higher POWER! We must become the answer.

Small detour, but this is also the meaning of "repent", in the bible, and in my opinion, that means leaving it <u>ALL</u> at the gate! In essence, "purified", or "baptized" moment by moment. Isn't baptism a CHOICE? Doesn't it symbolize the fact that <u>NOW</u>, our "sins" are washed away, and <u>NOW</u> we are new? A fresh start of sorts, a rebirth. We are NEW in this moment by leaving the old behind and showing up to NOW with an empty cup! Aren't we doing that by CHOOSING the narrow gate? If we leave them there at the gate, and arrive to NOW, the "selves" and their "sins" are no longer "within"! Once again, it comes down to being PRESENT and available to make a pivotal CHOICE! I think the word repent confuses people. It means showing up NOW and following the guidance (Not the "selves"), BEING LOVE vs anything else we might be inspired or "tempted" to BE. Be the instrument, GODs instrument vs anything less, which would be "sinful"! So having **FAITH** is not only a good idea, but also a requirement in order to receive proper instructions, real time, in this moment, NOW! We need it to get to the gate! Without it, we don't even arrive, presently, and so we are not "delivered" from anything!

### With faith, we are delivered...from our "selves" into the moment!

Without them, we do arrive TO the moment. It isn't that the selves aren't there anymore, but they are somewhat evanescent. Like the Lord's Prayer says, they have been acknowledged like loose fitting clothing and as requested, we are "delivered" from them, they are let go, they are no longer affecting us. Once FREE from their influence, restrictions and limitations, "evil" or the "devil" if you wish to call it that, faith carries us through the gate.

### FAITH gets us to the moment!

## We have been saved, potentially!

At that point, in this moment, we must be able to convert the instructions to a very REAL ACTION, NOW! This is where we must LISTEN, and it's not enough to just hear, we must BE IT. Trust, faith, love are not just nice words, they are an action plan TO LIVE BY! "LIVE BY" means what? We no longer try, we DO, we need to BE IT!! It is NOT a RE-action to life, we take higher "SELF" directed ACTIONS with very pure guidance, the TRUTH, as delivered by GOD! The actions are NEW, presently! This means that we had enough SKILL to arrive, we heard, we saw the instructions, and we ACTED! Faith puts us on the <u>EDGE</u> of NOW, in position, the gate is open... it is NOW all up to us! WILL "YOU" take that next step and walk through? CONNECT...HEAR, SEE, get the guidance, and then convert that into an ACTION! It is here and now that we must become the answer. It requires faith and trust to get there!

## <u>Mathew 17:20</u>

**"Because of your little faith," He told them "For truly I tell you, if you have faith the size of a mustard seed, you will tell this mountain, *"Move, from here to there"*, and it will move. Nothing will be impossible for YOU"[140]**

HAVE FAITH!!!! With it, and without the selves, in the moment, YOU have been UN-limited, or "delivered" from them! You have been saved. The answers are not in the past, and not in the future, yet that is where we are most of the time. Narrow is the gate to NOW, NOW you know where it is. Choose it. Step forwards, TRUST! Now is the time!

Jesus and others were examples of what is possible upon the union with GOD in Heaven. YOU must get past (or QUIET) the MIND to SEE and HEAR and BE this presence, NOW! It is always and eternally present! If you are in the past or you are in the future, you have essentially put the shackles on your "self". You have locked your own freedom doorway, and LIMITED yourself! If you are lost in thought, or unconscious, then maybe, just maybe you have locked yourself out of heaven in that moment?!? Did you ever think of it that way? What will you do with the next one?

Didn't **Jesus** state emphatically that:

**"The KINGDOM of GOD is WITHIN you"?[141]**

YOU HAVE THE KEY, LOOK WITHIN!!!! Stop focusing all your efforts "out there"! So many people, so many traditions say the SAME THING!! LISTEN, SEE, HEAR! BE! NOW!

Here are a few more examples:

**"Past and Future are in the MIND only—I AM NOW"[142]**
**"To know that you are a prisoner of your mind is the dawn of WISDOM"[143]**
**-Sri Nisargadatta Maharaj**

**"Unease, anxiety, tension, stress, worry—all forms of FEAR—are caused by too much FUTURE, and not enough PRESENCE. Guilt, regret, resentment, grievances, sadness, bitterness, and all forms of NON-forgiveness are caused by too much PAST and not enough PRESENCE. Most people find it difficult to BELIEVE that a state of consciousness totally FREE of all negativity is possible. And yet this is the liberated state to which all spiritual teachings point. It is the promise of salvation, not in an illusory future but right here and NOW"!**

**-Eckard Tolle, The Power of NOW[144]**

That liberated state that Eckard Tolle mentions = FREEDOM! Understanding comes with the removal of falseness with TRUTH, the removal of attachments to past/future selves (EGO) and the application of FAITH to arrive in the **eternal Present** with GOD. Here, NOW, with TRUST and FAITH, YOU can SEE with new eyes and HEAR with new ears the guidance that is needed and available, every moment of every day! In doing so, and by doing so, this SKILL affords YOU the understanding needed in this world, NOW. The effort and sacrifice it takes to master this skill truly show you WHY forgiveness is needed, and NOT just some lofty ideal! With this understanding, you will ultimately forgive your "self" and others when you/they fail and are unable (momentarily) to get to the moment fast enough...to get the guidance, to get the lesson. That may mean that they did not respond with or from LOVE, that doesn't mean that you can't! YOU CAN, and it must happen NOW!

You realize how hard it is, and the massive amount of effort and focus it takes to be "PERFECT". Lofty goal for sure...but we are human, right? So, inevitably, that is where we fail to bring the best version of our "SELF", in any given moment, and the result is less than stellar. We were looking at and responding to an illusion, understandable, it happens to all of us. forgive "IT", the "self", the mind!

As **Jesus** said:

## "Forgive them, for they know not what they do!"[145]

Please understand that this means more than implied. It is multidirectional. It means not only "out there", but "in here", WITHIN! YOU must forgive and LET IT GO! This includes you, the "selves" within when they take you over, and everyone else "out there" as well that may miss a moment and makes a mistake! UNDERSTANDING is POWER, pass it along! LOVE truly is the answer...and we can be the answer. BE THE INSTRUMENT!

Before signing off, I do want to Thank all the people who have influenced this perspective, I have referenced them throughout this write up. You are all SO very much appreciated! If you happen to read this, I welcome your thoughts and input!

Also, please continue on to some bonus sections that follow. I do believe that they will help you build an incredibly stable foundation and enhance the skill. Start from where you are, that's all you can do! This includes a top 10 ways to use this information, as well as some exercises, credits, and links. All of this is intended to help you along the way. Take the time to work at it! Don't go it alone, share this with the people you love! We are all here to help each other.

There are thousands of links to writings, songs, lyrics and more I should add, people that should be applauded, noted, mentioned, and thanked if I haven't done so already. You are all appreciated, **everyone I have ever met and known!** You have all contributed to this perspective, and my own growth, one way or another, and as a result I am hopeful this this book helps many more people as a result! Sending LOVE and massive appreciation! See also the official credits section that will follow at the end as more official end notes. It is much more than that though. Use it as a way to look these people up, as a source for more "stuff" to help, in some cases my thoughts about them, more knowledge, angles & helpful details. It has website links, and acknowledgements to the amazing people I reference in this book and resources to find them online! You all have affected me one way or another...so please forgive me if I haven't given credit to you here specifically! If you are offended, please observe WHO specifically (which "it" in the mind) is offended! LOL. Sending LOVE, as always!

As promised, here are a few links to some instructions from **Jaie Hart**. She is AMAZING and has some wonderful perspectives!!!!

http://dreamintime.blogspot.com/2015_11_01_archive.html[146]

Here is one on TRIGGERS that she wrote:

http://dreamintime.blogspot.com/2017/02/triggers-flashes-of-emotion-or.html[147]

### BONUS CHAPTERS TO FOLLOW:

- BEACH BALL / HOW TO SECTION

- ATTITUDES, IMPERMANENCE, AND FINAL THOUGHTS...

- TOP TEN WAYS TO IMPLEMENT THIS MATERIAL

- EXERCISES TO HELP YOU BUILD YOUR NEW SKILLSET!

- DEDICATION

# THE BEACH BALL / HOW TO

# BONUS CHAPTER

I AM NOT QUITE sure who it was that told me about this perspective, or where I read it or if I heard it in a course maybe? I tried to look it up and was unable to find the article I read. I think it may have been either Guy Finley, or Bill Harris that explained this in one of the courses I bought. Either way, Thank you! I appreciate the analogy immensely as it has helped me to understand what **Jaie Hart** explained to me so many years ago, that **"The obstacle is the path"**. She wrote about it too, among other insightful topics like **"The EGO is the Veil"**[148]. Thanks again Jaie! The ZEN proverb regarding the obstacle explains that you can't solve a problem by going around it! Avoidance is not a solution, YOU MUST FACE IT, in my words! Once again, that's the straight path...not left or right! Face it head on. In this example, the beach ball is the obstacle.

Furthermore, and in more detail, this is the way that I understand the beach ball analogy. It is a process, and as a starting point, when speaking of a mind type obstacle, it essentially needs to be deflated, in a manner of speaking, so check out this depiction. It's a great way to see it conceptually in the mind's eye as a visual tool or as an explanation of the perspective it offers, more completely, as it relates to the mind.

Consider the surface of the mind to be the water level in the pool, lake, sea, or whatever water you want to visualize. Your psychology, former "selves", programming, and the things that affect you, from a negative standpoint, (your baggage) is a beach ball, which is currently underneath the surface of the water. The sum total of your baggage is represented by how much air is in the beach ball. You could actually consider it to be many different beach balls that vary in size. Your PEACE of mind is represented by the status of the surface of the water. In other words, is it calm and peaceful, or is there a virtual hurricane going on? More than likely somewhere in between!

Wait, let me back up... We are all born with "stuff". In some philosophies, that is called Karma. I think I have heard it called a lot of things, law of attraction, the ID, the unconscious, the shadow, the dark side, the subconscious...whatever. It is there, I refer to it as the "selves" most often, and their baggage. Bottom line, most of us are not aware that it is operating in the background all of the time, without our awareness. It carries weight, as we drag this baggage around with us...and it does weigh us down! There are many books written about "shadow" selves. I kind of refer to them as the lower "selves", basically they are positionalities / perspectives / beliefs and programming within us. What it amounts to is a sum total of all our desires and fears and the stuff we stubbornly refuse to let go of. I should mention triggers and pain points, in particular! This "stuff" or baggage affects the water level in one way or another. Situationally, there is typically only 1 winner when these opposing forces go head-to-head and battle it out in the mind. Assuming the higher "SELF" has not reeled them in yet! That is going to be the one "self" that is carrying the most weight into the battle and arrives to make the decision this time!

So, what does the beach ball have to do with that? It's funny actually, the description makes me laugh. As we go through life, or lives, depending on your beliefs, we all run into negative situations, and unfortunately "bad" things happen. Stuff that we don't want happens, it just does! That reinforces the fact that we experience PAIN when those things that we don't want to happen, happen! Sometimes that means physically, but I am primarily talking about EMOTIONAL pain. In fact, I think that **Eckert Tolle** calls that the **"pain body"**[149] and it is a cumulative memory bank, so to speak of our baggage, in my words, although he explains it in quite extraordinary detail if you'll look him up.

My vantage point is that each time a negative thing happens, it tends to be a pain point if we don't process it completely. If that's the case, then it becomes a future trigger because we are adding it to this memory bank. As life goes on and we keep adding stuff, this "baggage" can get very heavy, and we can build up an enormous number of triggers too, if we don't know any better! Assuming we process things in an effective way, deal with them, understand them, and move on...it's not a real problem they don't carry a lot of weight. That doesn't always happen though does it, life moves fast, and we have some well-established mind tools like escapism, avoidance, distractions, and resistance, among others! Human nature is to bury it or avoid it because we are too busy, or it is too painful, or both. One way or another, due to timing, or our habitual nature, or an array of other reasons, we can't, won't or don't want to deal with it right now, we want to move away from it quickly and NOT think about it at all, as fast as possible. That is assuming we are conscious enough to see it and react to it to start with! Bottom line, that is NOT GOOD!!! When we don't process something, and that something carried with it a lot of weight...it MATTERS! If it mattered to you, in any way, it mattered to the beach ball! You will understand why momentarily.

The beach ball is this virtual "obstacle" in this example, or our baggage so to speak. When we run into the obstacle and GO AROUND the obstacle, and don't deal with it, because it's a little obstacle, we pump just a little bit of air into the beach ball. Not a big deal, well...not yet anyway... right? We have only added a little teeny bit of air to the beach ball...and that issue was just small potatoes!

As we go through life, that same scenario will present itself over and over again, in similar ways, in this life or the next, this MOMENT or the next...and WHEN that happens, YOU HAVE AN OPPORTUNITY. A couple of Choices:

1. You can deal with it, understand it, and process it...and GET THE LESSON or

2. You can resist it, avoid it, go around it, bury it, or in one way or another NOT deal with it, NOT process it, and by doing so you blow just a little bit more air into the beach ball. Again, not a real big deal...the beach ball only has just a little bit of air in it. SO, as this round of being human evolves, keeping that beach ball under the surface of the water (your mind) is pretty easy, especially when you are younger! Quite honestly, you may spend an entire lifetime avoiding dealing with that particular issue and NEVER process it and NEVER get through it. You can remain unconscious; it is actually possible. However, it may resurface in the mind for processing every other day if you are actively working on it. Either way, at this stage, it is not a real big deal, right? It is not causing you a big stir...there isn't a whole lot of air in the beach ball and it isn't causing a lot of waves in your pool, or within the mind! Nothing stirring anyway.

KEY ELEMENT HERE: In order to deal with the obstacle, YOU MUST meet it in the moment, or on the razor's edge of the NOW moment! Why? Because without seeing it actually step in, without the awareness of this happening, the MIND cannot choose, it is on autopilot! The "you" or lower "self" doesn't even see it, nor does it have a choice, it acts from what it is programmed to do! Let me say that again, in that scenario, without presence, **no choice is even available** until this higher "YOU", higher "SELF" becomes aware enough to see it. What does that mean? Situationally, and throughout our lifetime, we have been, and are continuing to unknowingly pump up the beach ball while we are unconscious or asleep at the wheel, so to speak! It is being inflated constantly when we are not AWARE, and not processing!

Not only that, we may have a whole bunch of different beach balls, all varying in size. Some of these make big waves all by themselves. Imagine if several of these beach balls all surface at the same time. This is the equivalent of waves and tides, possibly major chop on the water, where it is very difficult to gain our footing. It can certainly knock us off balance, take us out of the moment for sure, even with Sea legs (meaning we are used to it)! Yes, we do get somewhat accustomed to chaos over time, that isn't necessarily a good thing.

The NOW is the only place / time where this "change" can take place within us because that is WHERE and WHEN the choice is available. The NOW is where we don't pump up the beach ball. In essence, what YOU will be doing is front running the "thought". YOU will, for all intents and purposes, BEAT that thought to the moment. In doing this, YOU will leave "it" at the doorway to NOW, on the crest of the wave...before yesterday crosses into tomorrow. NOW! It may take a little while and a few tries before you actually see it happen, but it will happen! For a while, it may beat you there, and "it" will win. (The "programming", lower, or "false self" / shadow self, etc.) After a while, YOU will see it coming, and since NOW YOU are wise to it...YOU won't let it happen! YOU will be there ahead of "it", since the last time this situation occurred, YOU were present and got the lesson! Something I learned early in my sales career is that a strategy known is a strategy blown. This is why certain sales techniques don't work on other salespeople, they've been trained, or educated about it! If people know what you are doing with a certain action or statement, it just doesn't work as effectively, if at all. Once you see a particular strategy implemented, or someone shows you how it works, you are now alert to it! Similarly, once thieves of your mind actually steal the moment, YOU will not let them take you over again because you are wise to it, YOU will see it coming! At some point, YOU gain the ability to arrive "in the zone" and these former selves and programming have no influence there. IF YOU arrive IN the moment, you left them at the gate! That's the higher YOU unaffected by these lower selves!

So, Let's say that doesn't happen, you remain unconscious and the lower you is in charge, you have been asleep at the wheel, unaware, and that 1000 times this thing comes up and each time you blow it off, and each time you don't deal with it. Either you ignore it or bury it, or whatever else. Each time you go around the problem, resist it or avoid it in one way or another. This is essentially by choice, if we are aware of it and refuse to deal with it, or in all reality, and more likely, it is automatic in the mind before we have woken up and are even aware it is happening. Regardless of methodology, by resistance, ignorance, going numb, pure unconsciousness, or by burying it...the result is that you blow a little more air into the beach ball. Please understand this: By avoiding it, suppressing it...or going around it, one way or another you are giving it MORE leverage, more power for the next time it comes up in your life! Well, that beach ball when it resurfaces each time, it resurfaces with a little more air, and each time you give it a little more power. Each time you blow more air into the beach ball and inflate it a little more, you give it a little more power in your life to cause a major disruption! Each time that even LARGER beach ball resurfaces, it causes a little more of a stir on the top of the water when it "comes up" (that is as "stuff" comes up in your life)! In the beginning it isn't a real big deal, because the beach ball doesn't have much air in it... but when you get to 1000 times, the beach ball is HUGE! That is going to cause a commotion...IT IS UPSETTING!!!! Remember the mind is the surface of the water and that sh** is going to cause some waves! At some point, you will have to deal with it, and you know it, but those waves are just too much to deal with right now and so we make every effort to bury it again, and again we do not get the lesson! Well, I hate to say it, but you are going down a dangerous road, PAIN ahead! As a reminder, look up **Eckard Tolle**'s **"pain body"**, and what happens if we refuse to deal with it! He has a lot of books, and one in particular that I think may speak to this. That book is called **"The power of NOW"**[150]. Hmmm that sounds interesting. I think He may be onto something! Or Maybe I am? LOL

Moral of the story, deal with your sh** NOW and NOW and NOW...DO NOT BURY IT, whatever you do, do not pump more air into that beach ball! Decide in favor of getting the lesson...and NOT pumping up the beach ball. That is why we are here, to get the lessons. Quite honestly, that is why the same things, the same type people, and the same type situations show up in your life, so that you can get the lesson and process it, so to speak! This is one of the reasons why we are being so watchful and paying so close attention, so that we can see when we are triggered, when we hit an edge!

If you are awake and aware and CHOOSE to get the lesson, then you will no longer be blinded by that thing! You will be wise to it. Onward and upwards to that next thing, that next lesson. Awake and aware, with PRESENCE! Yes, it will resurface periodically to make sure you still get it, probably when you are low on energy or something, but at a minimum, just know that if you don't deal with it now and now and now...well then, it will come back later, and it will carry MORE

WEIGHT!!!! Each time is an opportunity to deal with it, process it, and move on.... take that step! The alternative is to postpone it and when it comes up the next time, it's going to be a bigger obstacle! The beach ball is going to cause more waves, bigger waves! You are giving the beach ball (The obstacle) your power, and each time you do, YOU GET WEAKER relative to it! Essentially, you are less capable of keeping that beach ball underneath the surface of the mind. It's going to come up more and more often and it is going to be MORE FORCEFUL each and every time until you wake up and see it. Each time you get a lesson you reverse that pattern ever so slightly, and that beach ball contains slightly less air...sounds like an action plan, right? Let's actively focus on and be sure to consciously deflate the beach ball! We need opportunities to do this, so as I say, we bring our "selves" to them, or they bring them to us! Let's be alert and ready.

It actually reminds me of a song I listen to, and it makes me laugh. I know by now you probably think everything makes me laugh. Well, not true, but a lot of stuff does and this one is more like a smirk. This song has a kind of a somber tone, for good reason, yet this is a very realistic and an amazing perspective that is similar to this process of seeing and deflating the beach ball, decluttering the mind, or removing yesterday's obstacles with awareness from a mind perspective. The way that I hear this song is as a conversation amongst the selves, higher SELF included.

With that as a preview, check out the song by **Evanescence**, **"HELLO"**[151] It's a kind of fun way to look at this education we are getting, in my opinion! As always, I can't promise that this is what they meant for it to mean, just the way I hear it and what it speaks to me. It seems as if it is a super cool portrayal of someone watching the mind, as if from this overseer perspective that I talk about so much. It is like as if someone is watching and greeting their lower "self" in the mind, as the higher "SELF" (Overseer)! Hello there, I see you in there...and then the lower self is kind of talking back to it! Kind of a funny perspective, I guess. So, it's basically a virtual playground when seen like this, and it is a whole lot easier to enjoy life if you don't take it so darn seriously! I hear this song as a description of the mind when you are looking at it from this "learning" perspective. If you consider the mind a playground, in which we are to LEARN, while on the playground having fun, then how can you take it too seriously? Kind of similar to wearing the world like a loose garment, right? Live and learn, pretty simple once you break it down. This makes it a little more comfortable, maybe even enjoyable!

The MIND is a playground, and as I have said previously, it can be quite comical and FUN when we are awake and aware and seeing this all happening within! We must take that overseer perspective though as the "witness" from ABOVE the

MIND, NOT IN IT...as in with awareness of thought, and PRESENCE rather than at the level of thought itself! It is a virtual classroom!

When the school bell rings, or we wake up because we are alerted to a lesson coming, we simply TURN THE LIGHT OF AWARENESS ON, class is starting! This song, to me, is a great reminder to wake up and GET in the classroom, the moment, to GET THE LESSONS! Better yet, stay present, like as in BE in class constantly, but make it a playground! It is a true education once you actually start watching from that vantage point! School is always in session as long as you are watching from awareness, above the mind. Making it a playground takes the stress out!

The somber tone of this song, in my opinion, speaks to the depressing realization that that a particular version of "self" is kind of sort of still stubbornly hanging around in the background, in the darkness which happens sometimes when we don't want to let go. While we know that we are no longer asleep at the wheel, it is a reminder that we can no longer be who we were. If we get trapped in the mind, that can bog us down and be somewhat depressing because we are essentially losing a part of ourselves that we were really identified with! What we end up seeing though is that whatever is carrying the most weight is going to win situationally...and we know it. That message comes through loud and clear to me in this song. In other words, our experience will be whichever "story" we are giving the most power. Our mind can only be in one place at a time! It can believe in the "good" or the "bad". We can focus on the desire or the fear. We can be present, or we can NOT be present. You can run your life from this new higher "SELF" perspective, or you can let whichever lower "self" shows up in the moment have its way with you! Just know if that if the lower "self" is running the show, the water is going to be a little ROUGH! Remember that "self" is focused on an illusion! Better brace yourself!

This song also reminds me that BELIEF matters, so I need to pay very close attention to what I am subscribing to in my mind! It is also a gentle reminder that the TONE of thought is often a good indicator of what I am subscribed to in the mind. Kind of like looking in the virtual mirror for what my face is doing, smile, frown, etc. Furthermore, it is a good reason to pay close attention to speed and tone in songs like this one. It can reflect a powerful message or vantage point if you can hear the tone, vocal intricacies, interpret speed as well as the lyrical components and gain insights from it all as it is combined and delivered! My take is that more than likely it is trying to portray a message of some kind, that's just my opinion! The mind does the same things, so pay attention! Speed, tone, themes, details...everything matters!

Pay attention to what the mind is doing, feeling, acting like, playing out, maybe even showing out...what is DRIVING this behavior, the reaction within, is it desire, or fear? Are you present, or NOT? WHY? What is and where is the belief? How much power does it have (emotion arising!) Where is this coming from? UNDERSTANDING is POWER. Remember that a strategy known is a strategy blown!

**STOP blowing up the beach ball.**
**Stop giving the "selves" all your power!**
**RECLAIM YOUR LIFE, your POWER! NOW!!!**

Here are a few other songs that I believe offer some powerful perspectives, ask important questions, and even throw in some sarcasm for fun. These songs, in my opinion, reflect an understanding, and hearing the messages in songs just makes it fun for me as key reminders of important lessons.

**Within Temptation**: **"See who I am"**, **"Pale"**, from **The Silent Force** album. **"The PURGE"**, and **"SHED MY SKIN"**[152] are newer singles. Be sure to see my comments in the end notes section on this and the other bands I reference for comments, links, etc. There are many more songs from this brilliant band, these are just the ones that come to mind quickly, and they are really good! They are very descriptive, add emphasis, some attitude, big themes, and wonderful angles on things... very cool songs! Thanks Sharon and team. I truly love and appreciate this music very much!

Try to see if you can really understand what they are saying, it is quite educational if you ask me! It's pretty powerful too. IMHO. Net, net, with understanding, we must, with all our power, all our focus and all our energy, HUGE amounts of awareness, USE THE SKILL, BE PRESENT, NOW and BE the change we wish to see in the world, our world! If we can't see it, we have to feel it. If we can't feel it, we have to hear it. One way or another, we have to SEE the "selves" and what they are up to!

This requires awareness, seeing who I am becoming in the moment! First, we are seeing these "selves" as the moment is unfolding, and then with understanding, shedding these versions of self that no longer serve us. We have grown out of them, like a snake shedding its skin, we are becoming NEW! To further the point, or as an alternate description, we SEE and then PURGE them. They no longer serve us, although we see them internally, we must leave them behind. So again, we are NEW! That is my interpretation, the way I hear the songs that I just referenced.

By doing this, quite naturally, we are deflating the virtual beach ball and each time it resurfaces, it does so with less and less force, less power. That means less of a disturbance on the surface of the water! Basically, we gain MORE POWER, as a result of this shedding and purging. We are, in other words, emptying our cup. We were full of our "selves", this is essentially saying the same thing in different words. Releasing, forgiving, shedding, purging, letting stuff go... which essentially means the "selves" that are holding onto the "stuff"!

Here is a slide in power point that I made for myself describing how to deal with this in detail so that I wasn't just pumping up the beach ball out of ignorance or resistance!

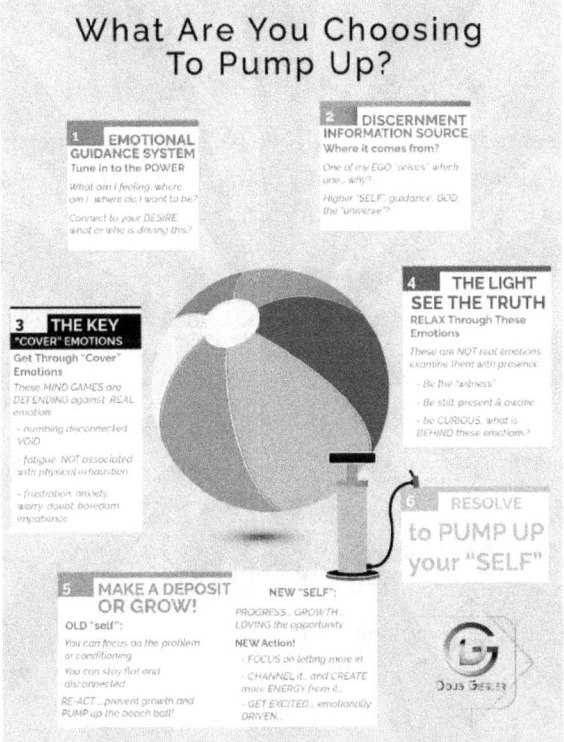

Bottom line is this: Little "you" has no choice. Big "YOU" has 2 choices. Pump up your "SELF" or pump up the beach ball and wait for a future "blow up" in your life that is inevitably coming soon! It's your decision. Once again, with your new SKILL, energy, awareness, and PRESENCE... YOU HAVE CHOICE!

Choose wisely!

Here are a couple more slides from my computer that I thought might help. I created a presentation for myself to remind me of some of these lessons...and a couple of acronyms I created.

GROWING:

FAITH: This is the UNDERSTANDING we need to be better at arriving in the moment! It's like an action plan. By doing this, it reveals the "selves" that are getting in our own way, the way of our truth, our faith!

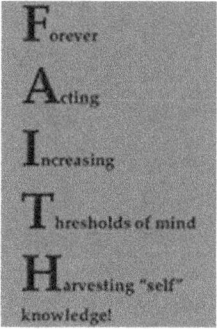

You can't stand still, keep moving, take that next step and GET THE LESSONs as you do!

## "Be up and doing, with a Heart for any fate"[153]

**Longfellow, The Psalm of Life!**

That means **UNATTACHED**

This is a screenshot of a visual I created for myself of the virtual vantage point I would visualize as the "overseer"! With the higher mind, as the "SELF" or watcher, the thoughts of the lower selves are powerless! HIGHER SELF is the over

SEER, seeing from above mind with the light of awareness fully on...PRESENT, Awake and Aware...NOW! Again, this is POWER! Why? Because YOU HAVE CHOICE and NOW highlighted (hi "light" ed) GUIDANCE! See the light!

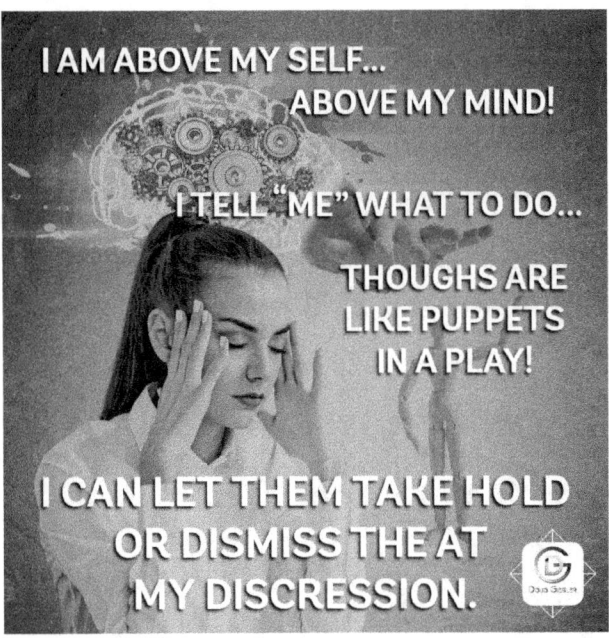

As each of the many beach balls surface for you to play with in this life playground or pool, have fun with it! Learning truly can be fun, it doesn't have to be treated with such a labor some attitude or like a grind! Be amused, cheer yourself on, and with each lesson gain some satisfaction within the process. With empathy, understanding and love, cradle that beach ball with kid gloves. Breathe, and with that next big deep breath, use the air and all the energy provided within that beach ball to PUMP UP your "SELF", your highest self that is! Use every ounce of energy that air provides to push you through to NOW! By arriving, you have just deflated the beach ball. In the process, you have increased faith & trust in the methodology. This experiential knowing is the ultimate trust factor and KNOWING will help you get in the zone more consistently, the moment, the NOW! The ZONE is where you can BE THE INSTRUMENT! Be the instrument :)

www.BETHEINSTRUMENT.com

# "We'd Love To Hear From You!"

Joelle and I know how much the information in this book has impacted our life and it would be a pleasure to hear about how it has positively impacted yours as well. Please take a few moments and write down YOUR story below. Then you have your choice in how you want to get it to us.

1. Go to this web link **BeTheInstrument.com/yourstory** and sumbit the story for consideration to be published in the next printing of this book or to be featured on our websites.

2. Scan or take a screenshot and upload it to our Facebook Community Page.
    *Facebook.com/groups/WhatTheFWords*
    **\*Make sure you tag me so I get notified.**

3. Tear out these 2 pages and send it to me by snail mail:
**Office Address:**
C/O Doug Giesler
316 Koons Street
Leesville, SC, 29070

_____

_____

_____

_____

_____

# MUSIC, ATTITUDES, IMPERMANENCE, AND FINAL THOUGHTS

## BONUS CHAPTER

## Music

To address impermanence, I am including an email that I wrote to my wife which was an effort to give her some mind strategies geared towards healing from loss. I have also included some song references, and links, because as you know, I am a music lover. I thought that these songs, and the powerful messages I believe to be in them, might help in a time of need. One of the cool aspects about music is that it can be played anytime, anywhere, these days...and if you are not connected to a device, or even wirelessly, it can simply be replayed in the mind! Surely, that would be a desirable feature at a time when no one else is available with a hug or a shoulder to cry on. It could act as a virtual pep talk!

Music can help us in many ways if we let it, which is why I am so appreciative to the folks that make it. I don't have a musical bone in my body, but I sure love to listen! It amazes me what these creative and talented people put together in so many different ways. Music can paint a picture with infinite combinations of tones and words. I love that aspect of it, some people and bands are just gifted at it, I suppose. They have a great talent with designing and delivering profound musical messages! I use the word brilliant a lot to describe songs, but in some cases, I don't even think that is a good enough compliment because, to me, it is so much better than that word conveys! The vocals alone in some cases are just incredible with the tones they can deliver, how they can convey a feeling, how long they can hold a note, or move from one to another, not to mention the range! My brain just gets captivated by it. Having the background music composed and played to provide the perfect landscape for that vocal delivery is just fascinating to me. I don't even know if I am using the right words, musically speaking, but all the elements just seem to come together, and it is extraordinary, magical even. I guess that's why I love certain bands so much, because they seem to do it with such amazing consistency, and not even in the same ways all the time, they mix it up and somehow, it still works! They do it in ways that really appeal to me, obviously. While I can't play music, or read it, whatever the musical sense in me is called hears it, is delighted by it, and it comes through me in such a way that I am simply awed, time and again! I must listen repeatedly sometimes, maybe to savor it, or because my mind is almost questioning how they could do all of that to begin with, no less convey something so meaningful, and so well in the process! Brilliant, and awesome just don't tell the whole story, not enough anyway, maybe we can add some more adjectives? ...dazzling, scintillating, vivid, imaginative, calculated, intense! Yep, I love it. I am sure glad that there are musical people in the world that can express themselves and communicate in ways that are so astounding! Very much appreciated.

The way I look at and hear music is naturally for the enjoyment, however that may not be for the same reasons in each instance or "session"! It depends on my mood really. That could mean as a casual listener for relaxation purposes periodically, but for me, that is not usually the primary driver. I hear and see messages in lots of ways, music is just one of them. More often than not, I am listening to something specific, or a particular band / album, for a reason. That meaning, for me, is most often because it contains a message or theme that is significant, or purposeful to me, and I want to be reminded of it right now and / or I really want to plant it in the mind again! Every moment is an opportunity, right? Sometimes we just need a boost in the right direction, particularly if today's energy level is subpar, or maybe something heavy is being processed, like a loss. It can have an uplifting effect, get some energy flowing, reposition things mentally, and maybe even help integrate them as an example. Music does that for me quite often. It acts as an incorporating influence, a mechanism for this assimilation process for various lessons and experiences! That's another reason why I appreciate these bands so much! I truly hope that they know this about their music, I welcome a call from any and all of them. I would love the opportunity to thank them from the bottom of my heart! Just sayin...THANKS a LOT!!!

While I tend to be pretty stable and balanced overall, I love the way music can enhance or highlight an angle, a way of looking at something, or show me something new relative to a present day happening, situation, or a life "pattern" I am seeing.

That might mean that I listen to the same song several times in a row because I just heard something I want to understand better, and it kind of brought it out from a corner of the mind for contemplation mentally. This could possibly be that a particular vantage point is being highlighted, and more thoroughly digested, because I am hearing it in a slightly new way! Sometimes that little tweak might mean it gives me an overall attitude adjustment too, like an AHA moment with a very specific thought that is sung in a beautiful or unique way, and as a result, it really hits home the way I needed to hear it, NOW, in that moment! It could also contain a super positive idea, or an energetic / happy speed or tone to it with unique musical components to highlight a subject or theme as a background for a lyrical message. It can be meaningful to me in a lot of ways really, another might be to just plant a seed. All it takes is one thought to change course on any given day, at any moment, in order to take that next step, sometimes in a new direction! May as well take it with some enthusiasm, maybe a little added internal vigor, faith & trust!!

Because of the way that I listen and hear, more often than not, music can provide me with a really powerful lyrical reminder of a lesson! To me, that's a boost and of course my patent pending chuckle emerges as a result. LOL. Joking of course, the chuckle is a real happening, no patent though, I want you to have fun with this and chuckle too! That's an aspect that I really like a lot, re-getting lessons! I have mentally sort of bookmarked a lot of songs as a way to hear them again, as a reminder, so I can reinforce an insight or understanding. Obviously, some songs are better at this than others, so I tend to replay these type songs quite often, even whole albums because I know that the theme of a particular album is related to something I am going through, or learned, and they deliver it in an appealing way. I pay attention to song, and album titles as well, because often times it may reveal a theme that the band is trying to convey within that song or series of songs! I think that is particularly true for the bands that I reference most, but of course, I can't be sure, and I can't speak for them. Seems true to me, based on what I hear though not only in the way that particular albums are laid out, but even the albums seem like a progression, theme wise! So cool. Now we can even use apps to group songs together as playlists, those playlists can be grouped by theme, imagine reinforcing a lesson, over and over again with 10 or 15 different songs. What a great way to learn and digest stuff in a fun way and it's all available with a click, or a verbal command!

I see lots of themes and mind stuff, be it resistance, emotion, power, dreaming, thought in general, waves of thought, ego perspectives and other stuff too! A lot of it is relative to mind gearing, in my opinion, and ways of looking at things. Some super powerful ideas are being delivered, or at least heard, from where I am standing. In my view, some are much deeper than others, to be sure. The thought has crossed my mind that maybe I am a little too eager for lessons sometimes. There is that saying, we hear what we want to hear right? There may be some truth to that. The stuff that is relevant to our "magnetism", demeanor, mood, or frame of mind, can really jump out at us much more prominently if we are leaning toward or away from something, not truly neutral, or 100% balanced. That's why we may hear different messages within the same songs when listening on a different day, for instance. We are essentially hearing with different ears, in a sense! I believe we all know how that can happen, right?

I'll listen to an album in its entirety as I am driving because the theme is something I am contemplating already or wish to revisit. I pay extremely close attention to the lyrics and how they are delivered within the songs. It isn't just what is said, or sung, but how, in what tone of voice, loud, soft, fast, slow, the emphasis, energy, attitude, etc. It may be that it is even delivered in another language, or another singer within the band joins in the delivery to demonstrate a meeting of the minds, marriage, joining or agreement. The alternative to that might be a conflict, a difference in opinion, or vantage point. In some cases, it feels as if there is another voice that talks back as if it was a conversation, or it even adds some drama and becomes argumentative! Hearing and reflecting on these differences can make things really interesting! They seem to want to ensure that we know there is a difference being conveyed, possibly an internal dark side, a lighter and brighter one, or perhaps just an exchange of some kind happening, so it is highlighted in order that we pay attention to it for some reason! It could be that it is coming from a different "voice", or vantage point "in here" within, or "out there" and being delivered to another person. We need to put the pieces of the puzzle together and try to make sense of it! What's the message? Who is it being directed at? I like that, puzzles... I probably hear things a bit differently as a result of this attention to detail, and sense of curiosity. My mind is trying to figure it out, decode it, and it is challenging my receptors and intuition! What I hear, interpret, or discern from particular songs, as I mentioned, is going to be somewhat dependent on what I am going through or processing at that time too. Joelle knows all of this, and relative to the email, these songs were included for a purpose. I just wanted to make sure that was understood. This way, you can also listen with a keen ear, so to speak, assuming you take the time to look at the lyrics, listen to the songs, or both. Just be attentive to what you are doing as you are listening, particularly if you are driving down the road. If you get too engrossed, that could be dangerous, keep your eyes and mind on the road! These songs can be quite captivating!

Relative to content & themes, I believe these musical references compliment the points delivered in the email, where they are provided, as well as the content of this book for that matter, else, I would not have included them where I did! As a reminder, my interpretations are my own. I do not know these people, the bands, or their intent! Their message, or the story they tell with the songs might have been designed with a different intent or target in mind all together. I am just saying what I hear, and I love it just the same! No offense is intended, regardless, but particularly if my interpretation is quite different. If that's true, my apologies! I will say that sometimes it does feel as if there are multiple messages, meanings, or angles that are being conveyed or can be perceived within the same song, and I think that to be true for a lot of things, not just music! We all see with different eyes and hear with different ears, so I just hope your ears enjoy it, and maybe you get a better feeling, or a powerful vibe, maybe even a message or lesson here and there as a result of listening in a way that suits you! I encourage you to listen with an open mind, that's all.

## Impermanence

The email below was from a period of time shortly after we lost our dog Kappi, for your reference. Tough stuff & not fun, so we tend to need whatever help we can get! I think this will help illuminate this issue from a mind perspective by giving you a very real example of some solutions as they were offered up to Joelle, my best friend and partner! As with most of my stories and / or examples, this does need somewhat of an introduction in order to interpret it more comprehensively. I want to make sure you get the understanding and guidance that is conveyed within the message. It is a pretty complicated topic, and not only relative to death...so a simple email about that type of loss is just not going to be enough to cover this subject start to finish, by any means. It is a prime example though. With that said, here we go with a more comprehensive introduction / discussion ahead of inserting the email.

Impermanence probably needs an entire book, quite honestly. This is for those who need some powerful ways to look at it sooner than later and also serves as a reminder of key earlier lessons! It can relate to so many things, because in essence, everything ends, but from a glass half full perspective it also means lots of new beginnings! So, as with much of this mind stuff, a different angle or spin can make all the difference when it comes to a generalized attitude, but that doesn't necessarily bring the underlying mind patterns into the light of day, particularly the ones that tend to want to avoid impermanence! Truth be told, the mind has an exceptional ability to sneak around impermanence vs having to see it, acknowledge it, or meet it head on. If it deals with it at all, it is with as little attention as possible, and then we quickly move on, as with other lessons.

As a result, the tendency is to miss valuable insights that are showing up quite often, probably more routinely than we might realize! I will broach this subject by explaining some of the ways it affects us, as well as discuss some ways to deal with it mentally in productive ways vs letting it hide out in the shadows and affect us adversely...and / or accumulate for a later date to weigh on us more heavily! As we know, missing lessons is not helping anyone! It's just that some "ends" are easier to meet than others, so we need to pay attention to all ends, big and small!

In understanding some of these vantage points, I am hopeful that integrating this knowledge will help you with fully grasping this complex topic, and of course, if needed, in getting through what might be a difficult time adjusting to an ending of some type in your life. I have purposefully positioned this towards the end for several reasons. First, because it can really bog people down, once we really drill down on it and see how often it affects us. It is always easier to learn about a valuable mind pivot before we need it vs after we need it, but any time is a good time for a lesson. It is a tough subject that impacts us in many ways, heavy ways! That said, it tends to get put on the backburner, so to speak. I encourage you to not do that! I promise you that before it gets heavy, the lesson is delivered in many more discreet and manageable ways! If it does get heavy though, don't dismiss it just because it is difficult to deal with, wrap your mind around completely, or just don't want to think about it right now. The second reason is because it can be very complicated, maybe even perplexing, and cumbersome to digest just how it is intertwined with just about everything, and we see it everywhere!

We just don't like things to end. We like things to feel good, consistent, comfortable, easy...and stay that way. It's called our comfort zone! The path of least resistance, right? We identify with it, it can become us, and more often than not, we want to stay within it, a sanctuary of sorts. Because of this, impermanence is highly relevant in a whole host of ways with many different inter-relationships which are not always the main issue! It might be several layers deep, or only be a minor part of some bigger "gearing" that is being exposed. In that case, seeing it would require a very acute awareness and highly developed perception! For that reason, having a base understanding of mind operations and a foundational platform with all the stuff we have explored so far seemed logical to me, ahead of trying to incorporate impermanence more thoroughly! Fact is we have talked about it quite a bit already, but we have not necessarily labeled it along the way each time. It makes it easier to see, acknowledge, process, and move on more productively, and more quickly, having received and absorbed the previous chapters and lesson keys. Otherwise, if not perceived and truly understood, then it cannot or would not be fully seen or integrated as impermanence shows up in its myriad of ways. Unfortunately, that would mean that the small lesson and the big lesson are missed. Assuming there were only two, they were just not seen, and we can't have that. We want to see ALL that we can see, right?

In fact, it is actually imperative that we not only see and understand impermanence but truly assimilate this very important lesson on an ongoing basis. We NEED to make these connections and associations moment by moment! That means that we need to wake up to it, with our heightened awareness and skill, we must see it, first! Fact is, we get this lesson over and over again in a lot of ways, we just don't realize it, don't want to acknowledge, or think about it for the most part (avoidance). Well, at least not NOW! I mean it is perfectly fine for some things to end, but not that _____ (fill in the blank with what you don't want to end), and certainly not ME! I don't want ME to end! As we see this come up over and over again, faster, and faster, the "selves" basically see their end coming, because we are outgrowing them! That's why they hang out in the shadows of the mind, they are hoping to not be seen or exposed to the light of day! If they are seen, they are done! For the "selves" and their wants, all ends they see are premature, well, except for the ones they don't like. When something we don't like ends, it is a blessing, right?! Hah!

So, the tendency on this one seems to be that we lean towards resistance or avoidance vs absorption, which is what is needed. The way that we mentally deal with it can change as we get older too, but it is generally more of a relaxed stance such as, Yeah Yeh, stuff dies, I get it! I am not dealing with that from a mental standpoint until I have to, not now anyway! I will have plenty of time to deal with that later, possibly when I am older, on my death bed, or maybe death is staring me in the face one way or another. The problem with that strategy though is that impermanence is about much more than death. The fact is that everything ends, nothing lasts forever, and when we don't pay attention to the ways that the mind deals with this, what does that mean? We are, or can become, unconscious to it relative to other things as well, if not almost everything as an adopted mind pattern, or "program" ...Uh Oh! That means we are missing even more important lessons along the way, right? As a general rule, it seems, we resist endings for the things we like!

I know you see the issue, right? It is not just death that's important relative to impermanence. It is because it relates to so much other mind "stuff", we most definitely need to pay attention, perk up our eyes, ears, and senses! In fact, the interconnectedness is a huge factor because as we know, if we are unconscious to the first link in a chain reaction we may just miss the whole thing, right? In fact, it is probably missed all together. If it is positioned somewhere else in the mind, or sequence, and the light isn't quite getting there, where it needs to be, well then that is where the missing link will be and then it gets past us, either way, we can't see it. Ahhh, the corners of the mind, yep...the cunning ego can tuck itself in there just fine! Fact is, this is predictable, but unless we are on the lookout for it, we won't see it happening. We need to get that floodlight in every dark corner! So, having said that, this impermanence thing comes into play with a great deal of situational mindset-oriented stuff and the way we look at things, a LOT of things! Comprehending impermanence at more than just a surface level will help us to make meaningful connections within and tie these things together for us in many important ways. As these associations are detected, and we become more aware of how we are treating them from a mind processing standpoint, it will connect the dots so to speak, within our mind, and enhance our skillset. In doing so, it will truly shed light on a lot of things that may not have been "lit up" previously!

This impermanence thing is often a <u>component of lessons</u>! This will be seen more readily as the lesson itself is spotlighted for observation, and essentially monitored within, using the skill we are mastering! In other words, it may not be the whole lesson, only an element of, or part of a lesson. Sometimes that part, from an awareness perspective, may be the KEY link which pieces things together in a more prominent way. This can ultimately shed light on an important interrelationship in which one thing is intimately tied to another. They may even be extremely dependent on one another and connected in ways we could not, would not, or did not see otherwise. Awareness can bring these interconnections into the light of day so that we can see it in the mind as it is processing! So, lets delve into this actively and consciously so that we can make some of these needed connections!

Let's do an exercise, to get started. Try, with a heightened curiosity, to put your investigator hat on. While doing this, look within the mind gearing at where impermanence may be positioned and possibly lost in a sequence, or "program" within. This is a process we take ourselves through in order to magnify certain mind perspectives as we take off on a journey and progress along a chosen path. It is an effort to understand how one thing relates to another within an overall framework of a mindset, and relative to our more personal stuff. The point in this exercise is to not only observe how impermanence relates to and is involved with how we "process", but how OFTEN it is meaningful, how, and how much it matters, like as in weight, and when/where it comes into play relative to our values! The exercise is to ask oneself a series of questions in an effort to uncover where these ends become more or less relevant to us. In fact, it is quite a simple process, and it can be very revealing.

EXERCISE: We ask ourselves in a progressive manner: "*If this happens, then what happens after that?*" (We answer) "*If that happens, then what?*" (Answer again) "*And then what happens?*" Don't stop at 2 or 3, take it out about ten or 15 levels or until you get to an official "end". There may be interim ends in the middle, and you may wish to pause and observe the "edges" where these turns happen, but then continue the exercise until there is no reasonable place to go from that point. The mind will see the end of that progression well before we want to acknowledge it. In fact, it will SKIP AHEAD....not only within this exercise, but as we are living our lives! It happens so fast experientially that often times we don't see the ends / edges in between, because of the speed. The mind can sometimes jump forwards mentally and be many steps ahead of us, in a flash! Just watch as it does this and see it. What happens when we skip something? If we don't see it, we can't recognize it as a connection, it is simply bypassed. This is how we miss lessons! In addition, since the mind skips ahead and sees something, it might just skip back, and turn in real life because it doesn't want that ending! This can all happen in a fraction of a second, and we don't see it because we are unaware! We need to see this kind of mind play as it is happening, that is why we need to have energy, focus and awareness. PRESENCE is just the ticket needed to get into the show...and we show our "selves" in the moment! We are basically shedding light on all those spots that the mind is skipping back n forth over, while we are unconscious, or daydreaming!

By doing this exercise we can see some of these connections more clearly, sometimes well in advance, and sort of play them out a little more slowly. When we play them out on the mind screen as life happens, and we stop momentarily and use that replay feature in order to get the lessons, it becomes easier to see them in real time the next time, like NOW! Our speed and skill evolve. It is as if all of a sudden, they are truly highlighted for us in a way we have never seen before, and we see it faster because it is more prominent, and we are dialed into it! We are teaching ourselves to do this by repeating the exercise consciously and seeing how the mind does these things. While we know we can't be asleep at the wheel, that doesn't mean it doesn't happen!

So, we can complete this exercise using different starting points. We can edit the internal settings, we can edit the different turns we took, etc. We can see where the edges were, the turns happened, or something ended but we skipped past it, didn't see it...or didn't WANT to see it! We can adapt the situational influences, people, places, things, etc. Something was said, but because I had an "END GAME" in mind, I didn't hear it. I had already skipped to the end! I encourage you to do this situationally and see the way that it can play havoc on the mind! The goal is not the havoc, obviously, the point is to show us some very important relationships within, as well as show the incredible amount of contrasting effects they have as the mind processes and moves through things experientially. Depending on which elements become involved, and / or various decisions, our values, the impacts they may have on one another could change the outcomes dramatically! In fact, statistically speaking, or in probability land, trying to play these odds out may just bog us down too much, and so that's another one of the reasons why we choose not to think about it at all. It's just too much, so we try to shut it off by various means. The thought becomes that I just need to deal with what's on my plate right now, so we put on these virtual blinders eliminating the peripherals! We have an attitude that says, "I don't have the time or mental capacity for all of that, can't do it", so we shelf it / avoid it. Lesson not learned, it's coming back...so it drives us batty as we try to go around it over and over again, or we go into overwhelm by allowing it to occupy the mind and take us over. Leave me alone, impermanence, I have other things to deal with right now! We all have different "coping" mechanisms, some healthier than others. UGGGGGH!

OK, so, we know we cannot ignore impermanence...we must see, recognize, and KNOW IT, intimately so that we can move through it in a productive way! Kind of like a stop sign, we need to observe where we are, if there is any oncoming traffic, and then when the coast is clear, proceed, awake and aware from a mind perspective! No matter where we turn though, it comes up, all kinds of stuff...so there's a lot of stop signs. Dang! Impermanence can affect the short, short term, to long range stuff, and everything in between. It relates to everything, and so we MUST learn to not only see how it affects these things, and us situationally, but digest it, understand it, and integrate it so that we develop our skill in a way that it is highlighted for us to see on an ongoing basis throughout our experiences. It's a lot of work, yes, but worthy! We (As the "selves") weigh some things much more heavily than others, and we NEED to see where this is impacting us. This helps us to see it in our "selves"!

The interesting thing about this is that if you really drill down on it, FAITH eliminates the need for us to be overly "concerned with" and get bogged down by impermanence.... but it must be seen in how it affects us first. Choice CAN be affected, but with awareness it doesn't have to be...it simply shows us where we are putting weight, possibly more heavily than we had noticed prior, or is warranted. It highlights these edges. The result is that we can enter situations with a more balanced approach rather than being overly aggressive, or resisting these things, as an example. We see things more clearly and can respond to life more appropriately as a result. Keep in mind that this can happen in reverse as well. As we open our eyes, we can see with remarkable clarity two differing angles, very prominently:

1. **There are things that we really don't want to end**, and as a result, we have developed mind strategies that steer us around having to deal with this mentally. Some strategies can be a little easier to see than others. Point is that we resist, and or avoid ends where what is ending is something we value! The alternative is to be so focused in on it that it overwhelms us, to the point where we aren't even enjoying the life we are in! We are caught in a sense of dread towards the future, and that projected ending. Double edged sword, right?

2. **There are things that we REALLY <u>DO</u> want to END**! With awareness, we can see how we relate to these things with a new eyesight that highlights our relationship to it. In some cases, we can see that we are giving it the power! In other words, because we want it to end so much, we are focused on it, drilled down on it, and we may even be internally complaining about it! That may even extend to external vocalizing of how much we hate it, want it to go away, or stomp our feet about it, physically or mentally! What does that mean? We are heavily dialed into it, focused on it, attention wise! By the nature of where we are focused, we draw it out. What we focus on expands right? So then, it lasts far longer than we would like. With an intimate understanding of impermanence and magnetism, this can all be understood and "LET GO" which eliminates the negative association, which eliminates the negative magnet! Just like the negative thoughts that seem to bring on more negative thoughts, situationally, the same exact thing happens. We tend to magnetize similar things, situationally. When we complain, we get more to complain about! If we use a true understanding of impermanence to our benefit, we can stop this bad mental habit because we see it happen! In fact, we can stop MANY bad mental habits with this level of awareness.

This all sounds very familiar, right? Yes, you got it, it is relative to where the mind is in TIME! We project forwards and backwards all the time, and impermanence plays a HUGE role in that! If we are in the future or the past, we are not present! This is why impermanence is so important to understand.

So, back to impermanence, relative to the email. I wrote this email to my amazing wife, that I love and appreciate so very much, because I can't stand to see her in pain! You might understand this relative to the people that are close to you and wanting to support or comfort them when they need it. On top of just wanting to help, we never want to see our loved ones in pain and losing a pet or a loved one can be excruciating. From a mind perspective it is unbearable in a lot of ways. The strain is not dissimilar to a muscle being hurt, or a bone broken. We can suffer from a broken heart just the same. Recovery methodologies are most definitely advantageous, if not a requirement. In fact, it has very real physical attributes as well, in that it can leave us quite literally with a heart that is injured, shattered, fragmented, or in one way or another "broken", seemingly in pieces sometimes. This can mean that we feel various degrees of hollow. It can quite literally take our breath away, maybe because of its proximity to the lungs, and / or being that it is somewhat broken, it is truly not functioning in the way it should! In an extreme case, where the love lost has had an extremely heightened value, or major significance in one's life, the vacuum effect created physically can leave a feeling of vast emptiness where the heart lies in the chest. This area truly aches with the vacancy left behind. It's actually strange because although the feeling is of an unbearable emptiness, the chest almost feels swollen, the whole thing! As a result of the love lost, the desolation we feel really does come out in physical ways, and we can feel this as true heartache, heart throb, or in other bad ways that don't feel good! The mental & physical attributes are challenging to say the least. Therefore, we need readily available mind tools to get us through it as the waves of grief can hit hard and quick!

Hugs & love help, even virtual ones from long distances, but let's face it, we are alone in our own worlds throughout much of our busy lives, and they don't stop for anyone! At times, in fact, many times, even while working we have travel time from here to there, or breaking points, where we are somewhat isolated with our own thoughts. Heaven forbid, please! Being un-accompanied and alone with our minds in such a state, without the strength and power of a higher SELF fully equipped and connected with mind tools that work to alleviate the pain can leave us stranded and powerless against a whole host of virtual demons! They can lash out and sting us, reach out and grab us, or simply lure us into their den of misery, if we let them do it! Once inside, the way out is masked or obscured, at best, and so we feel somewhat trapped in a bad place where one thought is replaced by another that is of like kind, or worse, and they aren't good to begin with. They almost seem to collaborate and seemingly, in a flash, the discomfort level advances even further downwards to torment and agony, in some cases. The chain RE-action advances in an insanely fast manner too, like supersonic...like a bat out of hell, right? Simply driving down the road again, and BOOM, a vision or memory pops into the mindscape and along with it comes a hurricane of tears (or fears)! Dangerous, not only physically if we are driving down an actual road, but mentally too. Not good! We need the SKILL with which we can find the calm within the storm, and we need it NOW!!!!

Our beloved Kappi was a gorgeous Fox Red Lab, and as always with our pets, it was very difficult to let go! When you open your heart and LOVE, giving it all without reservation, it most definitely invites the inevitable. It can be painful to see and feel it end in the physical, which creates suffering, if we let it. It takes time to truly process grief and look at it from a healthy perspective. If you like, I'll send you his website link or post it on my blog, social media, or website. He was a handsome boy, and please do visit me online![154]

Noteworthy is that Joelle gets these insights from me all the time, so she has a base understanding of this "stuff" already. Having said that, the email that follows is a much more condensed Doug notes version that serves as a reminder of some of these mind strategies. It is really just a revisitation of ideas we have discussed and "KNOW" already, hence the intro I am providing here seems warranted! Hopefully, by now you know this stuff pretty well too, so it is easier to soak this up. Sometimes when life smacks us in the face, we need a reminder of the good, and positive things in this human experience, as well as the mind angles that allow us to feel good again...preferably sooner than later!

It can be tough to "LET GO" of anything we place value on, no less cherish, and / or LOVE, no doubt about that! I sincerely hope that you, or someone you love may benefit from this vantage point, it helps to "process". Share the LOVE!!!! Keep in mind that while the email is intended to help another person "out there" so to speak, these mind angles are intended to be, and should be directed at the "selves", within. They need to be brought into the light of awareness, and truly seen, as they try to adjust to life after a meaningful "loss", whether that be a loved one leaving this earth, or a cherished situational thing ends, or whatever else. Clearly, impermanence can show up in our lives in many ways, and hit us very hard, quickly, without notice. Sometimes there is even expectational pain, because in some cases we can see it coming as an end of something approaches. In fact, because sometimes our eyes are not seeing 20 / 20 we can feel it ahead of seeing it. We may know it's coming one way or another, loss is troublesome in that way. It can weigh on us even before it happens if that's the case. We sort of project it forward in time in our minds, or our intuition feels it coming, and then we miss it even before it is gone. We may not know why we feel a certain way because we simply don't want to acknowledge it. Sometimes and unfortunately, this melancholy feeling can prevent it from being enjoyed while it is still here! We kind of know, but we don't want to look at it, even though it is staring us in the face and announcing itself, in more ways than one!

These are all things to be aware of and SEE "In here", as we look within and grow through various life situations, and lessons within which the primary teacher is impermanence. It could also be a key linkage in an impermanence progression as we have discussed, as a component.  This could range from the end of an employment situation, a life situation, relationship, home, a vacation, breakfast, dinner, a vehicle you don't want to part with, a simple as a bowl of ice cream or the last cookie! Wink. Not to belittle the MAJOR ways that impermanence affects us, I mention this here because we do need to realize that it relates to all things big and small and shows up in our lives constantly. Some are not noticed as much, or even acknowledged at all, because they just aren't as impactful to our lives. We barely notice, and what happens when we don't notice a lesson?  It comes back and we see it again, but the next time it shows up it makes bigger waves, right? We need to get the lesson and understand it well! These are all opportunities.

Impermanence is not only relative to things and situations, but all of us, our families, friends, and unfortunately our beloved pets as well! This is written with love and that certain level of understanding gained from having used the strategies and KNOWING that they work. An internal knowing is often difficult to convey in person, no less put into words, but imagine a vantage point that doesn't carry the pain of loss forward!  That would be valuable, right? Quite simply, and with a more detached perspective, grief is baggage, it is better to process it rather than to carry it forwards by adding it to the **"pain body"**[155] or blowing up the beach ball! It absolutely, 100%, still needs to be processed, which means that it must be seen and understood, within, as it is happening! Not easy at all in some cases, but no different than a lot of what we have covered in this book already. It is difficult to look at it from that vantage point though when it is fresh, close to us, and the waves of emotion continue to sweep over us in relentless succession. That fierce barrage can be quite overwhelming. The waves can carry a heavy burden and truly weigh on us in many ways! The tendency is to not want to feel it, because it hurts too much, so we do whatever we can to bury it, avoid it, or whatever methodology works best to NOT deal with it, or NOT think about it at all for that matter. Ultimately though, that doesn't work. It may postpone it, but it still must be processed.

Grief is a really tough one to deal with, and while lessons in general are typically not fun, especially in the beginning, impermanence is probably one of the most difficult of them all to get a handle on in order to unburden our "selves"! That is particularly true if you have experienced a lot of loss in this lifetime, or have experienced some major traumatic variations of loss, and not had the where with all, or the time / ability, for whatever reason, to process it all. It could also be that you just didn't know how to until now, so effectively, this new understanding will help begin that process.

Remember please that if it is not processed fully, it has a cumulative effect, and each new occurrence is MORE difficult, not less, as we blow up the beach ball, so to speak. That's not to say we can't work through it, we MUST, just like all the other lessons before it, as they resurface, in the moment! Impermanence is a life lesson to be processed and understood. Nothing lasts forever, and the alternative to focusing on the end of something, whatever that might be, is to enjoy life NOW while it is still here! This will not only enhance the here and now, but it will also aid in the prevention category, for other potential dark clouds such as regret, remorse, or even guilt because they may never have an opportunity to really grab and hold us, as a result. Impermanence is continually showing its face, it is undeniable. With this level of constancy, and a knowing that it will revisit us perpetually, we ought to know it, see it, and expect it. Let's make sure that we do it without inviting fear to our doorstep in the process. Understanding does that for us, and unfortunately, I must say, that does take some effort and a healthy attitude. Have faith! There is a new sign I have been seeing, it is being displayed here and there on yards around me. FAITH over FEAR, what a great concept! You may want to revisit that question about what faith is, and ponder it as I have, deeply! What is faith? Can you answer that, with understanding so thorough you could explain it to someone else? I know, we have already been through this...it is important though!

Relative to impermanence, once understood, faith is just the right tool though, and it can be relied on to deliver, it always does!! Understanding how impermanence affects us intimately and comprehensively, we evolve with resolve, and that's implemented with a heavy dose of faith! Faith overcomes, overrides, and seemingly absorbs! Sometimes it takes a little time to initiate, and escalate, to the point where we can feel like progress is being made, but it does materialize as we trust it to carry us through! Perspective, and awareness combined with our ability to implement our skill with determination make loss a little easier to process, in order to move on, when we look at it from a broader, higher-level frame of mind. Faith, however, may need to be built incrementally in some cases. It may take some time to spawn it, build it, and nurse it into being, which gains traction as we create that virtual distance and grasp for the energy we need. We need to muster something positive "WITHIN" to generate the spark which ignites that faith fire and actualizes it. Initially the pain can just be overwhelming, and so we are essentially cut off from the moment where this can happen. In that state of mind, we are fixedly drawn in and focused so closely on the pain that processing anything else just doesn't seem to happen. Faith can't get us there because the circuits are overloaded. More than likely, they are tripped because the negative energy is coming in avalanches, which completely overwhelms the system. The tears are literally drowning out our internal fire! The mind gets bogged down and can't see past it. It can seem as if we are almost instantly, from out of nowhere, struck by a crushing wave of emotion, tears are gushing, and we are experiencing a ridiculously heavy dose of grief. It can really knock us down and be a huge weight. So heavy, that the feeling truly drags us underwater with the wave when the "selves" get stuck on the side of PAIN vs switching over to appreciation, or a more positive mind angle, as an example.

If the wave actually knocks you down, guess what? That enormous beach ball just resurfaced. Recognize it!? Come back to NOW and realize where you just were, future, or past? RE-focus and try to stay present. The waves do have a way of distancing themselves over time, but the waves can still come at us for quite a while, particularly if we do not know how to process them or we choose to remain unconscious. That could mean we are attempting to use distraction techniques, avoidance, self-medicating, or other methodologies. Unfortunately, these can and will be "triggered" just like anything else when they are buried within the subconscious layers of the mind. They will resurface, and when they do, we must be ready, present, and hopefully just a little bit more balanced the next time it comes up!

This is a way to be just a little bit more awake and aware as this is happening which will help manage the energy. The process can be looked at as an effort to deflate the "obstacle", which kind of depersonalizes it in a way, if allowed. It shows the mind toggles that are available once we can bring on a state of awareness just stable enough to begin choosing a better thought, a better angle, and some level of understanding by standing above it, or "over it" and not trapped in it. We literally do need to "GET OVER IT"! That is a very real recommendation in that when we look at it from this more elevated vantage point, "over it" is a better place from which we can see, observe it, and "process"! That's the beginning of the recovery process, however, it does take time sometimes. If we back up enough to see this as a stage in the process of mastering the "SELF", and overcoming that particular obstacle, it does lighten the blow ever so slightly, in my opinion. Recognizing the fact that we must fight the good fight so to speak, kind of helps us fight it, and energizes the determination and resolve to make the effort. That little boost alone is a step in the right direction, as it is taking and shifting, or redirecting energy! While it feels as if we are walking up hill for a little while, and some of these waves keep knocking us back a bit, we pretty much expect it, know how to deal with it, and we are more energized to deal with it. Sooner or later the internal spark does light the flame.

Waves of tears and emotion are completely understandable though, and sometimes that is just what is required to process and deflate this "obstacle" as long as it is seen with awareness. They have to come; it is just a matter of how long it takes for us to process and get through it vs around it! You'll have to decide that for your "SELF", as to how long is appropriate or needed for you? You will know! Everyone is different, and each loss is different because we relate to it in unique ways! As we grow older and of course, depending on where we are in our respective lives, the accumulation of "loss" and impermanence lessons that have not been processed can be small or large! The difficulty gauge can change relative to our level of consciousness, and the degree with which we have mastered the ability to be the overseer and process "life" at this time from this more elevated vantage point! Bottom line, don't let it sink the ship. After the storm is when the beautiful rainbow appears, right? Keep your head above the virtual water and BREATHE until you can see it, in the eye of the storm! It may not be in the same place as the last time, stay alert.

Impermanence shows us two sides, doesn't it? If we look at the right side, it gives us an ounce of faith, that there are better days ahead, and that is super great news, just when we needed it! If we are in a bad place, we actually can look at the flip side of this currently ugly coin called impermanence which changes our mind! The mind can be shown that while the good doesn't always last, neither does the bad. The "rub" is that GOOD THINGS ARE COMING! How's that for some glass half full spin to look at the bright side? When I say rub, it is really just a thought, but the implied element of it is that in some cases it must be rubbed in, or massaged in, because when we are in these less than stellar states, the mind is not as receptive as it normally would be. It takes a little convincing sometimes. The tears need to stop dropping on the igniter within so that it can spark a new flame, a new thought.... new direction, and preferably not upstream! As we massage in these new ideas, the tears are dried out, and the spark can land on this new kindling (emerging thought) and fire us up again! We must get our internal fire going again, this is the means to do it.

YES, things end. They also begin, so there's the choice, with awareness and focus! Which way would you prefer to look at it? There is a choice there, NOW we can see it! I can say to myself that whenever something ends, it is the beginning of the rest of my life! What am I going to do with it? That question IMMEDIATELY forces the mind to answer a better question and the opportunity is presented for a better thought to occupy that space that was just created by asking the question. It opens the door so to speak, to see a new answer. See a new path! I think that the Godly perspective is that when GOD closes one door, He opens another! That to me is the faith perspective, an internal KNOWING this to be true! But that means we have to look for it. For me, that question helps me look for the door! The answer will typically give me a "new lease on life" by putting a more positive spin on things and it energizes me, gets that fire going. There is always a reason, I tell myself, and then I try with a certain conviction to find the open door. So, faith allows us to find the door, gets us to it, we just need to be inspired and skilled enough to open the door and walk through it with awareness to see all the new choices that are available. In the case of losing Kappi, and Real Estate slowing down, it has meant an opportunity for me to finish this book! I have wanted to do that for years. Faith delivers....and that doesn't mean I love Kappi any less, it just means that I can move on with my life while loving him and appreciating him just as much as I always did, with less tears! In fact, even better, with massive appreciation for having been so lucky to have had such an amazing dog to spend so much time with, fun times experiencing him and his love! These are good, empowering thoughts.

Even if momentarily, we choose to see an end, that doesn't mean we have to choose suffering relative to that ending, whether that be a person, pet, thing, or whatever "it" is. There may even be a feeling like there is a certain duty, or requirement to feel the pain and be miserable, to cry for some time in order to honor it. I have to ask this. How long would be good enough? Is that relative to a gauge of some kind? When is it ok to feel good again? Is someone or something determining this for us, or watching as if we will be punished for smiling too soon? This is ridiculous and must be seen and questioned! No one we love, nor would any pet we have ever had and loved, that loved us, EVER want to see us in pain! That would NEVER happen, so don't let the mind be deceived with these shenanigans!

The mind is funny like that though, isn't it? It will try to show, tell, and even sell us some wildly inappropriate stories. Like for instance, the thoughts may come that look or feel something like this: *"I need to show "it", him, or her, and everyone around me how sad I am that it is gone, and that I miss it...and so I must keep crying and shedding tears permanently graveside"*. While that thought may not be spoken internally exactly like that or in those words, the actions or feelings may be telling that story. Others might be *"I am so lonely, why did you leave me?"* or *"I can't stand it without you"*. There are many negative ways to look at impermanence, and an unconscious and /or tired mind will be susceptible to all manner of self-torture! The selves will argue the validity of the misery, undoubtedly, the question becomes whether or not we want to listen, and subscribe to the miserable thoughts. Cancel the subscription! You do that with choice.

We must wake up and see that these are not productive thoughts, assuming of course, that we would prefer to smile. They must be seen from a more elevated perspective though, and then acknowledged, and ultimately understood, processed, and integrated. While it may seem cold, stone hearted, unsympathetic, heartless, or any number of more descriptive adjectives, the reality of it is that these are just poor, distressing thoughts that take us to the past with a negative perspective! They leave us in a state that is less, sometimes much less than desirable! From a more detached perspective, such as the overseer, this is quite simply a really grim and bothersome way to look at things.

Higher SELF, with its extraordinary speed, perception, and skill, sees that we can choose a different thought all together! There is always a brighter more positive way to look at things, which must be seen in order to be chosen. We must realize that we are WORTHY and we can choose to SMILE, in spite of that "feeling" or thought / story that tells us to do otherwise. If that's not possible at this time, for whatever reason, possibly an extremely convincing excuse given by the mind, then maybe we can choose it in anticipation of a better thought, with faith. I know that sounds strange, but it may be beneficial to look at impermanence backwards in this case. Everything is impermanent, that includes pain and even bitterness. That is possible, of course, assuming that there is a sincere want for a smile, or a desire to feel a better feeling than that which we are entangled with currently. This may not be true from this "sense of self", and also why we need a different vantage point. That makes perfect sense, right? Mind tricks. Ha-ha, sometimes when dealing with the mind you have to beat it at its own games!

The better thought, better angle, is generated from a KNOWING, and a TRUSTING that with FAITH and LOVE, we can smile, laugh, appreciate, and enjoy even in hindsight by seeing this or some other experience that ended in the mind's eye with a different lens! Soon enough, once known and understood, that positive vantage point can be applied to this experience, or relative to this loss, as well as any others that have not been fully processed. In due time, we will be able to look back at this and laugh or think of it in a better light, one way or another. That may include an understanding that it is better to have loved and lost than to have never loved at all! That is the truth, and believe it or not, it can actually be the appreciation of that love that we just lost that will bring us out of this temporary darkness. In this case it would be a flip of a virtual switch, from PAIN to a genuine LOVE in hindsight, sorrow to APPRECIATION for having loved, and been loved, as examples. It is as if that love is somewhat captured or reclaimed in a way. There are many ways to spin it positively. It could be true happiness and appreciation for the JOY, for the fact that we got to have the experiences that we did, and while we do realize they just ended, we can look back with a smile and gratitude vs making and holding on to the other negative associations! Looking back with a different LENS can truly view this as the GIFT it was. It will have a much different effect on the mind, our outlook, our demeanor, and the way we see it and the world going forward!

You do realize that this has major consequences, right?! It could be the difference between seeking it out or avoiding it for the rest of our lives, and even thereafter if you subscribe to that line of thinking! If there was any JOY in it, that's a real eye opener. We see that a super positive experience, such as this, can be associated with pain, in the mind, or subconscious, and therefore avoided. NOOOOOO! Why would we deliberately choose to do this to ourselves? We don't, typically, but the "selves" do when they take us over! Wake up to it, see it, and from higher "SELF", don't do it, don't let it happen! Go right ahead and pursue it, knowing full well that yes, indeed, it may end one day but by golly I am sure as heck going to enjoy it today, NOW! That is the line of thinking that allowed us to get another dog in the first place. Had we not really understood this, and very deliberately chosen it, imagine all the amazing experiences we would have missed with this amazing dog, Kappi. Quite honestly, even if we did get another dog without an understanding at this deeper level, that might have come along with a sense of dread, or worse, as the selves just implant the thoughts or vantage point that sooner or later that dog will die, and the pain is anticipated. We may even avoid getting involved too deeply, or loving, as we know that will invite the inevitable pain when it ends. Rather than that, we enjoyed Kappi and spent MORE time with him, treated him like royalty, gave him every ounce of love we had, took him everywhere with us, and loved every minute of it! We took every opportunity to show him how much he was loved, in many ways, and of course, that allowed us to experience him more completely as well. The love and companionship of a dog is unparalleled! I am forever grateful to my wife for having introduced me to this aspect of life. It is something that I did not know or understand until I met her, and of course, it was amplified as we got each of our dogs! To be loved, you must LOVE! The more you LOVE, the more it reflects back to you...WOW! Now imagine if everyone employed this knowing and took every opportunity to BE IT in the world vs the alternatives! Would the world look different? I think so, but then I am the eternal optimist! Be what you wish to see, right?

So, impermanence is a lesson, and we need to look at it that way. This non-at-tachment, detached, or more elevated perspective allows us to see it in a different light, for sure. Whether we view it as a long-awaited lesson that was finally just learned, and quite painful because we waited so long to learn it, or we are having to deal with losing someone that was very close to us, it is still just a lesson! From that stance, digestion doesn't need to be indigestion! We can learn to CHOOSE to look at the bright side of that coin, that is the choice. Choosing to see the wonderful experiences we have had, the amazing people, things, pets and just smile joyfully and with appreciation of them is a choice. The same past can be viewed with joy, love, and gratitude vs pain because of a loss.

One way or another, as we know, energy is required to make a better choice. We need to generate that energy or use the available energy we have in more appropriate ways as these waves come in. That requires presence! Be attentive to what energy is being generated by this experience, how is it rolling in, and arriving in the mind? Is it just sadness, and distress, or is there more to it? Is this triggering something else within? Are you seeing any anger? Resentment? Sorrow? Regret? How is it hitting? What are the deeper feelings, thoughts, emotions? Not in general, but specifically, details matter. How are you choosing to process them in the moment? Just pay attention. Are you stuck in the past, or projecting towards the future? Where is the mind? Where is that relative to the pain? Whatever energy is available, it is more than likely arriving in waves, be ready to use it with your skills in the moment as it arrives and channel it. GRAB IT in the moment and redirect it in order to distribute it in whatever way it is possible to generate a more positive outlook. Just one thought, and then another. I know, mind SPIN...yep, you got it, and it works, if you let it. Part of letting it work is choosing a new thought, which means letting the previous one go, with awareness! That means, more specially to let the pain go, by choice! Use your internal fortitude and gather your strength, even if only for a moment! It takes fractions of a second to strategically elevate and implement an A/B testing scenario in the mind. As we employ this virtual assessment game mindfully, we put two different thought tracks in front of us and in essence, play them through to their likely conclusions. As we do, we see more options. The idea is that we can kind of play with the ideas. In order to make a new choice, ideally a more productive one, first we must see that at least one more viable choice is available. Once we see that there is a reasonable chance that this one, the one we have been choosing, is not the best choice available, then we can elect to make a new choice. Just by the nature of making oneself available in the moment like that though, by seeing that at least one other thought is available as a choice, quite miraculously many others are presented as options. We have to be present to see them though!

Perhaps you can muster a situational thing that inspired a shred of JOY within you, use that tiny bit of energy available and flip the switch to a more positive mindset. Energy can SPIN it quickly and efficiently, and you must have FAITH that it will. Presence creates choice. Walk through that virtual door, and see that within the moment of NOW, there is a CHOICE, if not MANY available choices. One, and only 1 of these choices is the choice is to stay with the pain. Yes, you can choose suffering. With awareness though, you will see the many other choices available which offer you the opportunity to take that virtual step forward, step UP and OUT of the pain, "get <u>over</u> it" and INTO something different, new.

Possible choices are typically stepped progressively, in a way. In other words, we may not go directly from misery to JOY. Self-torture, regret or remorse is a far cry from appreciation, love and other life affirming values. So, while these are possible choices, they are not likely seen as viable options at the starting gate so to speak. The point in this observation state is that joy, appreciation, and LOVE are among an infinite array of other choices that are NOT PAIN or suffering! By taking that step with awareness and faith into the moment, presence offers up many better alternatives. Having choice offers us a multitude of virtual mind toggles that allow us to move forward with a more positive attitude. Which we choose is up to us! As we progress it becomes easier to make larger advances faster because we know it more experientially. With practice, and a somewhat deflated beach ball, we may even be able to make that jump from tears to giggles in a heartbeat. Once we see the power in choice, and that it is available for us in that moment we decide to arrive with presence, whole heartedly, progress, or digestion happens almost before you can say GO! Remember also, that when an even higher power comes into play, it has infinite resources! Just imagine what can happen when we arrive to NOW, with trust and faith, WHOLE HEARTEDLY, right?! What percent is that? 100! In the beginning though, a stepping process is more than likely what will come more naturally as acceptance is only marginally "approved" at this point! The "selves" will be observable throughout the process as they release their grip on pain and other forms of darkness, and allow something else in, preferably a little lighter and brighter. It is ultimately a grand stairway, or an escalator of sorts...some just move a whole lot faster than others with much larger strides, if you will. You might even call it the stairway to heaven, just sayin, but you don't have to die to get there! Just take one more step in the right direction.

Look up the stages of grief, there are many powerful images online that lay out the basic stages using different words, colors, and themes. They even show the various progressions as examples, graphically in some cases, so the whole bottoming out process can be seen, and mind strategies generated accordingly. You may very well see the whole landscape better as a result of seeing how they stack up and relate to the other stages. In addition to identifying the stages alone, it can be beneficial to see by looking at a diagram, very clearly that in some respects we might be at or near one level, and in other respects, we are most definitely somewhere else in the processing of something. Some of these early states might include confusion, denial, fear, anger, irritability, and anxiousness and by looking at some of these diagrams, we can see what we are doing to ourselves. That may mean the difference between stepping further down the ladder and regressing vs calling a bottom and beginning the process of recovery! Then as we step up the ladder, or go up the escalator so to speak, we may be able to "choose" to tell ourselves a slightly different story. Gradually we "move on" and up from distress and guilt to bargaining with our "selves" for a reason to feel better! As we start to envision this differently, see it in a new light so to speak, new options become available, seen, and chosen. Each better feeling has a little bit better energy to it, which opens a new door to see new options, and another step forward is taken, chosen. We might move from mildly depressing thoughts and loneliness to somewhat more acceptable feelings, and then on to full acceptance, and a re engagement with life with a much more positive spin and grin on the whole thing!

With presence, pain is seen as a choice, whether looking forwards or backwards. It is also seen that there are different choices available that offer better paths forward, but they are not being chosen, yet. The choices are available, and sooner or later the realization will come that I am choosing pain, that I don't want to do that anymore, and so a new choice is made! Once seen though, this mind power tool can be tapped to overcome lots of mind hurdles. BY CHOOSING, we enable and empower the skill TO CHOOSE like this the next time! In fact, that will usually mean that the next time we see it, we see even more and better options with awareness! The choice ability becomes stronger and easier as a result, and so we become that better "SELF" quite naturally which opens us up to even better options! Choosing a smile can do wonders if we realize that a very powerful choice was just made, and we can do it again by taking that next step! Choosing new and better thoughts is emancipating. Just the action of doing this is freeing us from a former "self" that was previously stuck. That lower version of "self" just "ENDED"! This is a moment to treasure, and USE to inspire future growth! We just GREW UP! We got a lesson. Whatever had us stuck has just been released, by choice, and freedom from that level of thought is celebratory, even if only for an internal acknowledgement and a new satisfaction of what was just accomplished. It is a sense that now I know and have demonstrated a way out! Self-assurance, trust, and faith is built this way! We think: "If I can do it for that" Really, think about this, hard, one small step leads to the next. My mental muscles just got much stronger.

### "If I can do it for that, then I can do it for other things as well, big and small, the implications are astounding!"

With an understanding this powerful, and a knowledge that this has now been processed, the new LENS with which we look backwards, from time to time, offers a better vantage point. Not only do we not get stuck in that past with the pain, but alternatively, we can look back with massive appreciation, and that gratitude is the result of an initial pivot where we literally processed the data and SPUN our minds in order to look and see in a new direction! That SPIN, or turn, in an instant, generated CHOICE, that choice created a chain reaction which is what it ultimately took for us to make a genuine smile come to fruition, NOW! How fast can you make that happen? Seriously, how fast can you make a choice?

That whole transition could mean fractions of a second, but for some it can take much longer, possibly many years or lifetimes if we are subscribed to theories that require self-sacrificing & other forms of punishment! This comes in many elaborate styles, both physical and mental. BEWARE, or should I remind you BE AWARE! I will not poo-poo any strategy that works for you, but I will offer you a very powerful word that works in this regard. I also want to remind you of previous discussions surrounding this word, as you may want to review them. It has big meaning, and we can use it. The more we do, the more we realize how FREEING it is. It's called forgiveness. This word has the power and might to take someone full circle, in a flash. It has such effectiveness, that we can come fully around and make a U-turn in an instant. In doing so we are taken from miserably negative, to wildly positive. The ENERGY we needed to flip the virtual switch was tapped and used in the NOW moment. Find the gate to NOW, it's a mighty place to operate from! In this case, it is as if the negativity is surgically removed, that's a pretty powerful operation! You can be that surgeon, with a laser focus like this! Forgiveness, Faith, Focus...FFFFFFFFF...sounds like a plane taking off!

The MIND's eye sees with different eyes, and those eyes are now very grateful for the experiences, and the lessons that it just received. Consequently, taking that next step is JOYFUL, and the smile naturally returns to the face and stays there. Burdens, sorrows, dark thoughts, and their weight being removed is often a feeling of major relief. Leaving that lower "self" and its baggage behind is creating a new freedom...freedom from IT, that level of self! It is as if we just pulled up the anchor that had us pinned to the bottom. We no longer drag that self and its baggage along with us. The good experiences, and the lessons alone can be cherished, as a result, and they are!

The waves still do come from a looking back perspective initially. That's where we must be awake to pivot and turn, faster and faster. The initial thrust of emotion is going to be negative when it arrives, which is often very difficult because we are drawn to the past and whatever it was that was lost is still there. BUT, because we know and are ready, awake and aware, and now we have done it already, it now becomes easier to change that view and look at it from this new more positive lighted perspective. Each time, we do it with a little more speed and agility, a little more enthusiasm, and appreciation! If it was a love lost, that LOVE was cherished and missed with this person, animal, situation, or whatever it was that just ended. The choice can go from a depressed state of MISSING it and sorrow, to a realization that it can be seen with these NEW EYES! The choice is seen SOONER, that it can be treasured with a smile and a sense of JOY rather than associated with PAIN and carried forward in that way. This is what it means to "process" loss, being able to look at it with a perspective that truly understands the choices in vantage point! Sadness can be seen, in the moment, as a choice...and we can choose to stay there, if we want to, or we can make a new choice. There are others available when we are ready to take that step! A smile will emerge when we decide, and we do make a different choice!

Worth mentioning as a reminder too that it is not a dodging, or shunning of a feeling or state, as in "avoidance". It is an understanding of a choice that is being made. The choice is to deliberately, fully awake, and aware, move in a new way consciously, with understanding and a powerful, somewhat permanent smile as a result. The turn, in essence, is after receiving a lesson, not before. This is meaningful and important to understand. Makes a big difference, actually!

So, I hope that serves as a fair summary in an effort to present this mildly edited version of my email to Joelle. The minor edits were for clarity, and the addition of credits, that's all. My apologies for all the typos and highlights...I left those in it. I know that I write with a lot of highlighting in various ways, capitals, bold and all included, apologies if that was not understood until now. I figured you should see it in its "raw" form, to the extent possible, as this is the way I typically write, right or wrong! My wife gets me, but some of it was tweaked a bit to make it easier for you all to understand. Apologies for the long-winded explanation. I thought it would help to understand the email, because it does address several topics which all "stress" the mind! This includes impermanence, regret, work stress, pain, and much more all at the same time. I hope it helps.

I LOVE YOU, You Love You and GOD Loves You!!

Here are a few songs you can use in several ways:

1. YOU STAND BY YOU: Your higher "SELF" perspective. From the "OVERSEER" perspective, you have the ability to forgive all the little Tom Sawyers, little small "selves" in the mind, for all the mistakes they ever made...not that you've made many, if any! This could be from 50 years ago, or a month, or seconds and/or minutes ago...it is also the ability

to release any worry or negative thought! Forgiving Yourself ...releasing thoughts and attachments, whether to the past or future is the equivalent of FREEDOM from "STRESS"!!!!! Freedom is from being tied and anchored in negativity, (worry included) towards the past or future, with awareness! You have the ability to release your "self", let it go and BE FREE...every moment of every day!!! As a reference, there is that thing called the **"PAIN body"**[156] that **Eckard Tolle** speaks about, and being aware, and present, you are allowing yourself a reason to release the attachment. You are removing the reason for the tears / frown on your face to begin with IN THE MOMENT...and that can happen in a flash / an instant on the crest of the wave...NOW!!!! You just need to allow it and **change** the "belief". You do that with awareness. What You believe, deep down at your core, is revealed by your present thoughts NOW and always NOW...so pay attention...when you see it. It WILL BE HIGHLIGHTED and highlighted **_by a feeling_**, acknowledge it SMILE and just KNOW that You are getting a lesson, and that You are LOVED,  ALL IS WELL, ALL IS GOOD...night vs Day, Light vs Dark, smile vs. frown or any other negativity vs positivity is a choice and You just made it...every moment of every day. You have this power, ALWAYS(with awareness/presence) unless you give it away to Ole TOM SAWYER and the little "false" selves! Take the high road...SEE from this new vantage point, it makes all the difference...NOW!

2. I STAND BY YOU. I get it, there are events that happen, life is not all peaches and cream. LOL...and "dark thoughts" can haunt us at times. Impermanence is now revisiting us as a life lesson, while unfortunate, nothing lasts forever! We still have the power and the blessings that came with the amazing experiences we had with Kappi, and Ranger, and Chief, and your Father. It doesn't mean we stop loving them, and it takes a minute, sometimes, to get our power back, to force a smile, fake it till ya make it. It takes remembering that had we not loved, we would have missed out on a lot of wonderful things...GOOD TIMES! Better to have loved and lost than to never have loved at all. We now have these treasured memories to bring us JOY even in a dark moment or dark time in our life. Once again, just know, with all your heart and all your energy, that You ARE LOVED! I'll stand By YOU...and You must stand by You as the HIGHER SELF, and from the HIGHER SELF vantage point from ABOVE MIND: If You need a reminder, listen to this song, it says it well, by **The Pretenders**: **"I'll stand by You"**[157]: https://youtu.be/SuWAGT9ZkYE

3. GOD STANDS BY YOU. Finally, don't hold it all inside...GOD is always on your side, and ALWAYS wants the BEST for You. Understand though that ONLY YOU have the capability to allow ANYTHING into your life. You do that by RELEASING the PAST and RELEASING dark thoughts, dark attitudes, old beliefs that no longer serve you, or as it says in the song above, when the night falls on You (the darkness in spiritual philosophy)! Whether that be regret, remorse, fear, or simply the painful thought of impermanence and losing someone or something dear to us...basically any form of negativity! Bottom line is that Higher "SELF", GOD is ALWAYS able, by the flip of a switch in vantage point and attention to the positive thought vs. the choice to focus on the pain...or darkness. First become alert and aware of where you are in TIME (past/future..in the mind) STEP OUT OF THE MIND, above the mind and watch....rewind to a moment ago if you have to in order to see what just happened, SMILE...**RETURN TO NOW** (vs past / future, where the dark thought was) and know, You just grew out of the pain, by choice, with the help of your higher self, higher vantage point, awareness / presence GOD...co-creating Your life moment by moment by moment...NOW! The choice is always available, but only NOW, and NOW...and NOW! GGITM, God Guides in the moment! YOU NEED TO GET THERE...You cannot be with GOD, and You Cannot get the lesson if You are centered and focused in the past / future. Stress simply means You are not present, you are in the past or the future. STRESS does not exist in NOW! You leave it at the gate, NARROW IS THE GATEWAY TO NOW...it is a razor's edge, right after yesterday, and before tomorrow. That is where GOD LIVES, meet him there! ALL your stress disappears in an instant just KNOWING, YOU ARE LOVED and returning to NOW with presence and awareness! Leave it at the gate.

   a. Don't follow your MIND, follow your HEART. Your heart is GOOD, Follow it!

   b. Your FEELINGS are telling You that there is a lesson, PAY ATTE NTION...and return to NOW, GOD IS THERE...guiding See the **Scorpions: "Follow your heart"**: https://youtu.be/tMui4IVW0 BM[158]

4. This is the process described...Your mind may revisit the past, be watchful in the **"EYE OF THE STORM"**[159]. This is also the **Scorpions**... return to NOW...that is where you make the choice to LOVE, and are

loved, ALWAYS: https://youtu.be/_sTc82-FS78

5. Looking to the Higher SELF to GUIDE...to help You release the past and GROW...NOW! **"THE BEST IS YET TO COME"**[160] yep, You guessed it: **The Scorpions**: https://youtu.be/LFKWMRaI-ME

\*\*\* NOTE: Look up the lyrics, they are really good!

*LOVE YOU LOTS:*

Doug Giesler

# TOP TEN WAYS TO IMPLEMENT THIS KNOWLEDGE

## (And FUN ways to hear these perspectives in songs!)

1. **Watch your thoughts.** As often as you can muster the energy, over and over again, watch your thoughts. This "watcher" vantage point will shed light on an array of "you's" or little "selves", their storylines, attachments, and potentially "dark" thoughts. Pay attention, and with a detached focus, just WATCH!!!!

2. **CHALLENGE YOUR BELIEFS!** Make it a point to SMILE. Again, as often as you can muster the energy, SMILE in the face of whatever tells you to do otherwise. Whatever tells you otherwise is an imposter, a LIE... consider **it** one, and question its motives. Be skeptical of "it" vs "YOU" because it is stealing your life, the one you could live with a smile on your face. It is either a past "you" or a future "you" and they are trying to step into the moment and by doing so they are in fact, stealing your life. Don't let them do that by keeping you locked up in or limited to that storyline, whatever the lesson might be. Step above the mind/storyline and see it. This vantage point is available, and by smiling in the face of everything that tells you that you can't smile, the storyline will be revealed, along with the "false self" (it). You get the lesson, and as a result, you amplify your POWER to CHOOSE TO SMILE! That choice, that power makes all the difference, when you claim it! The sun is always shining, however, the "dark thoughts" in your mind are "CLOUDING" your vision so you can't see it. You can't "SEE THE LIGHT", so REMOVE THE CLOUDS! The clouds are the thoughts

that are blocking your smile, or the sun / light! This thought, emotion, line of thinking, or storyline you have bought into is the cloud hiding the sun...the "self" is doing it! That "self" is preventing your smile. WHY? You must see and KNOW! You remove the clouds by seeing these false 'selves' in the darkness and exposing them to the light of day, your awareness! Understanding, SEEING the LIGHT OF DAY, once the "night" or cloud is removed eliminates the darkness! Point is, YOU don't have to fight the darkness, the darkness is an illusion, and once you realize this, it just simply fades away as your light becomes brighter! With a really bright light, there is no darkness. SMILE, SMILE, SMILE...in the face of any darkness, even the darkest most violent thunder clouds can be squelched in an instant with this process! WAKE UP!!!! See the light and SHINE IT ON your "Darkness"!!

    a. ***** NOTABLE: As always, **RUSH** has a relevant song, the way I hear it. Check out **"Jacobs Ladder"**[161] if you feel so inclined. It is an amazing illustration of this phenomena in my opinion! Also, an interesting tidbit, in some philosophies Jacobs ladder represents the bridge between Heaven and Earth!! Do you think that there is symbolism here? RUSH lyrics are brilliant! This song helped me understand that vantage point as a visual...if you aren't making the connection, the clouds are the dark, limiting thoughts, and / or storylines. Behind the clouds is "The Light"! Check out the lyrics, very powerful!

3. **WITH AWARENESS, pay very close attention to these storylines in the mind and the extent to which you are "bought into" them.** Another way to look at them is to consider these thoughts as you might a "salesman". Get to know them, listen with a keen ear and be watchful of your own mannerisms as you react to the pitch!! Each salesman, or woman is pitching their idea, their product, which is in the form of a thought which is selling you a STORY, are you a buyer? The extent to which you might be a buyer, and how much you would be willing to pay as a buyer is a virtual scale weighing the extent and power of your "AT-TACHMENTS" to control you and your RE-actions relative to that thought or storyline! (This "theme", or pool of thoughts, is intended to keep you anchored in the storyline, that's where they want you to STAY! EGO) This is where your biggest motivations and resistance points will reveal themselves, in the storylines themselves! This is in essence showing you your blind spots and the various "BAGGAGE" you are carrying into the moment as a result of these storylines! Substitute storyline for

beliefs if you prefer.... they go hand in hand! Other examples might be paradigm, patterns, programming, archetypes, your ideals, standards, etc. Remember that a storyline can be a past regret, failure, or whatever else as well as a projection, as a hypothetical future you so just be mindful of all these potential imposters! What you need to see is that they are a figment of your imagination, a complete illusion and if / when they take you over, your mind will be elsewhere, and not NOW, not PRESENT! In addition, there may be a lot of these storylines cluttering up the mindscape and creating a lot of chaos and confusion! To whom, what or which belief shall I listen to this time? First You have to see them, then YOU have CHOICE. Are you a buyer? Pay very close attention to where, when, how, and what you BUY into in all kinds of situations, and then choose wisely!! This may change conditionally, how does that affect the "decider"? WATCH the MIND!

4. **With awareness and a detached focus: <u>LOOK OUT FOR THESE WORDS</u>: "I AM", or "I FEEL". When these cross your mind screen, it's a SET UP...pay very close attention to what follows after you say these words! "<u>I AM</u>" _____ or "<u>I FEEL</u>"** _____! Make sure you are watching for these; they are setting the tone for what comes next! In other words, once you fill in that blank that follows, you become THAT, and that defines the paradigm from which you respond to the moment! That is, one of the little selves or "You's" steps in and becomes you and acts AS YOU based on that set of beliefs (whatever that paradigm means and activates within you!). You must see it as it happens though in the moment. These are the little "selves" I speak of here in this book. Filling in the blank after I AM _____ is where you draw the virtual lines around what you can and can't do or BE! REALIZE, that by filling in the blank, you are defining <u>YOUR LIMITATIONS</u>! Be very particular about what you give your attention, and where your focus is. Your energy and your power are at stake here, and so is your SMILE, Peace of mind, and FREEDOM!! Watch out for these SET UPS! Let it be a cue to you, a ringing of the school bell, to really WAKE UP and be WATCHFUL! The lesson is starting... make sure you are in the classroom! (As the watcher)!

5. **Instead of working exclusively on "knowledge", and knowing, work harder on awareness and PRESENCE...the SKILL!** Book knowledge is great, understanding is power, and then you MUST take the next step, watch how that knowledge is literally affecting your life moment to moment and driving your decisions. You do this

with AWARENESS / PRESENCE. Knowledge can be VERY LIMIT-ING!!!!! Look at this very closely. Awareness is taking a higher vantage point than that of "thought". It is being the watcher OF THOUGHT vs. being the thinker! Exactly how has all of the knowledge you have acquired affected the various paradigms from which you respond to and live your life? What storylines and beliefs has this generated within you? Is it TRUE? Is there a chance that this tidbit of "knowledge" isn't even valid? Beware of false prophets... In other words, be AWARE! WAKE UP, evaluate, assess, shine your light on it, SEE and LISTEN and then discern / decide!!!!! Knowledge is great, and wonderful, useful...so is awareness, use BOTH!

6. **DREAM!** Think BIG...it is this process that will bring you to the next obstacles. By taking the next step in your personal expansion, it will show you the storylines and resistance points. They are generated by the EGO, mind, programming, and OTHERS TOO, that try to put their LIMITs on you. Realize that these limitations are SELF IMPOSED even if they come from someone else, because YOU SUBSCRIBED TO it and bought in to their story! That might just be their belief, and they may be seeing an illusion, right?!? Just see this, as the watcher, and walk right through these limitations! Stop telling yourself the same old lies, and just stop listening to these "false selves", particularly the ones of doom and gloom, and all the other miserable projections the mind comes up with for that matter!  DREAM, and whenever a roadblock comes into the mind, pay attention to the limits it is defining for you! You are defining your limitations when you subscribe to that level of thinking. In addition, if you are not paying attention, and / or you decide to go unconscious, or numb yourself out...your card is on auto pay! It is going through anyway, even if you are not paying attention, your limits are set and the next time you are PAYING MORE, with interest and you will be MORE LIMITED! Pay NOW, with your attention and awareness, control what grabs your "interest" so that it doesn't accrue! You will pay more dearly later! Looking the other way is really not an option to move forward, face it head on, NOW, awake, and aware!

7. **Pay super close attention to WORRY and / or FEAR, particularly when it is heightened.** BTW, MIND GENERATED worry and fear...they are the same thing, just varying degrees!! These are opportunities to confront your demons so to speak. There is a storyline here or something that you have bought into, and an underlying belief that is again <u>LIMITING you</u>! I can _____ or I can't _____,

fill in the blank. This is true to the extent that you BELIEVE it. Once again, COURAGE is not the absence of fear it is the understanding that in the name of growth, I MUST walk right through it. The virtual promised land is on the other side of FEAR/EMOTION. This is not to say you can or should go out and do life threatening things, in the name of conquering fear. Don't stand in a furnace or walk off a tall building as an example, the result will not be good, and that's not what I mean by stare fear in the face! Don't be going out and trying to prove that you can do something stupid! In fact, I would advise against that personally, but if you do decide to challenge yourself physically, please do it safely! I am not condoning craziness/stupidity, there are human limits that are valid, for the record! If there is a tiger chasing you, that FEAR is REAL and if it bites your head then it is very likely that you are dead! What I am trying to show you is that you can SEE <u>false</u> fear in the mind, and from above the mind, you can see it and challenge it without risking your life! There is a difference between real fear, such as the fear that gets you out of the way of something dangerous, and a mind generated illusion! This is an understanding of "virtual" mind generated road blockages and obstacles that are thrown into your path as dark and false thoughts by your "selves"! This is a virtual bridge over the raging river of thought so you can look down on these selves and see what's going on, what they're up to! This is how to get there, a path through fear with understanding and not around it! Once you truly understand and SEE that this fear, the fear I am talking about, is not real, it is an illusion that is built into and generated by the storyline, YOU can walk right through it. Your belief in the storyline is what stops you at the virtual wall, and NOW you can walk right through it because NOW you actually see that the wall is an illusion. It is just another self-imposed limitation! Have faith and trust that this is true, it is TRUE!!!! Need I even say this, I am not talking about REAL walls here! Bottom line, I can't be who I was and who I intend to be at the same time. I can ONLY move forward if I take the next step. Growth only happens by making new decisions, taking a NEW ACTION vs RE-acting as my "old self"! I MUST BE NEW...in THIS MOMENT!! Once you arrive to NOW, you will <u>understand</u> that you just left that old "self" and fear at the gate...and that offers you the ability to move forward with your life, <u>you got the lesson</u>, and <u>CHOSE A NEW THOUGHT</u>!

8. **Watch your emotions. Don't discount them, don't bury them, don't disconnect, don't look the other way, and definitely don't**

**numb them out with your favorite recipe for food, drink, or whatever else! Emotions are there for a reason...PAY ATTENTION, a lesson is at your doorstep!!** These are thoughts and situations that are showing you yet again, some "belief" that you have bought into, is it REAL?! These emotions carry weight, and that weight varies with your level of attachment to what is driving that emotion. The more attached we are, the more weight they carry! We can FEEL this with the level of the emotion. This "stuff" must be processed. You do that with understanding and seeing the storyline that generated the emotion! You have to be present to do it though. **AVOIDANCE is NOT AN OPTION!** DO NOT bury these emotions in food, alcohol, drugs, or whatever other distraction the mind can come up with (tv, social media, endless scrolling, etc.). These are usually attractive alternatives that do one of two things: They numb you out to avoid dealing with it or distract you from having to think about it. Either way, you are finding a way to get it out of the mind to avoid the underlying emotion. This is not going to help you move forward and will steer you right around growth mode. In fact, you will be progressively and increasingly limiting yourself vs growing! If you want the lesson, which you really do NEED to move forward with your life, wake up and pay attention when these alternatives present themselves!!!!! Emotions will be the driver, and they show us "the devil" so to speak. That cunning character is kind of disguised though, and you may not recognize him. "HE" is disguised as US, the "selves"! In other words, the former and future little "you's", all dressed up in their storylines.... watch out for them!!!! We are the self-imposed "devil" (limitations) to ourselves, and we get in our own way! YOU really have to see this on the cutting edge of the moment of NOW, that fraction of a micro second, as you step into the moment as your new "SELF vs old "selves"!!!! Once seen, YOU can't unsee it! YOU have all the power in the world to move forward with your life. **STEP INTO YOUR POWER**! "The devil" or dark thought has no power here, YOU leave them at the gate! How? YOU DO IT by watching your emotions and NOT avoiding them, NOT burying them! By using them as clues to heighten your awareness, you begin to understand the storyline that generated these emotions. UNDERNEATH the emotion is the story. As you realize that it is simply a line of "BS" that we had formerly bought into, YOU FREE YOUR SELF from that limitation and no longer carry that weight forward! HOW? Emotion arising= STOP, pay attention, see underneath it, understand it (the story/belief) ...heal, RISE UP above this level of thought, and take that next step...INTO

THE MOMENT without them!!!! YOU are enough, YOU have the power …don't give it away, leave them at the gate! For a "devilish" song to challenge the way you think, check out the song by **Karliene**, **"We're the devils"**[162]. We create our own evils, for sure! (Devils, right?) Check out the powerful lyrics in this amazingly well-done song. We absolutely DO tell stories well, extraordinarily well, so well that they are believable! If we really look, and pay attention, the beast can certainly be seen within us. BUT, we don't have to subscribe to those stories, nor do we need to become the beast, right?! Great job Karliene, I think you got it right, BIG TIME! Love the ominous tone to the song too, so appropriate! In the end, once we see the "selves" and what they are up to, we have CHOICE. We can either subscribe to what they are selling, be it fear, or whatever else, or we can FORGIVE our "selves", for they know not what they do, right?! The little selves are unconscious, we are NOT! The "selves" are in the darkness, SHINE YOUR LIGHT ON THEM, those cunning little devils! They need to be SEEN, in the light, understood, forgiven, and LET GO!! Problem is, we don't even see them until we know where to look, and we may need to dig a little, underneath these surface emotions to see the whole story. This is where we gain UNDERSTANDING! The emotion is just the clue… dig deeper. Thanks, a lot Karleine, great song!

9. **SEEING and HEARING is happening every moment of every day, instead of seeing and hearing with a vantage point and a focus that is "OUT THERE" so to speak, LOOK IN!** Pay attention to what's going on out there, YES…and watch the wheels spinning around in your own head as well. See the gearing and the processing going on AS IT IS going on. In other words, as life is happening, maintain a "PRESENCE" that is ABOVE THOUGHT! With this presence YOU will see life happening yes, but more importantly you will see this sort of double view, **out there and in here**! This is highlighting for you where your attention is, and **"Where attention goes, energy flows"**[163]. With this vantage point you will see the storylines and the "selves" or "you's" with amazing clarity, and the ball will truly be in your court as to what to do about it. CHOICE is now available. Where moving forward previously was impossible, an unknown, or at a minimum, difficult to see, now the path is truly lighted and highlighted… emphatically! For a musical angle to this vantage point, check out the following songs:

   a. **"SEE WHO I AM"**[164] **Within Temptation**. This is a very cool song from the album **"The Silent Force"**. This, to me, is a reminder to be on the lookout for and SEE these "selves". FREE YOUR

MIND from them and BE the change!!! Not only does Sharon Den Adel have an amazing voice, but the song lyrics from this band are INCREDIBLE! My compliments to them and THANK YOU! I listen to this music all the time and I love it! To me, it's like listening to lessons, in the lyrics, and it's fun as well as entertaining, quality music! You may wish to check out the song **"The whole world is watching"**[165] also by **Within Temptation**, because in it they seem to amplify the point that <u>time</u> is a really key element. This MOMENT, <u>NOW</u> can change EVERYTHING!! Brilliant. As I said, powerful lyrics and lessons are in these songs if you choose to use them for an education like this! As I say, I can't promise that this is what these bands intended with their music, but these are the messages I hear. You may gain an even more important lesson from music because you hear it slightly differently than I do, so as always, pay attention. There may be a lesson in it for you as well.

b. I must also refer you to the **RUSH** song **"Natural Science"**[166]. It is an amazing song. To me it seems like it describes the mind really well, and it is a great reminder on how it processes with all the gearing and what not! Take the time on this one and really READ the lyrics, they are incredible! Consider the perspective that if it were talking about thoughts, what that might mean? In fact, the speed, tone, and delivery in this song are brilliant as well, have a listen when possible. Thoughts, and storylines generated by these lower "selves", and the mind gearing can be quite complex, right?! I guess that's my opinion anyway! From above thought and seeing thoughts we can see them forming and even collecting as pools of thoughts that are similar in nature! We can see these with awareness as the mind is processing. After seeing all of that, the song even seems to imply that we have an opportunity to LEARN! If we fail to learn, or expand, grow...well then, in my words, we missed the lesson and then life goes on just as it was, which is similar to the conclusion of the song! So TRUE, YOU MUST take that quantum leap, and step into the NOW! GET THE LESSONS.

10. <u>**WAKE UP, take the step!!**</u> In song land: **Be the "PRIME MOVER"**[167] **of your life!** This is another **RUSH** song I love, and again, for fun... look it up! Great lyrics, as always. My take, the way that I hear this song is that the prime mover is YOU & I, acting as the higher "SELF" that is SEEING and HEARING from this new and HIGHER level of awareness and watching as thoughts form in

the mind. It seems to show us this amazing vantage point that can be activated. As you know already, once you activate this window that is ABOVE THE MIND, you then have this powerful overseer perspective and everything changes! Try to visualize this vantage point as if the song is talking about thoughts! Answers and insights are available, this allows you to see them as life is happening! It is showing where and how to SEE and HEAR on an ongoing basis! Answers or the "TRUTH" is not generic or static, as a one and done type deal, like once you know you know. Um, NO... That's not the way it works! Once YOU learn how to see & hear with awareness, it is an ever-available flow....and the "TRUTH" is available in the moment when you are the watcher OF THOUGHT, rather than IN amongst the thoughts themselves! You can't solve the problems that thoughts generate from their same level, in my opinion, you must step above them and out of the mind, and watch it process. As you do that, the "light" truly turns on. It's like walking in a dark room and turning a flood light on! All of a sudden you can see stuff you never saw before WITHIN! That includes showing you your own beliefs and where they limit you. Unfortunately, you won't see this until or unless you arrive at the gate and see it happen with a watchful eye on the cutting edge of time, right as today is crossing into tomorrow. This is that ever important edge we need to be alert and present to! It's a fraction of a second, as shown. It is right before "NOW" that the "old" self or "selves" show up and STEP IN to be the "you" instead of real "YOU" arriving to the moment and making a new "action" vs a RE-action. It is the difference between old selves' responding vs the new higher "SELF" having an opportunity to make a new choice, take a new ACTION! It helps you truly see the "you's" as they try to step into the moment and be "YOU"! That's where this light of awareness, the "watcher" SEES, and that is "en**LIGHT**ening"...once you "see the light"! As you proceed through life with this new vantage point, every moment is an education, an ever-unfolding lesson...it truly teaches us our own self-imposed limitations! **RUSH "PRIME MOVER"**[168] seems to speak to this activation of that window as the watcher, from above the mind, which is very cool. If you don't see it in the song, the clouds, in my opinion, are the "programming" I refer to, beliefs, or the little "you's", or the "selves", basically thoughts in the mind! The window is the vantage point as the watcher, above them :) Check out the lyrics online, you may see something important for you and / or learn something from it. You may see or hear something different, which is also fine!

11. BONUS: **Register on my website**, www.BetheINSTRUMENT.com. I will be developing this over time, so check back periodically and if you register, I'll make sure to keep you in the loop on any new stuff! I intend to have some more materials geared towards "visualizing" properly, with MAXED OUT super amplified manifesting & CO-CREATING MOJO, if that is of interest! I also have some other songs that are quite amazing that I'll share with you, if not already included here. More of these mind angles, how to live from this perspective! There are more and more people "waking up" in this world, which is truly a great thing! There are quite a number of bands that sing about it with very powerful lyrics! I am "SEEING" and "HEARING" more and more all the time, I hope and expect that you are too! Let me know if you hear a good one! ALL THE BEST, the best is yet to come!

# EXERCISES

## PREVIEW AND EXPLANATION OF THE GOALS:

T HE PURPOSE OF THIS chapter is to give you a path forward, a condensed, more specific way to explore your beliefs, and put this philosophy to work in your life. It will help you to really drill down on the main "me", "you", "self" or "selves" and their drivers that could potentially be pushing and pulling you in DIFFERENT directions. The intent by doing these exercises is to reveal to your higher "SELF", the activities, thoughts and gearing of the lower "selves" in the mind. It is an enlightening process, and this will really help you to implement these strategies!

By doing this, your next step, and next step, will be revealed over and over again and as it is, you will gain more clarity in any given moment. Some of your "stuff" will be fairly obvious, but you MUST DIG DEEPER! Ideally, by doing so, this digging and drilling down process should help you to discover some of the more powerful and limiting underlying "themes" (beliefs and storylines). These are very important things to bring into the light of day, and that is why doing the exercises is so important! With that being said, this is the **WORK** section, and please know that this is a beginning, not an end to the process!

Understand, going in, that the limitations, roadblocks, and obstacles that have stopped you thus far, or hampered your abilities from time to time to perform at your best (to date), are a part of your "selves" and their associated storylines. These "selves", or "you's" or the little self, as I refer to them, are all limited in DIFFERENT ways! This process is an effort to understand these ways and to develop ways to grow through them, with understanding. We are in essence, making every effort to remove our "blind spots"! Blind spots are triggers that take us out of the moment. This limits our ability to grow through them primarily because we can't see them while we are unaware / unconscious of them. Once we fully wake up and see them, then we can help our "selves"!

In the grand scheme of things, as you go through these exercises and this process you will come to a major realization, at some point. That realization is that in order to be completely FREE, you need to arrive in the moment without all of your baggage, without these limited perspectives and "knowledge"! Knowledge, while wonderful and helpful to a point, is ultimately still limiting, and will not get you across the finish line! The SKILL you are developing is to leave these limitations at the gate!

In order to do that, you need to know what they are, when they show up in your life, and why they are there to begin with. You will see, with awareness, how they are limiting you if not eliminating your ability to make a choice all together! By bringing them into your awareness, you are shining that virtual floodlight on them and what was formerly "in the dark" is no longer lingering around as the unseen and unknown, in the shadows of the mind! PRESENCE is very powerful because with it you are SEEING and understanding these "selves" and it is gradually revealing your blind spots as you become more and more AWARE! Please understand that each moment is a new opportunity for a new lesson, and Rome wasn't built in a day! It is a process, and it takes time! Some revelations come in unexpected ways, in unexpected moments, and in very powerful life changing ways, so always be vigilant, and aware!

These exercises are an effort to develop a SKILL, more quickly! The SKILL is to understand these "selves", their storylines(beliefs), and what DRIVES them to do the things that they do! By understanding this, we are uncovering the software that is running behind the scenes, between the ears, and outside of our awareness, UNTIL NOW! This skill will develop over time into a TALENT. The talent is ARRIVING IN THE MOMENT, FASTER...without the baggage! SELF MASTERY is about as good a description as I have heard to describe this ability. SELF mastery is the skill to ARRIVE in the moment to SEE and BE, as described in the book. Hopefully you understand this really well by now, this is simply a workbook summary and action plan to help you get there more consistently!

When the light really turns on and starts glowing, gleaming even, you naturally change your vantage point on the virtual time wave as yesterday is crashing forwards into today, and ultimately tomorrow as well! You will see with all new eyes and hear with all new ears from this heightened perspective, as to where you are relative to that wave! It is AMAZING! This vantage point, to the extent that you can get there, and maintain your presence there is the SKILL! It shows you, consistently, major insights & realizations; one of which is that FREEDOM is available! The interesting thing is that it is not by refining beliefs, and / or creating new "better" ones, although in the beginning that is very helpful. FREEDOM is available by arriving in the moment WITHOUT these self-imposed LIMITA-TIONS all together! In the beginning, the goal is to uncover them, SEE THEM, and dissect them, with understanding. At that point, you are then beginning a new challenge. The challenge from that point on is to take that skill to the next level, and with massive amounts of energy, focus and awareness, leave them at the gate! This is the ultimate availability, a blank slate, fully available for instruction and guidance in the moment. Fully balanced, unbiased and aware. PRESENCE!

Right before yesterday crosses into tomorrow, be NEW, with TRUST and FAITH and please just watch what happens. A whole new world is opening up to you and is at your fingertips, DO GOOD!

# EXERCISE #1

Credit to my dad, **Gerry Giesler**[169], for not only suggesting the idea to create these exercises for you, but also for generating the first version of the exercise! So here we go:

Beliefs: What is a belief and what is MOST IMPORTANT to ME!?! Ready to turn on your night vision?

1. Look up "belief" on your favorite search engine or dictionary online.

2. Write down the definition you like best, or what it means to you, more specifically! There are no wrong answers here, this is for you to develop a game plan, everything helps at this stage! It is a process...and it is truly an illuminating brainstorm session! The important part is that you DO IT and WRITE IT DOWN!!!

3. What are your TOP TEN most important beliefs, and WHY? Where did they come from? Briefly. Know that this may change over time. There are MILLIONS of potential beliefs! We are just looking for a top ten here, your big motivators, drivers, for now. You can further develop this over time, here are some examples:

a. My personal integrity is most important to me

b. Being right, I hate to be wrong...particularly if someone TELLS ME I am wrong!

c. Being a good person is who I AM

d. Winning is all important

e. Making money is the most important thing in the world

f. I will NEVER _____. Fill in the blank

g. I AM _____ or, I AM NOT _____. Fill in the blank.

h. What are my BEST qualities?

i. What are my WORST qualities?

j. What are the "storylines" that have developed in my life that are driving the above "beliefs" and how important are these to me? Secondly, what beliefs are tied to what storylines? How impactful is that, and how much "stress" would it cause the "me" if that were to change? (This is the equivalent of measuring your "attachments"!)

4. There are more than likely **"ARCHETYPES"**[170], or variations of them, that drive the answers you gave in exercise number three. Thank you, **Carl Jung**! These archetypes DRIVE who we want to BE, and who we ARE in any given moment! NOW, THINK HARDER, dig a little deeper! The following will help you explore more in that regard and help you to see more clearly your personal "character", personality types/ archetypes! These will be the things that color the lenses in your eyes, and SET YOUR FILTERS! They determine how and what you see "out there"! We want to pay attention when they do one of two things. #1 They give you major motivations to move TOWARDS something. OR #2 They are a major deterrent and push you AWAY from something! These will likely be to KEEP a particular storyline going and maybe amplify it OR MOVE AWAY from one that is a hard negative. (Something you really don't want!)! You shouldn't really need to put too much weight on the ones in the middle of the pack at first, until or unless they become more of a priority for you, and situationally that would mean that they are carrying more weight because something has changed in

your life! You want to know the "STUFF" that is carrying the most significant amount of weight, FOR YOU, right NOW...ever presently! The IMPORTANT "stuff"! This may very well be attachments to the more important people and situations in your life too, so keep that in mind!

    a. Look up Archetypes online and pick the ones that you really admire in people, then the ones that you despise in people. (BE HONEST with yourself!) While these may be similar to the stuff identified in step 3 it may add some additional perspectives and considerations. Write down a top 5 that you would NEVER exhibit, with every ounce of your being, and the top 5 that YOU FULLY EXPECT and make every effort to BE!

    b. There are archetypes that you exemplify, or aspects of these archetypes that you WANT to exemplify, what are they?

    c. There are archetypes that you really don't like, or don't even want to see, no less BE, what are they?

    d. What are the archetypes, or aspects of an archetype that you really want to exemplify but you really don't yet?

    e. What are the archetypes, or aspects of an archetype that you really can't stand, and / or when you see them in people you either shut them out or run the other way?

    f. Is there an archetype, or personality trait, that has not been defined that is important to you, if so, include it, and define it!

    g. Have you any examples of these type people in your life that you can picture in your mind that "represent" these for you? Make a note of that.

5. REALITY CHECK! REVISE THE LIST according to your TOP priorities/beliefs. You want the TOP 10 motivators in your life and the top 10 things you absolutely 100% want to avoid! Once completed, discuss this list with someone you know and trust. This someone MUST know you well, and yes...this is somewhat of a "GUT TEST", so BE HONEST! If this someone knows you as well as you know yourself, this should be an easy process. If they are your "friend", they will be honest, and don't blame them for doing so, that's what you want! You don't gain

anything by leaving out a major motivator or demotivator! If nothing else, look in the mirror, BE the friend you need to be, to your "self". And again, be honest!

6. REFINE the list. Write it in BOLD and give it some major consideration. I mean really think about what it was that developed these perspectives, priorities, motivators, and demotivators? What do these things really mean to you and why are they so important? Maybe spend an entire day thinking about one of these at a time, pay attention to how often it comes up, and then move on to the next! Remember please the goal here: UNDERSTANDING! This is your present day "Character", and it needs to be understood! From the me perspective, or "I": I understand that I am going to be bringing my higher, NEW version of "SELF" into the moment from this point going forward. I want and NEED to know WHO, and / or what version of "ME" that is, presently! As an example, I may love my grandmother very much, but I am not going to bring that "mindset" into a BATTLE! Your grandmother may be more of a warrior, mine was not:)

7. Use **Gerry Giesler's**[171] **Priority setting TOOL**, as detailed below. You are going to do these exercises at least three ways as follows below. Once you will do it for your Primary and biggest MOTIVATORS. Secondly, you will do this for your Primary and major DE-MOTIVATORS, or the things that repulse or repel you! So, things you are attracted to first, and the things you like, and then the things that you avoid or things you don't like! Lastly, once you have done this and gone through it, take your top 5 and do this again with your top five motivators vs your top five demotivators.

As an alternative, there is another way to potentially fill these in, and that would be by writing out a top ten that says I AM _____, and a then a top 10 that states, I AM NOT _____ and fill in the blank.

Lastly, a very simplified version would be I like vs what I don't like and weigh them vs one another. You can do this in every one of these ways. Each is beneficial as it is uncovering the "selves"! The goal here is to uncover drives, motivations, and deterrents to see what is carrying the most weight on your life, right now! These are the selves that need to be SEEN! So here is the exercise that helps you do this, thanks DAD!

**Priority setting tool:**

**a. Draw a 10 x 10 grid of boxes.**

**b. List each of your beliefs in order at the left of a horizontal row, number them 1-10.**

**c. List each of your beliefs in the same order at the top of a vertical column, number them 1-10.**

**d. Compare each of your beliefs to each of the others and put the number of which is more important in the corresponding box.**

**e. Note that prioritizing one belief over another does not diminish that belief, it's all relative.**

**f. Add up the times each number appears in all the boxes.**

**g. Write down your beliefs in the resulting sequence. This is a weighted result, what carries the most weight in the mind, YOUR MIND!**

**h. Now do this again, with the good vs bad beliefs, likes vs dislikes, motivators vs demotivators. You can do this many ways and it is very helpful in establishing a base knowledge of your drives and motivators. Some of these motivations will be more powerful as a NEGATIVE, vs a POSITIVE. Pay particular attention to these!**

**i. Pat yourself on the back...and then RE ASSESS!**[172]

8. Create a workable goal sheet or "model" for your "Psychology". This is your NEW personal approach to life! MIND management. This should be FUN, not a chore! This is exciting and is setting you up for success. Understand that you wear multiple hats in any given day, as we all do, and this will inevitably be situational. That said, you can have more than one of these, and you probably should, depending on what hat you need to be wearing in any given moment! Remember that each and every moment is different, and to be successful in this crazy world we really need to be a chameleon, right? I can't be the same person in all situations, doing everything the same, without adjusting my skillset or mindset right? The point is, knowing who and what skillset / mindset we are bringing into the moment! We MUST be the WATCHER of this! Here (below) is the "model" I created years ago for myself, relative to trading, and life too! I was noticing certain behaviors in myself while I was making trades, and living life so to speak, and so I really took a deep personal assessment of myself in that time period because I was seeing my weaknesses, REAL TIME! I mean I was really disappointed in myself for having these "flaws"! It was a total eye opener, and I did

kind of "sulk" about it periodically because I didn't understand how to address them. This is HOW, with awareness! This is how you UNDERSTAND THEM and DEFLATE the beach ball! WATCH, as the watcher and over time the beach ball just starts losing its buoyancy, there's just no air in it anymore, and it is FUN! This process is geared to bring these "you's" into the light of day, so that you can see them. At first, they are kind of lingering around and just popping up here and there to show their faces (in the mind). With awareness, you are slowly letting the pressure out of the beach ball...by letting them go! After a while, and a lot of effort to pay attention, these "you's" are no longer in the shadows, or darkness and the beach ball that was coming up to haunt you, is NO MORE!!!! Why, because IN THE MOMENT, they are essentially dissolved in the light of day, with your awareness fully on and your SKILLSET entirely at your fingertips! You NOW have ACCESS to the moment.... the little "self" the little "you" did not BUTT you out of the way to gain access to the moment and STEAL IT! YOU have ARRIVED, and NOW where you formerly had no choice, all of a sudden YOU do HAVE CHOICE! The pond surface is consistently calm and quiet, and the moment anything comes up to disturb the water level, this new "SELF" sees it, instantly! And then what happens? The higher "YOU" LETS THEM GO! In other words, you just grew into a better version of you, less limited, and more powerful! How? By letting go of the previous version of you that was MORE LIMITED!

Here is an example of what my priorities looked like some years ago. Please remember that you don't need to "like" a person to see a quality in them that you admire! My list may or may not be a list of "likes" personally, that's not the important thing here, so please don't "judge" the people I picked. If you do see the mind wanting to do that, pay attention to why! This is a model for the "psychology" and / or SKILLSET that I would like to bring to the moment in certain situations! You don't need to like these people to get the lesson. Pick different people that mean something to you if you prefer. That will be more powerful! When you read the psychology of a trader(below), please understand that my mentality back then was that there was a virtual committee in the mind (the Me's, or little selves). I was acting as the RULER, giving direction to the little selves as they showed up in the mind, and effectively deciding which skill set I was going to bring to the moment! Which "self"! Make sense?

## Psychology of a Trader:

WE ONLY MOVE FORWARD, WE ARE ALWAYS PRESENT, and WE ARE FOREVER in the NOW
MOMENT! We are the inner archetypes driving us forward!

Be aware of us and prosper, let us work in the shadows and you'll never know our strength!

COURAGE of a BraveHeart (Alertness, Strength, Determination)

FOCUS of Michael Jordan (Mastery, Concentration Poise)

WISDOM of my Higher SELF (Guidance, Awareness, Power, Understanding)

Mental Agility of my Higher SELF (Nimbleness, Balance, Non-Attachment, FOCUS...Intuition)

Strength and Stamina of Pele' (Persistence, TALENT, Mastery)

Confidence of George Bush (RULER, Poise, Peace, Purpose, Power, Positivity, Non-attachment)

Understanding and Persistence of my Father (RULER, Achievement, Determination, Strength of Character)

Intuition of my Mother (Faith, Patience,

*I The Ruler, take responsibility for all of the below Archetypes and all their decisions!*

*Once made, CAREGIVER will ensure that there is no backlash on any decision, by any one, any time, or any how!*

*Inner critics ARE NOT*

*Welcome here!*

Understanding, Awareness, Unconditional LOVE, CAREGIVER)

## AMPLIFY these Qualities:

**RULER:** DISCIPLINE, NON-ATTACHMENT, POISE, Ability to DELIGATE, Strength to make tough choices, to LEAD!

**WARRIOR:** COURAGE, Adrenalized ACTION, STRENGTH and FOCUS toward a GOAL.

**SAGE:** IMPARTIALITY, NON-ATTACHMENT, PATIENCE, INTUITION, Calm detached WISDOM!

**CAREGIVER:** Understanding, Unconditional LOVE, Silencing of the inner critic, Encouragement, Positivity!

*With my inner HEROES, I ACT from STRENGTH, WITH CONFIDENCE and LASER FOCUS..... Re-actions are for the other guy!*

*NO REGRETS !(or you'll be dealing with my MOMMA!)Trading is a PROBABILITIES GAME...Curtis Arnold and GERARD say take the trades, Dad says PULL THE TRIGGER!*

# EXERCISE #2

After doing exercise #1 and then living life for a period of a time, you be the judge of how long this is, then re-assess! You may not need to go through the entire exercise again, and if you do that's not a bad thing. Go ahead and do it again! This is a process, and your Peace of Mind is at stake here, so make the effort!

Exercise two is about arriving in the moment more and more consistently. Knowing all the results that you came up with in step one, pay attention in the mind as these various archetypes and personalities jockey for position and TRY to decide on your behalf. This is where the RULER of the mind, the higher "YOU" vs the lower "you" MUST be the traffic director in the mind, or above the mind. You are essentially CHOOSING which skillset and which "self" has the authority and power to make the best decision and you are bringing the highest "SELF" to the moment! You had better do it fast though because you only get a fraction of a second to choose! Life happens FAST! That is one of the reasons why I love that song **"Faster"**[173], by **Within Temptation**! Not because we need to live it faster, but because the mind moves so fast, we miss stuff, so we need to see it faster! In other words, we need to be faster than IT, and be able to process it all! So, as we are seeing it, we see it faster to BE IT faster!

Question #1: Are there times when the "I" that shows up to decide is from archetype "A" and in reality, choosing from archetype "B" would have been more appropriate? Substitute archetype with "belief" if you prefer.

Question #2: In any given situation, did I bring into that situation a situational bias based on a storyline that was driven by my beliefs? Which ones, and how did that affect my decision-making capability? Was it effective? If I dropped that bias or belief, what opportunities, doors, or windows would that open up? With that freedom, what new choices would become available?

Little by little, step by step...eliminate the "beliefs" that no longer serve you! This is not intended to be a vicious predator type attack on yourself and beating yourself up in any way! That's not the point of this and is counterproductive. It's resistance, not good...but do pay attention when or if this happens! This is the stuff we need to see, and then wake up to these tendencies & triggers that are especially prolific, these are most definitely notable! What we do want is a calm awareness and a processing or "LETTING GO" of these non-serving attitudes, archetypes, and beliefs with "understanding"! This includes behaviors that are not doing us any good! Empathize, process, understand, let go...repeat!

# EXERCISE #3

**Repeat, Rewind and Replay**! In a moment where you missed it, in other words, you were not fast enough, and did not arrive in the moment, QUICKLY, go back and in your mind, DO IT OVER! Virtually, of course. Go back and try to watch super quickly what happened, why you missed it? Use your imagination, and SEE it through, with all the available options, and pick the best one, as if it happened that way, in the mind. This is not to JUDGE; this is an exercise that will allow you to release the version of self that didn't **"GET IT DONE"**! This is a lesson, and this process of discovery is showing us the element of mind that did not allow the higher version of self that was required into the moment, so that the next time this situation presents itself, we can ALLOW and GAIN access to the moment.

We need to be THE WATCHER of the mind, as these little selves try to take us over by LOOKING WITHIN!! The mind in a state of panic, or confusion, or rage, or any heightened emotion can't help itself! That's why this is such a powerful process, why? Three reasons, maybe more:

1. This process is not making a demon of the "me" that didn't get it done. (resistance). This is not to be critical of the "self".

2. This seeing and understanding is giving us a LESSON that there is a "me" that could have gotten it done but that "me" didn't show up. This is actionable intelligence, an understanding, for the next time!

3. This replay feature, re-visualizing, is showing us how to part the sea of thought and see, within that moment that just happened, the lightning bolt that just hit us! (Trigger) With PRESENCE, this education will help us to be more prepared and balanced the next time! That lightning bolt (your baggage and emotions) generated a flash and maybe even a ROAR of thunder that got in your eyes/ears and temporarily blinded you! You literally could not hear and / or could not see at that time! The "processing" part of this is that while we may have missed it real time, so to speak, this way we didn't miss the opportunity to learn from it.

The reason that the higher / better "me" didn't show up was because someone or something got in my way! It was me, my trigger, my lack of FOCUS! I got taken out of the moment and need to understand why, how?! There is an underlying issue. Pay ATTENTION, and NOT just OUT THERE, certainly not in blaming someone, or something exterior to the self. We do need to see what "out there" happened, and then REALIZE what happened within the MIND as a result! YES, something OUT THERE happened, indeed... What this exercise is doing is revealing to you the following RE-action, INSIDE and who or what version of "you" it was, that responded. Seeing INWARDLY, is the KEY...as in which "you" made the decision or allowed a less than effective decision to be made! LOOK WITHIN! The processing part of this is the essential learning element that is geared to enable a higher version of SELF to be more prepared and balanced the next time this situation presents itself. We are deflating the beach ball.

Each and every moment is an opportunity to get the lesson, we must be available and PRESENT, with AWARENESS. That requires ENERGY, STAMINA, and FOCUS! By doing so, you arrive for class, and you get the lesson! Class is held at a particular time each day, it's called NOW! Need I say it again? LOOK WITHIN!!!!

# EXERCISE #4

Pay attention to EMOTION! NOW, do that with a different lens, and a different AGENDA. Inevitably, you will fail! Over and over again, you will fail to arrive in the moment. The good news is that you will SEE IT AS IT IS HAPPENING, OR JUST HAPPENED a moment ago! This is really GOOOOOOD! Ever heard of the light at the end of the tunnel? It is getting brighter! As you see it, and realize you failed again, you'll see emotions come up. USE THEM! The funny thing is that early in the process the emotions are the things that tend to blind you. NOW the game has changed, and you will be USING THEM in your favor. How? Emotions carry with them something really useful: ENERGY!!!! You need it and must redirect that energy and channel it in a POSITIVE WAY towards your awareness, attention and focus to amplify your SKILLS!

As an example, instead of getting "frustrated", which is a toned down, MUTED version of anger, I am going to use a redirect as the RULER of the mind! Pay very close attention here as this is important. RESISTING the anger, trying to "be good" and not demonstrating or showing it out, turns it into frustration! That's no fun, right? Instead, there is a better way to "process". I am going to EM-BRACE the anger, and USE IT to **amplify my SKILLS and FOCUS**!! THIS IS a HUGE difference, why? Remember that what we resist tends to persist, or repeat in our lives, because we are giving it the power! TAKE IT AWAY, and USE IT! IMMEDIATELY, go back and visualize / imagine, how that could have gone differently! Listen to the song, **"Prime Mover"**[174]! **RUSH**. This, once again, in my opinion, is a lesson in a song, describing this process! What you will find in doing this is rather remarkable. It takes a negative emotion that formerly blinded you in the moment, giving it a POSITIVE "SPIN" that is now PROPELLING YOU INTO THE ZONE! This is a major contrast, as follows:

1. RESIST / AVOID / ACT OUT: anger, not processed, not understood, can become frustration as an example. The mind cannot dissipate this "bad" energy if it is ignored, or buried, and so it builds up inside. As you have just pumped a good amount of air into that beach ball, it pops right back up again and frustration turns into MORE FRUSTRATION,

probably VERY SOON!! Anger, acted out, is a just a poor use of energy! That usage is dissipating it, or offloading it, usually onto someone else because we just don't know what to do with it, how to process it, and that typically doesn't end well. The consequence is a movement, yes, but usually it is backwards! We either have to go back and fix something because we made a decision in the state, and from a bad state, and got a comparable result, or we just dug a bigger hole for ourselves and have to climb out of it by burying the emotion and postponing the lesson! Net result: Backwards, or sideways at best! We also missed the lesson!

2. EMBRACE / UNDERSTAND / PROCESS / STEP FORWARD: Anger, processed, understood, redirected, can be used to amplify our skills and focus. This is done with PRESENCE! This is an opportunity to not only get a lesson, but to move forward in the same instant, CHANGING a potentially negative situation into a positive learning and growing experience! Net result = GROWTH, which means FOR-WARD! YAY!

Congrats, GOOD CHOICE! Way to go.

To expand on this conceptually and revisit the diagram in the middle of the book, this is taking you from anxiety, through arousal, and then using that ENERGY that is generated in a positive and productive way! When you are pushing like this, the body creates adrenaline when you bump into these obstacles! You are going to TAP, bottle, and USE the ENERGY that is created from it! Awareness creates the opportunity to basically grab that energy, channel it, and use it, as long as you are PRESENT to see the opportunity! It's going to happen real fast though, so get your higher "SELF" READY, awake, and aware! If embraced, channeled, and used properly, the ENERGY joins the team and gives you the added focus and awareness you need. This literally pushes YOU into FLOW, the ZONE! What is true for anger may show up a little bit differently for other emotions. Emotions show up in different ways, with different energy...the point is that they have ENERGY, USE IT!

The important part of the above example is to understand that each situation is going to be slightly different. What will be consistent is that you are making a very clear and conscious choice in how to process emotion ONCE YOU SEE or FEEL IT, or both! So, pay attention, AS emotion shows up, what is it and what type of energy is it bringing? Not all energy can be processed in the same way. Sometimes this may show up as adrenaline, other times it may show up as simple nerves, or a mannerism, or a self-protection quirk like tapping your feet, toes, fingers, the desire to go eat a cookie, etc. Something! It will show up in the body in one way or another, like "NERVES" and it will be different based on the situation. It might be butterflies, a little uneasiness, stomach churning / upset, throw up, sweat, you name it...you may even start shaking and quaking... Doesn't matter what it is, just use it as the WAKE-UP CALL, to pay attention, wake up and get in the classroom! (As the over SEER) The stronger emotional reactions are the equivalence of a more MAJOR and important LESSON! That may have been postponed for a LONG time, it's time you got it and moved through it! To do so, you must USE THIS ENERGY; this is a major opportunity here! It needs to be seen as one vs. letting the emotion, or fear win, AGAIN! Breathe, deep! SUCK IT UP BUTTERCUP! Seriously, a major victory is in sight.... put a positive spin on this thing / event/ personal challenge, whatever it is and take the next step to understand, process and gradually move through it with understanding! You know why you need to do this, and must do it NOW! The moment you walk through this, you will see that on the other side is a NEW FREEDOM from the self- generated illusion! (Limitation)

We are putting ourselves in a position to make a NEW decision! CHANGE is possible. GROWTH is at stake. Personal expansion can and should be FUN, make it fun! As an example, you could use this strategy as a model: Decide that from this point forward, you are going to be the traffic light coordinator in the mind as thoughts are streaming through it. You are the "COP" if you will! Your position in time is right before the moment arrives. With the backing of an amplified and heightened focus and awareness generated by the emotion "Triggered" in the moment, YOU now have control at the gate and of the gate!! YOU control the FLOW of energy, of attention, of focus, and of awareness! When you can muster and direct the focus, awareness, and attention, AMPLIFY them with the ENERGY created in each situation by the EMOTION of it, really fast... guess what happens? Your PRESENCE, or ability to BE PRESENT and arrive in the moment gets better and better! It's a SKILL...work on it!

Be alert as to how you are USING, or DISSIPATING energy. Are you making best use of it, or wasting it? This needs to be seen and managed diligently. I'll tell you this, once you start to NOT WASTE so much energy, your days and moments can become a lot more productive. Your tasks are completed in a much more efficient manner as well! Talk about optimizing, holey moley. You'll amaze yourself. This adds major productivity, longevity, endurance, focus and fuel for awareness! This could also mean that you need less sleep as a result. That's adding more fruitful hours to your day!

# EXERCISE #5

Now that YOU have this new SKILL, play with it, and amplify its POWER at every opportunity! Wake up with this INTENT, every day, and bring it into every moment! How? With more and more awareness, and each time it is with a new twist, and a new realization. Every situation is dynamic! Your influences, and influencers are in a constant state of change, and nothing is static. As we progress down this road, more and more selves are going to be let go. This is wonderful, and powerful, because it allows us to see more clearly in general. Exercise #5 is to really drill down on the moment, situationally and to look at it with a new twist.

## Pay attention SITUATIONALLY:
## Observe which version of "self" or "me" I AM allowing into any given moment, as it is unfolding!

Ask the following questions:

1. Which version of "I" is arriving at the gate?

2. Which "ME" am I CHOOSING to allow into the moment?!

3. Am I arriving as my best and highest "SELF"?

4. OK, NOW, step forward into the moment.

Your skillset is getting really good, now. In order to use it just a little bit more effectively, to amplify its power just a little bit more, take one more step just a little higher on the wave. Use this newfound vision and perspective to SEE and HEAR even better, even clearer! Take that one step, but this time, take it BACKWARDS, wait what???? All this progress now backwards? Let me explain what I mean. I am talking about a virtual reality in which you are envisioning your physical placement ON THE TIME WAVE. As the wave is crashing forwards in time, your vantage point on this virtual wave matters. If you take one step backwards on the wave, like as in away from the shoreline the wave is moving towards, your vantage point is moving up a little higher ON THE WAVE and as this wave is starting to curl forwards. From this new perspective you can literally SEE better from here, above the little chop below and moving a little bit FASTER too! It is higher, you are no longer surrounded by the tumultuous water below. The wave is gathering steam, volume, and momentum... Paddle ...Paddle ...Paddle... Paddle, you are almost there! Man, you are moving, and you are going to catch this wave and ride it! You are slightly elevated and can literally see forward toward where you are going and to what's coming! It is as if you have a new vision, and an amazing surfboard. You can see the ride ahead and can project your "selves" into the future! The wave is juuuuuuuust barely, ever so slightly starting to curl forwards...just on the brink of >>>>>> now you fill in the blank space. PAUSE: Now think, with massive awareness, massive focus, using every ounce of energy you can muster! You literally have just a fraction of a second here, so make it count. YOU, your mind, and only ONE version of self is going to be allowed onto this wave. Where's this wave headed? Am I headed straight towards a rock... ABORT ABORT>>>>or is this clear sailing ahead, RIDE IT OUT!  In other words, YOU NOW have CHOICE, a choice with a VISION ahead of the upcoming result and potentials/probabilities of "success". Are you kidding me? NOPE. It is stupendous! Who, as in what version of self, are you going to allow on this wave? THIS IS CHOICE! What are you deciding? What thought, what action? NOW is almost here, what's it gonna be? NOW, is here... completely open, and WILLING, wide awake and aware, as the highest version of "SELF" you can arrive with, STEP UP onto the wave just as it is about to crash forwards into the moment. Un-pause. You can position yourself anywhere you want on the wave, just make sure to enjoy the ride! Have a great time, enjoy the journey!

Can you see that by stepping into the moment in this manner, your "processor" just went from 8 megabytes to 100 gigabytes, and then in a flash of a lightning strike of a moment it took a giant leap to a terabyte, petabyte....or maybe even an exabyte of processing power! Talk about a quantum LEAP! Holey MOLEY! In fact, and BY FAR, you are processing from a less "limited" perspective. You just went from using a dated computer and waiting for an answer, to a super-comput-er that is fully tapped in, turned on, connected, and it has produced a virtually optimized set of choices that is available INSTANTLY. That's GUIDANCE! As you arrive to the moment, over and over again in this fashion, your SKILL level, and your TALENT to "BE" are forever increasing. Ultimately, with readily available guidance, from the highest power in existence, you step out of your own way, and YOU BECOME the answer, the INSTRUMENT! Imagine processing without limitation! The "processor speed" as the instrument is UN-LIMITED! Is your "thinking" model up to the task? You want access to a better processor? BE THE INSTRUMENT! Much power is available for use, YOU, this higher "I" must be up to the task! BE willing to BE the choice.

www.BEtheINSTRUMENT.com

# EXERCISE #6

## BE THE INSTRUMENT! By doing so, you gain MASSIVE POWER! Use it wisely, please!

SIN, in my opinion, is where we are LIMITING GOD! Guess who does this. Yep, YOU got it, the "selves"! The selves are essentially putting bad "code" into the machine (your mind) and processing from this limited perspective. Not only is the processor bogged down and WEAK, but the code is also bad! Fight it if you must... but come back to use these exercises to identify the weak / bad code and update your processor in the moment! Do this over and over again! Bring your best "SELF" to the moment, consistently and progressively. As you LET GO of these former "selves" that were not up to the task, your SKILL at being the instrument will improve. Your HEART and SOUL will thank you. Please remember that while it is a wonderful goal to BE THE INSTRUMENT, we are human, and we make mistakes. That is what forgiveness is for. Forgive your "self" and try again! In fact, forgive the other guy/girl as well, and know that they've done their best in that moment. You know what, don't just forgive them, grab your GOOD HAT, go the extra yard, and HELP THEM! Do unto others, as YOU wish to be done to YOU! What would you want, what would you NEED? Be the instrument!

Please share the LOVE! Help make this world a better place for everyone!

www.BEtheINSTRUMENT.com

# DEDICATION
# Thank You!

Everyone I have known has contributed in one way or another to what I now know, and ultimately that has landed on these pages! While I appreciate everyone, I really do, I want to take this opportunity to acknowledge some of the people that have been more influential. These are the people that are really close to me, I have had or still have close relationships with, and have helped me tremendously over the years. I want to thank my family in particular, although I have had some very close friends that have really had a big impact on me too. Life isn't always easy, and it sure is better with friends, particularly GOOD ONES. I have been fortunate enough to have some great ones! Thank you to my friends, you are so loved, I mean it, and YOU KNOW IT too. I hope as life settles down; we can reunite on occasion! I cherish the fact that when we do talk, even though it isn't as often as it should be, it is as if we left off yesterday.

My family is AMAZING, I LOVE YOU ALL so much, and you are all very much appreciated, for more ways than I will ever remember to write here.  Although I tell you all the time, I wanted to also acknowledge that without your love and support, I would not have had the opportunities that I have been so lucky to have. Consequently, that has given me the opportunity to share this book!

My parents, Dottie Giesler & Gerry Giesler teed things up for me over and over again in my life! Thank you, Mom & Dad!  Your love has truly helped me in every stage of my life! You are so appreciated, and I am forever grateful. The situations and times are countless, that you gave me not only love, but encouragement, opportunities, recommendations, consolation, advice, and even money, when I needed it. Also readily available was your laughter, smiles, fun spirit & the joyful experiences that go along with such amazing people. You gave all, words are inadequate, and I am so grateful. He-hem, a little too much food though. Ha-ha. Joking. You were always there for me, in every way and any way that was needed, always timely too, I might add. The sacrifices you made for me could not be repaid in many lifetimes. I can't thank you enough. Nothing seems like it would be sufficient.

My sister Donna Giesler (Tangolics is her married name) has been a best friend to me, in many ways. Thank you, Donna for all the FUN TIMES, and the many long, good talks. It has been a solid give and take through the years, always! Good stuff. Your family too, Steve, Troy and Tyler are all amazing! Just knowing all of you has been a blessing to me, lessons abound! I am very fortunate to have all of you in my life, and I love you!

Finally, my loving wife, Joelle, and her family! Jean & Jim, Denise & Fred have all blessed my life in various ways. You have helped me understand things that I would not have known, had I not had the opportunity to know and love you too! I would not be able to explain these things to the extent that I can because I understand them better as a result. You are all very much appreciated and loved! Rest in peace Jim, we love you!

I am very thankful and blessed to have such an amazing family that have all contributed to ME, who I am!! Not that I am anything special, I just love you all very much. I have the most sincere and joyous feeling of gratitude in my heart for all the love you have all given me. I could extend this book for another 5000 pages with all the various lessons you have brought me to and through! I'll keep it short though, I think you get the point! I Love you!

Yes, there's MORE! Of course, needless to say, my wife Joelle is my best friend. I wanted to focus down on her a little more, not only because I love her so much, but because it is impactful in ways that may help you to understand this material even more. There is knowing someone, and then there is really KNOWING someone. TRUST and LOVE matter. FAITH in someone MATTERS. I met Joelle in 1987, so that makes for a long time with 1 person. Thank you, Joelle, for your cherished and treasured love, which makes my life better every day. Thank you for sharing your dreams with me. Thank you for understanding me and giving me the space to be ME! Mostly, thanks for LOVING ME, and helping me to be a better ME! How lucky I am to have you in my life! One more thing too, an extra special thanks which is an extension of you. Thank you for introducing me to something that has meant the world to me! DOGS! Had I not met and fell in love with you, I would have never had dogs at all. I was always allergic to them, and I would have avoided them. In fact, I was bit in the neck by a dog, in high school, and fortunately, lived to talk about it. It bit me 3 times and missed my jugular by only a small margin. For the fact that you loved dogs so much, I truly wanted you to have them, and that enabled me to get past all of that. In getting past that, I was able to, over time, get an incredible number of additional lessons from our amazing animals and enjoy them with you. The joy of having such amazing pets is alone enough, for 1 person. We had 3, so far, all were ideal, what more can I say, they were the best dogs a guy could ask for! You cared for them, and gave them all they needed, with LOVE! Eventually, that even resulted in me deciding that I wasn't going to have allergies anymore! That's how powerful the lessons were. The unconditional love of a dog is something to behold! Quite the opposite of fear. The many experiences we have had with our dogs are cherished, in so many ways. Our dogs have been amazing additions to our family in that regard, each has been remarkable in their own special ways. The smiles and laughs they bring, even in hard times...simply irreplaceable.

I have really appreciated our dogs in ways that you might not expect though. It was not only their loyal companionship and friendship that I cherish. They taught me the full range of human emotion, and that is truly only the beginning. In the extreme positive, they demonstrated unconditional love, which is the most amazing thing to experience, I am so grateful. They also took it all the way to the extreme opposite, and upon their passing, the sheer agony, emptiness, and pain associated with loss. Each of our amazing dogs has brought with them even more though, and as with everything else in life, if you are open to it, messages and lessons will come at you from all sides, in many ways. You just have to be listening. My amazing furry friends were no different, in fact, my BEST friends they were, right beside YOU, Joelle! Talk about trust and love. Joelle, and her dogs exemplify love, PURE LOVE! Mutually, always. How is that not educational, and in incredible ways too. While our dogs are not with us anymore, each of them has shown me important life lessons in dramatic fashion, on top of all that! I cannot even say how incredibly timely their lessons were given, it brings tears to my eyes, once again, not for the pain associated with the fact that they are not here anymore, but in the appreciation for what they gave me, showed me! Happy gracious tears, of JOY for the benefit of knowing them, and enjoying them in my life! IN ORDER, and appropriately so, this is EXACTLY how it has unfolded for me. Coincidence? I think NOT!

**Ranger: Beautiful Yellow Labrador!**

**Lesson: EXTREME positive, blinding optimism. Happy Go lucky!** The positive exuberance alone just makes you smile. Everything about Ranger was HAPPY! So much fun. The downside to that is when it gets to an extreme like this, can be blinding just from the enthusiasm side and the overwhelm of positive energy. This dog would wag his tail no matter what. The EXTREME positive, BLIND optimism. He could have easily been hit by a car chasing a ball or something else, thankfully he was not. I don't think he thought that anything could hurt him though. This is the type of dog that was so happy, you could accidentally step on his toe, and he would wag his tail. If he farted, wag. He stood at the glass door when we came home, wag. Anyone else showed up, wag. He had such an enthusiastic wag that his whole body would wag, not just his tail. Sometimes the wag was so crazy his tail would be going in circles it seemed. Full body wag. SO HAPPY, always! Thank you, Ranger for showing me the most amazing and contagious enthusiasm! You are forever the epitome of what that word means to me, a prime example of the breed, and why it is so popular! Thanks, Ranger!

### Chief: Gorgeous Deep, Dark Chocolate Lab!

**Lesson: Not extreme, but general anxiety type FEAR and how that can affect perception negatively.** Thankfully Chief had Ranger, and we rescued him from a family that maybe didn't understand him! Fortunately for him, and for ME personally, I was able to decipher the lessons he was to give me. Ranger and Chief both enjoyed full lives, relatively unscathed and unharmed, well fed, well cared for, and very well loved! Chief was fast, and agile! When Ranger chased him playing, they'd be running full steam, Chief would turn, and Ranger would just keep going in the direction they were going. He just couldn't turn that fast. He was amazing. He tried to chase down a cow one time in Virginia though, and that cow didn't budge...He just stood there chewing his cud, not phased in the least. Chief was running full speed and then tried to slam on the breaks when the cow didn't move, but the grass was wet! His resulting slip and slide ended up going like 30 ft in the grass, almost right up to and through the cows' legs. It was hilarious to watch, and thankfully no one was hurt. That situation, looking back on it, was even insightful. We do that same thing in our minds, and we look like a hot mess sometimes doing it! Chief was a trooper, and while he did have some nerves, he did not let it affect his enjoyment of life! I think Ranger was a big factor in that, and of course, we gave him everything he needed too! I think Chief was a thinker, made me wonder what was spinning around in there. Physically he was flexible, and athletic. He could go under the fences, where Ranger would need to go around! That flexibility and athleticism was very beneficial as this agility provided the means to maneuver much more quickly, with speed, and change directions faster as well. From a mind perspective, this would have obvious and lasting benefits! Just think about speed and agility relative to seeing and tracking the ego, as an example...that would be beneficial, for sure, if not a requirement! Thanks, Chiefy.

**Lesson:** We lost Ranger and Chief 30 days apart, the same year. Thanksgiving and Christmas. Joelle and I felt a substantial hole in our chest for quite a while. Grief is a challenge, the LOVE lost, and the gaping cavity it leaves is gut wrenching. The feeling of emptiness and misery was a whole new kind of suffering for me, at a time that was already a challenge! When it rains it pours right? So true, at least now we know why! At that time though, I had never felt anything like this before, not at this drastic level. This was piercing, and blunt at the same time. It seems to hit every ounce of your being, and it was overwhelming. EVERYTHING was affected. My intent is not to belittle this, but I do want to point something out that is very important to understand about it. While I was going through this agonizing period, that felt like complete torture, I noticed something within it that was strikingly familiar. Not immediately, but after a short period, I noticed that the "PANGS" of grief would come in waves. In fact, if I was tired, I had no control, tears were relentless. Otherwise, the waves started to distance themselves, ever so slightly, and be further apart each day. It was interesting to me that the way they kind of crept up on me and exploded in tears was very similar to the way that "withdrawals" from nicotine happened when I quit chewing tobacco. That also came in waves, and when I was tired, I had less resolve, but yet I conquered it. The "self" that wanted to keep doing it was seen, acknowledged, understood and released. I had to let it go. Not in the same manner, but in a similar manner, I understood the pain, and what that "self" was doing to me. I think that understanding helped me see this through to the other side, just the fact that it wasn't insurmountable. With the understanding and the RESOLVE to quit that stuff, and come out the other side, I could do this too. It was a mind perspective. What I did was change the vantage point. Instead of focusing on the pain that was associated with the dogs not being in my life anymore, I focused on the appreciation I had for the fact that they were in my life. These were true feelings. I focused on the LOVE I was able to experience as a result of knowing them. For a minute, the tears still came, but they were different tears. These were not tears of pain, they were tears of JOY, PURE JOY, and true THANKSGIVING. This changed my life!

If, at the flip of a switch, I can move from PAIN to JOY...by changing what I focus on, then what else is possible here on this earth? In this mind! It really made me think. I am not talking about turning off emotion, I am talking about a VERY REAL movement in perspective, from pain to appreciation. Pain to JOY. Pain to Happiness. So happy, in fact, that tears of joy were running down my face. That's a powerful understanding. HUGE LESSON! Thank you, Joelle,

Ranger and Chief. One of the most painful periods of my life gave me one of the most powerful lessons I could ever learn. There is no way I could have even seen this without the experience, and what it showed me. The EXTREMES, seeing them for what they are, how they are, and how they show up in the mind! WOW, what a lesson... to SEE, HEAR and FEEL and then have the capability to bring in a higher-powered emotional management system. TRUE processing! EMPOWERED is an understatement. It took years for this to really sink in as I used it WITHIN, from above, as a skillset. As I did this, it grew more and more powerful!

It took Joelle and I two years to really process this amount of "stuff" and be ready. It was heavy, and it most definitely, was not easy. With understanding, full on knowledge and confidence that it was the right thing to do, we got another dog. We fully understood the consequences of what we were signing up for, meaning loss and pain at the end, but now with understanding we knew we could get through it again. Not only could we get through that, but we could enjoy the experience prior! The JOY and LOVE of our dogs is worth it, every bit. Enjoy the Journey, right? I did not want to tarnish the image and memory of Ranger and Chief by getting another yellow or chocolate, and so we started looking at other options. We are true Labrador fans, and so we ultimately found the Fox Red variation. OMG, they are truly stunning, and the temperament was exactly what we were wanting! MELLOW! **Keepsake Labradors**[175], here we come. We bought Kappi before he was born and watched the whole litter grow up via webcam. We had to wait 8 weeks, and it was so much fun. The joy and anticipation. Talk about a new mindset. Then, of course, we went out and met Kappi. We sat with the whole litter. He picked us, I thank GOD for that!

**Kappi: Very Handsome Fox Red Lab!**

**Lesson: AWARENESS, and UNYIELDING CORE HAPPINESS!** NOTH-ING and I mean NOTHING phased Kappi. We had some affectionate names for KAPP! Bubbs. Kapp Dog. Kaptain was his official name. Ultimately, we called him Kappi. In reality, it was ZEN KAPPI, and in fact, we have statues of a meditating dog in our house now to remind us of him because that is just the way he was. Kappi taught me so much, to name a few: CORE stability, balance, and unwavering PEACE are possible! He exemplified it. In fact, Kappi just resonated calm, composed, happy, and it always felt like he just didn't need a darned thing, well, until it was mealtime anyway. LOL. His EYES, OMG his eyes were amazing; DEEP, "steely eyed", and beautiful. That Kappi stare was really intense, PENETRATING. If he wanted something, you knew it. It was as if he communicated on a different wavelength. He was happy as a clam, really didn't need much of anything...and he loved his food! Kappi also lived a very long lab life, happy, healthy, well fed, and well loved, by ALL! Everyone in our subdivision loved Kappi.   Kappi taught me so much, friendship, companionship, loyalty, trust, and patience! Over and over and over again, Kappi taught me patience. There's time, and then there is KAPPI time. Kappi was so slow and deliberate, even when he was younger but particularly when he was older. I will get there when I get there, never, EVER was he in a rush, well...except at dinner time. LOL. Even then though, he didn't bark...in fact, we could hardly even get him to bark. Imagine, a dog that doesn't bark! Are you kidding me.  We had to train him to bark, and even then, He really didn't want to, he was just doing it to appease us and get a treat!  Oh, yeah, he loved his treats for sure. Kappi was full of LOVE, and just happy, like CONTENT happy though. It was different.  It wasn't that overenthusiastic / overexcited full body wag like Ranger. It was this CORE unwavering PEACE. Nothing got to this dog, I mean NOTHING! There was a time he was peacefully laying in our front yard, and one of our neighbors' dogs had gotten out. It was across the street. Kappi stood up and took notice, which was actually odd, because normally he would just lay there and stare out and watch the neighborhood. Kids, cars, etc. This dog caught his eye though. Just like that, the dog charged him, from 100 yards away. Kappi didn't move, like the COW when chief charged it, unwavering, STILL...unafraid and statuesque. The dog ran up tried to bite Kappi, growling and all, but Kappi didn't move. Right up in his face and at his neck.  He just stood there, as if nothing was even happening. Thankfully I was right there and chased it away quickly. It upset me and amazed me at the same time. I was shaken, but he was not. I learned something that day too, how fast the brain can be overcome with emotion! Overwhelm, is real, and fast...the influx of energy must be managed! We must be ever vigilant. READY for life, it happens at lightning speed.

Last story. Kappi was diagnosed with cancer at age 7. They said he wouldn't live much longer. This sends shivers down your spine, 7 is too young for a lab. So here comes another lesson. Don't believe everything you hear. Fear can send you into a downward spiral, quick if you let it. We didn't. We got another opinion. Maybe a change in beliefs helped? Maybe a bit of faith and love, some brilliant Doctors, and maybe we got a little assistance from a higher power. I won't take you through the whole dissertation, but with a whole lotta love & care, a bit of faith, and some money, Kappi lived a long healthy life, with not much more than a speed bump at that crossroads. Kappi lived almost to 14...and he never changed, happy and healthy. Kappi was a little slower than most dogs, I'd say, and Zen Kappi even amazed the Vets with his composure and stillness. Amongst all the chaos at the vet clinic, Kappi was still Kappi. UNWAVERING CALM! He enjoyed every bit of it too, right up until the last day, when he told us with his eyes. That's one of the worst feelings on this earth. Kappi's eyes ...oh Kappi's eyes were amazing! They were deep, and certainly told you a story! He didn't have to say a thing, we knew. Always, this was no different, just takes your breath away for a moment. Maybe two.

Dogs will take you to the extremes of human emotion. The extraordinarily joyful ups and the inevitable downs too. Cycles of life I guess, and thankfully, my dogs introduced me to myself, or shall I say "selves", and my feelings. They taught me what they were for, how they registered, when, and of course what it meant. The alerts it triggers within, the pain they bring, and how to "process"! This is applicable to the whole range of human emotion. In the end, it comes down to a fairly simple although not always easy, CHOICE. Do you want to SMILE or FROWN? Which version of self is choosing? Do you want to stay in the pain and / or suffering or are you willing and able to CHOOSE JOY and APPRECI-ATION?! Who decides? While I still can't promise you a tear will not flow from my eyes relative to our dogs, I promise you this. If and when they do, they are tears of JOY. I am so appreciative, THANKFUL for every moment I had with my dogs, as well as everything that they have taught me about being HUMAN!

GOD is GOOD! We get exactly what we need, exactly when we need it. If only we can wake up and see it in the moment it is provided. If only we are able to believe and receive! We can, by making the effort, faster and faster! I can only think that the world would be a much more joyous place to live, and people would look at people with a whole lot more LOVE as we grow together! Maybe the news could report the GOOD, and the focus of the entire world would be on what we want MORE OF. Appreciation, forgiveness, joy, laughter, fun, faith, trust, and ultimately LOVE. People HELPING people vs the alternatives.  I am certainly not perfect, but my dogs have helped me to be better at it.

Thank You all! Sending love :)

# ABOUT THE AUTHOR
## Doug Giesler

How to Unlimit your limit, attain massive success in your personal and professional life while enjoying extraordinary PEACE of MIND, which is often elusive in this fast-paced world!

Doug's real-life experience in consistently generating top performance while helping others has inspired several books. His proven mind hacks, spiritual techniques and attitudes provide real life skills geared towards making limits a thing of the past and creating idealized futures where our world is a better place to live and play! Every day, every moment is an opportunity to understand and UNlimit a limit.

Doug provides a virtual tool chest for heightened self and situational awareness allowing you to overcome obstacles, break through barriers, overachieve and Self-actualize! He teaches a win-win philosophy with a big smile, and a positive attitude. Grab this opportunity, study this philosophy and WIN!

*Follow Doug on Amazon for updates and new releases!*

**a**

amazon.com/author/douggiesler

**in**

linkedin.com/in/doug-giesler/

# WHERE TO FIND DOUG

**WEBSITE:**
www.UNlimityourlimit.com

**LINKEDIN:**
https://www.linkedin.com/in/doug-giesler/

**AMAZON:**
https://www.amazon.com/author/douggiesler

# DOUG'S OTHER WEBSITES:

www.BeTheInstrument.com

www.SCLakehomes.com

www.RealEstateLakeMurray.com

www.RealEstateLakeMonticello.com

www.RealEstateLakeCarolina.com

www.RealEstateLakeWateree.com

# ENDNOTES

## CREDITS, ACKNOWLEDGEMENTS, AND LINKS

The following references to the sources of these books, articles, essays, poems, lyrics in songs, artists, bands, authors, and all of this is an effort to give credit where credit is due. These are incredible people and I appreciate them and their messages so VERY MUCH! Massive appreciation to everyone here, as they have inspired me, showed me things about myself, and taught me many lessons, progressively! I do not make any claim as to their intent within their content, nor do I claim to be a Doctor, or professionally anything, other than human, so take my advice as you may. Where explanations are offered, these are my own interpretations, which are based on my own experiences, and they are 100% valid for me. They may be completely different than what may work for you, as they are based on the way that I personally see things. Please do not assume that the interpretations I have offered are the same as the intent of the folks I am crediting! Their meanings, intention, direction, context, etc. may be slightly different, vastly different, or completely different in some cases! Context matters, and remember, everyone looks at things with different eyes. I expect you to as well :) I have done my best to offer up "official" links to their content, in the hopes that I am giving you their direct links, however, there is a sea of content providers out there, and fan pages as well, so please excuse me if there are any errors w/ links. I hope it is helpful. These folks are easy to find on many platforms. All the BEST to ALL, Everyone. Blessings and LOVE!

1. Jung, C. G. 1991. *The Archetypes and the Collective Unconscious*. Translated by R. F. C. Hull. 2nd ed. Collected Works of C.G. Jung. London, England: Routledge. Carl Jung, https://www.jung.org/who-is-carl-jung NOTES: This is just a reference to his body of work. He proposed a number of primary "Archetypes". I am proposing that there are possibly more, maybe infinite "patterns" that could occupy the mind, conscious & unconscious.

2. James Redfield, book, *The Celestine Prophecy*, New York, Boston, 1993, re-release 2018 Grand Central Publishing, https://www.celestinevision.com/, https://www.grandcentralpublishing.com/titles/james-redfield/the-celestine-prophecy/9781538730263/

3. Napoleon Hill, book, "*The LAW of success*", TarcherPerigree, 1937, 2008 https://www.naphill.org/

4. Napoleon Hill, book, "*Think and Grow Rich*", Combined Registry Co., 1937, 1961 https://www.naphill.org/

5. Claude M Bristol, book, "*The magic of believing*", Pocket Books, 1969. https://www.penguinrandomhouse.com/books/317479/the-magic-of-believing-by-claude-bristol/

6. Tradestation Technologies, technology, trading software: This is the name of their programming language, "easy language". https://www.tradestation.com/

7. Bill Harris, product: HOLOSYNC, Centerpointe Research, https://www.centerpointe.com/, 2020.

8. *Within Temptation*, Band. https://www.within-temptation.com/, 2023. Reference to SONGS; Stand My Ground, VIDEO LINK: https://youtu.be/4sCkAvh50Vs They have many more amazing songs. NOTES: Pay close attention, their Lyrics are super powerful, and the band is really good! Sharon Den Adel has serious vocal talent! Check out their stuff, and pay attention to everything, tone, speed, the videos, and the themes! Super powerful lyrics and a band that really delivers the message in a powerful way! Pay attention to who is singing, and who the song is being directed towards...is it someone else, or the alter EGO? I find this extremely thoughtful music and lyrics, well played out themes, even in the contents of each album! As an example, *The Silent Force, The Heart of Everything*, etc. They are, again, very powerful mental angles being played out in themes, and songs, just my opinion! Makes you think about thinking. The videos are also compelling with a lot of symbolism IMHO!

9. James Redfield, book, *The Celestine Prophecy*, New York, Boston, 1993, re-release 2018 Grand Central Publishing, https://www.celestinevision.com/, https://www.grandcentralpublishing.com/titles/james-redfield/the-celestine-prophecy/9781538730263/

10. Ken Roberts, book, "*A Rich Man's Secret*", St. Paul, MN, Llewellyn Publications, 1998, https://kenroberts.com/

11. James Redfield, book, *The Celestine Prophecy*, New York, Boston, 1993, re-release 2018 Grand Central Publishing, https://www.celestinevision.com/, https://www.grandcentralpublishing.com/titles/james-redfield/the-celestine-prophecy/9781538730263/

12. Rush, the band, song; Limelight, Album, Moving Pictures https://www.rush.com/ VIDEO LINK: https://youtu.be/ZiRuj2_czzw

13. Gerry Giesler, My Father, The Dadaroo! Quote from Dad!

14. John E. Sarno, M. D., *Healing Back Pain*, Warner Books, Feb 1991. *The Mindbody Prescription*, Warner Books Inc. Oct, 1999.

15. James Redfield, book, *The Celestine Prophecy*, New York, Boston, 1993, re-release 2018 Grand Central Publishing, https://www.celestinevision.com/, https://www.grandcentralpublishing.com/titles/james-redfield/the-celestine-prophecy/9781538730263/

16. Bill Harris, product: HOLOSYNC, Centerpointe Research, https://www.centerpointe.com/

17. Rush, band, song; Vital Signs https://www.rush.com/ VIDEO LINK: https://youtu.be/nnLJoBU9 cLw 2023

18. Bill Harris, product: HOLOSYNC, Centerpointe Research, https://www.centerpointe.com/

19. Bill Harris, book, *Thresholds of The Mind*. Centerpointe Press, 2007. With Centerpointe Research approval I also reference his blog article on "Flow states", which had the diagram & chart I reproduced. It is commonly used, but his article made me think about the chart referenced in the getting in the zone section. Plug for the company, I use their product called Holosync, their meditation program, as a lifetime member, every day! AMAZING! Check them out: https://www.centerpointe.com/, https://www.centerpointe.com/products/thresholds-of-the-mind-totm-paperback/

20. Bill Harris, Blog, flow states. Relevant book; *Thresholds of The Mind*, 2007, Centerpointe Press https://www.centerpointe.com/ , https://www.centerpointe.com/products/thresholds-of-the-mind -totm-paperback/

21. Alan Greenspan, Federal Reserve Chairman, Speech Quote, The Challenge of Central Banking in a Democratic Society, American Enterprise Institute speech. 1996 (This was during the dot com bubble)

22. Esther Hicks, Audio CD. https://www.abraham-hicks.com/ CDs https://www.abraham-hickslaw ofattraction.com/cds-and-tapes.html NOTES: I remember listening to her speak of this paddling upstream vs downstream concept quite a bit, and I liked it, relative to thought, and the dialogue was very powerful!

23. Within Temptation, Band, Song; Faster https://www.within-temptation.com/ VIDEO LINK: http s://youtu.be/iQVei5C2N4E

24. Bill Harris, BLOG, https://www.centerpointe.com/, Centerpointe Research Institute. 2020

25. NIKE, company slogan/ad campaign, "Just DO IT" 1988, https://www.nike.com/ NOTES: Branding used by the company. https://www.nike.com/jordan

26. Bill Harris, BLOG., https://www.centerpointe.com/ , Centerpointe Research Institute. 2020

27. Glenn Phillips, CEO: Lake homes Realty, https://www.lakehomes.com/ Image he posted on Facebook.

28. Michael Jordan, video clip, @JayMJ23, Michael Jordan "Failure" Nike Commercial, 2023: https ://www.nike.com/jordan VIDEO LINK: https://youtu.be/GuXZFQKKF7A NOTES: The man is AMAZING, I loved watching him play basketball! Talented!

29. GOOGLE, www.GOOGLE.com: Online definitions and synonyms: Notes: GOOGLE rocks, I use it all the time, for just about everything! These words were provided more specifically by: "Oxford Languages", Oxford University Press via the dictionary box on google, as well as "Thesaurus.com", dictionary.com, LLC. www.thesaurus.com accessed 3/14/2023. www.dictionary.com

30. Merriam-Webster, Merriam-webster, Incorporated, 2023 https://www.merriam-webster.com/ online definition accessed 3/14/2023.

31. Within Temptation, song; Stand My Ground. Album, The Silent Force. https://www.within-tempt ation.com/ VIDEO LINK: https://youtu.be/4sCkAvh50Vs

32. *The Wizard of OZ*, movie clip, David Johnson. original movie: Vidor, King, Victor Fleming, George Cukor, Richard Thorpe, Norman Taurog, and Mervyn LeRoy. 1939. The Wizard of Oz. United States: Metro-Goldwyn-Mayer (MGM). Notes: Movie character: The Cowardly Lion. YouTube video link https://youtu.be/LEEyijiTW-I

33. *The Wizard of OZ*, movie clip, David Johnson. original movie: Vidor, King, Victor Fleming, George Cukor, Richard Thorpe, Norman Taurog, and Mervyn LeRoy. 1939. The Wizard of Oz. United States: Metro-Goldwyn-Mayer (MGM). Notes: Movie character: The Cowardly Lion. YouTube video link https://youtu.be/LEEyijiTW-I

34. Within Temptation, Band, Song; Faster https://www.within-temptation.com/ VIDEO LINK: https://youtu.be/iQVei5C2N4E 2023

35. Within Temptation, Band, song; Shed My Skin. https://www.within-temptation.com/ VIDEO LINK: https://youtu.be/mP0TVptLDQE 2023

36. Within Temptation, Band, song; Where is the edge, Album: The Unforgiving. https://www.within-temptation.com/ VIDEO LINK: https://youtu.be/zcF8441U5xM 2023

37. RUSH, band. Song; The Trees. https://www.rush.com/ 2023 VIDEO LINK: https://youtu.be/8_D0wkLyCXE Notes: Reference to Neil Peart, Alex Lifeson, and Geddy Lee

38. Neale Donald Walsch. Email quote, Newsletter Subscription, http://www.nealedonaldwalsch.com/ NOTES: This is from an email he sent to me, reprinted with approval. Love his positive inspirational messages!

39. Within Temptation, Band, song; Where is the edge, https://www.within-temptation.com/ VIDEO LINK: https://youtu.be/D0npkAdnjMk 2023

40. Visions of Atlantis, Band, Song; Master the Hurricane https://www.visionsofatlantis.at/ VIDEO LINK: https://youtu.be/d9wwC93Lzuw 2023

41. Disturbed, Band, song; The Light. https://www.disturbed1.com/music VIDEO LINK: https://youtu.be/e1UUAhZ3JzM 2023

42. Jackie Robinson, Baseball player, Quote. https://jackierobinson.com/

43. Evan Longoria, Baseball player. YouTube video; https://www.youtube.com/watch?v=eCH4zelZFNk Note: thanks to Evan, All the contributors & Mental Training, Inc for providing the video! https://mentaltraininginc.com/ (I was unable to find a website for Evan Longoria)

44. Mental Training, Inc., https://mentaltraininginc.com/ YouTube video link; https://www.youtube.com/watch?v=eCH4zelZFNk 2023, Note: thanks to Mental Training, Inc. for providing the video! https://mentaltraininginc.com/

45. Dr. Ken Rivizza, Sports Psychologist, https://kenravizza.com/ Reference to YouTube video; https://www.youtube.com/watch?v=eCH4zelZFNk Note: Thanks to Mental Training Inc. for providing the video. https://mentaltraininginc.com/

46. Reinhold Niebuhr, (1892-1971) The Serenity Prayer, widely known, used, and quoted. Note: Many relevant sources of information on this prayer are online, here is one: https://en.wikipedia.org/wiki/Serenity_Prayer accessed 3/16/23

47. Jaie Hart, http://www.jaiehart.com/, Jaie said that this was a ZEN proverb, and she wrote about it. She is AMAZING! Check her stuff out online. Check out her book, or books, here is one I liked: The EGO is the Veil, https://www.lulu.com/shop/jl-harter/the-ego-is-the-veil/paperback/product-21734045.html?page=1&pageSize=4

48. Franklin D. Roosevelt, Quote, 1933 inaugural address, President of the United States. Note: This is widely known and quoted, here is one source: Goodreads, Inc. March, 2023 https://www.goodreads.com/quotes/432909-first-of-all-let-me-assert-my-firm-belief-that

49. RUSH, Band. Song; Tom Sawyer. https://www.rush.com/ Note: Neil Alex and Geddy are the band. Reference to Neil Peart, Alex Lifeson, and Geddy Lee. VIDEO LINK: https://youtu.be/auLBLk4ibAk

50. Simon and Garfunkel, Band, Song; Bridge Over Troubled Water https://simonandgarfunkel.com/ VIDEO LINK: https://youtu.be/4G-YQA_bsOU

51. Henry Wadsworth Longfellow, 1807-1882, Favorite Poems of Henry Wadsworth Longfellow, NY. Doubleday, 1947: A Psalm of Life. This is widely known and quoted. Here is a source for more information 3/2023: https://en.wikipedia.org/wiki/A_Psalm_of_Life

52. Henry Wadsworth Longfellow, 1807-1882, Favorite Poems of Henry Wadsworth Longfellow, NY. Doubleday, 1947: A Psalm of Life. This is widely known and quoted. Here is a source for more information 3/2023: https://en.wikipedia.org/wiki/A_Psalm_of_Life

53. Henry Wadsworth Longfellow, 1807-1882, Favorite Poems of Henry Wadsworth Longfellow, NY. Doubleday, 1947: A Psalm of Life. This is widely known and quoted. Here is a source for more information 3/2023: https://en.wikipedia.org/wiki/A_Psalm_of_Life

54. Henry Wadsworth Longfellow, 1807-1882, Favorite Poems of Henry Wadsworth Longfellow, NY. Doubleday, 1947: A Psalm of Life. This is widely known and quoted. Here is a source for more information 3/2023: https://en.wikipedia.org/wiki/A_Psalm_of_Life

55. Rush, the band, song: Marathon. https://www.rush.com/ VIDEO LINK: https://youtu.be/yJPcKg2NSwI

56. Rush, the band, song: Mission. https://www.rush.com/ VIDEO LINK: https://youtu.be/If9gFVnmQ8c

57. Theosophical origin, unknown author. NOTE: Much debate online as to where this originated, and many variations of this statement, with no clear answer as to whom it is to be attributed!

58. RUSH, the band. Song, The Spirit of The Radio. https://www.rush.com/ VIDEO LINK: https://youtu.be/g_QtO0Rhp0w

59. The Bible, The New Revised Standard Version. 1 Thessalonians 5:16-18

60. The Bible, New International Version, John 14:12

61. The Bible, King James Version. Mathew 5:39

62. Phillip Arnold, Quote. No official website found. This is quoted in many places online, here is one source accessed 3/2023: https://www.epicquotes.com/you-will-never-be-free-until-you-free-yourself-from-the-prison-of-your-own-false-thoughts-philip-arnold/

63. Franklin D. Roosevelt, widely quoted online, Here is one source: Goodreads, Inc 3/2023: https://www.goodreads.com/quotes/45529-men-are-not-prisoners-of-fate-but-only-prisoners-of

64. James Redfield, book, The Celestine Prophecy, New York, Boston, 1993, re-release 2018 Grand Central Publishing, https://www.celestinevision.com/, https://www.grandcentralpublishing.com/titles/james-redfield/the-celestine-prophecy/9781538730263/

65. The Bible: English Standard Version. Mathew 13:13. Note: This is stated in many places in the bible, in a whole host of varieties and written many ways!

66. Rush, the band, song: Marathon. Album, Power Windows. https://www.rush.com/ 2023 VIDEO LINK: https://youtu.be/MUcdRLn3bgM

67. Within Temptation, Band, song: Entertain You: https://www.within-temptation.com/ VIDEO LINK, 2023: https://youtu.be/a7-8hK2f_So

68. Whitney Houston, Singer, Song; One Moment in Time. simply AMAZING! https://www.whitney houston.com/ VIDEO LINK: https://youtu.be/96aAx0kxVSA

69. Rush, Band, song; Vital Signs. https://www.rush.com/ VIDEO LINK: https://youtu.be/MUcdRL n3bgM

70. Whitney Houston, Singer, Song; One Moment in Time. simply AMAZING! https://www.whitney houston.com/ VIDEO LINK: https://youtu.be/96aAx0kxVSA

71. The Bible: New International Readers Version, 1998 John 8:31-32

72. Visions of Atlantis, Band, Song; A life of Our Own https://www.visionsofatlantis.at/ VIDEO LINK: https://youtu.be/mNn_7COkKj0

73. Rush, the band, song: Natural Science https://www.rush.com/ VIDEO LINK: https://youtu.be/3 xe3It9DFDQ

74. Dottie Giesler. Doug's childhood. Mom quote, from when I was a kid: THANKS MOM!

75. William Shakespeare, English poet & playwright, As you like it, Act 5, Scene 1. Also notable: widely quoted online. Here is one source, 3,2023: https://www.folger.edu/explore/shakespeares-works/as-y ou-like-it/read/5/1/ And another: https://www.goodreads.com/quotes/71-the-fool-doth-think-he-i s-wise-but-the-wise

76. Yoda, The Jedi master, LUCASFILM Entertainment Company LTD. Movie: The Empire Strikes Back, 1980 film. https://www.starwars.com/databank/yoda

77. The Bible, English Standard Version: Luke 23:34

78. Rush, Band, song: Tom Sawyer https://www.rush.com/ VIDEO LINK: https://youtu.be/auLBLk 4ibAk

79. Esther & Jerry Hicks, book, "Ask and it is given", Hay House Inc. Oct 1, 2004 https://www.abraha m-hicks.com/

80. Styx, Band, song; Boat on the River https://styxworld.com/ VIDEO LINK: https://youtu.be/K9Q s8-BkiLw

81. Rush, Band, song; Time Stand Still https://www.rush.com/ VIDEO LINK: https://youtu.be/dMS FqXGZ5TQ

82. Rush, Band, song: Tom Sawyer https://www.rush.com/ VIDEO LINK: https://youtu.be/auLBLk 4ibAk

83. The Bible, American Standard Version, Exodus 14: 21-22 Note: Moses. This is something He did on the TV show as well, I was just acknowledging the action as symbolism. This is simply my opinion!

84. Scorpions, Band, song: Send Me an Angel https://www.the-scorpions.com/ VIDEO LINK: https://youtu.be/1UUYjd2rjsE

85. Jaie Hart, said that this was a ZEN proverb, and she wrote about it. She is AMAZING! Check her stuff out online. http://www.jaiehart.com/, Check out her book, or books, here is one I liked: The EGO is the Veil, https://www.lulu.com/shop/jl-harter/the-ego-is-the-veil/paperback/product-2173 4045.html?page=1&pageSize=4

86. Scorpions, Band, song: Winds of Change https://www.the-scorpions.com/ VIDEO LINK: https://youtu.be/n4RjJKxsamQ

87. Guy Finley, book, The Courage to be FREE, 2010, Page 109-111, Weiser Books www.GuyFinley.org

88. Science of Mind Magazine, Quote, Richard Bach, July 2017 Issue, Daily Guides. https://scienceofmind.com/

89. Reverend Karen S. Wylie, Page reprinted from Science of Mind Magazine with her permission as well as Science of Mind. Her website is here: http://karenswylie.com/ and her book: https://www.amazon.com/Into-Me-See-Daily-Inspiration/dp/150853103X/, Science of Mind Magazine: www.scienceofmind.com is a monthly print publication.

90. Reverend Dr. Ron Fox, Page reprinted with approval from Science of Mind Magazine and Ron Fox, Quote: Ron Fox, August 2017 issue, Daily guides https://scienceofmind.com/ Here is a link to Reverend Dr. Ron's book on Amazon as well: https://www.amazon.com/dp/1943581231/?col iid=I3K6J1BINWX3ZL&colid=1PBAJTE8JF4RA&psc=1&ref_=lv_ov_lig_dp_it, Science of Mind Magazine: www.scienceofmind.com is a monthly print publication.

91. Dr. Reverend Ron Fox, Page reprinted with approval from Science of Mind Magazine and Ron Fox, Quote: Ron Fox, August 2017 issue, Daily guides https://scienceofmind.com/ Here is a link to Reverend Dr. Ron's book on Amazon as well: https://www.amazon.com/dp/1943581231/?col iid=I3K6J1BINWX3ZL&colid=1PBAJTE8JF4RA&psc=1&ref_=lv_ov_lig_dp_it, Science of Mind Magazine: www.scienceofmind.com is a monthly print publication.

92. Dr. Reverend Ron Fox, Page reprinted with approval from Science of Mind Magazine and Ron Fox, Quote: Ron Fox, August 2017 issue, Daily guides https://scienceofmind.com/ Here is a link to Reverend Dr. Ron's book on Amazon as well: https://www.amazon.com/dp/1943581231/?col iid=I3K6J1BINWX3ZL&colid=1PBAJTE8JF4RA&psc=1&ref_=lv_ov_lig_dp_it, Science of Mind Magazine: www.scienceofmind.com is a monthly print publication.

93. The Bible: New American Standard, Mathew 8:13 Jesus. Note: There are many variations of this quote!

94. Sri Nisargadatta Maharaj, I AM THAT, book: Chetana Private LTD. Dec 5,1999, https://www.maharajnisargadatta.com/, https://www.amazon.com/Am-That-Talks-Nisargadatta-Maharaj-dp-818530 0534/dp/8185300534/ref=dp_ob_image_bk

95. Sri Nisargadatta Maharaj, I AM THAT, book: Chetana Private LTD. Dec 5,1999, https://www.maharajnisargadatta.com/, https://www.amazon.com/Am-That-Talks-Nisargadatta-Maharaj-dp-818530 0534/dp/8185300534/ref=dp_ob_image_bk

96. Sri Nisargadatta Maharaj, I AM THAT, book: Chetana Private LTD. Dec 5, 1999, https://www.maharajnisargadatta.com/, https://www.amazon.com/Am-That-Talks-Nisargadatta-Maharaj-dp-8185 300534/dp/8185300534/ref=dp_ob_image_bk

97. Sri Nisargadatta Maharaj, I AM THAT, book: Chetana Private LTD. Dec 5, 1999, https://www.maharajnisargadatta.com/, https://www.amazon.com/Am-That-Talks-Nisargadatta-Maharaj-dp-8185 300534/dp/8185300534/ref=dp_ob_image_bk

98. Ernest Holmes, The Science of MIND, book, TarcherPerigree, August 24, 1998. quote, Note: This is also the magazine my wife and I read daily: Science of Mind Magazine, monthly publication: https://scienceofmind.com/

99. Ernest Holmes, The Science of MIND, book, TarcherPerigree, August 24, 1998. quote, Note: This is also the magazine my wife and I read daily: Science of Mind Magazine, monthly publication: https://scienceofmind.com/

100. Ernest Holmes, The Science of MIND, book, TarcherPerigree, August 24, 1998. quote, Note: This is also the magazine my wife and I read daily: Science of Mind Magazine, monthly publication: https://scienceofmind.com/

101. Ernest Holmes, The Science of MIND, book, TarcherPerigree, August 24, 1998. quote, Note: This is also the magazine my wife and I read daily: Science of Mind Magazine, monthly publication: https://scienceofmind.com/

102. Emerson, Essays: The Oversoul, Ralph Waldo Emerson, www.EmersonCentral.com Web Marketing Now. Accessed 3/13/2023 https://emersoncentral.com/texts/essays-first-series/the-over-soul/

103. Marshall Sylver, Passion, Profit & Power. Audio Cassettes, January 1, 1993. 6 cassettes and a workbook. https://sylver.com/ This was a course I bought years ago. Passion, Profit, and POWER was the name of the course. In the video presentation he demonstrated this principle. It was very cool; the man is talented! He also has a book by the same name, Passion Profit Power, January 21, 1997. Simon & Schuster Paperbacks.

104. Within Temptation, Band, song; Supernova https://www.within-temptation.com/ VIDEO LINK: https://youtu.be/Z3nb_r18ug0 2023.

105. Johnny Nash, song, released 1972, I can see clearly Now. VIDEO LINK: https://youtu.be/b0cAWg TPiwM

106. The Bible, King James version, Mathew 13:12

107. Louise Hay, book: You Can Heal your Life. Hay House. 1984, Website: https://www.louisehay.com/

108. The Bible, Legacy Standard Bible, Mathew 8:13

109. Ralph Waldo Emerson, 1803-1882 Peter Pauper Press, White Plains, NY. Essays, The Oversoul, Accessed Online 3/13/2023 via https://emersoncentral.com/texts/essays-first-series/the-over-soul/ and downloadable here: https://emersoncentral.com/ebook/The-Over-Soul.pdf

110. Ralph Waldo Emerson, 1803-1882 Peter Pauper Press, White Plains, NY. Essays, The Oversoul, Accessed Online via https://emersoncentral.com/texts/essays-first-series/the-over-soul/ and downloadable here: https://emersoncentral.com/ebook/The-Over-Soul.pdf

111. Ralph Waldo Emerson, 1803-1882 Peter Pauper Press, White Plains, NY. Essays, The Oversoul, Accessed Online via https://emersoncentral.com/texts/essays-first-series/the-over-soul/ and downloadable here: https://emersoncentral.com/ebook/The-Over-Soul.pdf

112. Ralph Waldo Emerson, 1803-1882 Peter Pauper Press, White Plains, NY. Essays, The Oversoul, Accessed Online via https://emersoncentral.com/texts/essays-first-series/the-over-soul/ and downloadable here: https://emersoncentral.com/ebook/The-Over-Soul.pdf

113. Ralph Waldo Emerson, 1803-1882 Peter Pauper Press, White Plains, NY. Essays, The Oversoul, Accessed Online via https://emersoncentral.com/texts/essays-first-series/the-over-soul/ and downloadable here: https://emersoncentral.com/ebook/The-Over-Soul.pdf

114. Ralph Waldo Emerson, 1803-1882 Peter Pauper Press, White Plains, NY. Essays, The Oversoul, Accessed Online via https://emersoncentral.com/texts/essays-first-series/the-over-soul/ and downloadable here: https://emersoncentral.com/ebook/The-Over-Soul.pdf

115. Ralph Waldo Emerson, 1803-1882 Peter Pauper Press, White Plains, NY. Essays, Spiritual Laws https://emersoncentral.com/texts/essays-first-series/spiritual-laws/

116. Ralph Waldo Emerson, 1803-1882 Peter Pauper Press, White Plains, NY. Essays, Spiritual Laws https://emersoncentral.com/texts/essays-first-series/spiritual-laws/

117. Ralph Waldo Emerson, 1803-1882 Peter Pauper Press, White Plains, NY. Essays, Spiritual Laws https://emersoncentral.com/texts/essays-first-series/spiritual-laws/

118. Ralph Waldo Emerson, 1803-1882 Peter Pauper Press, White Plains, NY. Essays, Spiritual Laws https://emersoncentral.com/texts/essays-first-series/spiritual-laws/

119. Ralph Waldo Emerson, 1803-1882 Peter Pauper Press, White Plains, NY. Essays, Spiritual Laws https://emersoncentral.com/texts/essays-first-series/spiritual-laws/

120. The Bible, Legacy Standard Version, Mathew, 26:41

121. Ralph Waldo Emerson, 1803-1882 Peter Pauper Press, White Plains, NY. Essays: Self Reliance https://emersoncentral.com/ebook/Self-Reliance.pdf Credit to John Fletcher as well as this is from a quote from "An Honest Mans Fortune" John Fletcher,1579-1625, edited by Ralph Waldo Emerson, 1803-1882, An Honest Mans Fortune, Parnassus, An Anthology of Poetry, Boston, Houghton, Osgood and Company 1880; Bartleby.com 2013. Accessed 3/13/2023 here: https://www.bartleby.com/371/266.html

122. Ralph Waldo Emerson, 1803-1882 Peter Pauper Press, White Plains, NY. Essays: Self Reliance https://emersoncentral.com/ebook/Self-Reliance.pdf

123. Ralph Waldo Emerson, 1803-1882 Peter Pauper Press, White Plains, NY. Essays: Self Reliance https://emersoncentral.com/ebook/Self-Reliance.pdf

124. Ralph Waldo Emerson, 1803-1882 Peter Pauper Press, White Plains, NY. Essays: Self Reliance https://emersoncentral.com/ebook/Self-Reliance.pdf

125. Ralph Waldo Emerson, 1803-1882 Peter Pauper Press, White Plains, NY. Essays: Self Reliance https://emersoncentral.com/ebook/Self-Reliance.pdf

126. Ralph Waldo Emerson, 1803-1882 Peter Pauper Press, White Plains, NY. Essays: Self Reliance https://emersoncentral.com/ebook/Self-Reliance.pdf

127. Ralph Waldo Emerson, 1803-1882 Peter Pauper Press, White Plains, NY. Essays: Self Reliance https://emersoncentral.com/ebook/Self-Reliance.pdf

128. Ralph Waldo Emerson, 1803-1882 Peter Pauper Press, White Plains, NY. Essays: Self Reliance https://emersoncentral.com/ebook/Self-Reliance.pdf

129. Ralph Waldo Emerson, 1803-1882 Peter Pauper Press, White Plains, NY. Essays: Self Reliance https://emersoncentral.com/ebook/Self-Reliance.pdf

130. Ralph Waldo Emerson, 1803-1882 Peter Pauper Press, White Plains, NY. Essays: Self Reliance https://emersoncentral.com/ebook/Self-Reliance.pdf

131. Ralph Waldo Emerson, 1803-1882 Peter Pauper Press, White Plains, NY. Essays: Self Reliance https://emersoncentral.com/ebook/Self-Reliance.pdf

132. John Fletcher,1579-1625, edited by Ralph Waldo Emerson, 1803-1882, An Honest Mans Fortune, Parnassus, An Anthology of Poetry, Boston, Houghton, Osgood and Company 1880; Bartleby.com 2013. Accessed 3/13/2023 here: https://www.bartleby.com/371/266.html

133. John Fletcher,1579-1625, edited by Ralph Waldo Emerson, 1803-1882, An Honest Mans Fortune, Parnassus, An Anthology of Poetry, Boston, Houghton, Osgood and Company 1880; Bartleby.com 2013. Accessed 3/13/2023 here: https://www.bartleby.com/371/266.html

134. Ralph Waldo Emerson, 1803-1882 Peter Pauper Press, White Plains, NY. Essays, The Oversoul, Accessed Online via https://emersoncentral.com/texts/essays-first-series/the-over-soul/ and downloadable here: https://emersoncentral.com/ebook/The-Over-Soul.pdf

135. Lindsey Stirling, featuring Rivers Cuomo & Lecrae. Song. Don't let this feeling fade. Album: Brave Enough. 8/19/2016 Lindseystomp Records: https://www.lindseystirling.com/, https://riverscuomo .com/home , https://lecrae.com/ VIDEO LINK: https://www.youtube.com/watch?v=zKutaKjG-Zw

136. St. Francis of Assisi, quote / saying. Origination date and publication unknown.

137. The Bible, English Standard Version, Romans 12:2

138. The Bible: "The Lord's Prayer", Mathew 6:9-13 and similarly Luke 11:1-4

139. The Bible: "The Lord's Prayer", Mathew 6:9-13 and similarly Luke 11:1-4

140. The Bible, Christian Standard edition, Mathew 17:20

141. The Bible, American Standard version, Luke 17:21

142. Sri Nisargadatta Maharaj, I AM THAT, book: Chetana Private LTD. Dec 5, 1999, https://www.m aharajnisargadatta.com/, https://www.amazon.com/Am-That-Talks-Nisargadatta-Maharaj-dp-8185 300534/dp/8185300534/ref=dp_ob_image_bk

143. Sri Nisargadatta Maharaj, I AM THAT, book: Chetana Private LTD. Dec 5, 1999, https://www.m aharajnisargadatta.com/, https://www.amazon.com/Am-That-Talks-Nisargadatta-Maharaj-dp-8185 300534/dp/8185300534/ref=dp_ob_image_bk

144. Eckhart Tolle, book, The Power of Now. New World Library, 2004. Notes: Reference to his idea of the "Pain Body". He talks about this quite a bit. "The power of NOW", "A New Earth" are the books I read although He has a lot of material available! https://eckharttolle.com/

145. The Bible, King James Version, Luke 23:34

146. Jaie Hart, said that this was a ZEN proverb, and she wrote about it. She is AMAZING! Check her stuff out online. http://www.jaiehart.com/, Check out her book, or books, here is one I liked: The EGO is the Veil, https://www.lulu.com/shop/jl-harter/the-ego-is-the-veil/paperback/product-2173 4045.html?page=1&pageSize=4

147. Jaie Hart, said that this was a ZEN proverb, and she wrote about it. She is AMAZING! Check her stuff out online. http://www.jaiehart.com/, Check out her book, or books, here is one I liked: The EGO is the Veil, https://www.lulu.com/shop/jl-harter/the-ego-is-the-veil/paperback/product-2173 4045.html?page=1&pageSize=4

148. Jaie Hart, said that this was a ZEN proverb, and she wrote about it. She is AMAZING! Check her stuff out online. http://www.jaiehart.com/, Check out her book, or books, here is one I liked: The EGO is the Veil, https://www.lulu.com/shop/jl-harter/the-ego-is-the-veil/paperback/product-2173 4045.html?page=1&pageSize=4

149. Eckhart Tolle, book, The Power of Now. New World Library, 2004. Notes: Reference to his idea of the "Pain Body". He talks about this quite a bit. "The power of NOW", "A New Earth" are the books I read although He has a lot of material available! https://eckharttolle.com/

150. Eckhart Tolle, book, The Power of Now. New World Library, 2004. Notes: Reference to his idea of the "Pain Body". He talks about this quite a bit. "The power of NOW", "A New Earth" are the books I read although He has a lot of material available! https://eckharttolle.com/

151. Evanescence, Amy Lee. Song "Hello". This is just one of MANY very powerful songs and Lyrics by this AMAZING band! https://www.evanescence.com/home/ VIDEO LINK: https://youtu.be/9MHG tlEYZBA

152. Within Temptation, Band. https://www.within-temptation.com/ 2023. Reference to SONGS; See who I am, Pale, The Purge, Shed My Skin. These are just a few of the AMAZING songs that they have produced recently. Pay close attention, their Lyrics are super powerful, and the band is crazy good! Sharon Den Adel has serious vocal talent! Check out their stuff, and pay attention to everything, tone, speed, who is singing, the videos, and the themes! Super powerful lyrics and a band that really delivers the message in a powerful way! Pay attention to or question who the song is being directed towards...is it someone else, or the alter EGO maybe? I find this extremely thoughtful music and lyrics, well played out themes, even in the contents of each album! As an example, The Silent Force, The Heart of Everything, etc. They are, again, very powerful mental angles being played out in song, just my opinion! Makes you think about thinking. The videos are also compelling with a lot of symbolism IMHO! VIDEO LINKS VIA THEIR CHANNEL: https://www.youtube.com/@wtofficial

153. Henry Wadsworth Longfellow, 1807-1882, Favorite Poems of Henry Wadsworth Longfellow, NY. Doubleday, 1947: A Psalm of Life. This is widely known and quoted. Here is a source for more information 3/2023: https://en.wikipedia.org/wiki/A_Psalm_of_Life

154. Doug Giesler, This book. Be The Instrument. 2023. My website: www.BeTheInstrument.com

155. Eckhart Tolle, book, The Power of Now. New World Library, 2004. Notes: Reference to his idea of the "Pain Body". He talks about this quite a bit. "The power of NOW", "A New Earth" are the books I read although He has a lot of material available! https://eckharttolle.com/

156. Eckhart Tolle, book, The Power of Now. New World Library, 2004. Notes: Reference to his idea of the "Pain Body". He talks about this quite a bit. "The power of NOW", "A New Earth" are the books I read although He has a lot of material available! https://eckharttolle.com/

157. The Pretenders, Band, song: I'll stand by You https://thepretenders.com/Homepage/ VIDEO LINK: https://youtu.be/nobHZ3nOp38

158. The Scorpions, band, song: Follow Your Heart https://www.the-scorpions.com/ VIDEO LINK: ht tps://youtu.be/tMui4IVW0BM

159. The Scorpions, band, song: The Eye of the Storm https://www.the-scorpions.com/ VIDEO LINK: https://youtu.be/_sTc82-FS78

160. The Scorpions, band, song: The Best is yet to Come https://www.the-scorpions.com/ VIDEO LINK: https://youtu.be/LFKWMRaI-ME

161. RUSH, the band, yet another really cool song with amazing lyrics! Jacobs Ladder https://www.rush.com/ VIDEO LINK: https://youtu.be/z3gvOV40ccU

162. Karliene, song and Lyric, We're the Devils, https://karliene.com/track/2708320/we-re-the-devil s VIDEO LINK: https://youtu.be/vuyedPuH5wY

163. James Redfield, book, The Celestine Prophecy, New York, Boston, 1993, re-release 2018 Grand Central Publishing, https://www.celestinevision.com/, https://www.grandcentralpublishing.com/titles/james-redfield/the-celestine-prophecy/9781538730263/

164. Within Temptation, Band, song: See Who I Am https://www.within-temptation.com/ VIDEO LINK: https://youtu.be/VMhhAzD5rvo 2023

165. Within Temptation, Band, song: The Whole World is Watching https://www.within-temptation.com/ VIDEO LINK: https://youtu.be/mf97F-SpBQU 2023

166. Rush, the band, song: Natural Science. https://www.rush.com/ VIDEO LINK: https://youtu.be/3xe3It9DFDQ

167. Rush, the band, song: Prime Mover. https://www.rush.com/VIDEO LINK: https://youtu.be/n95r64HhLOQ

168. Rush, the band, song: Prime Mover. https://www.rush.com/ VIDEO LINK: https://youtu.be/n95r64HhLOQ

169. Gerry Giesler, My Dad, He generated an example exercise from which I created this section. Thanks Dad!

170. Jung, C. G. 1991. The Archetypes and the Collective Unconscious. Translated by R. F. C. Hull. 2nd ed. Collected Works of C.G. Jung. London, England: Routledge. Carl Jung, https://www.jung.org/who-is-carl-jung. I am referring to his idea of themes in the mind relative to "archetypes". I like it, and kind of created my own when I modeled my own psychology.

171. Gerry Giesler, Dad, Priority Setting tool.

172. Gerry Giesler, Dad, Priority Setting tool.

173. Within Temptation, Song: Faster https://www.within-temptation.com/ VIDEO LINK: https://youtu.be/iQVei5C2N4E 2023

174. Rush, the band, song Prime Mover. Just referenced the song again. https://www.rush.com/ VIDEO LINK: https://youtu.be/n95r64HhLOQ

175. Judy & Josh McCormick, Elizabeth, WV 26143 https://keepsakelabs.com/index.html (724) 602-1802 This is where we got Kappi :)

www.ingramcontent.com/pod-product-compliance
Lightning Source LLC
Chambersburg PA
CBHW071705120626
46550CB00001B/109